HUMAN
ENCUMBRANCES

DAVID P. NALLY

HUMAN ENCUMBRANCES

Political Violence and the Great Irish Famine

UNIVERSITY OF NOTRE DAME PRESS

NOTRE DAME, INDIANA

Manufactured in the United States of America

Library of Congress Cataloging-in-Publication Data

Nally, David P.
 Human encumbrances : political violence and the Great Irish Famine /
David P. Nally.
  p. cm.
 Includes bibliographical references and index.
 ISBN-13: 978-0-268-03608-9 (paper : alk. paper)
 ISBN-10: 0-268-03608-X (paper : alk. paper)
 1. Ireland—History—Famine, 1845–1852. 2. Famines—Political
aspects—Ireland—History—19th century. 3. Poverty—Political
aspects—Ireland—History—19th century. 4. Ireland—Rural conditions.
5. Ireland—Colonial influence. 6. Political violence—Ireland—History—
19th century. 7. Social control—Ireland—History—19th century.
8. Great Britain—Colonies—Administration—History—19th century.
9. Great Britain—Foreign economic relations—Ireland. 10. Ireland—
Foreign economic relations—Great Britain. I. Title.
 DA950.7.N35 2011
 941.5081—dc22

                                                              2010052723

CONTENTS

Famines are wars over the right to existence.

—Mike Davis, *Late Victorian Holocausts:*
El Niño Famines and the Making of the Third World

The vice which is inherent in our system of social and political economy is so subtle that it eludes all pursuit, that you cannot find or trace it to any responsible source. The man, indeed, over whose dead body the coroner holds an inquest, has been murdered, but no one killed him. There is no external wound, there is no symptom of internal disease. Society guarded him against all outward violence;—it merely encircled him around in order to keep up what is termed the regular current of trade, and then political economy, with an invisible hand, applied the air-pump to the narrow limits within which he was confined, and exhausted the atmosphere of his physical life. Who did it? No one did it, and yet it was done.

—John Hughes, *A Lecture on the Antecedent Causes of the Irish Famine in 1847*

"I got to figure," the tenant said. "We all got to figure. There's some way to stop this. It's not like lightning or earthquakes. We've got a bad thing made by men, and by God that's something we can change."

—John Steinbeck, *The Grapes of Wrath*

This book begins from the position that both the genesis and effects of food crises, like the construction of food systems themselves, ought to be analysed and understood from within "the political realm of human affairs." This phrase is gleaned from the political writings of Hannah Arendt, for whom "neither violence nor power is a natural phenomenon." While Arendt insisted that "violence" and "power" are far from the same thing, she also admitted that nothing is more common than to find both forces operating in concert. "Even the most despotic domination we know of," she cautioned, "the rule of master over slaves, who always outnumbered him, did not rest on superior means of coercion as such, but on a superior organisation of power—that is, on the organized solidarity of the masters."[1]

Arendt's comments, I want to suggest, provide an important background for understanding the nature of "political violence" and its role in the creation of famine. A person or population can be "dominated" through brute force, but they might also be dehumanised or reduced to a position of virtual rightlessness through harmful economic policies, debilitating institutional programmes, prejudicial legislative actions, or misguided political doctrines. In the first example, subjugation would require the repressive presence of a police force or an army; in the second instance, domination is achieved through greater organisation and political design, or what Arendt termed the "solidarity of the masters."

This typology of political violence provides a helpful way to think about mass starvation. It is relatively easy, for example, to find cases where famines are the direct outcome of brute force. In the medieval period the ritual of "slash and burn" practised by retreating armies is an obvious case in point. And the ongoing crisis in Sudan provides a more recent illustration of the synergies between armed conflict and mass starvation. The violence of hunger can result from other sources, however, including, for instance, colonial policies, market crises, state and corporate food control, inequitable labour regimes, and so forth. These examples of "structural violence," to use Paul Farmer's helpful term, might not appear as obvious as a civil war or an armed conflict, but evidence shows that they are in fact a more common cause of protracted famine.[2]

And herein lies the crux of a larger problem: not only are structural factors more difficult to identify, their *complex* and *composite* nature makes it very difficult to isolate and distinguish the parties responsible. To view, say, a bureaucratic system as the principal cause of a particular famine can generate the false view that neither agency nor design is involved in the catastrophe. This is not just a problem for scholars to ponder, as Pierre Spitz makes clear. Certain mechanisms like tariffs, poll taxes, rent systems, and usurious credit practices are easily identified as "extractive forces" that strip populations of their assets, leaving scarcity and hunger in their wake.[3] In these situations the populations directly affected are usually able to identify those responsible—that is, tax collectors, moneylenders, large farmers, and landlords—a fact that explains why these figures are very often the target of agrarian violence. The complex character of other kinds of extractive forces, however (for example, price structures, declining terms of trade, or the rising costs of farm inputs), makes them far less easy to analyse and identify. In other words, the multifaceted and compound nature of political violence often renders its operations opaque.

Whilst the complexity of political violence needs to be recognised—and we owe a debt to Spitz, amongst others, for pointing this out—it would be wrong to deduce from this, as is often the case, that food crises simply happen.[4] In his excellent book *The End of Food,* Paul Roberts, drawing on John Thackara's work on urban sprawl, makes a very powerful point about food crises that is worth quoting at length:

> Nobody seems to have designed urban sprawl, it just happens—or so it seems . . . On closer inspection, however, urban sprawl is not mindless at all. There is nothing inevitable about its development. Sprawl is the result of zoning laws designed by legislators, low density buildings designed by developers, marketing strategies designed by ad agencies, tax breaks designed by economists, credit lines designed by banks . . . data mining software designed by hamburger chains, and automobiles designed by car designers. The interactions between all these systems and human behaviour are complicated and hard to understand—but the policies are not the result of chance.[5]

For Roberts, food crises, like the phenomenon of urban sprawl, are the outcome of a complex political process. Disasters do not happen; they are designed. Behind the structural causes of hunger lie the machinations of politicians, legislators, workhouse guardians, usurious creditors, apathetic landowners, and utopian economists. The challenge is to determine the key sites of agency and action from the "sprawl" of compound forces.

The interaction between cognitive designs and human decisions—between ideology and conduct—is a central feature of what I describe in this book as *political violence*. In many ways, as we shall discuss, the Irish Famine was viewed as an instrument of cure, a form of social prophylaxis, that would finally regenerate what was perceived to be a diseased body politic. Even before the Famine reached its deadly apogee, a wide array of social commentators believed that Ireland's peasant culture (hinged on a "degenerate" potato diet) was fundamentally incommensurable with enlightenment norms of civilisation and progress. Objectified as a "redundant" people, Irish peasants were thought to be preventing the long-term modernisation of Irish society. To the economists and public officials who embraced this dehumanising logic, the potato blight was literally a godsend: a "secret scourge," to adapt a well-known phrase from Edmund Spenser, that would mark the beginning of a process of political, social, and economic amelioration in Ireland.[6] A great deal has been written about such providential readings of the Famine, but another reason why these claims gained political currency was that they drew on an earlier colonial ideology that equated civility with the imposition of English norms and values. That is, to be civilised Irish society must be anglicised, and for this to happen the soil must be swept of its *human encumbrances*.[7]

For these reasons I place particular emphasis on the role of colonisation as a factor in the genesis and progression of famine in Ireland. The occlusion of colonisation (both as an ideology and as a practice) is often bemusing to scholars viewing Irish studies from the "outside," where potent connections are frequently drawn between events in Ireland and subsistence crises in the colonised regions of the global south. Here special mention needs to be made of Michael Watts's pioneering work on northern Nigeria and Mike Davis's seminal study, *Late Victorian Holocausts*.[8] In different ways, both accounts explain how colonial occupation, confiscation, and displacement left local populations bereft of the means of production and thrust back onto precarious modes of subsistence. In addition to undermining residual safety nets and coping mechanisms, colonial ideologies produced formidable boundaries between "ruler" and "ruled" that severely attenuated, and sometimes negated, more positive humanitarian impulses.

The emphasis in this volume, therefore, is on the importance of engaging in comparative analysis, particularly with regard to the institutional responses to famine across the British Empire. Without denying the specificity of the Irish Famine, there are clear lessons to be drawn from other colonial contexts. Writing in 1880, for example, as India was experiencing a series of catastrophic famines, Charles Trevelyan told readers of the *Times* that the earlier events in Ireland were "full of instruction on the present occasion."[9] "At the commencement of the Irish Famine," Trevelyan recalled, "there was the same popular desire to prohibit the exportation of grain, but it was successfully resisted." By adhering to orthodox economic theories, "a great famine was stayed, and the stamina of the population was restored."[10] "The result in Ireland," concluded Trevelyan, "has been to introduce other better kinds of food, and to raise the people, through much suffering, to a higher standard of subsistence. We shall see how it will be in India."[11] It is indeed peculiar that modern scholars have been reluctant to pursue the colonial connections that were so regularly rehearsed by well-known Victorian commentators.[12]

As well as threading together what might first appear as discrete historical and geographical phenomena—"first" and "third world" hunger—my argument also develops key insights originating from the relatively new and vibrant field of "Famine Studies."[13] This work includes the "entitlements framework" developed by the Nobel Prize–winning economist Amartya Sen (including emerging critiques of Sen's methodology), as well as a very diverse corpus of work that falls under the conceptual umbrella of political ecology.[14] With one or two notable exceptions, this scholarship has been ignored in recent accounts of the Great Irish Famine. There is, I want to suggest, a significant "opportunity cost" to overlooking this body of theoretical work, not only for researchers working on Irish Studies but also for those scholars labouring on the politics of hunger in the present. It does not seem to me too fanciful to suggest that analysing an historical famine might help us to better understand contemporary hunger and food insecurity; as the pioneering economist George O'Brien recognised, "the distress of the lower classes in Ireland in the early nineteenth century is a commonplace not merely of Irish but of world history."[15] And, in much the same way, more recent case studies and conceptual innovations might cast new light on the Irish past.[16]

I should add that although I incorporate postcolonial and modern famine theories to support the claims made in this book, I am primarily motivated by the interpretations offered by contemporaries (principally British and Irish observers but also American and European commentators) who vehemently protested against the injustice of famine and the suffering of the Irish people. The record of these disagreements comprises a rich and valuable trove of contemporary famine theory developed *in situ* and in response to specific grievances. While the intellectual basis for these critiques was quite diverse (republican, anticolonial, socialist, philanthropic, and so on), the crucial point is to acknowledge the presence of famine theories that predate the advance of modern Famine Studies. The tendency to attribute social failings to "natural" environmental causes or to judge famines as "the fiat of the Almighty," for instance, was both undermined and satirised by a number of Victorians.[17] In fact, many of the cornerstones of famine theory today—including the distinction between the immediate antecedents and the deeper underlying or structural causes of famine—were made with remarkable sophistication by contemporary observers. Although the "entitlements framework" and postcolonial perspectives help to develop a substantial critique of British famine policy, they certainly are not a precondition for this critique.

The reclamation of these contemporary voices is also a powerful antidote to the still prevalent belief that the Irish Famine was in some way "inevitable." This view comes perilously close to the Malthusian view—popular though fiercely contested in the nineteenth century—that famines are a "natural" outgrowth of unrestrained reproduction. Too many people plus too little food equals famine, as David Arnold condensed the problem.[18] Although arguments about population size are not inconsequential (the *reasons* for population growth certainly deserve scrutiny), it is simply erroneous to think that hunger and mass mortality were utterly unavoidable. Not everyone fiddled while Rome burned, and to insist otherwise is to confuse fatalism with historicism. More seriously, this view diminishes the significance of political decision making—in terms of directing specific outcomes—and renders irrelevant the aspirations of those who consistently disputed the discourses and policies of the British government. Being mindful of the pitfalls of teleology (what E. P. Thompson memorably described as the "enormous condescension of posterity"), this book tries to restore—and indeed amplify—those voices usually thought to be at the margins of mainstream political and economic opinion.[19] From the perspective of these witnesses, the Irish Famine, and its attendant social miseries, was a direct consequence of human affairs—"a humiliating homily on modern state-craft," according to Archibald Stark, and an act of "class extinction," in S. G. Osborne's view.[20] Indeed, from a diversity of perspectives, "famine" enters the political imaginary not as a "natural scourge" of the population but as a *crisis of government.*

Finally, the fact that many of these critical statements hail from English observers reveals another important point: disapproval of British famine policy was never the exclusive product of nationalist analysis. As Catherine Nash insists, power and violence are contested in the centre as well as the periphery.[21] Nash's sharp observation is well illustrated in the persistent challenges to the dominant aetiology of famine and through the stubborn insistence that there is nothing "natural" about "natural disasters." There are, clearly, alternative worlds of political critique, parallel to the dominant one, that need to be taken seriously if we are to restore the contingency of history and see the past anew as a site of possibility.[22] Although the significance of different perspectives and countervailing voices might appear obvious enough—after all, the pauper and politician will scarcely view hunger in the same way—I hope to show that these differences offer a rich critique of the positivistic orthodoxies that have dominated the historiography of the Great Irish Famine.

ACKNOWLEDGMENTS

The arguments presented in this book owe an enormous debt to the encouragement and assistance of numerous colleagues and friends. I would like to extend my sincere thanks to Stuart Basten, David Beckingham, Chay Brooks, Padraig Carmody, Nessa Cronin, Caoimhe Nic Dháibhéid, Eamon Duffy, Jim Duncan, Nancy Duncan, Matt Farish, Mary Gilmartin, Derek Gregory, Philip Howell, Al James, Willie Jenkins, Gerry Kearns, Stephen Legg, Denis Linehan, Joanna Long, Francesca Moore, John Morrissey, Pat Nugent, Eric Olund, Natalie Oswin, Geraldine Pratt, Amrita Rangasami, Ray Ryan, Rebecca Smith, Richard Smith, Anna Stanley, Ulf Strohmayer, Juanita Sundberg, Steve Taylor, Karen Till, Andy Tucker, and Bhaskar Vira. For their time, energy, and perspicacity I am very grateful. In researching this book I have also made ample use of cyberspace as a collegiate network. Chris Vanden Bossche, James Donnelly (whom I later had the pleasure to meet at the Institute of Irish Studies at the National University of Ireland, Galway), Melissa Fegan, Christine Kinealy, Amy Martin, Kerby Miller, and Cormac O'Gráda were kind enough to answer my queries regarding sources, interspersed with impertinent questions regarding their own interpretations. Kevin Whelan went one step further and furnished me with what were then unpublished materials. For the "kindness of strangers" I am very grateful. Chapter 5 is a substantially reworked version of my paper "'Eternity's Commissioner': Thomas Carlyle, the Great Irish Famine and the Geopolitics of Travel," *Journal of Historical Geography* 32, no. 2 (2006): 313–35. A portion of the argument in chapter 3 first appeared as "'That Coming Storm': The Irish Poor Law, Colonial Biopolitics, and the Great Famine," *Annals of the Association of American Geographers* 98, no. 3 (2008): 714–41. I would like to thank Mike Heffernan and Audrey Kobayashi, respectively, for their encouragement and editorial advice. I hardly need add that any faults that remain are solely my own.

For their cartographic work and technical assistance, I wish to acknowledge and thank Eric Leinberger, Owen Tucker, and especially Philip Stickler. Staff at the National Library of Ireland, the National Archives of Ireland, and Cambridge University Library have been magnanimous and efficient with all my requests, although I should make special mention of the research librarians at the University of British Columbia (UBC). This book would not have been possible without their detective work and the tremendous interlibrary loan service that UBC provides.

Thank you also to my friends at the Department of Geography, University College Cork, who made it possible for me to spend a short time there as a visiting lecturer. Many of the ideas expressed in these pages really began to gestate as I struggled to articulate them to an undergraduate audience. I owe a tremendous debt to Willie Smyth, friend and interlocutor during my first postgraduate years at Cork. Without his indefatigable support, I would not have made the journey from the "old" world to the "new"—and back again. Here also, perhaps, is the appropriate place to acknowledge the generous financial support provided by the National University of Ireland through their travelling scholarship scheme. Since this initial grant I have also benefited from a scholarship programme, administered by the University of British Columbia, as well as from smaller funds kindly provided by the University of Cambridge and the Department of Geography.

Since my arrival in Cambridge in October 2006, I have been made to feel welcome and very much at home. For this I have to thank my colleagues in the Department of Geography as well as the Master and Fellows at Fitzwilliam College. Within the Department of Geography, the members of the research cluster on "historical and cultural geography"—especially Jim Duncan, Phillip Howell, Gerry Kearns, Andy Tucker, Richard Smith, and Nancy Duncan—as well as a changing but always challenging cohort of graduate students, have been crucial in creating a regular space for critical reflection. I have also benefitted enormously from conversations with Steve Taylor and Chay Brooks, two exceptionally bright PhD students.

I want to express my wholehearted thanks to the staff at the University of Notre Dame Press, particularly my editor, Barbara Hanrahan, who has shown great faith in this project and whose patience was surely stretched as multiple deadlines were missed. In Christina Lovely I was blessed with a friendly and meticulous copyeditor, and Rebecca DeBoer, Wendy McMillen, Kathryn Pitts, Emily McKnight, Elizabeth Sain, and others at the University of Notre Dame Press each worked assiduously to nurse the manuscript through production. I am also very grateful for the efforts of three anonymous reviewers whose comments encouraged me to reconsider my arguments and clarify certain lines of reasoning. Their critical remarks helped to improve the manuscript enormously.

I hope those cited above will not mind me singling out for special mention the friendship and support of Gerry Kearns, John Morrissey, and Derek Gregory. Gerry has patiently read and listened to every argument contained in this book, and his suggestions and unrivalled insights have improved virtually every page. John's own work on early modern Ireland, and his more recent forays into geopolitics and international relations, are a model example of critical scholarship. At a late stage he agreed to read through sections of the manuscript, and no doubt his efforts have saved me from a number of embarrassing omissions. Derek has encouraged and guided this project from its very inception. He was the first to suggest that my early writings would make the basis for a great book. I'll leave for others to decide how well I have lived up to his expectations, but I do know for sure that the present work would be immeasurably inferior without Derek's help and inspiration. It is a lovely honour to finally pay tribute to his influence.

Finally, I wish to thank my family, especially my parents, Elizabeth and John, who have given me so much love and support. In my early days as a graduate student I recall my parents once joking that I didn't seem to care about money, possibly because I was so used to spending theirs! Although I laughed at the time, deep down I knew that there was more than a grain of truth to this quip. Isn't this, after all, what Albert Einstein was getting at when he said that our inner and outer lives depend on the labour of others? Certainly, the abiding memory from my childhood is the very strong emphasis my parents placed on my schooling. In secondary school, when I was struggling to keep up, extra tuitions were paid for without the slightest complaint. Later in adult life, when most of my peers were busy working toward promotion, my parents encouraged me to pursue my doctorate, even though this meant sacrificing their own retirement plans, not to mention long overdue holidays. I am truly at a loss to find the right words to acknowledge the near-pathological concern they have shown for my well-being over the years. They have had to put up with much, in return for so little, and all with consummate grace and good humour. I am so very grateful for all that they have done to educate and nurture me.

The research for this book was begun in Vancouver, British Columbia, and completed in Cambridge, United Kingdom. Along the way innumerable friends and colleagues have helped and provided intellectual support. There are a thousand acts of tenderness and tolerance that never find their way into footnotes yet are so necessary for the task of scholarship. But the real bedrock in my life has been the loving companionship of Estelle Levin. My first and most important interlocutor, Estelle has been the sounding board for every idea expressed in this book. Were it not for her unwavering belief in this project I would have given up long ago. With much love, therefore, I dedicate this book to her and to my mother and father.

INTRODUCTION

Colonial Biopolitics and the Functions of Famine

In Ireland the consequence was Famine—a calamity which cannot befall a civilised nation; for a civilised nation . . . never confines itself to a single sort of food, and is therefore insured from the great scarcity by the variety of its sources of supply. When such a calamity does befall an uncivilised community, things take their course; it produces great misery, great mortality, and in a year or two the wound is closed, and scarcely a scar remains.

— Nassau William Senior, *Journals, Conversations and Essays Relating to Ireland,* Volume 1

Dark whisperings and rumours of famine in its most appalling form began to reach us, but still we could scarcely believe that men, women, and children were actually dying of starvation in their thousands. Yet so it was. They died in their mountain glens, they died along the sea-coast, they died on the roads, and they died in the fields; they wandered into their towns, and died in the streets; they closed their cabin doors, and lay down upon their beds, and died of actual starvation in their houses.

— William Steuart Trench, *Realities of Irish Life*

TRAUMATIC HISTORY

In 1843 a mysterious blight, now known as *Phytophthora infestans*, was observed in the potato harvest in America. Within two years the blight had crossed the Atlantic (most likely on a freight ship), quickly spreading

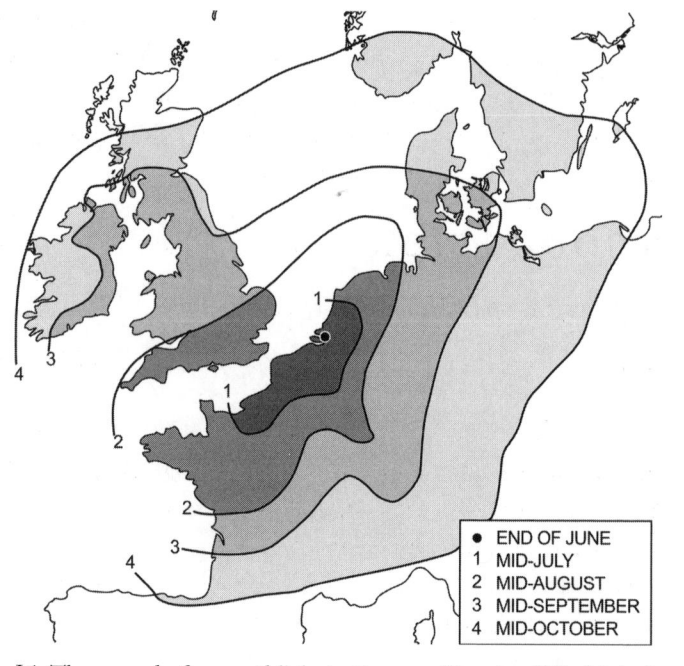

Figure I.1 The spread of potato blight in Europe. (Bourke, *"The Visitation of God,"* 142)

to many parts of Europe and first appearing in Dublin in August 1845. Over the next five years the Irish potato crop failed four times, the exception being the year commonly referred to as Black '47. During this period one million Irish people perished—approximately one-eighth of the population—while an additional two million ploughed the seas in search of new beginnings in places as far-flung as Canada, the United States, Australia, England, Scotland, New Zealand, South Africa, and further afield. Thus, in a relatively short period of time, three million people—largely destitute smallholders, cottier tenants, and day labourers—were either dead or gone.[1]

The sojourn of *Phytophthora infestans,* the potato-killing pathogen, to Irish shores was in itself unremarkable (figure I.1). Indeed, parts of Belgium, the United Kingdom, the Netherlands, and Scandinavia, not to mention North America, were also affected.[2] In regions where potatoes were an extensive part of inhabitants' diet, as in the Scottish

Highlands, the crisis was acute and starvation deaths occurred in significant numbers.[3] In Ireland, however, the failure of the potato harvest resulted in national rather than regional calamity.[4] Historian Peter Gray has said that "no peacetime European crisis since the seventeenth century, with the possible exception of the Ukrainian famine in the early 1930s, has equalled it in intensity or scale"; and more recently the Indian economist Amartya Sen has argued that the mortality rate during the Great Famine was higher than in any other recorded famine, anywhere in the world.[5] Certainly the Famine was larger than anything the European continent had endured for centuries, blunting John Post's suggestion that the earlier food crisis of 1816–17 was the "the last great subsistence crisis in the Western world."[6]

The occurrence of a mass famine in Ireland, at a time when European subsistence crises were thought to be a relic of the past, continues to provoke acrimonious debate. Especially controversial is the relationship between Ireland and Great Britain. As the Great Famine drew to a close, over one million international visitors poured into London to witness the Great Exhibition (1851), where Britain's "technical, industrial and financial supremacy" was proudly arranged and displayed.[7] The exhibition was a spectacular reminder that the catastrophe of famine occurred when Ireland was constitutionally linked to Great Britain, considered by contemporaries to be the "workshop of the world" and a beacon of democratic government, with one of the most socially interventionist governments of its day. The question remains, How could one of the world's worst famines occur in the backyard of the world's most economically advanced nation?

BETWEEN THE STOMACH AND THE PURSE: THE AETIOLOGY OF FAMINE AND THE POLITICS OF BLAME

Modern scholars tend to agree that famines do not necessarily *begin* with crop failures, droughts, or equivalent climatic hazards; rather, their violence is coordinated much earlier, when a population is made progressively vulnerable or slowly brought to the point of collapse. According to this aetiology of hunger, droughts, floods, and crop failures are "trigger factors," though not necessarily an "underlying cause," of famine.[8] For David Arnold famines are "a symptom rather than a cause of social weakness," a viewpoint that raises deeper questions concerning social and economic inequality, collective vulnerability, and uneven power relations.[9]

Despite the fact that the Great Irish Famine is now a major field of scholarly enquiry, there has been little attempt to engage with these critical perspectives, which are derived principally from famine experiences in colonial and postcolonial contexts. Cormac Ó Gráda acknowledges that "themes central to mainstream famine history research have until recently been ignored in Irish work." Ó Gráda references in particular Sen's distinguished treatment of famines as "entitlement failures" and Ambirajan's consideration of colonial bureaucracy and classical political economy, neither of which has been greatly discussed in what Ó Gráda characterises as the "serious" literature on the Irish Famine.[10]

This lack of attention to a "comparative phenomenology of famine" may partly explain the resilience of historical accounts emphasising the "natural" causes of the Irish Famine.[11] Lingering neo-Malthusian arguments claiming that nineteenth-century Ireland was overpopulated (and, therefore, a cull through mass starvation was largely unavoidable) are an extreme case in point.[12] More common is the tendency to focus attention on the sudden shock of the potato blight, a move that implicitly, if not explicitly, assigns the real meaning of events to an unruly nature.[13] For instance, one popular account of the Great Famine claims that Irish deaths were the result of "a tragic ecological accident." "In the end," the author concludes, "the Irish were desperately unlucky."[14] More recently, the Famine has been characterised as a series of "malign coincidences," a phrase that appears to echo this environmental reading.[15] Similar to Malthusian arguments, these accounts place the events of the Famine beyond blame because, as Eagleton writes, "a blankly indifferent Nature is not even enough of a subject to be malevolent."[16]

Besides attributing social failings to natural causes, another tactic of deflecting blame is to suggest that it is unfair—even "anachronistic"—to pass judgement on state officials who viewed the Famine as an "act of God," or condemn civil servants who zealously supported market responses to Famine management, on the grounds that such views were "commonplace" in the mid-nineteenth century. For instance, Margaret Crawford argues that it is "simply anachronistic" to think that the state "could have interfered with private markets," while Mary Daly believes that it would be inappropriate "to pronounce in an unduly critical fashion on the limitations of previous generations."[17] The distinguished historian Roy Foster goes so far as to claim that an embargo on food exports "was not adopted *anywhere*, and would have been considered an economic irrelevance at the time."[18] Woodham-Smith concluded her classic account with a caveat similar to Mary Daly's, while Robin Haines has argued that Charles Trevelyan's (1807–86) providential reading of the Famine was "theologically commonplace" and should therefore be excused.[19] More guardedly, but summing up the same mood, Peter Gray accepts that "historians risk falling into gross anachronism in attempting to pass judgement on long-dead individuals."[20]

In raw form these charges of "anachronism" imply that we should be less critical of ideologies that were popularly endorsed by the Victorians. This moral relativity is deeply problematic, however. The fact that many people approved of slavery and supported racial apartheid—to take two separate examples—tells us absolutely nothing about its propriety.[21] As Hannah Arendt has noted, critical judgement is an act of great political importance—an argument that is as true today as it would have been in the 1840s.[22] Furthermore, the allegation of "anachronism" seriously underestimates *contemporary* expressions of moral outrage made by English *and* Irish peers. In the House of Commons, for example, the leader of the opposition, George Bentinck (1802–48), charged that "They [the government] know the people have been dying in their thousands and I dare them to enquire what has been the number of those who have died through their mismanagement, by their principles of free trade, yes, free trade in the lives of Irish people."[23] The English traveller James Johnson (1777–1845) observed a popular refutation of providential reasoning and a tendency to consider hunger as a social phenomenon: "It would require philosophy—and 'something more,'" he exclaimed, "to convince the sufferers or even

the bye-standers, that this stupendous inequality in the lot of mankind, is the fiat of the Almighty, and not the effect of some injustice in
human laws."[24]

The scepticism of the "sufferers" was shared by several observers of Irish events. "Is this [Famine] to be regarded in the light of a Divine dispensation and punishment?" asked the Quaker William Bennett (1804–73). "Before we can safely arrive at such a conclusion," he
reasoned, "we must be satisfied that human agency and legislation, individual oppression, and social relationships, have had no hand in it."[25]
In a public lecture, Catholic Archbishop John Hughes (1797–1864)
dismissed the view that this was "God's Famine," blaming instead
"the invisible but all-pervading divinity of the Fiscal, the unseen ruler
of the temporal affairs of this world."[26] Hughes contrasted the new
"political economy" ("the free system,—the system of competition,
the system of making the wants of mankind the regulator for their supplies") with what he defined as a more progressive "social economy"
("that effort of society, organized into a sovereign state, to accomplish
the welfare of all its members").[27] Hughes went on to distinguish the
"antecedent circumstances and influences" from the "primary, original
causes" of hunger, thus anticipating, by nearly a century and a half, the
general theoretical thrust of modern Famine Studies.[28] Hughes's sentiments were echoed by Archbishop John Mac Hale (1791–1881), who
reproved the prime minster for endorsing the "political casuistry"
of economists who promoted the "unchristian doctrine that the lives
of the people are to be sacrificed, rather than interfere with the cruel
speculations of [the] mercantile lobby." In Mac Hale's view economic
liberalism was "as wrong in principle as it is inhuman in practice."[29]

Similar arguments where advanced by English critics when faced
with the problem of food shortages in Britain. In a searing account
of the food crises following the conclusion of the Napoleonic Wars,
the economist John Wheatley (1772–1830) maintained that the widespread deprivation was not the result of a "Visitation from Heaven,"
nor the "blow of a foreign enemy," nor had it "originated in [natural]
calamities, against which human foresight could provide." Having dismissed his fellow economists for fastening blame to such easy tar-
gets, Wheatley went on to impugn the "blind policy" and "incapacity
of [government] Ministers" who both produced and exacerbated the

food crises by doing "nothing they ought to have done, and every thing they ought not to have done." "It is not easy," Wheatley reprimanded, "to forgive ourselves for having so tamely and needlessly submitted to their errors."[30] Although he was a vociferous advocate for free trade, Wheatley's judgement of his peers and their "tame" submission to what he considered to be false dogmas (blaming in turn "nature," "foreign enemies," and "providence") shows that sophisticated appraisals of subsistence crises were available to Victorians decades before the Great Irish Famine. Indeed, many of the themes addressed by Wheatley were subsequently developed in the political writings of the Young Irelanders—not to mention certain critical comments collected within the Parliamentary Papers, memories assembled in the folk archive, and the opinions of numerous travel writers, pamphleteers, and contemporary observers—who in a commensurate way protested against the blind policies and meek submissions they witnessed in the 1840s. The point made here is that from the present perspective, what might seem to be an incontestable orthodoxy or dominant ideology was in truth challenged and undermined from a range of *contemporary* standpoints.

Nonetheless, the question of "anachronistic" viewpoints is not simply a matter of historical accuracy. The tendency to underplay the disputes over environmental and providential readings of famine (or the propensity to consider laissez-faire doctrines as an immutable fact) naturalises the violence of hunger by obscuring the role of actors and agents in securing particular outcomes. Take, for instance, Crawford's view that it is historically inaccurate to believe that the government could have interfered with private markets. Crawford's claim is only tenable if one ignores a vast body of evidence demonstrating direct government interposition to *maintain* the sanctity of private property and to *support* a system of propertylessness. Critics such as the English MP George Poulett Scrope never tired of singling out the hypocrisy of such "laissez-faire" pronouncements:

> It is a common fallacy—though a very natural one for an Englishman to be deluded by—to deprecate all interference between landlord and tenant, as contrary to sound economical principle, which "should leave their relations to be determined by voluntary

contract" . . . [But] the law, as it stands at present, is the result of *innumerable interferences in favour of the landlord, and against the tenant.* Some sixty acts of this one-sided legislation stand catalogued in the statute-book. Repeal all these acts, and restore the old common-law relation of landlord and tenant and something might be said against interference with their free bargaining.[31]

For Scrope, laissez-faire economics does not imply that "everything is left alone." In contradistinction to neoclassical theories, the liberalisation of the food system—"not interfering, allowing freedom of movement, letting things take their course"—is made possible through the meticulous elimination of all non-market behaviour that is considered aberrant or undesirable.[32] Indeed, laissez-faire was not only "planned," as Karl Polanyi famously insisted; its imposition required an increase in repressive measures, as labourers, peasants, and smallholders were forced to bear the costs of *market regulation.*[33] The assumption that markets are "natural systems" operating outside of power and politics is itself an invention of the nineteenth century.

It stands from this that if "free markets" are the product of human design, they must have a history and geography—and a fraught one at that, if we are to treat Polanyi's arguments with the seriousness they deserve. Before the dominance of laissez-faire, most European governments (and indeed many societies beyond Europe) operated what Michel Foucault has described as an "anti-scarcity system."[34] Foucault is alluding to the customary mechanisms or traditional entitlements for ensuring that interventions in times of dearth were considered "an inevitable extension of general state functions."[35] The means of accomplishing these so-called moral economies differed substantially between societies, but they more often than not included a mixture of price controls, limitations on exportations, proscriptions against hoarding, the operation of public granaries, the duty-free import of victuals, and prohibitions on the use of provisions for the distillation of alcohol.[36] Significantly, these practices were considered *preventative* rather than remedial. In other words, the maintenance of an "anti-scarcity system" was designed to stop food shortages from occurring in the first place.

However, the tensions between a nation's subsistence and the "economic management of society" become increasingly evident in the eighteenth and nineteenth centuries, first in the doctrines of the physiocratic politicians in France and later in the writings of free market theorists like Adam Smith (1723–90) and David Ricardo (1772–1823) in Britain.[37] In France the panoply of measures formerly used to guarantee stocks and promote grain price stabilisation were gradually abolished in favour of techniques designed to enhance the free circulation of provisions and capital. This new programme of regulation was the "practical consequence of economic theories" advocating that the "free circulation of grain was not only a better source of profit, but also a much better mechanism of security against the scourge of scarcity."[38]

The guiding tenets of economic liberalism were also making political inroads in Britain. In a letter directed to the statesman William Pitt (1759–1806) and entitled *Thoughts and Details on Scarcity,* Edmund Burke (1729–97) relates the issue of food supply—"one of the finest problems in legislation"—to the subject of responsible government. For Burke public provision in times of dearth was both naïve and dangerous: "Of all things, an indiscreet tampering with the trade of provisions is the most dangerous, and it is always worst in the time when men are most disposed to it: that is, in the time of scarcity."[39] According to Adam Smith, restricting the freedoms of the market by "the violence of government" was the most certain method of prolonging famine.[40] Similarly, David Ricardo's views on comparative advantage—suggesting that regions and states should specialise in a single niche product to gain a competitive edge—reinforced the case for interdependent global markets and unrestricted private enterprise.[41] Referring euphemistically to the "Irish emergency of 1847," the liberal economist J. S. Mill (1806–73) endorsed market mechanisms as the optimal scheme for addressing food scarcity. In his widely praised *Principles of Political Economy,* Mill warned against "direct measures at the cost of the state, to procure food," favouring instead "private speculation."[42] These pronouncements reflected the class interests of a newly politicised urban bourgeoisie, who resented measures designed to promote price stabilisation and guarantee food stocks because these same methods might also precipitate adverse exchange rates, restrictions on credit, and even runs on banks.[43] In general, as governments promoted the class interests of merchants and industrialists, they became less willing to interfere in food markets in order to protect poor peasants. The question of collective food provisioning was fast turning into a political war between the stomach and the purse.

It is important to underscore the extent to which laissez-faire doctrines represented a sea change from the "anti-scarcity systems" that dominated food structures before the nineteenth century.[44] During the severe famine of 1740–41, for example, an embargo was placed on food exports from Irish ports, while Parliament prevented severe scarcity once again in 1765 by prohibiting exports of corn and the distillation of alcohol.[45] Similar food embargoes were enacted by most European governments during the subsistence crisis in 1816–17. In the Netherlands, for example, the government allocated 6 million florins for the purchase of rye; the French government spent 164 million francs on imported provisions, whilst the British authorities imported 700,000 quarters of grain (much of it commandeered from Ireland) to address acute shortages in England. In Europe such interpositions were essential for keeping overall mortality levels similar to seventeenth-century famines.[46]

The history of the 1743–44 relief campaign in Zhili (now Hebei), China, demonstrates that similar "anti-scarcity" policies were common in supra-European contexts as well. According to Pierre-Etienne Will, two million peasants were maintained for over eight months until the return of the monsoon made agricultural production possible again. Indeed, Will estimates that 85 percent of the relief grain was shipped from tribute depots or public granaries located outside the main area of drought. This was a massive government-assisted campaign of food redistribution.[47] To cope with the pressures of harsh climatic conditions, peoples in the Hausaland district of northern Nigeria were encouraged to develop farming practices and redistributive systems to ensure their collective food security.[48] And in India, prior to the imposition of colonial doctrines and laissez-faire principles, the "importation of food, fixation of maximum prices and punishment and/or torture of offending grain dealers were the usual methods employed in fighting famines."[49] Obviously, these examples demonstrate very different kinds of "anti-scarcity" programmes, ranging from government policies (geared toward redistributive food relief and risk mitigation) to household and communal strategies (directed toward mutual dependence and collective provisioning). Notwithstanding these differences, the evidence suggests a surprisingly broad recognition of what might be described as an implicit "right to food."

In one of the earliest reflections on the Irish Famine, Anna Parnell (1852–1911) drew attention to the abnegation of government responsibility for food provisioning that laissez-faire implied:

> In old times the duty of the ruler to protect his subjects from extermination by hunger was taken for granted. When Joseph had interpreted Pharaoh's dream to him, Pharaoh did not talk about political economy, or disturbing the balance of economic conditions, or of laws of supply and demand, but passed at once to the question of meeting the evils foreshadowed by Joseph, whose advice he promptly and successfully acted on . . . it is rather interesting to compare the ideas of the old Pharaoh and those of Queen Victoria regarding the obligations of sovereigns.[50]

The point of Parnell's comparison is quite evident: historically the right to food was guaranteed through political action rather than the hidden hand of the market.[51] The erosion of this "anti-scarcity system," and its gradual replacement by a liberal market economy, is the crucial context for assessing the deficiencies of the government's relief programmes and the vexed question of food supply and exportation during the Great Irish Famine.[52] Although there is a general consensus that British famine relief was remarkably parsimonious (Donnelly condemned the "endowed but miserly treasury," and Mokyr described the government's relief funds as a "mere pittance"), discussions of food availability and supply are considerably more polarised.[53] The Irish republican John Mitchel (1815–75) notoriously claimed that "a government ship sailing into any harbour with Indian corn was sure to meet half a dozen sailing out with Irish wheat and cattle," and in the House of Commons Irish landlord William Smith O'Brien (1803–64) protested that "the people were starving in the midst of plenty, and that every tide carried from the Irish ports corn sufficient for the maintenance of thousands of the Irish people."[54] The economic historian Cormac Ó Gráda disagrees with these claims, arguing that the issue of "grain exports is of more symbolic than real importance" and that "food imports dwarfed food exports" during the famine period.[55] Transferring all the grains to the starving masses, Ó Gráda maintains, would have made "only a small dent" in the nutritional gap left by the potato, leading him to conclude that the Irish Famine was "a classic case of food shortage."[56]

By contrast, historian Christine Kinealy has strongly condemned the "food shortage" thesis. "The Irish poor did not starve because there was an inadequate supply of food within the country," she writes; "they starved because political, commercial and individual greed was given priority over the saving of lives in one part of the United Kingdom."[57] Kinealy argues that the historical emphasis on the exportation of "grain" actually amounts to a focus on corn, ignoring the exportation of other foodstuffs from Irish ports, particularly oats (already the largest item exported in 1841), wheat, and large quantities of livestock. Calls to prohibit the exportation of these provisions, Kinealy reminds us, were met "very coldly" by the British government.[58] Secondly, the continued distillation of alcohol—which requires grain—amounted to what Kinealy calls an "averted supply of food."[59] In 1847 alone, 7,952,076 gallons of spirits were exported from Irish ports.[60] Similarly, the fattening of livestock on foods that could have been consumed by humans distanced resources from nutritional needs. Furthermore, the Navigation Laws, which legislated that food must be imported on board British ships, remained in place until January 1847, contributing to exorbitant freight charges and what Kinealy terms an "artificial shortage of shipping."[61] Finally, it should be remembered that the Famine years marked a difficult period for most European governments, with several reacting by (temporarily) limiting the exportation of staple foods.[62] At the very least these arguments show that what was *offered* to Ireland in terms of relief was drastically inadequate, and what was *withheld* from Ireland, by dogmatically insisting on the principles of free trade and "noninterference" in Irish food markets, had deadly repercussions for the poorest and most vulnerable members of Irish society. In sum, the government showed no inclination to initiate anything resembling the traditional "anti-scarcity" measures used to mitigate the worst horrors of famine around the world.

The artificial encouragements to free trade, outlined above, make it difficult to support the view that laissez-faireism amounted to a crude policy of noninterference or that the market functioned as a "natural" regulator of social life. The late suspension of the Navigation Act, the closure of Irish food depots, the repeal of the Corn Laws, the Rate-in-Aid Acts, the failure to prohibit food exports, and the enactment of the Gregory Clause, which facilitated the legal confiscation of Irish property—all are evidence of a series of politico-economic interventions designed to regulate trade and relief in favour of specific outcomes. When looked into a little, it becomes evident that laissez-faire was a *policy choice:* it required a liberal, future-oriented, and proactive administration rather than the conservative and reactive outlook that "nonintervention" seems to imply. Hence one of the principal aims of this book is to extend David Keen's thesis that famines have *functions as well as causes.*[63] The fact that some people are *denied* entitlement to food—and are as such "entitled to starve"—is the result of governments upholding the rights of some at the expense of others.[64] The point that "the law stands between food availability and food entitlement" and that famines may reflect what Sen calls "legality with a vengeance" was forcefully underlined by contemporary observers of Irish affairs.[65] Discussing the legal processing of famine evictions, Scrope asked, "Does the law, then, protect the Irish peasant?" And then answering his own question, "Not from starvation!":

> All is done in the sacred name of the law. The sheriff, the representative of the majesty of the law, is the actual exterminator. The officers of the law execute the process. The constabulary, acting under the orders of the magistracy, stand by to prevent resistance; and, if any is expected, the Queen's troops are brought to the spot to quell, with all the power of the Throne, what would amount to an act of rebellion. It is absurd to cast the blame of these foul deeds, and the horrible results, upon a few reckless,

bankrupt landlords. It is to the law, or rather the Government and legislature which uphold it, and refuse to mitigate its ferocity, that the crime rightly attaches; and they will be held responsible for it by history, by posterity—aye, and perhaps before long, by the retributive justice of God, and the vengeance of a people infuriated by a barbarous oppression, and brought at last TO BAY by their destroyers.[66]

Scrope was not the first to condemn the sovereign violence of the law, nor was he alone in suggesting that famine deaths—resulting from evictions and land clearances—were the positive outcome of policy and ideology.[67] Isaac Butt (1813–79) described "free trade" as a legislative experiment, which meant that "for the first time [the Irish people] started into existence as elements of calculation in the economic problem of the supply of Ireland's food."[68] These observers recognised that the blight triggered a massive subsistence crisis, but at the same time they thought it unjust to ignore the considerable impact of fiscal, administrative, and legislative policies that obviously contributed to Irish suffering.

Despite what is said about so-called natural disasters, in practice calamities *tend to authorise a high degree of political control and intervention.* Indeed, as I wish to argue, the modern association between disaster and opportunity—the idea that famines can serve a strategic function—recapitulates earlier colonial arguments about "improving" and "anglicising" Irish society. The assistant secretary to the treasury, Charles Trevelyan, reminded readers of this fact when he approvingly cited the poet Edmund Spenser, who in the seventeenth century declared that "some secret scourge" was necessary for the regeneration of Ireland.[69] Like other key figures in government, Trevelyan came to view state relief as a Benthamite "science," which if orchestrated correctly could improve the habits of a rebarbative people and launch the "transition" from subsistence farming to agrarian capitalism. This belief in a redemptive crisis took hold in powerful sections of government and civil society. In addition, politico-cultural factors such as racial stereotyping (especially pseudo-biological accounts of poverty and racialised understandings of "redundant labour") became key components in discursively reproducing "bare lives" in need of historical transformation. I want to argue that this suturing of disaster and improvement actually encouraged the state to become closely involved in the "administration of bodies" and the "calculated management of life."[70] Drawing on the ideas of Michel Foucault, I term this *colonial biopolitics.*

COLONIAL BIOPOLITICS

The concepts "biopower" and "biopolitics" were first systematically theorised by Foucault in the last chapter of his well-known study *The History of Sexuality.*[71] There Foucault explains how both the principle of government and the exercise of sovereignty acquired a new, modern meaning by the end of the eighteenth century. Prior to this period, "government" usually meant managing a territory and controlling its inhabitants, while the principal characteristic of sovereign power was the right to decide over life and death. The power of the sovereign over individual lives was an ancient right named *"patria potestas* that granted the father of the Roman family the right to 'dispose' of the life of his children and his slaves."[72] In time sovereign power was gradually diminished or circumscribed, until only the defence of the sovereign and his continued survival justified its invocation. If external enemies threatened the sovereign he could legitimately wage war and require his subjects to take part in the defence of the state. Without directly proposing their death, he was empowered to "expose" their life to likely fatality: "Power in this instance was essentially a right of seizure: of things, time, bodies, and ultimately life itself; it culminated in the privilege to seize hold of life in order to suppress it."[73]

Foucault subsequently developed these preliminary thoughts on modern government to include what he called "biopolitics," defined as the careful control and supervision of life, death, and biological being—a form of politics that places human life at the very centre of its calculations.[74] By the nineteenth century, Foucault claims, sovereign power takes control of life in order to *reinforce and optimise* its existence rather than to seize and suppress it. This does not mean that the "old power of death" is totally abandoned but rather that violence must now be justified by the "notion of improvement."[75] As evidence of this important shift in governance, Foucault points to the rise of mercantilism (followed by the promotion of a capitalist economy), the birth of statistics, the science of demography, and the rapid spread of public health campaigns in the eighteenth and nineteenth centuries.[76] A biopolitical regime of governance is therefore a very general form of population management, which obviously has significant implications for our understanding of state power and sovereignty vis-à-vis subject populations.[77]

Significantly, in a series of lectures on food provisioning, Foucault argues that the new emphasis on the vitality and improvement of populations does not mean that famines and other catastrophes will be prevented in the future; on the contrary, he suggests that "there will no longer be any scarcity in general, on condition that for a whole series of people, in a whole series of markets, there was some scarcity . . . the scarcity that caused the death of individuals not only does not disappear, *it must not disappear.*"[78] To valorise the belief that some will have to starve for the benefit of others, a radical distinction between "peoples" and "populations" must be introduced. For Foucault the population includes those members of the community who adhere to the new rationality of market regulation, even promoting it as a means to attain greater security. The people, on the other hand, are those who "disrupt the system" and "throw themselves on the [food] supplies." They reject the new liberal order, and because of this they are perceived as political outcasts and delinquents, "threats, either external or internal, to the population."[79] According to Foucault, in a liberal biopolitical system "killing or the imperative to kill is acceptable only if it results not in a victory over political adversaries, but in the elimination of the biological threat to and improvement of the species or race"[80] Put differently, famine is permissible if it provokes a desirable social and economic change. Those who stand in the way of progress, or refuse to be assimilated, are deemed to be worthless degenerates—in a word, *human encumbrances*—thwarting the civilising currents of capitalist modernity.

It should be evident that when Foucault describes "killing or the imperative to kill" he does not mean simply murder as such but "every form of indirect murder: the fact of exposing someone to death, increasing the risk of death for some people, or quite simply, political death, expulsion, rejection, and so on."[81] Tania Murray Li fruitfully employs Foucault's unique genealogy of state power to analyse the violence of development practices aimed at encouraging purer morals and better habits among supposedly backward peoples. Significantly, Li concludes that the colonial will to improve was "difficult to reconcile with high mortality, although not, it seems, impossible."[82] Studies by Eric Stokes and Mike Davis similarly detail how millions of famine deaths were the outcome of normative economic theories designed to "advance" native capacities rather than any programme of direct killing.[83] A comparable understanding of political violence can also be found in Maybury-Lewis's assessment of colonial rule, which concludes that "widespread dying resulted not so much from deliberate killing but from the fatal circumstances imposed by imperialists on the conquered."[84] These studies speak volumes about the ways in which colonial regimes can undermine indigenous food systems through, for instance, the commercialisation of agrarian practices, the erosion of customary entitlements, the denial of political voice, or the failure to implement "anti-scarcity" programmes in times of crisis. Even the supposedly higher goal of stimulating socioeconomic reforms can cause or exacerbate human suffering by suppressing alternative conceptions of development or by crushing more progressive humanitarian impulses.[85] Ensuing famines may not be the result of any direct killing (in fact, very few famines are "genocidal" in this sense), but it does not follow that food crises are "natural" occurrences outside the realm of human affairs.[86]

What is being emphasised here is the shifting context of government regulation: modern famines are distinguishable from previous subsistence crises insofar as they take place *within* new systems of production, modalities of representation, and regimes of power.[87] "Modernity may have promised that hunger would be vanished," writes James Vernon, "but its dogged persistence produced a constant reinvention of the problem."[88] In Ireland this sense of "reinventing" the problem of famine is played out in different theatres of political conduct. These include contestations over (a) *discursive authority,* particularly the ability to define populations as savage, backward, and degenerate; (b) the development of *institutional power,* including the potential to control and regulate social behaviour; and finally (c) the mobilisation of *politico-legal action,* which is necessary to regulate or compel subject populations. As we shall see, the famine situation contributed to the extension of state power (augmenting an earlier shift from local to centralised methods of control), which together with the expansion of biopolitical norms, enabled the colonial state to target the Irish social body *under the pretext of reform.*

OUTLINE OF THE BOOK

Chapter 1 examines Ireland's colonial status. By all accounts, Irish poverty was acute by the mid-nineteenth century, and I make the case that the colonial experience is central—not incidental—to this situation. In particular, I want to show how the making and taking of space—politically, socially, and economically—is directly related to Irish vulnerability, especially the capacity of peasants and smallholders to cope with what Mokyr calls "exogenous shocks."[89] The larger argument is that there is a radical shift in colonial governance toward biopolitics and more meticulous methods of superintending Irish life, land, and resources.

Chapter 2 offers a critical account of how contemporaries responded to pre-Famine Irish life and how a discursive space opened up between "the satiated" and "the emaciated." The chapter is intended as an analysis of popular geopolitics, one that takes seriously Amartya Sen's contention that "the sense of difference between ruler and ruled—between 'us' and 'them'—is a crucial feature of famines."[90] I explore how empathy can be rhetorically disabled by focusing on what might be called "instrumental knowledges" about Ireland and the Irish, as developed in political pamphlets, contemporary travel accounts, and reports commissioned by the British government. Rather than treat these accounts as merely "descriptive," I show how they contribute to making Irish life *visible* so that it might be more *governable.* Similar to modern scientific knowledge, these accounts attempt to "bring distant objects close to hand, rendering these transported objects manipulable and predictable."[91] The resulting distinctions—between those who represent and those who are considered incapable of representing themselves—shaped the terms for dealing with the Irish poor.

Chapter 3 discusses the drafting and implementation of an Irish Poor Law in 1838, four years after the overhaul of the English Poor

Law and just seven years prior to the first appearance of *Phytophthora infestans*. The Poor Law was a new social experiment meant to better manage and regulate pauperism; however, the Irish system differed in crucial respects from its English counterpart—a divergence that was valorised by appealing to anthropological accounts of Irish difference (as discussed in chapter 2). I then explore how the government responded to the appearance of blight in Ireland, focusing on the plethora of institutional spaces—and legislative initiatives—designed to address the problem of Irish hunger. A major part of this response involved the co-opting of the Poor Law as a famine relief strategy, a decision that had very severe consequences for the poorest and most vulnerable sections of Irish society. I argue that the government's relief operations enabled the state to virtually monopolise the means of subsistence, thus assuming control over a radically depotentiated form of life. In other words, the administration of relief slowly merged with the biopolitical regulation of what Agamben terms "bare life."[92]

The emphasis on corrective regulation is quite deliberate; in chapter 4 I show how temporary aid structures were bound up with long-term goals aimed at radically restructuring Irish society. The desire to break the pattern of small, subsistence-based landholdings and cultivate a tripartite division of labour among landlords, capitalist tenant farmers, and landless wage labourers (as had happened in England) was well expressed and theorised prior to the arrival of the potato blight. Influenced by these views on agrarian transition, the Irish Famine was increasingly interpreted as a productive crisis, an occasion when "great organic changes"—as the author of the Irish Poor Law termed them—could be effected with conceivably less resistance from Irish smallholders hoping to hold on to their social positions.[93] This chapter shows how relief operations facilitated depopulation and dispossession and how "formerly unacceptable means and sacrifices were justified by the overriding importance of the ultimate goal": the long-term modernisation of Irish society.[94]

Chapter 5 examines Thomas Carlyle's journeys in Ireland. Carlyle's opinions on Ireland and the Irish are significant for a number of reasons. First, the timing of his visits is immediately striking. Carlyle travelled to Ireland first in 1846 and then again in 1849. These dates profile the beginning and the deadly culmination of the Great Irish Famine,

and Carlyle's response to these different "faminescapes" is important. The chapter also considers Carlyle's economic thinking. Although
known as a vocal critic of laissez-faire, Carlyle left Ireland extolling the
virtues of the market as a disciplinary mechanism capable of restoring
moral order. This shift in Carlyle's economic thinking parallels his propensity to qualify human value through environmental and racial readings of the Famine. Finally, I consider Carlyle's relationship with the
well-known nationalist Charles Gavan Duffy, who accompanied him
on both of his Irish tours. Duffy published his own account of their
sojourn, and it offers a vivid counterpoint to Carlyle's perspective. A
close reading of their journey—and subsequent quarrels—helps us
understand how particular political rationalities are forged at the "contact zone" of two cultures. Such calculations take us into the domain
of biopower and capitalist political economy, the two most powerful
forces directing the government's response to the Irish Famine.[95]

The final chapter revisits some of the main arguments of the
book by exploring the contradictions between the ideology of improvement and the huge and lasting devastation caused by the Great
Famine. Recent historiography has been mired in contentious debate
over the relative culpability of the British government. Most scholars
of the Famine reject the extreme nationalist charge of genocide, but
beyond that there is little consensus. I argue for a more nuanced understanding of "famineogenic behaviour"—behaviour that aids and
abets famine—that draws distinctions between the effects of political
indifference (a policy of "letting die") and reckless conduct (including
utopian plans to radically reconstitute Irish society), whilst acknowledging that both kinds of behaviour can produce extraordinary levels
of violence. The *context* of causality is therefore important, not only in
terms of redefining the discussion of culpability but also in terms
of taking seriously the alternatives to the British government's famine
policies.[96] The fact that famine and malnutrition continue to haunt a
depressingly large portion of humanity illustrates how far we are from
understanding the legacy of the nineteenth century and how important
it is to explain the forces that shape vulnerability and determine overall
famine mortality. This book is an effort to open up this indispensable
enquiry.

CHAPTER ONE

FATAL CIRCUMSTANCES

Colonialism and the Origins of Vulnerability to Famine

Strange it is that this poor hungry Ireland, in which so many actually die of hunger every year, and in whose bills of mortality and hospital books "starvation" is as regular a heading as any other cause of death; — strange it is I say, that this country should, above all things, be destined to feed so many strangers on her soil.
— J. G. Kohl, *Ireland, Scotland, and England*

The mass of the people struggle against the same poverty, flounder about making the same gestures and with their shrunken bellies outline what has been called the geography of hunger.
— Frantz Fanon, *The Wretched of the Earth*

COLONIAL ENCOUNTERS

Most accounts of the Great Famine begin their analysis in 1845 — coinciding with the appearance of potato blight — and among the many books now available, very few choose to situate the story of hunger within an historical geography of colonisation and population management.[1] In 1975 Peter Gibbon declared "The occasion for all this [suffering] is well known — successive failures of the potato crop, the staple diet of half the population. Less well known are the circumstances in which this situation arose, and their relation to British colonialism."[2] Precisely twenty years later, marking the sesquicentennial commemoration of the blight, Kevin Whelan could still justifiably assert that the "colonial context . . . [is] too often ignored in our recent analyses of nineteenth-century Irish life."[3]

While this outline is accurate enough, more recent publications have begun to question and overturn this historiographical tradition by exploring, for example, the connections between Irish and Indian famines and by interrogating the ideological assumptions shaping the British administrative system in the nineteenth century.[4] Also noteworthy is the fact that scholars working on other colonial famines have observed strong connections with Ireland in the 1840s.[5] By and large, however, this research remains quite marginal to the mainstream historiography of the Irish Famine, a fact that partly reflects the fractious and ongoing debate regarding the applicability of colonial models to Irish history more generally.[6]

It is odd, then, that the most popular account of the Famine and possibly the most widely selling Irish history book of all time, Cecil Woodham-Smith's *The Great Hunger,* frames the Great Famine in relation to Ireland's political subjugation. Arguably, it is precisely this focus that some scholars find so jarring. For instance, Liam Kennedy critiques the Irish mythology of "incomparable oppression" resulting from an unhealthy reliance on a small, but quite vocal, coterie of nationalist writers.[7] Published in 1962, Woodham-Smith's *The Great Hunger* is usually seen as emblematic of this "mythological" tradition.[8] Indeed, in contradiction to the facts, D. G. Boyce goes so far as to suggest that "writers as diverse as Cecil Woodham Smith and the IRA leader, Ernie O'Malley, shared a common view of the Famine as a kind of genocide."[9] Until quite recently historical accounts loosely following Woodham-Smith's interpretation were characteristically derided as "emotive," a designation that disregards certain historical interpretations whilst promoting other, presumably more "objective," readings.

There are no doubt important exceptions to this trend. I have already mentioned the beginnings of comparative research on "colonial famines," to which I should now add the diverse writings associated with "The Field Day Company," which are on the whole exceptionally attentive to the implications of colonisation. Beyond this diverse group of scholars, historians Peter Gray, Christine Kinealy, and Kerby Miller have all published research that explores—sometimes directly, though more often implicitly—the relationship between colonialism and the Irish Famine. Kinealy's *A Death-Dealing Famine,* for example, writes the history of the 1840s back into the Irish experience of "dispossession and disunity."[10] Significantly, none of these accounts has prompted anything like the ridicule heaped upon Woodham-Smith.[11] While recent research has come closer to agreeing with many of Woodham-Smith's original conclusions, a great deal of theoretical and substantive investigation remains to be done.[12] *The Great Hunger* was published just before the wave of decolonisation in the non-European world and the advent of postcolonial studies as a vibrant research field in its own right.[13] Meanwhile, in Ireland the sesquicentennial commemorations have come and gone, but we are still without a substantial monograph addressing the Irish Famine as a *colonial experience.*

This chapter does not—and cannot—attempt to redress this fact; however, it does make the case that a *historical* perspective on how space is seized, occupied, and reconstituted is necessary for understanding the genesis and progression of the Great Famine. As Cameroonian political scientist Achille Mbembe reminds us, colonisation is an innately spatial process, involving the violent transformation of indigenous polities and social structures:

> *Colonial occupation* itself was a matter of seizing, delimiting, and asserting control over a physical geographical area—of writing on the ground a new set of social and spatial relations. The writing of new spatial relations (territorialization) was, ultimately, tantamount to the production of boundaries and hierarchies, zones and enclaves; the subversion of existing property arrangements; the classification of people according to different categories; resource extraction; and, finally, the manufacturing of a large reservoir of cultural imaginaries.[14]

The colonial rewriting of spatial relations, as described by Mbembe, can be read productively alongside recent work in critical famine theory, which urges scholars to look beyond the "end game" of famine (that is, mass mortality) to focus instead on the recasting of agrarian relations in ways that undermine rural livelihoods or facilitate expropriation. Considering famine as a process, not an event, puts greater emphasis on the *transformations* taking place in rural social relations—changes that must ultimately affect the viability of certain ways of life and the susceptibility of particular populations to exogenous shocks.[15] The point argued here is that colonisation is itself a formative social force with lasting implications.

It has already been suggested that the unprecedented upheaval in landownership, particularly in the sixteenth and seventeenth centuries, had a precipitous impact on nineteenth-century Irish life.[16] Critics of this argument sometimes point to other instances of agrarian dispossession, particularly the enclosures in the English countryside, which concentrated land ownership and facilitated rural proletarianisation. There are clear and irrevocable distinctions between the English and Irish experiences, however. In England the position of peasant proprietors was more commonly undermined through a process of *appropriation* ("buying out" by landlords), whereas in Ireland the shift in control over land was accomplished through a system of *expropriation* involving military occupation backed by an expansionist state.[17] The use of state power and violence as the leverage of social change suggests that more accurate comparisons might be drawn with other colonial contexts. In Indonesia, for example, "agrarian differentiation" was accomplished through "forced markets" rather than market forces: "It took intervention, by force and law, to transform land into private property that could be bought, sold, and accumulated, and to transform people into wage labourers available for hire."[18] Examining the agrarian question in Karamoja, Uganda, Mamdani shows how British colonialism began with the "forcible acquisition of land," leaving local people bereft of the means of production and thrust back onto precarious pastoral modes of existence.[19] In his account of colonial Ceylon, geographer James Duncan similarly highlights the exceptional control over labour necessary to insert (racialised) bodies into the process of surplus production and the unique role of the state in restructuring markets to encourage export-oriented agriculture.[20] While the exercise of colonial power was never absolute—and peasants continued to resist through a multitude of subversive tactics—it is hardly in doubt that agrarian relations were profoundly transformed through colonial encounters and that these changes often had negative consequences on the political and economic trajectories of colonised societies.

In the discussion that follows, therefore, I prioritise three colonial encounters in Ireland: the foundation of the Pale, the plantations and confiscations during the sixteenth and seventeenth centuries, and the Act of Union made law in 1801. I describe these colonial encounters as iterative performances—serial "acts of union"—that attempted to make good an original claim of possession. The privileging of these encounters serves to highlight the fact that colonial rule often differed remarkably in terms of social vision and political methods.[21] Admitting the heterodox nature of colonisation in practice should not obscure the fact that its ideological character rested on a relatively unquestioned set of core beliefs. These included the presumptions that native populations were fundamentally incapable of autonomous development (hence colonial subjects required constant remedial intervention) and that, in certain situations, violent methods may be necessary to stimulate political reform and socioeconomic development. Indeed, colonialism continually spun on a *dialectic of conversion and coercion,* at times preferring military pacification as an engine of modernisation, while on other occasions favouring a "milder enlightenment ethos of order, progress and rationality" as the most expedient harbinger of social change.[22] We begin now with the scene of colonisation where these rival tensions were originally articulated.

COLONIAL LAW AND THE PALE

Ireland's colonial history is both long and complex. Early raids by Scandinavian Vikings brought Ireland its first settler populations since the Celts arrived in 400 BCE, but the country's political association with England did not begin until the Norman conquests (1169–1315).[23] Like the Vikings they succeeded, the Norman settlers preferred to seize the fertile lowlands and consolidate their power in urban centres. Their settlements were inevitably piecemeal, and in time they merged with the indigenous Irish, often adopting their language, customs, and *brehon* laws. As late as the fifteenth century, English rule was effectively confined to a small tract of land commonly known as "the Pale." At this time the boundaries of the Pale extended north from Dublin to Dundalk and inland from the coast as far as Naas, before winding south to include the settlement of Bray (see figure 1.1).

Reflecting the failure of colonisation as much as anything else, the parliament attempted to criminalise the use of the Irish language and other autochthonous customs considered barbarous by the new settler-colonisers. The Statute of Kilkenny (1336), for example, decreed "that no alliance by marriage, gossipred, fostering of children, concubinage or by amour, nor in any other manner, be hencefoth made betweeen the English and Irish."[24] To ride a horse "otherwise than on a saddle in the English fashion" was deemed illegal, and to sell horses or military armour to the Irish was a treasonable offence. The sale of victuals was to be "reasonably regulated," and merchants were ordered to present themselves to state officials to negotiate trade prices and taxes. Significantly, those who breached these ordinances were liable to have their "lands and tenements" legally seized and confiscated—an early example of the use of statutory law as an aid to expropriation.[25]

Although the Statute of Kilkenny seems to repeat earlier legislation to the same effect, its occasion and tone hint at the growing realisation that brute force would not be enough to subdue and govern Ireland.[26] It is worth remembering that the statute also attempted to shape the behaviour of the settlers themselves, who were now forbidden to adopt Gaelic modes of living. In making acculturation a criminal offence, early colonial officials recognised, however implicitly, that Englishness, like Irishness, was never a stable identity.[27] The cultural porosity of the contact zone—what Canny refers to as "the permissive frontier"—meant that colonial demarcations of difference would require vigilant surveillance and constant reaffirmation.[28]

The Pale was therefore a material expression and spatial manifestation of "the dark fears of the classic embattled settler."[29] It was with reference to the recalcitrant Irish living outside its borders that the English phrase "beyond the pale" (meaning "beyond the law") originated. As Heidegger recognised, however, the proliferation of boundaries does not necessarily imply a process of political retrenchment: "A

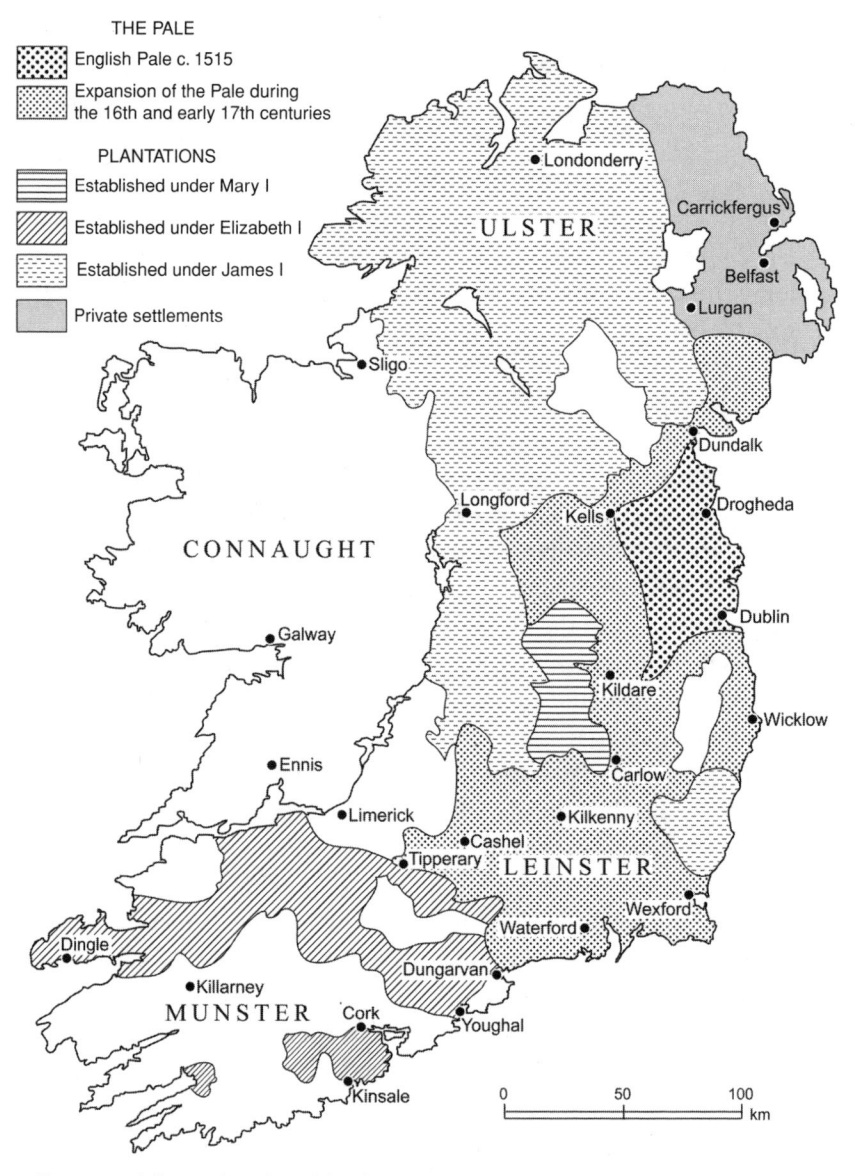

Londonderry

ULSTER

Carrickfergus

Belfast

Lurgan

Sligo

Dundalk

Longford

Kells

Drogheda

CONNAUGHT

Dublin

Galway

Kildare

Wicklow

Ennis

Carlow

Limerick

Kilkenny

Cashel

Tipperary

LEINSTER

Dingle

Killarney

MUNSTER

Wexford

Waterford

Dungarvan

Cork

Youghal

Kinsale

0   50   100
km

Figure 1.1. The Irish colonial landscape

boundary is not that at which something stops, as the Greeks recognized, the boundary is that from which something begins its presencing."[30] As we shall see, the Pale was an early attempt at policing cultural difference through *presencing* new political structures, legal codes, cultural norms, and economic policies. Properly speaking, the Pale was neither a perimeter nor a frontier. Rather, it was an inside-outside dialectic—at once topological and topographical—that constructed differences (the "civilised" and the "barbarous," those inside the law and those beyond it) precisely as it attempted to erode those distinctions.

The establishment of colonial distinctions gathered pace under the Tudor regime. Following Henry VIII's break from Rome (1534), Catholic Ireland was thought to be a strategic threat to the Crown. As a consequence, Henry duly proclaimed the Kingdom of Ireland (1541)—replacing the earlier Lordship of Ireland—and embarked upon a series of "plantation" schemes that were later continued and expanded under the reign of Elizabeth I (see figure 1.1). Henry sought to convince many of the Gaelic and Anglo-Irish lords beyond the Pale that he could guarantee superior security by presenting them with new legal titles to their lands. Forty of the most influential lords "surrendered their lands to the crown and received them back *in capite* by regrant."[31] The policy, known as "Surrender and Regrant," proved to be a successful but limited platform for colonisation during the Tudor period, primarily because the "principle of primogeniture that underpinned English common law—the system by which the eldest legitimate child succeeds to all property and titles—ran directly counter to Irish practice, where bastard sons had as much right as legitimate offspring."[32] Rather than continue to force "square pegs into round holes," colonisation took on a more coercive character with the confiscation of Irish lands and the replacement of indigenous farmers with English and later Scottish planters. This new policy was practiced when Edward VI (1537–53) imprisoned O'Connor of Offaly and O'More of Laois and declared their lands forfeit. Shortly thereafter, 160 families, mostly from the Pale and England, were granted estates in these territories. Initially, Gaelic resistance was strong, and the lands bordering the newly planted estates suffered internecine strikes that ultimately led to the settlements' failure. In other instances, small colonies of English farmers were "planted" with the expectation that the Gaelic populations living in the surrounding countryside would emulate these ideal farming communities. These exemplary plantations are an interesting prototype of nineteenth-century colonial policies promoting civilisation by example.

Plantation policy gained greater momentum under Queen Elizabeth's rule. When the Earl of Desmond was killed during a rebellion in 1583, Elizabeth saw an opportunity to recreate "the world of southeast England" in Munster.[33] Accordingly, in 1586 she confiscated 374,628 acres in counties Cork, Limerick, Kerry, and Waterford.[34] This massive land grab was followed by an equally ambitious project of re-territorialisation: landed estates of 12,000; 8,000; 6,000; and 4,000 acres were awarded to thirty-five English landlords and some twenty thousand settlers "who vowed to introduce English colonists and to practise English-style agriculture based on grain growing."[35] Although the "Munster Plantation" was only moderately successful (just a small share of the confiscated lands were actually settled and even this was not financially rewarding), it served as an important lesson in colonial governance. The scheme was far more systematic than any previous plantation attempt, and it proved the rule that large numbers of settlers were vital if plantation-colonisation was to be successful. By the end of the sixteenth century, an estimated twelve thousand settlers were actively engaged in farming on the confiscated estates.[36]

The lessons gleaned from the Munster scheme proved valuable to planning the much more extensive colonisation of Ulster. Elizabeth's successful conclusion of the bloody Nine Years War (1594–1603), and the later flight of the Ulster aristocracy to continental Europe (an exodus known as the "Flight of the Earls"), produced a power vacuum that the newly appointed King James I moved to exploit.[37] In contrast to earlier schemes, the plantations in Ulster involved the confiscation of huge swathes of land. Six counties were involved in the official plantation: Armagh, Fermanagh, Cavan, Coleraine (renamed Londonderry), Donegal, and Tyrone.[38] Of the 3.8 million acres confiscated, 1.5 million acres were either partly or wholly infertile (see figure 1.1). This marginal land was to be regranted to the indigenous Irish, the lowest of the three divisions of settlers listed in the Articles of Plantation

(1609). Within the colony only a small number of native settlers would be retained and only on condition that they assumed English modes of dwelling and farming.[39] This ordinance was meant to encourage the new colonists to "plant" in groups rather than on isolated islands or pockets of land.

In practice, however, the Irish population was neither completely removed nor wholly anglicised. Although new English and Scottish planters did arrive in substantial numbers, they often had to accommodate Irish tenants in order to make their estates economically viable. In addition to these state-sponsored schemes, private plantations were established in Antrim and Down that proved to be remarkably successful. By 1618 the Scots population of Ulster was estimated to be forty thousand.[40] Before the end of James I's reign, additional plantations were established in Leitrim, Westmeath, King's County, Queen's County, Longford, and Wexford, although with only limited success.[41]

This cascade of plantations helped establish and fortify the power of a new elite, loyal, and largely Protestant aristocracy. At the end of the Tudor monarchy, and despite the early attempts at plantation, 90 percent of the land remained under Catholic ownership. By 1641, mainly as a result of the Ulster plantations, there were estimated to be 100,000 Protestant settlers in Ireland (comprising 30,000 Scots and 70,000 Welsh and English).[42] Still vastly outnumbered by Catholics (by around 15:1), the colonists now controlled 41 percent of the land. However, the most devastating legacy of the Tudor confiscations lay in the reshaping of Irish rural society:

> The defeats of Desmond and the Ulster lords rang the death knell for the medieval societies of Gaelic and Gaelicized Ireland . . . [T]he Crown proscribed the *brehon* laws, abolished traditional Irish titles, and forced the native Catholic gentry to observe English rules of inheritance and succession. In addition the government strove to abolish the networks of traditional obligations which had knit medieval Irish society together, replacing them with purely commercial, contractual relationships: new laws not only required Irish landowners to pay cash rents to retain their properties but obliged them to demand the same from their tenantry. Perhaps most important, the Elizabethan conquest inau-

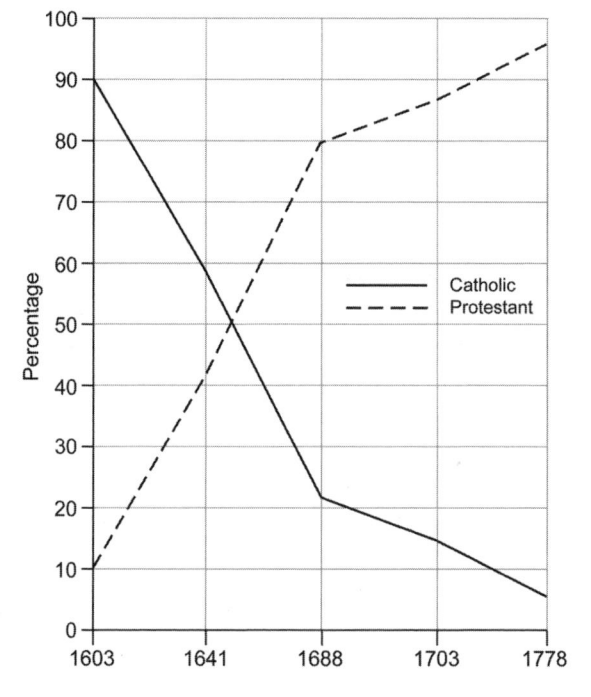

Figure 1.2. Transfer of land ownership in Ireland (adapted from Edwards and Hourican, *An Atlas of Irish History,* 164)

gurated the belated commercialization of hitherto pastoral and subsistence-oriented Irish rural economy . . . To enforce these new patterns, the crown modernized and expanded its administrative machinery, thereby bringing the island under closer control by the Dublin government—itself a creature of English policy and New English ambition.[43]

The removal of the former owners of the land was the primary engine driving these transformations. By the time of James II's accession to the throne in 1685, the new settlers possessed nearly 80 percent of the land (figure 1.2).[44] Oliver Cromwell's brutal suppression of another rebellion in 1641, and the subsequent Jacobite war in Ireland, prefigured a further round of displacement and dispossession. Surviving Irish officers surrendered on terms that allowed them to recruit for military service overseas. Those driven into destitution by the conflict were rounded up and transported to the West Indies, where they served as household servants and indentured labourers. "Within a few decades," writes S. J. Connolly, Ireland became "the main source of white plantation labour in a climate shunned by better placed migrants."[45] Of the landed class, the few who were permitted to retain their estates were to be uprooted west of the river Shannon, where they were to be relocated on the bog lands and marginal soils of Connaught and Clare. Forbidden to appear within four miles of the sea and ten miles of the Shannon, Cromwell was said to have driven the Irish "To Hell or to Connaught," though according to some descriptions there was little difference.[46] In all, 11 million acres were expropriated across Leinster, Munster, and Ulster, not to mention the significant confiscations within Connaught and Clare, as nearly two thousand displaced Catholic landowners competed with local inhabitants for the scarce resources on the western seaboard.[47] Of huge consequence, too, was the confiscation of all properties in towns and cities previously held by rebel forces. As a result of these measures, Catholic merchants were excluded from local government and, therefore, from the main arteries of political and economic power.[48]

This long cycle of confiscation and banishment paved the way for what became know as the period of "Protestant Ascendancy."[49] Future rebellion was to be quashed by a complex body of anti-Catholic legislation, collectively known as the Penal Laws, that were enacted from the end of the seventeenth to the middle of the eighteenth century. In addition to proscribing the Catholic faith, these codes disqualified Catholics from civic pursuits, barred them from voting and obtaining an education, and stipulated that Catholic estates were to be distributed by "gavelkind"—that is, divvied up among all the sons of the family. If one son were to convert to the Protestant faith, he could become the sole heir.[50] Unable to rent or purchase land, Catholics were "denied access to the most secure source of profits in a still overwhelmingly agrarian society."[51] By the eighteenth century Irish land ownership had fallen to a mere 5 percent (figure 1.2), and it is around this time that English descriptions of Irish poverty became more common. A celebrated political economist of the period, William Petty (1623–87), described the majority of Irish as living in "such cottages as themselves can make in 3 to 4 days; eat such food (tobacco excepted) as they buy not from others; wear such clothes as the wool of their own sheep, spun into yarn themselves."[52] Such misery was commonly attributed to slovenly habits, although the English traveller Thomas Campbell (1733–95) rebuked his countrymen for failing to consider the legislative aids to Irish indigence:

> We keep the Irish dark and ignorant, and then we wonder how they can be so enthralled by superstition; we make them poor and unhappy, and then we wonder that they are so prone to tumult and disorder; we tie up their hands, so that they have no inducements to industry, and then we wonder why they are so lazy and indolent. It is in vain to say that these severe laws restrain Catholics within the bounds of allegiance, and clip those wings, which, if fully fledged would be hatching new rebellions: for the very contrary seems to be their tendency; they are restraint, not from doing evil, but from doing good . . . No wonder that it should be part of the Irish character that they are so *careless of their lives,* when they have so little worth living for.[53]

Even more guarded assessments admitted that the Penal Laws "interfered with almost every mode of dealing landed property by those who professed that religion [Catholicism], and by creating a feeling of insecurity, directly checked their industry."[54] A series of Catholic Relief Acts in the eighteenth century corrected many of these injustices, but even so by 1828 Catholics held only 5 percent of the minor political offices available to them.[55]

These sectarian acts were buttressed by a number of important economic sanctions. The Navigation, Cattle, and Wool Acts were especially important in securing what Denis O'Hearn terms a negative "path dependency."[56] For example, Navigation Acts in 1660, 1663, 1670, 1671, and 1696—"a rather invisible episode in Irish colonial history"—excluded Ireland from importing most plantation commodities.[57] High-value Caribbean products (including tobacco and sugar) could only be landed at British ports.[58] Although Petty recognised that "Ireland lieth well for sending butter, cheese, beef, fish, to their proper markets which are southward, and the plantations of America," in practice it benefited little from the expanding networks of Atlantic and imperial trade.[59] The Cattle Act of 1665 prohibited the exportation of live cattle to England, and the Wool Act of 1699 banned the export of Irish wool to any country other than England.[60] These acts had disastrous consequences for Irish trade; in the case of live cattle, exports plummeted from 37,544 heads in 1665 to 1,054 in 1669.[61]

O'Hearn insists that the *exceptions* to these acts affected Irish economic development every bit as much as the restrictions they imposed, particularly in terms of controlling Irish production. The Wool Act, for instance, cushioned the English market from competition on the continent and, at the same time, *accelerated* the transition to linen production in Ireland. Similarly, by restricting Irish exports of cattle "on the hoof," the Cattle Acts encouraged a transition to the provisions trade (including the exportation of barrelled beef, butter, and pork), expansions in sheep husbandry, and the exportation of wool to England.[62] "In the decades after 1688," writes Connolly, "it seems perverse to suggest that the cutting off of two of the most obvious sources of profit for hard-pressed Irish farmers and manufacturers, English demand for food and European demand for woollen cloth, did not have a negative impact."[63] For O'Hearn, "trade restrictions were designed not only to suppress Irish competition with England but to encourage Irish production of commodities that were crucial to England's Atlantic commercial project."[64] Properly speaking, these "acts of union" were *regulatory* rather than punitive: they suppressed certain economic behaviours whilst inciting others deemed more conducive to colonial and metropolitan expansion.

These asymmetries in trade are indicative of a more momentous shift from a traditional economy based on a "subsistence ethic" to a more commercialised economy determined by market forces largely beyond the control of poor peasants.[65] Although bartering continued as a mode of exchange and indigenous patterns of agrarian organisation persisted well into the nineteenth century, the old verities of rural life creaked under the weight of an expanding commercial economy. For Kerby Miller, "the relative pauperization of the Irish was a direct consequence of the process of commercialization itself, occurring as it did in a colonial appendage to the world's most advanced industrial economy, and under a grossly inequitable system of landownership."[66] The upheavals of the sixteenth and seventeenth centuries had installed a new landowning class eager to anglicise Ireland by introducing new scientific farming methods to what was increasingly considered to be a degenerate rural economy. Under the auspices of "improvement" a new form of political control was gathering momentum.

CROWN CONTROL AND THE FORCE OF LAW

In his *History of the Poor Law in Ireland,* George Nicholls (1781–1865), the Irish poor law commissioner, glosses this tumultuous period of Irish history in a very revealing way. From the eighteenth century, Nicholls avers, "we no longer see any allusion to the 'Irishry' as a separate race. All are brought within the pale of the law, or it may rather be said that *the law and the pale have become conterminous.*"[67] Above we suggested that the Pale was neither a perimeter nor a frontier but rather a boundary or point from which new structures, codes, and norms begin their presencing. By this reading, the taking of land is a perpetual process of inclusion and expulsion as the state first incorporates and then transforms polities and social structures formerly beyond its domain.

Reviewing this history of conquest, Nicholls saw that violence does not simply make way for politics and the rule of government. In a colonial context, politics itself becomes the continuation of conquest by other means.[68] Formerly beyond the law, the "Irishry" were forcefully placed under English jurisdiction and gradually governed by its edicts and norms.[69] The early colonial policy of "Surrender and Regrant," for instance, extended the principle of primogeniture (which underpinned English common law) by giving the state a degree of control over Irish property relations. Later Mary Tudor planned to re-people the land with loyal subjects, not as an act of military security but as a way of broadening English rule. The use of conquest to rewrite political, social, and economic relations seems to bear out Arendt's point that "violence has always been the *ultimo ratio* in political action and power has always been the visible expression of rule and government."[70] By claiming that the Pale was not overwritten but writ large upon the colonial landscape, Nicholls was observing the importance of force as a catalyst for social change and insisting that violence is constantly internalised within the new political structures established by the colonisers.

This insightful formulation of colonial conquest is suggestive of the historical geography of capital accumulation. Building on Marx, who identified colonial plunder ("primitive accumulation") as a precondition for the emergence of capitalist modes of production, David Harvey has argued that capitalism perpetually seeks something "outside of itself" in order to continue to accumulate—what he elsewhere describes as a "spatial fix."[71] To maintain a cycle of endless accumulation, objects formerly outside the production process (for example, peoples, regions, and resources) are continually brought into the sphere of capital's influence. For Harvey, therefore, force is not simply a *precondition* for primary accumulation; it is the *chronic feature* that distinguishes capitalist modernity itself. As Luxemburg famously observed, "the accumulation of capital, seen as an historical process, employs force as a permanent weapon."[72]

It would be wrong to reduce the history of conquest in early modern Ireland to the prerogatives of capitalism or industrialisation, but without attending to the history of accumulation by confiscation and dispossession, it is impossible to understand many of the features that came to define the Irish agrarian landscape in the nineteenth century.[73] Nor is it possible to comprehend British responses to Irish problems that continued to draw inspiration and political lessons from the past. In the post-Union period, as we shall see, Ireland continued to function as a "social laboratory," although the emphasis shifted from a policy of military conquest and plantations, which was found to be costly and only partially successful, to a programme of political, social, and economic amelioration to be accomplished through administrative and legal reorganisation.[74] In fact, many of the structural weaknesses of Irish society in the nineteenth century—including the grossly inequitable land tenure system, the reliance on vulnerable forms of monoculture, the presence of an "alien" and largely absentee landlord class, intense demographic pressures, and the gradual collapse of domestic industries — can be thought of, on the one hand, as a material legacy of conquest and, on the other hand, as an effect of more recent efforts to secure political and economic hegemony. In the following section I want to concentrate on how these transformations rendered Irish society less able to cope with "exogenous shocks" and, therefore, more vulnerable to famine.[75]

ACTS OF UNION: IRISH QUESTIONS AND COLONIAL ANSWERS

On New Years Day 1801, the Act of Union came into effect and a new political entity, the United Kingdom of Great Britain and Ireland, was born. The immediate motive for the Act was an unsuccessful insurrection in 1798, which nearly proved the old rebel axiom that "England's difficulty is Ireland's opportunity." The American colonies had been lost and a war of attrition was about to begin with Napoleonic France. The Irish rising might have been crushed, but the knowledge that Irish soldiers marched to the tune of the "Marseillaise" (they were assisted by French armaments, troops, and money and were exposed to Republican ideology) remained frighteningly fresh. Any future Franco-Hiberno alliance had to be prevented, and the Act of Union was fashioned as the most practical legislative response. But because the Act was neither popular nor consensual, a divide-and-rule strategy was devised: if the Protestant Ascendancy could be bought and secured, then the Catholic majority could be ignored. The Ascendancy feared the Irish Catholics more than they resented the intrusions of the British government, and the lure of prestigious posts and titles proved enough to secure the deal.[76] It is estimated that government bribes amounted to over 1.25 million pounds, "a scale of expense enormous even by contemporary standards," according to historian Gearóid Ó Tuathaigh.[77]

The Act effectively wrested *formal* political autonomy from an Anglo-Irish (almost exclusively Protestant) minority in Dublin and placed it under the guardianship of Westminster. The "injured lady" of Ireland, to employ Jonathan Swift's sobriquet, was married at last.[78] Other contemporaries described the act as a brutal rape, comparing Ireland to an "heiress whose chambermaid and trustees have been bribed, while she herself is dragged, protesting, to the altar."[79] "From the present perspective," one historian writes, "the act seems most startling for its assumptions that union could be decreed, that Ireland could be made politically one with England [*sic*], and that modern politics and economic necessity could override the enduring distinctions between both islands."[80] In fact, the "enduring distinctions" were crystallised in the very naming of the "United Kingdom of Great Britain and Ireland"; here the awkward conjunction "and" seems to inscribe the very difference it seeks to erase.[81] Given that colonial acts of naming are notoriously unstable, further rituals of authentication (from the re-narration of history to the implementation of new institutional structures) were required to both justify and normalise the original act of dispossession.[82]

According to the labour historian W. P. Ryan, the Act of Union legislated Ireland "into a dreary absurdity."[83] Politically Ireland was to be represented by a mere 100 MPs out of a total of 656 in the House of Commons, whereas by population and revenue the Irish people should have been entitled to 175 MPs.[84] On religious grounds the vast majority of Irish remained politically rightless. As part of the relaxation of the anti-Catholic Penal Laws, a forty-shilling franchise had been extended to Ireland in 1793.[85] This gave Catholics with at least a forty-shilling freehold the right to vote, although they were still disqualified from sitting in Parliament.[86] In the absence of secret ballots and with the threat of eviction hanging over them, tenants were easily intimidated into voting with their landlord and against their own class interests.[87]

Demographically this was a volatile situation, and increased Catholic pressure—headed by Daniel O'Connell and the Catholic Association—led to the eventual granting of Catholic Emancipation in 1829. In a cynical move, however, the government used the occasion to raise the voting franchise, from 40 shillings to £10, in an effort to undercut O'Connell's electoral base. "At one foul stroke," declared Charles Gavan Duffy (1816–1903), "the electors of Ireland [were] reduced from 200,000 to little more than twenty thousand."[88] Under the new rating system smallholdings were no longer politically useful. Formerly "the more voters the greater the political power and influence of the landlords; so small holdings found favour in their eyes."[89] No longer of any electoral value to their landlords, smallholders found themselves to be, as Karl Marx put it, "mere accessories to the soil."[90] Here begins what the Devon Commission later described as the "clearance system," as landlords attempted to remove the "superfluous populations" from their estates.[91] Even after the Reform Act in 1832, only about one person in every eighty-three was entitled to vote; the Franchise Act of 1850 increased this to one vote for every forty persons.[92]

There were additional ways the Act of Union proved to be a political setback for many Irish people. Important concessions such as the Renunciation Act (1793)—which had recognised the jurisdiction of the Irish courts and acknowledged the exclusive right of Ireland to legislate for itself—were rolled back as Whitehall and Westminster assumed charge of Irish affairs.[93] Although the British parliament maintained a right to repeal the Union, Ireland was denied the selfsame privilege.[94] The granting of Catholic Emancipation did little to diminish their widespread grievance for having to pay a tax for the upkeep of the Established Church of Ireland. Under Penal legislation anyone working the land had to pay a tithe, usually amounting to 10 percent of the agricultural produce, for the maintenance of the Anglican Church (the knowledge that this practice was common in countries where the Catholic Church was in the ascendancy did little to appease Irish Catholics).[95] Many landholders were simply unable to make payment and the Irish Constabulary regularly collected tithes under force of arms.[96] The distrainment of property and the seizure of livestock in order to pay the salaries of Protestant clergy ("whose ministrations they never attended and whose religion they [Catholics] detested") became the source of great bitterness and sectarian strife (see figure 1.3).[97] By 1834 the Anglican Church in Ireland was employing no less than twenty-two bishops and four archbishops, even though its Irish constituency was less than the English diocese of Durham. The clergy of these "ghost parishes" claimed national revenues amounting to nearly

DRIVING CATTLE FOR RENT BETWEEN OUGHTERARD AND GALWAY.

Figure 1.3. Driving cattle for rent between Oughterard and Galway (*Illustrated London News,* December 29, 1849)

£800,000. Three-quarters of this sum came from taxes paid by more than six million Roman Catholics, while their own priests depended entirely on voluntary contributions.[98] These difficulties led to the Irish Tithe War of 1831–36—what Irish socialist James Connolly saw as the "first move against the forces of privilege" in Ireland.[99]

Notwithstanding the importance of these religious tensions, the greatest controversy lay in the terms of economic amalgamation. The Act of Union established a "free trade" zone between Ireland and Britain, with a few duties preserved for a finite period in order to protect Irish manufacturers. Originally the financial systems of the two countries were to remain distinct, but shortly after the Napoleonic Wars, in 1817, the British and Irish exchequers were amalgamated, and in 1826 a common currency was legislated. Whether an independent Ireland would have been able to withstand the competing power of its rapidly industrialising neighbour is of course debatable, but the union of two vastly unequal trading blocks, the exposure of Irish proto-industrial manufacturing to international competition, and the shift from domestic production to large-scale industrialisation amounted to something akin to "shock therapy" for large sections of the Irish economy. The market logic of specialisation and rationalisation contributed to the decline of the rural, largely cottage-based spinning industry. The linen trade especially suffered, while the cotton industry eked out a more protracted existence owing to the continuance of duties for the first two decades after the Union: "By the 1820s the Lancashire cotton industry, like the Yorkshire woollen, was gradually strangling all opposition in the British Isles."[100] The well-known exception to this story was the industrial belt based around Belfast, where a mechanised linen trade greatly profited from commercial expansion.[101] For some contemporary observers, the Ulster example was proof of a Protestant work ethic rather than the result of a shift in comparative advantage.[102]

The city of Dublin was especially hard hit. Its traditional manufacturing sectors of shipbuilding and silk were virtually wiped out, while its coachmaking, glass, and tannery industries were substantially reduced.[103] The popular author Henry Inglis (1795–1835) reviewed the situation in 1834: "Dublin formerly possessed an extensive, safe, and very lucrative commission trade from both the West Indies and England; but the facilities of steam-navigation are now so great, that the country dealers throughout Ireland, who formerly made their purchases in Dublin, now pass over to England, and there lay in their stocks."[104] This shift was witnessed in many of the smaller towns across Ireland, where in-migration from rural regions only added to the general misery.

Notwithstanding the atrophying of rural livelihoods and significant out-migration from the countryside, Ireland was predominantly an agrarian society in which the potato economy reigned supreme. The root had originally functioned as a supplementary food (ironically as a standby in case of famine) amidst a more varied diet of vegetables, milk, butter, and occasionally, where wages permitted, pork and fish.[105] During the eighteenth and the nineteenth centuries, however, the Irish diet underwent "profound changes" as the reliance on the potato substantially increased.[106] Ireland produced a variety of foodstuffs, including various grains, cattle, pigs, and dairy produce, but as alternative sources of income dwindled and the produce that formerly diversified the Irish diet was sacrificed to supply an export trade in cash crops and livestock, the Irish increasingly turned to the potato for the bulk of their calories.[107] In such circumstances the potato proved a practicable alternative: it was easy to grow, highly productive, relatively free from disease, suited to the Irish climate, and required minimal capital investment since it produced its own seed for next season's crop.[108] The potato also allowed "under-capitalized tillage farmers to secure the extra labour necessary on their holdings without having to pay cash."[109]

Though estimates of potato consumption vary (ranging from seven pounds to a staggering fifteen pounds per person per diem), research has shown that the pre-Famine diet was nutritionally sound, especially when supplemented with milk or butter (the popular mode of consumption) and occasionally with oatmeal, fish, or eggs.[110] Some contemporary opinions agree with this picture. Travelling through Ireland in 1825, Walter Scott found Irish men "stout and healthy" and the women "buxom and well-coloured" even though for food "they have only potatoes, and too few of them."[111] Although monotonous, this diet became the mainstay for the poorest two-thirds of Irish society. On the eve of the Famine, Irish potato acreage amounted to 2.1 million statute acres; however, a large proportion of this crop (as much as 33 percent, or 0.7 million statute acres) was indirectly exported through the fattening of livestock for overseas markets.[112] For the poorest classes pigs were the farm animals of choice, and small stocks were sold at Ireland's many fairs in order to earn the money to pay rent.[113]

As the potato crop rose in importance so did the possession of land. The situation was exacerbated by the fact that the vast bulk of Irish people worked on the land but did not own it. Pre-Famine Ireland had between eight thousand and ten thousand landlords, most of whom were Anglican Protestant and tended to identify with the lifestyles of their peers in England.[114] Although the problem of landlord absenteeism had been a pronounced feature of Irish society before the Act of Union, the political, cultural, and economic decline of

Dublin, coupled with the grandeur of London life (and in some cases the duty to attend parliament), kept increasing numbers of landlords away from their Irish estates.[115] It is estimated that one third or more Irish landlords resided more or less full-time outside Ireland.[116]

Most landlords preferred letting their estates under long leases, and in the absence of restraint, individual tenants sublet the land, creating the notorious "middleman" system. In addition to encouraging subdivision, this practice tended to increase the cost of land to the point where the actual "cultivator's rent per acre might be several times greater than that of the middleman." Moreover, existing legislation "made it possible for the landlord to distrain against any of the tenants, so that a cultivator who had punctually paid his rent to the middleman might find himself subject to distress or eviction through the middleman defaulting."[117]

In 1826, the same year Ireland abandoned its own currency, the government passed an Act of Parliament that proscribed lessee subletting.[118] The ensuing war on the "middleman system" provided head landlords with an opportunity to consolidate holdings and introduce more rigorous methods of "scientific farming" popular in England and Scotland since the mid-eighteenth century.[119] Land consolidation had long been touted in liberal economic circles as the great panacea for Ireland's backwardness; however, legal curbs (leases), political expediency (the forty-shilling franchise), and aristocratic custom (absenteeism) retarded attempts to concentrate land ownership and commercialise agricultural production. The Subletting Act of 1826 and the raising of the freeholder franchise in 1829 provided both motive and incentive to consolidate smallholdings, anglicise farming practices, and encourage commercial practices more generally.[120]

In some parts of the country efforts in agrarian improvement were already apace. In 1823, for instance, a Select Committee reported on consolidation and its humanitarian costs: "That this alteration of system [consolidation] may ultimately be beneficial, and that it was actually necessary to prevent the indefinite subdivision of land, before in progress, may be admitted; but the first effect of the alteration has been to make a sudden change in the peasant's mode of life, depriving many of their former homes, and making it extremely difficult for them to obtain a new habitation."[121] Seven years later another Select Committee put the matter more forcefully:

> It would be impossible for language to convey an idea of the state of distress to which the ejected tenantry have been reduced or of the disease, misery, and even vice which they have propagated in the towns wherein they have settled . . . They have increased the stock of labour, they have rendered the habitations of those who have received them more crowded, they have given occasion to the dissemination of disease, they have been obliged to resort to theft and all manner of vice and inequity to procure subsistence; but what is perhaps most painful of all, a vast number of them have perished of want.[122]

Clearly, for some small farmers the penetration of commercial practices into the Irish rural economy precipitated a decline rather than an improvement in their conditions. While the Devon Commission lamented such blatant injustices, it felt compelled to add the caveat that any interference with the landlords' powers to distrain and eject would "greatly weaken the just rights of property."[123]

Most landlords refused to grant long leases, or any lease whatsoever, in order to make evictions easier. More indulgent landlords paid for their tenants to emigrate (known as "assisted emigration"). In fact, out-migration proved a thriving industry in post-Union Ireland. Travelling around Ireland in 1823, the American John Griscom recorded passenger fares as low as £2 owing to increased competition. Griscom also recounted the lies fed to destitute emigrants and the perilous packing of ships, allegations that resurfaced with force during the Great Famine.[124] The town of Youghal recorded its highest rate of emigration in the first six months of 1834. According to one witness, those who left were "chiefly agriculturalists," while those who remained were often the poorest members of society: "I noticed in one of the poorest cabins, in the neighbourhood of Youghall [*sic*], where scarcely any furniture was to be seen, one of the printed bills, announcing the approaching departure of a ship for Canada, stuck upon the wall. This is a very little circumstance, but it is full of meaning."[125] Despite the financial obstacles, emigration remained the only hope for many—reminding us of Friedrich Engels's remark that the only solution the ruling class can ever find to its problems is to constantly move them around.[126]

Although many tenants now held land directly from their landlord (who now employed agents to manage their estates), few landlords granted leases and absenteeism continued. "The most general, and indeed almost universal topic of complaint brought before us in every part of Ireland, was the 'want of tenure,'" declared the Devon Commission.[127] On the eve of the Famine, and the year before the Devon Commission published its findings, James Johnson (1777–1845) echoed a popular belief that "ABSENTEEISM appears to be, in some respects at least, to Ireland what POETRY was to Goldsmith. 'It found him poor, and helped to keep him so.'"[128] The truth of the matter is more complicated, however. Resident landlords would have made little difference to the welfare of Irish tenants so long as tenure remained insecure. Peasant proprietorship was almost nonexistent in Ireland, and, in contradistinction to England and Scotland, where farm buildings, fences, and gates were provided for and maintained as part of the terms of rental, Irish landlords typically leased only the "bare soil" to their tenants.[129] This had two precipitous effects on peasant livelihoods. First, prospective tenants—invariably with little capital—were made responsible for all the improvements to their property. Furthermore, the law "afforded no right of compensation to the tenant for such investments, which became the property of the landlord at the conclusion of tenancy." This tenurial arrangement encouraged apathy and thrift because the least sign of improvement might encourage eviction or force an increase in the rent.[130] Second, incumbent property arrangements led to a common practice known as "the hanging gale." "Gale" was the term used for the regular payment of rent. The hanging gale allowed an incoming tenant to leave his rent in arrears—in other words "hanging"—in order to finance rudimentary investments on the property (bearing in mind that not infrequently a cabin had to be erected).[131] Edward Wakefield, a well-known economist of the period, described the practice as "one of the great levers of oppression . . . the lower classes are kept in a kind of perpetual bondage . . . this debt hangs over their heads . . . and keeps them in a continual state of anxiety and terror."[132]

The striking exception to this rule was Ulster, where some security of tenure was indirectly afforded by the tradition known as "tenant-right." By custom an outgoing tenant was entitled to sell his "good-will" to an incoming tenant, making it possible to recover capital spent on improvements. In sum, tenant-right recognised, albeit implicitly, the accumulation of capital and "dead labour" in the land.[133] In Ulster quantities equal to between ten and fifteen years purchase upon the rent were frequently given for tenant-right.[134] Elsewhere in Ireland, however, this custom was scarcely recognised.[135] "Anomalous as this condition is," the Devon Commissioners concluded, "if considered with reference to all ordinary notions of property, it must be admitted that the district in which it prevails has thrived and improved, in comparison with other parts of the country."[136]

To understand the lives of the majority of Irish tenants, it needs to be remembered that in an overwhelmingly agrarian society (six people out of seven lived in rural areas), where the nonagricultural sector had been demolished and the land-letting system was hugely discriminatory, the production and control of space was a deeply political affair.[137] The fact that "the country was farmed by tenants rather than owners" had its origins in the plantations and confiscations of the sixteenth and seventeenth centuries, which placed landownership almost exclusively in Protestant hands.[138] To some observers the peasant-gentry relations seemed feudal in nature:

> The Irish landlords are . . . still worse than the great Polish and Russian proprietors; for *they* so far take an interest in the affairs of their dependents, as to assist the peasant in the repair of his cabin; and are also compelled to furnish him with sustenance in time of famine. But this is not done by the Irish landlord. Yet his tenant is a *free* man: he can go away whenever he chooses. He has almost all the inconveniences of slavery (he is entirely dependent on his master; the lash only is wanting—a fact which must be thankfully acknowledged,) without enjoying the advantages resulting from the sympathy and kind foresight of his master. So,

also, he has all the inconveniences of freedom, (want, care, hunger,) without being able to enjoy one of its advantages.[139]

Almost all contemporary accounts admit that Ireland sorely lacked a class of substantial tenantry. From the census data collected in 1841, Mokyr estimates that over two-thirds of the population were "without capital, in either money, land, or acquiring knowledge."[140] If one includes the class above them (that is, small farmers who held between five and fifty acres of land), this accounted for 97 percent of the entire population.[141]

The small farmers typically held land from a landlord (or middleman) and paid a money rent for it. Farmers lucky enough to hold above forty acres typically required one permanent labourer in their service.[142] Labour was hired at a nominal rate—not more than 6d. to 8d. per diem, varying regionally and seasonally—although by most accounts money rarely exchanged hands. Instead, the labourer was given a cabin and a small plot of manured ground to raise potatoes, and the rent was worked out in labour.[143] Given the immense competition for land, and the crippling necessity of planting some potato seed, labourers often agreed to the highest possible rent on small slips of land, placing the lowest possible value on labour.[144] According to one economist, a tenant might work as much as 250 days to pay for a cabin plus one acre of manured potato ground and might still be expected to provide petty commodities, like poultry and eggs, or perform services like threshing corn or drawing turf when requested. These exactions significantly "increased the real, as distinguished from the nominal rent, paid by occupiers" and ensured that less time could be devoted to the nutritional needs of the peasantry.[145]

Few labourers, however, were fortunate enough to have a permanent engagement of this kind, and many more had to find hard cash in order to hire land in "conacre." The terms of letting conacre varied (as do definitions), but in general it involved leasing manured land to a landless labourer for the potato season only.[146] The English Quaker William Bennett (1804–73) summarised the typical lot under conacre leasing: "The average rent in Ireland at which arable land is let, is probably more than double the same in England; so that what with the conacre rent for his land, and Gombien [usurious] price for his seed, and ditto for his food, while he tills the land, it is not surprising that the Irish peasant has been kept at the lowest verge of pauperism; for all the inducement to industry, beyond the barest living, is in fact withdrawn."[147] The Devon Commission reported that "in many districts their only food is the potato, their only beverage water, that their cabins are seldom a protection against the weather, that a bed or a blanket is a rare luxury, and that nearly in all, their pig and manure constitute their only property."[148] Despite these horrific conditions, tenants typically paid £10 and sometimes as high as £12 or £14 per acre, making conacre, from the labourers' perspective, "virtually a speculation in subsistence."[149] Where the occupancy of land was the "*sine quâ non of existence,*" Irish landlords held "a summary power of deciding the fate, the life, or the death" of their tenantry simply through the service of an eviction notice.[150]

If life was a constant gamble between penury and starvation, the summer months were especially grim. Potatoes did not keep after early summer, but the new crop was not harvested until September.[151] On occasion food was secured on credit from a larger farmer or local usurer called a "gombeen-man." Rates were often 30 or 40 percent above the market fee. According to William Thornton (1813–80), indebted labourers still figured themselves "lucky" because their creditor would employ them in order to guarantee payment of the debt.[152] For most labourers the prospects of local employment were slight; during the "hungry months" between potato harvests, thousands of Irish labourers migrated to England and Scotland to work the land while their families fell to begging and charity to survive.[153] William Thornton relates how Irish women and children were seen to travel many miles before begging, "for the sense of shame is most acute, in spite of all their wretchedness."[154] Travel writers—most of whom arrived during the "hungry months"—met crowds of ill-clad peasants lining the coach-ways and thronging the towns (figure 1.4). It was reported that some peasants dug their potato patch early, consuming potatoes "so small that only hunger could see them"; others resorted to eating half-cooked foodstuffs to slow down their digestion.[155] There are many descriptions of labourers turning to the noxious weed called "pressagh,"

Figure 1.4. Traveller and beggars in Muckross (W. M. Thackeray, *The Irish Sketch Book,* 138)

which gave its victims a shameful yellow hue. "What can we do?—can we starve?" lamented one witness. "If this would kill us, we should have been dead long since, for many's the time we have put up with worse."[156] For those who could obtain neither employment nor credit, food shortages became an unavoidable part of everyday life.

The Irish subsistence economy, although extensive, existed side by side with a class of substantial farmer-landlords who hired and leased land to the former. This is what economists usually describe as a "bimodal" distribution pattern or a "dual economy."[157] Throughout Leinster and Munster, for example, pasturage and tillage relied on cheap labour from the subsistence sector, forming a "patchwork quilt" of very large and very small farms "intertwined and mutually dependent."[158] This substantial class of "peasantariats"—consisting of small farmers and semi-proletarianised labour—was central to the productivity of the top layer of Irish agriculture, the so-called strong farmer class.[159] "From the pores of his skin," wrote W. M. S. Balch, "oozes out the sweat which circulates life . . . [and] supports the petty aristocracy, so abundant in all Irish towns . . . and then [the smallholder] is called *lazy, indolent, and worthless,* and sneered at as unfit to live in such a bountiful and beautiful country."[160]

As surely as the Act of Union affected the political, social, and economic conditions *within* Ireland, it also facilitated wider networks of trade *beyond* it. The "pig and potato economy," Christine Kinealy explains, fed a commercialised export sector responsible for the maintenance of a growing industrial urban class in Britain:

> Paradoxically, the reliance both of potato production and tillage on low subsistence wages (literally a potato wage) and labour intensive methods, also proved to be a barrier to technological and agricultural innovation within Ireland. Nevertheless, in the decades after the Union, high quality corn was grown extensively in Ireland (predominately in the south-east). Like linen, it was grown primarily for sale and export, mostly to the bread-hungry towns of industrial England. By 1841, oats was the largest single-item exported from Ireland and, in total, Ireland was exporting sufficient corn to England to feed 2 million people. This high level of dependence on Irish agriculture led to the description of Ireland as the "bread basket" of the United Kingdom. Ironically, it was the existence of the much despised potato economy which allowed English workers to enjoy cheap bread, probably ignorant of its origins."[161]

Karl Marx tellingly described Ireland as "an agricultural district of England, marked off by a wide channel from the country to which it yields corn, wool, cattle, industrial and military recruits."[162] Ministers and public officials were likewise well aware of the importance of the Irish subsistence sector to the British economy. In 1819 a Select Committee suggested that a refined transportation network should be at the top of the list of government priorities for Ireland on the grounds that it would "insure to England supplies of grain at moderate prices, which might render it wholly independent of foreign countries for the food of its manufacturing population."[163] Four years later yet another Select Committee reported on the circumstances of the peasantry. The potato crop had failed the previous season, and although exact calculations were difficult, the committee reckoned that "the distressed districts were equal in extent to one-half of the superficial contents of all Ireland."[164] According to the commissioners, the poorest were starving even though "there was no want of food of another description for the support of human life":

On the contrary the crops of grain had been far from deficient, and the prices of corn and oatmeal were very moderate. The export of grain from ports within the distressed districts of Ireland, was considerable, during the entire period from May to August, infinitely exceeding the imports during that period; and those districts in the south and west presented the remarkable example of possessing a surplus of food, whilst the inhabitants were suffering from actual want.[165]

The conditions described above suggest that the poor starved from an inability to command food through market transactions rather than from an overall dearth of food supplies—a situation that is inseparable from the transformation of colonies into economically subordinate suppliers of commodities for the colonial metropole.[166] "As would be expected in an agrarian, export-based economy," Kerby Miller explains, "nearly all major [Irish] towns were seaports: in 1841 Kilkenny, the largest inland town, had only 19,100 people—compared with Dublin's 232,700 and Cork's 80,700."[167]

Anticipating Amartya Sen's comments on "exchange entitlements failures," the Irish commissioners highlight the structure of ownership in a market economy and its crucial role in determining the allocation of vital provisions. In contradistinction to Sen, however, the commissioners mask the violence of such practices, preferring to eulogize the "meritorious patience of the Peasantry" who declined to breach public order to secure food supplies.[168] While it was extraordinarily common for the ruling classes to salute the stoicism of the poor, such praise rings particularly hollow in the context of widespread starvation ("suffering from actual want" and "distressed districts" were the conventional euphemisms used). Indeed, the same Select Committee unanimously agreed "that a state in which an *inequality of conditions* offers the natural rewards of good conduct, and inspires widely and generally the hopes of rising and the fear of falling in society, is unquestionably the best calculated to develop the energies and faculties of man, and is the best suited to the exercise and improvement of human virtue." Significantly, the Irish commissioners were (anonymously) citing the demographer and political economist Thomas Robert Malthus (1766–1834)—a common occurrence, as we shall discover, when it comes to justifying free market policies in the face of acute suffering.[169]

Not surprisingly, nationalist writers like Thomas Davis (1814–45), James Fintan Lalor (1807–49) and John Mitchel (1815–75) pointed to the self-serving nature of the logic that renders inequality a virtue. These writers insisted that the system itself was rotten, linking the worst excesses of free trade to the imposition of colonial rule. Influenced by the ideas of John Locke (1632–1704), Lalor asserted: "We owe no obedience to laws enacted by another nation without our assent; nor respect to assumed rights of property which are starving and exterminating our people."[170] In the pages of the *Nation* Mitchel fired a stinging condemnation:

> The free trade and competition—in other words the English system—is pretty well understood now; its obvious purpose and effect are to make the rich richer and the poor poorer, to make capital the absolute ruler of the world, and labour a blind and helpless slave. By free trade the manufacturers of Manchester are enabled to clothe India, China, and South America, and the artisans of Manchester can hardly keep themselves covered from the cold. By dint of free trade Belfast grows more linen cloth than it ever did before; but the men who weave it hardly have a shirt to their backs. Free trade fills with corn the stores of speculating capitalists, but leaves those who have sown and reaped the corn without a meal. Free trade unpeoples villages and peoples poorhouses, consolidates farms and gluts graveyards with famished corpses.[171]

These epistles condemn the destructive nature of colonial trade, but it is equally important to recognise that capitalism was also a *productive force*, bringing economists, politicians, philosophers, travel writers, and civil servants together to debate the future administration of Irish society. Significant in this context are the growing references to Ireland as a "backward" country in a "transitional" stage of socioeconomic development. In 1830, for example, a government report commented that "The present difficulties of the situation of Ireland rather appear to be incidental to a transition from one system to another, than any which can be considered as permanent."[172] The commissioners continued to cite the opinion of economist James Ebenezer Bicheno (1785–1851)—later a querulous member of the Irish Poor Law enquiry led by Richard Whately—who remarked, "In examining the old authors, about the time of Elizabeth and James, all the facts that are stated by them bear me out in saying that the condition of the peasantry in this country [England] in the fifteenth and sixteenth centuries was very similar to what now exists in Ireland." The commissioners felt that Bicheno's "analogy certainly tends to establish the fact that Ireland is now in a transition state, the ultimate consequences of which will be useful to the country, however severe the pressure may be for the time on individuals."[173] This "denial of coevalness" became a powerful means of Othering that helped valorise novel efforts to stimulate Irish development.[174] While the rhetoric had moved on from the early modern emphasis on repeopling the land, there is no mistaking the fact that behind the new language of amelioration lay the longstanding desire to anglicise Irish society. In sum, the civilising mission resurfaces in the guise of a new colonial "will to improve."[175]

COLONIAL IMPROVEMENT

"It must never be forgotten," wrote the Devon Commission on the eve of the Great Famine, "that an improved cultivation, with the consequent increase from the produce of the soil, and of comfort to the occupier, are not matters of private and individual interest only, but are intimately connected to the preservation of public tranquillity, and the general prosperity of the whole empire."[176] This sentiment signalled the new, vital place of agrarian capitalism in the theory and practice of empire.[177] Agrarian improvement gradually superseded military force as the cornerstone of colonial policy and the *modus operandi* of the civilising mission. However, agrarian "improvement" entailed its own form of political violence. In particular, the steady commercialisation of the Irish economy was considered an unequivocal good regardless of the vulnerabilities and inequalities that emerged. As alternative sources of income were abandoned—and survival strategies radically contracted—the Irish economy became increasingly reliant on the potato as a cheap, reproducible source of calories. The fact that the vast majority of Irish tenants were "without control of the land and the means of life generally" added greatly to the levels of vulnerability.[178]

I have argued that colonisation is central to how poverty is produced and how susceptibility to famine is framed, but is it possible to measure the *extent* of poverty and the *degree* of vulnerability in Irish society? This is a question posed by the economic historian Joel Mokyr. For Mokyr traditional proxy measures, like income per capita, are especially problematic when it comes to assessing food security. He notes that it is perfectly possible to experience a rise in income per capita accompanied by an increase in the inequality of income *distribution*. In this scenario poverty might be increased even though the statistics detailing income per capita would obscure this fact. To avoid this problem Mokyr chooses to measure poverty as the probability of any individual dropping beneath subsistence levels at any given time. The brilliance of this alternative formula is that it considers the *frequency* and *severity* of food crises as a central factor in the measurement of poverty.[179] According to this standard, Irish society was both chronically poor and exceptionally vulnerable. In the century prior to the Great Famine, for instance, Ireland suffered subsistence crises in 1725–26, 1727–28, 1757–58, 1765–66, 1770–71, and 1782–84; according to David Dickson, the famine of 1740–41 (known as *blian an áir* or "year of the slaughter"), may have equalled the Great Famine in its relative magnitude and scale. During the early nineteenth century, Ireland also experienced "partial famines" in 1800–1801, 1811, 1816–17, 1821–22, 1830, 1838, and 1842.[180] The structural weakness of the Irish economy is all too evident when the vulnerability to famine is taken into account. "Famine years," as George O'Brien rightly noted, "were simply the years in which the chronic symptoms became acute."[181]

This chapter has argued that colonial rule forged an entirely new social order that affected the very fabric of social life in Ireland. For William Smyth the process of property confiscation was matched in "no other European country of the period," forcing him to turn to the "scale and ruthlessness . . . of Soviet Russia's land appropriations" for comparable purposes.[182] The usurpation of indigenous land was the prelude to, and necessary condition for, the development of modes of rentier capitalism, the penetration of unstable commodity markets, and the diffusion of exploitative labour practices. The superimposition of these "modernising" social structures resulted in massive socio-economic dislocation as "relatively self-sufficient communities and localities" struggled to cope with the uncertainties of an increasingly commercialised agrarian economy.[183] Furthermore, after decades of grinding poverty and rural stagnation, the elements of Irish society most resistant to imposed change—day labourers, subsistence farmers, cottiers, and those who leased conacre—were least able to resist the forces of social improvement unleashed during the eighteenth and nineteenth centuries. Seen this way, the violence of conquest prepared the ground for the development of a capitalist economy across Ireland—the final cornerstone in the anglicisation of Irish society. As we shall discover, the plans to reconstitute the Irish countryside developed in tandem with new governmental techniques for disciplining unproductive labour and reclaiming Irish nature from a host of deviant social influences.[184] Before turning to this unquestionably modern colonial project, however, I want to examine more closely the formation of a discourse of regeneration, which became apparent in the pre-Famine decades and played a decisive role in shaping the institutional response to the Irish Famine.

CHAPTER TWO

DEFINING CIVILITY

On the Poverty of Others

*All accounts of travellers in Ireland represent the most striking characteristic of
the labouring poor to be extreme indolence. The man frequently passes his days
stretched on the floor of his hovel, raising himself, and hardly that, only to join in
the universal repast round the eternal potatoe-bowl.*

— George Poulett Scrope, "Poor Laws for Ireland"

*The poor were treated and despised as if they were beings of quite a different creation.
The satiated never understand the emaciated.*

— Hugh Dorian, *The Outer Edge of Ulster*

MAKING UP PEOPLE

The phrase "making up people" is used by the philosopher Ian Hacking to describe how certain ontological categories (for instance, insanity) are historically constructed.[1] I borrow the term here to draw attention to the ways in which Irish life was socially constructed and, in particular, how an *imaginative geography* of Irish poverty helped to shape and valorise new forms of colonial regulation.[2] In chapter 1 of this volume I showed how colonial policies radically reterritorialised rural life, leaving Irish society increasingly vulnerable and the poorest facing seasonal hunger from a position of virtual rightlessness.

This chapter is premised on the idea that famines always exceed any narrowly defined structural reading. The economist and Nobel Laureate Amartya Sen has argued that the *perception* of peoples, places, and cultures is central to shaping government conduct. Institutionalised prejudices and racist attitudes—particularly the tendency to "blame the victim"—often determine the nature and extent of relief programmes, thereby creating or exacerbating human suffering.[3] Accentuating the moral, cultural, and biological differences between "the satiated" and "the emaciated" (to adopt Hugh Dorian's terms) enables state officials and relief workers to justify the violence of inaction and overlook the harm caused by their own prescriptions.[4] This is not simply a matter of saying that difference and deviancy are socially constructed; the task is to show how language is deployed as a political weapon in the transformation of society.

Certainly there was never any shortage of self-appointed experts on pre-Famine Irish life.[5] Travellers, government commissioners, novelists, economists, and politicians all ventured their opinion on the condition of Ireland.[6] In what follows I focus primarily on travel accounts written between the Act of Union and the Great Famine, although I will also make reference to more "official" narratives published either as political pamphlets or archived in the government's Blue Books.[7] Although it is fair to say that some accounts reveal a genuine compassion for Irish suffering, in the majority of cases Irish destitution was explained as an obdurate moral failing—the symptom of a broader culture of domestic degeneracy—that required swift remedial action. The Irish were rendered vulnerable and then derided as backward and improvident, and these views set the terms of the first Irish Poor Law and, shortly thereafter, the government response to the Great Irish Famine.

ROUTES AND ROUTINES OF COLONIAL TRAVEL

A major impediment to "social reform" was thought to be the lack of accurate knowledge about the social, political, and economic condition of Ireland. Toward the end of the eighteenth century, the agricultural reformer and writer Arthur Young (1741–1820) declared that to be ignorant of the condition of the labouring classes, and the poor more generally, is to be wanting in the first rudiments of political knowledge.[8] Nearing the end of the following century, the English traveller Arthur Bennett (1862–1931) could still confidently announce that "At the root of Irish difficulty lies the prevailing ignorance concerning the country."[9] Yet in the intervening years the thirst for instrumental knowledge was unrelenting. Between 1800 and the outbreak of the Great Famine, for instance, no fewer than 114 commissions and 61 special committees were instructed by the British government to report on Ireland.[10] The Devon Commission travelled 3,126 miles, visiting each county and sitting in 96 districts, where the board examined approximately 1,100 witnesses over 1,217 hours.[11] One economic historian has described the commission's work as "the most thorough and comprehensive investigation carried out by any nineteenth-century *ad hoc* agency."[12] This is surely an excellent example of what Nicholas Thomas describes as state power "turned upon inscription, upon the absorption of events into a prodigiously dispersed writing machine."[13]

This paper landscape functioned not only to describe Irish life (its conditions of existence, habits, customs, and so forth) but also to make it visible in ways that strengthened the hand of government. As James Scott outlines, the will to know and render visible is one of the fundamental differences between the premodern and modern state:

> Where the premodern state was content with a level of intelligence sufficient to allow it to keep order, extract taxes, and raise armies, the modern state increasingly aspired to "take in charge" the physical and human resources of the nation and make them more *productive*. These more positive ends of statecraft required a much greater knowledge of society. And an inventory of land, people, incomes, occupations, resources, and deviance was the logical place to begin.[14]

According to Scott, "society" was being incorporated into widening grids of inscription and intervention. The modern state's interest in everyday life required a form of governmentality that could circulate and gain access to peoples' lives—"discovering," defining, and investing life with meaning. In other words, the state was now "making up people."

CHAPTER XII.

Figure 2.1. Excerpt from the table of contents of Henry Inglis's *Ireland in 1834*
(viii)

These developments are of great importance to the history of
travel. Even a cursory look at the table of contents of nineteenth-
century travelogues demonstrates that travellers were also conducting inventories of "land, people, incomes, occupations, resources, and
deviance," and often in ways that broadly complement what Scott
terms the "more positive ends of statecraft" (see figure 2.1). Travel
accounts are seldom objective and almost never benign; it seems important, therefore, to consider these productions as something more
than mere descriptions of contemporary life. "What requires attention," writes Nicholas Thomas, "is the wider range of textual devices
that present others in particular terms; difference is produced, not
simply distorted."[15] For Stephen Greenblatt the overriding interest
and investment in travel "is not knowledge of the other *but practice upon
the other*": the construction of difference and deviancy was important
precisely because it could authorise programmes for controlling, policing, and regulating colonised peoples, whose very existence seemed
to necessitate such extraordinary intercessions.[16] Building on these insights, I want to consider what might be gained in taking the study of
travel knowledge into the realm of *use.* How do discourses produce,
reinforce, and validate regimes of intervention? How is the production of knowledge related to the geopolitics of conquest?

Travel writing was peculiarly suited to gathering useful intelligence. Travel books could and did lay claim to the privilege of presence, and like the investigations of state officials (which they mim-
icked), they preferred to market their opinions as "objective." Henry
Inglis (1795–1835) advertised his travelogue as a "truth telling book"
not a "party book," detailing "stern realities" and opposing "poeti-
cal fancies."[17] "In narrating my investigations," wrote Anne Plumptre

(1760–1818), "I have looked to fidelity as my polar star."[18] Claims to objectivity were always open to contestation, but in terms of influence travel writers possessed a real advantage in that their opinions were meant to be purchased and read far more widely than the government's Blue Books.[19] Indeed, popular commentators such as the "*Times* Commissioner" (Thomas Campbell Foster, 1813–82) satirised the numerous government reports that "have passed away like an Egyptian dynasty, buried under pyramids, not of stone, but an equally wasted material,—of printed paper."[20] Foster could speak with some licence, for as Peter Gray notes, his views were more widely read, and incited greater controversy, than the government's Devon report.[21] Henry Inglis's travel account went through several editions, and he was subsequently quoted as an "authority" in Westminster. The sustained popularity of authors such as Arthur Young (1741–1820), William Thackeray (1811–63), Asenath Nicholson (1792–1855), and Harriet Martineau (1802–76) is evidence that travelogues were an important means of geographical education for Victorian readers.

The will to describe and inventory Irish life was significantly boosted by the development of cheap and convenient transportation networks. In particular, the development of steam transport had a dramatic effect in terms of regularising contact between Britain and Ireland. "Yesterday in London—an Englishman; and to-day in Dublin—an Irishman. Success to steam!" declared the German Jacob Venedey (1805–71) in 1843.[22] Contrast this with Arthur Young's journey in 1776—which lasted twenty-two "tedious" hours—and we get a sense of the enormity of this transformation.[23] Of the various routes between Britain and Ireland, Holyhead to Dublin was by far the most popular. Having arrived in the capital, visitors could choose from among the thirty coach roads and two canals radiating from the city, giving travellers unprecedented access to the country's main towns and villages.[24] By 1841 only a few areas on the remote western seaboard were more than ten miles from public transport, while the train journey between Dublin and Cork was estimated to be just six hours.[25] New technologies of movement meant new scales of travel and a different intensity of engagement with other peoples and places (figure 2.2). This too was part of a wider trend whereby the space and time of communications and politico-cultural contact was radically

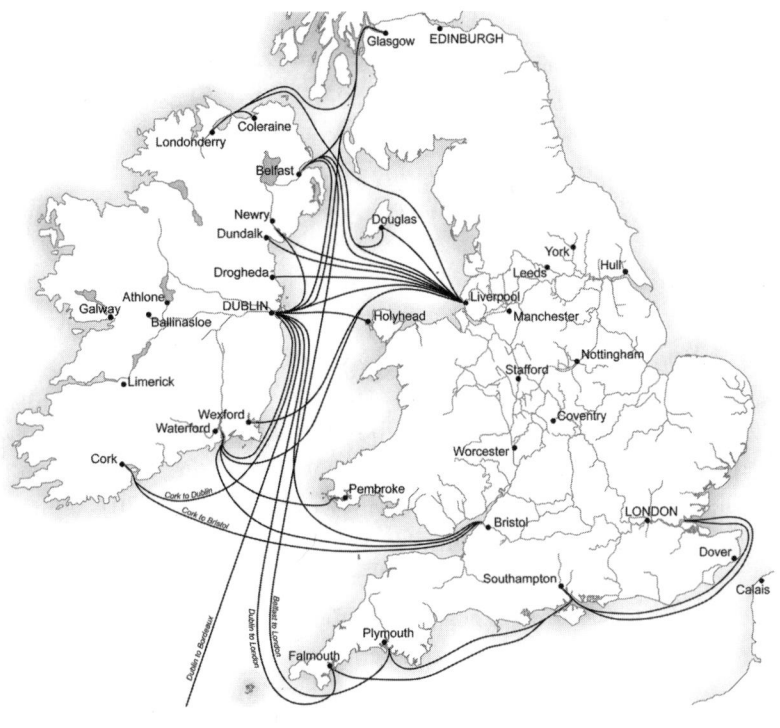

Figure 2.2. The annihilation of space by time (based on "Third Report of Evidence from the Select Committee on the State of the Poor in Ireland. Minutes of Evidence," 1037)

imploding—a process that has been termed "time-space compression."[26] Visitors regularly remarked on the cheapness, convenience, and efficiency of Irish transport, and several, such as Reverend John Ashworth (1795–1882), openly mused on the civilising potential implied by these achievements:

> Now that the internal communications are daily opening out the country . . . it becomes a self-evident fact that Ireland cannot remain as it is; propinquity to better things will induce imitation; and that spirit of enterprise which has already converted so many far distant deserts of the earth into smiling and prosperous colonies, cannot and will not suffer one of the loveliest and most fertile islands of the world, only a few hours' distance from our own

shores, to remain a mere waste, inhabited, as it is, by a hardy, intelligent, but ignorant and semi-barbarous population.[27]

Making peoples and places less remote—and opening them up to civilisation—was seen as an important task for social commentators, who could describe, inventory, sketch, and map secluded Irish hamlets and towns for which only the vaguest descriptions were available.[28] "Judging by myself," wrote Inglis, "our ignorance about the second and third-rate Irish towns is extreme. There are only some few we ever hear of. Leaving Cork, Waterford, Limerick, and Belfast out of the list, less I think is known of the other towns, unless by the gentlemen of the army."[29] It was widely felt that for the state to be an effective regulator of the social milieu, accurate information was needed on the rudimentary conditions of Irish life. As a popular form of social analysis, travel literature could contribute to the production of useful knowledge, and many travel writers began to self-consciously characterise their roles in quasi-official terms. In his four-volume travelogue on Ireland, for example, Arthur Bennett described himself as an "amateur Commission of Enquiry."[30] Inglis's only slightly slimmer two-volume tour deliberately anticipated the government's Poor Law Commission of 1834 by devoting a full chapter to his own uncommissioned "report." Thomas Carlyle (1795–1881) undertook two separate journeys to Ireland, first in 1846 and then again in 1849, and selected for himself the ominous moniker "*Eternity's* commissioner."[31] As noted above, the *Times* newspaper dispatched a special journalist to Ireland to submit weekly reports as the "*Times* Commissioner."[32] In these and other accounts, the line distinguishing "correspondent" and "commissioner" was clearly blurred, a fact that suggests the degree to which observers were now viewing Irish conditions with a mind to influence government-led social reform.[33]

An Amateur Commissioner

Henry Inglis's sprawling account of Ireland, *Ireland in 1834: A Journey throughout Ireland, during the Spring, Summer, and Autumn of 1834,* is a case in point. Having dabbled as a journalist, editor, and novelist, more-or-less without notice, Inglis turned to foreign travel and reporting to earn a living. At the time of undertaking his Irish tour, he had published a number of travelogues — including *Narrative of a Journey through Norway, Part of Sweden, and the Islands and States of Denmark* (1826), *Solitary Walks through Many Lands* (1828), *A Tour through Switzerland* (1830), *The South of France and the Pyrenees* (1831), *The Tyrol, with a Glance at Bavaria* (1833) — and had met some critical and commercial success. In his account of Ireland, Inglis managed to fill two volumes with thirty-two chapters, researched over a period of nine months (the spring, summer, and autumn of his title), and by his own admission he journeyed through virtually every county in Ireland (figure 2.3). Throughout the book the author is at pains to point out that his account of Irish conditions stands in contrast to his previous travelogues:

> I have not studied to make this an agreeable book, so much as a useful book. It has neither the romantic incident, which, *malgré moi,* diversifies my work on Spain, nor the scenic which I have introduced into my books on the Tyrol, or on Norway. This is not because I could not find romance to amuse the reader with, or scenery to describe to him; it is I trust, for a better reason. Irish legends, Irish novels, we have in abundance. Irish character, condition, and manners, have been presented to us in many agreeable forms of fiction . . . But why jest, when occupied with so grave a subject? why endeavour to amuse, when I desire to interest? why raise a smile, when I would rather induce meditation, and serious thought? God knows, there is little real cause for jocularity, in treating of the condition of a starving people.[34]

The self-appointed "narrator of truth" was not unaware of the immense challenges ahead: "I was everywhere informed that Ireland is a difficult country to know."[35] To avoid making a "shipwreck of truth," Inglis carried from Dublin an arsenal of "upwards of one hundred and thirty letters of introduction," and during his journeying he delivered at least three times in excess of that number.[36] These letters permitted two essential practices. First, they allowed Inglis to stage himself from mansion to mansion among the network of the Anglo-Irish

Figure 2.3. Inglis's nine-month tour in 1834

ruling class.[37] Secondly, they were decisive in obtaining constructive information on Irish grievances. The letters permitted access "to persons of all ranks, from the peer to the farmer" (to the peasant he introduced himself), and to individuals of all opinions, "from the orange magistrate of Down and Derry, to the Catholic repealer of Kilkenny and Tipperary; from the protestant dignitary to the country curate; from the Catholic bishop to the parish priest."[38] While these introductions ensured access to information, they also, to a large degree, conditioned perceptions.

It so happens that 1834, the year Inglis undertook his tour, was also the year the British government appointed a Royal Commission to investigate the condition of the poorer classes in Ireland.[39] Inglis was well aware of this fact, and through the intercession of friends he was able to procure "all the papers which the government intended should guide the inquiries of the commissioners."[40] The penultimate chapter of his book is devoted to addressing the terms of the government's commission. Moreover, though many commissions had been sent to report on Ireland, there was an exceptional degree of anticipation surrounding this report. The English Poor Law had been reformed the same year, and it was widely expected that a similar structure would be extended to Ireland.

Inglis's penultimate chapter is therefore significant. The author takes great care to qualify his "extraordinary presumption" that "the statements of an humble individual like myself are more entitled to carry weight with them than the report of the government commissioners." The reasons offered are both strong and varied, ranging from his "practice and experience" to his cagey admission that he conducted the entire journey in the company of his wife (if an Englishman in Ireland immediately begets suspicion, "the appearance of a female as quickly disarms it").[41] Of foremost importance is Inglis's belief that the "unpretending traveller" elicits none of the suspicions of government officials: "There is one sad omission in the instructions delivered to the commissioners.—There ought to have been printed in the front, and in large characters, these words: 'Upon no account, let your official character be known among the country people, from whom you wish to receive true information.'"[42] Unlike government officials,

I [Inglis] had not to cloak my dignities, and achieve a triumph over my own importance, before I could make myself useful. I could freely take a glass of illicit whiskey with the farmer, and a potato with the labourer; and take a turn with him, in digging his turf: I could sit down in the hedge whiskey-house; and jest with the landlady, and dance a jig with the daughter . . . In order to win the confidence of an Irish peasant, the free and easy is absolutely essential.[43]

Inglis also pointed out that he possessed the advantage of being able to work comparatively. Typically, government officials were dispatched to different counties or districts to report on local conditions, leaving the general report "framed from materials unequal in their value" and lacking any real synthetic quality.[44] It was Inglis's opinion that a lone reporter with sufficient "practice and experience" possessed distinct advantages. This was especially important as the Irish were reputed to be incorrigible liars. Even the most experienced traveller could be hoodwinked, as William Thackeray was warned:

Ask about an estate you may be sure almost that people will make misstatements, or volunteer them if not asked. Ask a cottager about his rent, or his landlord; you cannot trust him. I shall never forget the glee with which a gentleman in Munster told me how he had sent off M. M. [Alexis de] Tocqueville and [Gustave de] Beaumont "with *such* set of stories." Inglis was seized, as I am told, and mystified in the same way. In the midst of all these truths, attested with "I give ye my sacred honour and word," which is the stranger to select? And how are we to trust philosophers who make theories upon such data?[45]

I spend some time discussing Inglis's travel book because the terms of its production raise important points regarding the dissemination of knowledge on Ireland. First, Inglis's lengthy rationalisations establish the point that *truth itself is a journey* — it is something to be "arrived at," as Inglis put it, in and through particular performances.[46] Even so, there is the distinct sense that the social landscape is inert without Inglis's presence, and local voices are almost entirely absent from his narrative. The Irish appear as ventriloquised subjects, and local opinions, where ventured, are invariably filtered by Inglis. Stephen Greenblatt's remark that indigenous peoples often seem "most silent at those rare moments in which they are made speak" seems entirely apposite here.[47] Like other literature from the "contact zone," documents *about* the people were seldom *for* the people. Indeed, the "public" addressed by Inglis—always in the singular—is resolutely British. This does not mean that Inglis's statements are ipso facto misrepresentations, but it does make it necessary to question his conclusions in light of his position and outlook on Irish affairs.

Inglis's reaction to Ireland was a mixture of sympathy and revulsion. He was "not at all surprised that a people suffering all the extremities of human privation, should catch at straws."[48] Yet he never thought it harsh or contradictory to denigrate the rural poor for making marriage "a very commercial concern."[49] Although he grasped that "the chief wealth of the poor, seemed to be the dung-heap before their door," he rebuked the Irish for "too many evidences of idle, slovenly habits."[50] He was appalled by the clear examples of perjury witnessed at the Ennis assizes, but he also had the perspicacity to observe that where the law had lost its legitimacy, "false oaths are the substitutes for weapons."[51] He protested that he was not anti-Catholic, though he concluded that Lough Derg, a Catholic pilgrimage, was a "famous resort of ignorance and superstition" and believed "Protestantism the better religion for the people, and safer for the state."[52] At times he could apprehend the grim realities of poverty, yet he described the poorest regions in the west as "the land of romance" and a place where "gallantry and superstition divide life between them."[53]

It remains a challenge to reconcile these conflicting statements. The knowledge that Inglis had to speak on Ireland exactly as he saw it—*en passant*—is significant, but nine months was considerably more time than most visitors spent in Ireland.[54] Likewise, the vagaries of cross-cultural interpretations, although important, do not adequately account for his mixed response to Irish life.[55] Clearly, other interpretations are needed.

LANDSCAPES OF REFORM

Following the Act of Union a noticeable paradox seemed to suffuse British opinions on Ireland. On the one hand, Ireland was habitually proclaimed "an object so near to us as a SISTER," while on the other hand, Ireland appeared all the more anomalous and strange because its intractable domestic culture continued to confound the view that political annexation would precede the conversion of Ireland into a smiling and flourishing colony.[56] Distinct from previous centuries, however, the so-called Irish Question became less and less about military security and much more about "agricultural malaise, proto-industrial collapse and rural over-population"—all of which were now linked to the small matter of colonial governance.[57] Thus the "great question" of the day: "How can Ireland be rendered prosperous, and her people tranquil and happy?"[58] For Charlotte Elizabeth Tonna (1790–1846) the answer was "a tormenting enigma, baffling the utmost skill of worldly men, and paining the hearts of those who look beyond the passing pageant of time," a sentiment that found numerous sympathisers throughout the long history of British-Irish relations.[59]

Nevertheless, the question itself presumed that Ireland, in its assigned role as younger sibling, was not meeting expectations. The so-called partial famines of 1816–17, 1821–22, 1830, 1838, and 1842, not to mention the migrating masses of Irish suddenly alighting in British towns—as T. R. Malthus predicted and Thomas Carlyle polemicized—confirmed British suspicions that Ireland was, in a word, "underdeveloped."[60] Lord Grey stated the matter plainly in 1846: "Ireland is the one weak place in the solid fabric of British power; Ireland is the one deep (I had almost said ineffaceable) blot on the brightness of British honour. Ireland is our disgrace."[61] Grey was writing during the second year of the Great Famine, but his telling blend of property and propriety—"our disgrace"—was based on commonly held views that stretch back to pre-Famine decades. Commission after commission had collected and reproduced evidence on Irish poverty and all were in agreement that Irish destitution was intolerable.

Passing through Dublin in 1804, an anonymous writer found that "on every street the most shocking spectacles present themselves."[62]

The thoroughfares were "crowded, in the day-time, with the lowest prostitutes, whose appearance betray squalid misery; and who either starve, or by their numbers prove the city to be depraved to an almost incredible extent."[63] In Dublin's hinterland the author found a "land of misery" before him: "I would not have given sixpence for the whole apparel of any man, woman, or child whom we saw all along the road."[64] His conclusions were severe: "To the poor, no experiment can be hurtful: for in comforts and in morals, they are already in the lowest state of degradation to which it is possible for the people to be sunk."[65] In 1817 Anne Plumptre travelled through Ireland "to understand . . . its customs and manners, its civil and political state, that we may be enabled to compare them with our own, and judge between them and ourselves."[66] At Skibbereen, a town subsequently synonymous with starvation, she witnessed "whole streets, and not very short ones, consisting entirely of the wretched mud cabins of the peasants."[67] As part of a protracted European tour, the American John Griscom arrived in Belfast in April 1819. Making his way toward County Armagh, he witnessed a ragged, barefoot population, the worst anywhere, "save some Italian villages." At Lurgan he found "deplorable appearances of wretchedness" and houses that were literally "hovels of mud" (figure 2.4).[68]

Walter Scott (1771–1832), who had long promised to visit Ireland, eventually arrived on Irish shores in 1825. At this time Ireland was already synonymous with degrading poverty, yet Scott was completely unprepared for the extremities of want and hardship:

> There is much less exaggerated about the Irish than is to be expected. Their poverty is not exaggerated; it is on the very verge of human misery; their cottages would scarce serve for pig-styes, even in Scotland; and their rags seem the very refuse of the rag-shop, and are disposed on their bodies with such ingenious variety of wretchedness that you would think nothing but some sort of perverted taste could have assembled so many shreds together. You are constantly fearful that some knot or loop will give, and place the individual before you in all the primitive simplicity of Paradise.[69]

Figure 2.4. The hut or watch-house (*Illustrated London News,* February 13, 1847)

Fellow novelist and artist William Thackeray had frequent occasion to describe a "shabby sauntering people," who moved about "bare-legged" and "bareheaded."[70] "Nothing could convey to the stranger a stronger impression of wretchedness and untidiness," wrote John Forbes (1787–1861), "than this vicarious costume of the Irish, disfiguring at once to the person of the wearers, and calling forth in the mind of the observer the most disagreeable associations. Even when not in holes, as they too often are, those long-tailed coats almost touching the ground, and those shapeless breeches with their gaping knee-bands sagging below the calf of the leg, are the very emblems and ensigns of beggary and degradation."[71] Jacob Venedey "had often, when looking at the garments of the beggars in Dublin, been greatly puzzled to think, how it was possible for them to find their way, right into them, through the labyrinths of holes and rents."[72] Andrew Bigelow (1795–1877) admitted that he never knew what the paupers of London did with their clothes until he arrived in Dublin.[73]

The "bareness" or "nakedness" of Irish life is consistently invoked, combined with a sense of dread that "some knot or loop will
give," as Walter Scott worried.[74] The Act of Union was supposed to
be cathartic, but the inescapability of hardship meant that eyewitnesses had to regularly confront what has been called the "darker
side" of civilisation.[75] This confrontation with the realities of impoverishment could have a rousing effect, as in S. G. Osborne's comment
that "The British lion has indeed here so mangy an appearance, that
every Briton of common decency would have inclined to disclaim
all connection with the unhappy animal."[76] In most accounts, however, Ireland reflected "civilisation" precisely by being the site of its
absence.

The picture of poverty painted by the many government commissions was virtually the same. In 1830 a Select Committee recorded
that three-quarters of the population of Kerry were "destitute of the
means of subsistence."[77] Desperate peasants built their hovels on cliff-
fronts in order to spot shipwrecks off the stormy coast: "they considered them part of their means of subsistence."[78] Similarly, Asenath
Nicholson was told how storms blew good luck for the poor because
they threw up seaweed that was used for food and manure for conacre
land.[79] Another individual giving evidence before the Select Committee recalled groups of peasants employed as "lifters." Their job was
to assist the cattle in the district who were so starved they could not
rise without aid.[80] Besides depictions of habitual hunger, the wretched
hovels of the peasantry were consistently remarked upon. The 1841
census identified four grades of housing in Ireland. The fourth grade
consisted of single-roomed, windowless mud cabins, which nearly
half of all the rural population occupied (see figures 2.5, 2.6, and 2.7).[81]
Living standards were appalling, as William Bennett's (1804–73) narrative makes clear:

> Many of the cabins were holes in the bog, covered with a layer
> of turves, and not distinguishable as human habitations from
> the surrounding moor, until close down upon them. The bare
> sod was about the best material of which any of them were con-
> structed. Doorways, not doors, were usually provided at both

Figure 2.5. Common Mayo mud cabin (Barrow, *A Tour Round Ireland,* 159)

Figure 2.6. Worst sort of Mayo stone cabin (Barrow, *A Tour Round Ireland,* 162)

ends of the bettermost—back and front—to take advantage of the way of the wind. Windows and chimneys, I think, had no existence. A second apartment or division of any kind within was exceedingly rare. Furniture, properly so called, I believe may be stated at *nil*... Outside many were all but unapproachable, from mud and filth surrounding them; the same inside, or worse if possible, from the added closeness, darkness and smoke.[82]

Figure 2.7. Hovel near the Foot of the Reek (Barrow, *A Tour Round Ireland,* 180)

Some travellers were so perturbed they did their best to avoid such scenes of misery. Osborne confessed that he enjoyed Clifden all the more because of the absence of people.[83] Thackeray took pleasure in Torc waterfall at Muckross because "savages won't pay sixpence for the prettiest waterfall ever seen, so that this only was for the best company."[84] The "ruinous supplications" of beggars were notorious. In a rare moment of scorn, the American philanthropist Asenath Nicholson declared,

> They are like Pharaoh's frogs; they compass the whole length and breadth of the land, and are almost as much to be dreaded as the whole ten plagues; they leave you no room for escape on any hand; dodge where you will, they are on the spot, and the ill-fated stranger needs a fathomless bag, who ventures on a tour among those hunger-armed assailants.[85]

In discerning letters addressed to his former wife, the Prussian Prince Pückler-Muskau (1785–1871) described Irish beggar boys "humming

Figure 2.8. An outside jaunting car as Inglis described; note the beseeching beggars (Barrow, *A Tour Round Ireland,* frontispiece)

about like flies and unceasingly offering their services."[86] Travellers used different ploys to rid themselves of this onslaught. Some scattered coins (figure 2.8). Alexander Somerville (1811–85) warned prospective travellers not to journey without being "armed" with bread.[87] But it was clearly difficult to avoid what was everywhere present, as Archibald Stark was to learn:

> It [poverty] involves the very existence of every class of society. It meets the tourist at every turn, whether he will or no; it is written in legible characters on the roofless cabin of the peasant—on the counter of the shopkeeper—on the desk of the merchant—and on the marble pillars at the threshold of the aristocrat. If the tourist were blind, it would be rung in his ears in a thousand different cries of agony; therefore, the tourist who has any regard for truth, may not pass it over.[88]

In a sneer aimed at Thackeray, Stark added that even "the frivolous butterfly-class of travellers, who float from place to place on pinions of pleasure," could not possibly avoid the worn face of dearth.[89]

The barb was mostly justified. In his travel account Thackeray confessed to being "haunted by the face of popular starvation":

> In this fairest and richest of countries, men are suffering and starving by millions. . . . Strong countrymen are lying in bed "*for the hunger*"—because a man lying on his back does not need so much food as a person a-foot. Many of them have torn up the unripe potatoes from their little gardens, to exist now, and must look to winter, when they shall have to suffer starvation and cold too. The epicurean, and the traveller for pleasure, had better travel anywhere than here; where there are miseries that one does not dare to think of; where one is always feeling how helpless pity is, and how hopeless relief, and is perpetually made ashamed of being happy.[90]

This is a significant passage. The author admits that suffering and starvation is "not the exception, it is the condition of the people." Moreover, the knowledge that other human beings are reduced to conditions of bare subsistence made him perpetually "ashamed of being happy." This sense of anomie, however, is never honestly confronted. A genuine politics of recognition is foreclosed, and like many observers, Thackeray's shame quickly switches to intolerance and bigotry. He frequently derided the Irish: "a doubtful, lazy, dirty family vassal—a guerrilla footman." Elsewhere he lampooned the "very mean, mealy-faced, uneasy looking subaltern," descriptions that led to a temporary fallout with the Irish novelist Charles Lever (1806–72).[91] In general Thackeray thought the Irish were poor guardians of their futures: "the people like their freedom, such as it is, and prefer to starve and be ragged as they list."[92]

Similarly, John Griscom remarked that the Irish have acquired "an habitual indifference" to destitution "and will make no exertion themselves to live in greater decency and comfort, when it is in their power."[93] James Johnson lamented a distinctly Irish "patience in poverty," while Anne Plumptre described an acquiescent peasantry, who exhibited "*patterns of patient endurance,* suffering but scarcely complaining, almost even kissing the rod by which they are scourged."[94] Visitors were clearly confounded by scenes of sociability amongst the poor.[95] The ever-sceptical German Jacob Venedey confessed that "wherever we see it we consider it unnatural, and we immediately believe there must be hypocrisy in them, and deceit practised upon ourselves."[96] Concern for the misery of others vied with widespread fears of "dissimulation and dishonesty" as well as suspicions regarding an innate indifference to social improvement.[97] These impressions were influential in defining an Irish Poor Law capable of responding to endemic poverty and managing traits thought to be uniquely Irish. Indeed, the nationalist writer John Mitchel claimed that "the vague and blundering idea that an impudent beggar was demanding their money with a scowl in his eye and threat upon his tongue" determined the course of relief policy during the Famine.[98]

From Hunger to Habit

Irish poverty was very often attributed to native "improvidence." According to James Johnson, "Whiskey-drinking swelled and accelerated the stream of population, not by making the people more productive, but by rendering them less prudent, less wise, less cautious in the contracting of early and improvident marriages."[99] There was also an underlying sense that Irish poverty was a result of Irish nature. As Thackeray pointed out,

> Kings and law don't cause or cure dust and cobwebs; but indolence leaves them to accumulate, and imprudence will not calculate its income, and vanity exaggerates its own powers, and the fault is laid upon that tyrant of a sister kingdom. The whole country is filled with such failures; swaggering beginnings that could not be carried through; grand enterprises begun dashingly, and ending in shabby compromises or downright ruin.[100]

Ireland boasted an "imaginary commerce" that reflected the profligacy of the people rather than the asymmetries of the market: "Mill-owners over-mill themselves, merchants over-warehouse themselves, squires over-castle themselves, little tradesmen about Dublin and the cities over-villa and over-gig themselves, and we hear sad tales about hereditary bondage and the accursed tyranny of England."[101] Archibald Stark sarcastically noted "Irish 'enterprises of great pith and moment,' between splendid beginnings and indifferent results."[102] "Everything in Dublin is pomp or poverty," wrote another traveller, who blamed the Irish gentry for having "no notion of economy, or of the frugal high living of the English."[103]

The discourse on poverty was shifting from depictions of hunger to searing critiques of Irish customs and habits. This personalisation of poverty helps explain the importance attached to descriptions of Irish cabin life. In *An Outline of the Science of Political Economy,* first published in 1836, Nassau Senior (1790–1864) declared, "We have no doubt that a well regulated gentleman's family, removing the prejudices, soothing the quarrels, directing and stimulating the exertions, and awarding the praise or blame to the conduct of the villagers round them, is among the most efficient means by which the character of a neighbourhood can be improved."[104]

The same arguments were translated from the country estate and applied to the peasant's cabin. "As the wretched hut debases a man's character," wrote John Wiggins (1822–52), "so the decent house lifts a man in the world: his sons and daughters marry better; he gets a better class of servants, who serve him better, and he prefers his house. The business of the house is better done, and with greater economy both of expense and consumption, and the man's position is alerted for the better." "Why also could not the state of cottar's cabins be subject to inspection under sanitory [*sic*] regulations," he wondered, and if found unwholesome, "competent authorities should enforce the repair of them upon the tenant of the farm. This would tend to improve the tenants' houses by force of example, and by the operation of pride."[105] Observers began to draw connections between "internal economies" and national economies, between domestic space and national territory, between the body proper and the body politic. As the government directed its attention to the reformation of domestic culture, social commentators began detailing the intimate spaces of Irish life. On the eve of the Famine, James Johnson provided this "exact survey" of an Irish cabin's "internal economy":

It was twelve feet in length, by eight in breath—the walls of mud, and the roof of wattles, thatch, and sods, black with smoke and soot. There was a little fire-place, in one corner, under the tin-pot chimney—a few shelves in the other corner—and I found that the bedstead, which was raised a foot from the ground, occupied half the cabin. It was therefore eight feet in length (being across the hovel) and six in breadth. The bed consisted of heath and hay, covered by a clean coarse cloth. On this bed eight people slept at night—the woman—six children—and the child of a neighbour, whose parents were down with the fever.[106]

To such accounts were added ethnographic observations depicting mounds of manure in front of cabin doors and animals living cheek-by-jowl with peasants—descriptions that did little to endear Victorian readers to the Irish rural life (see figure 2.9).[107] These environmental readings of poverty were often mixed with moral prescriptions for social improvement that were strongly feminised:

to enter their cottages, and to talk to them about the mismanagement of their children and their domestic concerns: to shew them economic modes of preparing their meals; to point out the mischief of uncleanliness and idleness; to set them an example, to rebuke and commend them according to circumstances, and to exercise that beneficial influence which higher position, and the power to do little acts of kindness, and the voice free from harsh tones of party and religious difference, naturally give.[108]

The English economist and journalist Harriet Martineau thought that Irish people required patient domestic instruction: "There seems to be nothing wanting, as far as the visitor can see, but the presence of a matron, or the occasional visits of ladies, to see the opening and cleaning of windows, and some domestic niceties; and we emphatically declare the encouragement of a wider notice and appreciation of this highly important institution a matter of national concern."[109] According to Forbes, "a little management, with the aid of more well to do neighbours to plan for them and to act for them," would soon transform Irish domestic arrangements. "Then should we see Paddy

Figure 2.9. A Kerry cabin and its inhabitants (Barrow, *A Tour Round Ireland,* 107)

'his very own self' . . . no longer transmogrified into that vile trav-
esty of a man, which has become the butt of the stage and the standing theme of caricaturists."[110] Distributing food aid during the Famine, one visitor confessed, "sometimes we thought proper to exercise
the right of lecturing; and made the levelling of the mud floor, the
filling in some filthy puddle, or the removal of some abominable
heap from *in* to *outside,* the condition of our gift" (see figure 2.10).[111]
Most observers conveyed an unmistakable level of repulsion at what
they saw. "What can be expected from ideas first formed in an Irish
cabin?" quipped Anne Plumptre.[112] She was stating the increasingly
popular viewpoint that the Irish Question was as much personal as
political.

    It is difficult to assess how the Irish reacted to having their homes
"surveyed," or how they felt about being rebuked for their apparent

Figure 2.10. Miss Kennedy distributing clothing at Kilrush (*Illustrated London News,* December 22, 1849)

"mismanagement" of domestic space.[113] A rare conversation is detailed by Asenath Nicholson:

> "Why don't you," said I to a widow who had an acre of ground, "make things about your cabin look a little more tidy? You have a pretty patch of land, well kept." "But, lady, I have but one little slip of a boy of fifteen years of age, and he toils the long day to rair [*sic*] a bit of vegetable to carry to market, and he helped me to put up this little cabin, and if I make it look nice outside, the agent will put a pound more rent on me, or turn me out and my little things; and I couldn't pay the pound."

To this testimony Nicholson added the following: "These are the facts all over Ireland. If the poor tenant improves the premises, he must be turned out or pay more. If he does not improve it, he is a lazy, dirty Irishman, and must be put out for that."[114]

The increasing tendency to explain Irish poverty in terms of essentialised Irish habits was sometimes tempered by more sober reflections on the prevailing socio-economic conditions in Ireland. The Devon Commission argued that the history of "confiscations and colonisations," and other "extrinsic events," meant that the Irish labourer bore "sufferings greater, we believe, than the people of any other country in Europe have to sustain."[115] Spencer Hall (1812–85) concluded that Irish poverty was determined by "circumstance as much as race," while Charlotte Tonna adopted the Benthamite position that Ireland could be made prosperous, tranquil, and happy if the government would replace "methods of compulsion" with "mode[s] of moral management."[116] While these writers appealed to the liberal norms of progress and enlightened supervision, their claims were often accompanied by racial prejudices. "Oh, surely the Englishman *is* a favoured man," declared Tonna, "and surely he may bless God every hour of his life for it, who comes to Ireland, and settles her soil, alike minded and enabled to be a blessing to her children!"[117] Social and moral explanations of Irish failings were reconciled to some degree during the Irish Poor Law debates, when moral management *and* social correction were achieved by extending the workhouse system to Ireland. In the following chapter we will see how the Poor Law institutionalised a method of regulated social engineering—what I call "colonial welfare"—but it is first necessary to say something about the growing racialisation of poverty that so clearly defined debates on Irish conditions.

"A DIFFERENT RACE OF MEN": THE RACIALISATION OF POVERTY

In his influential study *Apes and Angels,* L. Perry Curtis Jr. argued that racial depictions of the Irish were uncommon until the latter half of the nineteenth century. Recently, several scholars have challenged this argument.[118] In different ways they argue that racialised depictions of difference existed, but they operated outside the paradigm of "scientific racism" usually associated with social Darwinism (figures 2.11 and 2.12). It has been suggested that after the ratification of the Catholic Emancipation Bill (1829), state discrimination on the basis of religion decreased, while racial and cultural constructions of difference became

Figure 2.11. Early racialisation of the Irish (*Illustrated London News,* October 3, 1847)

Figure 2.12. Daniel O'Connell conjures up the Irish Frankenstein (*Punch,* November 4, 1843)

more common.[119] This is true to a point, even though it is not difficult to find evidence of anti-Catholic bigotry after 1829. Thackeray
wrote several disparaging passages about the Catholic clergy in 1842,
and the rabidly anti-Catholic Charlotte Elizabeth Tonna believed that
the Irish priests were actively fomenting rebellion. "Take away Pop-
ery," she was convinced, "and Ireland as she ought to be will stand
out in all the beauty that is now shrouded in corruption."[120] Travellers
in the post-Famine decades continued to describe Catholics as "lam-
entably deficient in that practice called common sense, persevering
industry, and taste for the decencies and comforts of life, which constitute . . . 'civilization.'"[121]

Indeed, it would be more accurate to say that racial and cultural
prejudices were reinforced and amplified by preexisting suspicions
about the loyalty, morality, and industry of Roman Catholics. Particularly important are travellers' responses to the northern counties
of Ireland, notably the area around Belfast, which was seen to be a
haven of Protestant virtues. The vast majority of visitors approached
the north having already visited the south and west of the country
and usually having witnessed depressing scenes of poverty. In the circumstances it is unsurprising that the relative prosperity of this region would be highlighted. Assessing the countryside between Derry
and Coleraine in 1804, one traveller recorded that shoes, stockings,
and chimneys were more common and that "the natives" appear
"more civilized."[122] "Belfast," James Johnson enthused, "is the Athens
of Ireland — the Manchester of Ulster — the Glasgow of Antrim."
He found that the "fiery excitability" he witnessed in the rest of Ireland was in the north "softened down to sober sense."[123] Travelling in
this direction, Inglis also noticed that "the poverty-stricken appearance
of the Irish towns was fast disappearing. I perceived that I was verg-
ing towards the north, and getting among a different race of men."[124]
As he approached Strabane, County Tyrone, he was

> greatly struck by the course of the day's journey, with the very
> improved appearance of the peasantry . . . The farm-houses,
> too, were of superior order; I do not mean merely that they
> were larger, or better built; this can be accomplished by an im-

proving and considerate landlord. *The improvement was visible in things which depend of the occupant* . . . the epithet, "slovenly," could rarely have found any subject for its application.[125]

These initial impressions were later confirmed: "It is impossible that Cork, Limerick, or Waterford, should ever become altogether like Belfast because the character of the Scotch and the Irish is essentially different."[126] Indeed, as early as the 1770s Arthur Young described the habits of lassitude supposedly characteristic of southern Catholics, who "only work to eat, and, when provisions are plenty, will totally idle away so much of their time that there is scarce any such thing as getting work done."[127] While it is true that non-British travellers like Venedey also found the north, especially Belfast, "clean, broad, and well lighted," they tended not to attribute this fact to the natural superiority of the inhabitants.[128]

It has been suggested that English racism "drew deeply on the notion of the *domestic* barbarism of the Irish as a marker of racial difference." Referring to "an exemplary image" of an Irish man and woman lethargically sitting in front of their hovel (figure 2.13), McClintock describes how the simianization of Irish physiognomies and the "slovenly lack of dedication to domestic order" became a surrogate sign of moral decay.[129] McClintock is referring to an image composed in 1882, when scientific racism was clearly in the ascendancy; however, her emphasis on the Irish domestic scene helps explain why the hovels of the poor were so captivating for pre-Famine travellers. Where skin colour proved "imprecise and inadequate" as a marker of degeneration, domestic disorder and public hygiene could be fixed on as a positive sign of Irish barbarism.[130]

Race was a particularly popular tool for travellers to use in approaching the realities of poverty in the south and west of Ireland. "To an Englishman," remarked one witness, "journeying westward across Ireland it almost seems that he is retrograding from an age of science and civilization to one of ignorance and barbarism."[131] Stark found the boys and girls at a Waterford Poorhouse "as ignorant as Ojibbeway Indians."[132] Johnson compared the guides in Killarney to "Hindoos and Mahomedans on the beach at Madras," while the houses

Figure 2.13. "The King of A-Shantee" (*Puck* 10, no. 258 [February 15, 1882]: 378)

in the fishing village of Claddagh were "wig-wams."[133] Hall described peasant dwellings in County Clare as "partaking somewhat in their style of the united orders of the Indian wigwam and the Hottentot kraal."[134] In Bantry Thackeray found the "beggars' houses" impossible to sketch: "one might as well make a sketch of a bundle of rags . . . I declare a Hottentot kraal has more comforts in it: even to write of the place makes one unhappy, and the words move slowly."[135] Over and over again, material difference was expressed as *civilisational distance.*[136]

Racial arguments were sometimes laudatory. "Amid the extreme neglect and indigence," wrote William Bennett in 1847, "the fine figures, the elevated features, and the native grace and beauty of many a Kerry peasant girl, is often striking. The whole race of peasantry are perhaps among the most simple and affectionate, harmless and peaceable, hardy and intelligent, of any within our islands."[137] These descriptions of "romantic primitivism" were not exceptional.[138] Certain peculiarities of Irish life were represented in mawkish terms (for example, "Irish bulls"), while other features were discussed with a mixture of fear and revulsion (for instance, funeral keening, whiskey drinking, and faction fighting). The contrast between Bennett's noble "race of peasantry" and Thackeray's feckless Celts reminds us that racism invariably rests on a series of movements between the strange *and* the familiar, proximity *and* distance, engagement *and* estrangement, inside *and* outside—what Edward Said described as a "geographical disposition."[139] Anthropologist Nicholas Thomas helpfully suggests that racism "ought to be seen as discourse that engages in conceptual and perceptual government, in its apprehension and legislation of types, distinctions, criteria for assessing proximity and distance, and in its more technical applications—in, for instance, notions stipulating that certain forms of labour are appropriate to one race but not another."[140]

Thomas's impression of "conceptual and perceptual government" usefully suggests how racial discourse influenced popular opinion on Ireland. Robert Knox's (1791–1862) influential study *The Races of Men: A Philosophical Enquiry into the Influence of Race over the Destinies of Nations* (1862) is an interesting case in point.[141] The book contains revealing thoughts on the Irish (and the Celts more generally) and suggests much about racism as a popular discourse for engaging with the Irish Question. The motive for the book is neatly encapsulated in the epigraph by Alexander Pope—"The proper study of mankind is man"—together with Knox's own mantra, repeated in various formats throughout the book: "Race is everything: literature, science, art—in a word, civilization, depends on it."[142] According to Knox it is humankind's biological make-up, zoological history, and propensity to act as a living, racialised being that holds the key to understanding life in its totality. To this extent, racial theories quite literally seize hold of human life by channelling it *inside* a system of power-knowledge (acts of "conceptual and perceptual government," including the will to identify, describe, categorise, and so forth), while at the same time placing life *outside* the zone of positive human influence since our species' being is seemingly pregiven. This "legislation of types" works to isolate and divide the human from the seemingly nonhuman or less-than-human. In Knox's account, biology, common to all human beings, is the most convincing explanation of human variation.

In the "Celtic race" Knox observed "furious fanaticism; a love of war and disorder; hatred for order and patient industry; no accumulative habits; restless, treacherous, uncertain: look at Ireland." He added, "As a Saxon I abhor all dynasties, monarchies and bayonet governments, but this latter seems to be the only one suitable for the Celtic man."[143] Knox's arguments were published in 1862—a decade after the Great Famine—but the lecture tour from which the book derived began in 1846. In fact, in the introduction to *Races of Men,* Knox insinuated that Thomas Campbell Foster (the influential "*Times* Commissioner") plagiarised his original arguments, travelling to Ireland to "discover" what Knox had already revealed: namely, the existence of two separate and distinct races in Ireland. The fact that Knox is aware of the formative power of travel narratives suggests that the line between scientific racism and more "cultural" appropriations of racial arguments was always blurred.[144]

In the popular domain racial theories of degeneracy mingled freely with crude Malthusian theories of overpopulation. Malthusian arguments are significant in at least two respects. First, as noted by Donald Winch, Malthus shifts "the terms of debate from political culture towards biology by grounding his laws of nature on a population principle—an ever-present propensity for population growth to outstrip the means of subsistence."[145] Second, just as racial arguments describe life at the *species* level, after Malthus it became more common to assess human *populations* with natural tendencies that need to be itemised and understood in order to be better regulated.

Although Malthus himself said surprisingly little about conditions in Ireland, an oft-cited letter to Ricardo written in 1817 gives a good sense of his position: "the land in Ireland is infinitely more peopled than in England; and to give the full effect to the natural resources of the country a great part of the population should be swept from the soil."[146] In the sixth edition of *An Essay on the Principle of Population,* Malthus reaffirms this position: "If, as in Ireland, Spain, and many countries of the more southern climates, the people are in so degraded a state, as to propagate their species without regard to consequences, it matters little whether they have poor-laws or not. Misery in all its various forms must be the predominant check to their increase."[147] Malthus's bleak prognosis was memorably characterised by William and Paul Paddock as a never-ending struggle between the "stork" and the "plough."[148] Mass starvations occur when the stork gains the upper hand, which Malthus predicted as inevitable.[149] Such forecasts stand in contrast to previous centuries, however, when Irish underpopulation was used to justify British settler colonialism and plantation policies. In the 1670s William Petty described Ireland as "thin-peopled" and warned statesmen against transplanting laws and norms "made and first fitted to thick-peopled countries."[150] Although by the mid-nineteenth century the population-resource relationship was thought to have reversed, the same problems of deriving governing principles from very different social circumstances persisted.

Even when observers of Irish conditions rejected the specifics of the Malthusian doctrines, they often borrowed his alarmist flavour or clung to the position that the Irish population required moral training.[151] "Wealth does not accumulate; but men do," wrote James Johnson, "*teste* nine million of population—two million of paupers—and four million of the 'finest pisantry in the world' living on wet potatoes, with or without salt." "In no country on the face of the globe," Johnson continued, "is emigration more necessary or more beneficial than in Ireland, where the very poverty and idleness of the inhabitants tend annually to swell the streams of a redundant population!"[152] With his mind's eye firmly fixed on Irish conditions, the economist John Wheatley urged statesmen to check the growth of "supernumerary hands": "Every country will be rich in proportion as it pursues a restrictive system [of population control], because its produce will be so far above population; and every country will be poor in proportion as it pursues a stimulative system, because its population will be so far above production." "To colonize the poor of Ireland, and prevent their reproduction," Wheatley concluded, "is the only mode by which the condition of the poor can be made what it ought to be."[153] Citing Robert Malthus and Arthur Young as authorities, George Cornewall Lewis (1806–63) accused Irish peasants of marrying early, living on the scantiest of foods, and being "indifferent" to the moral obligations of civilised life: "Far removed from the brutality of those half-civilized nations, which have practised the exposure of new-born infants, they [the Irish] nevertheless performed only the animal, and none of the moral duties of parents."[154] Such was the power of this discourse that by the mid-1840s even a compassionate observer like William Bennett was convinced that the Famine was an unavoidable check on unrestrained population growth.[155] These are striking examples of how a form of power-knowledge fixes upon human life at the *population* level and at the *species* level, making this discursive move the foundation for specific economic principles and political strategies.

CORRECTIVE REGULATION

A number of conclusions may be drawn from the foregoing discussion. First, I have tried to show how the "massive inscription of social knowledge" was central to the extension of state power.[156] Moreover, the gathering of intelligence about Ireland was based on the presumption that Irish people, especially the poorer classes, were incapable of representing themselves. This supposition is common to other colonial situations. In his influential book *Orientalism,* Edward Said invokes Marx's dictum: "They must be represented, they cannot represent themselves."[157] In choosing these words Said was attempting to underline "how the garrulous discourse of representation interposes itself between the curious reader and the silent (silenced) subdued/passive Orient."[158] Writing about Irish conditions, Harriet Martineau insisted on instructing the pauper peasants "till they shall have become qualified for the guardianship of their own interests," a statement that rejects the possibility that Irish people were competent to understand and represent "their own interests."[159] In a similar vein those authors who declared themselves "narrators of truth" typically presumed that "truth" was a unilateral matter with little or nothing to do with what the Irish might think and say about themselves.

These asymmetries in the production of knowledge also extended to more official circles. Most government commissions were thoroughly unrepresentative. The Devon Commission, appointed to enquire into the nature of land tenure, consisted entirely of landlords. In conducting its enquiries the first Poor Law Commission paired "a native of Great Britain with a resident native of Ireland," this method of working being "the only mode of combining the national knowledge possessed by the one, with the impartiality almost certain of the other."[160] Mirroring the political belief that Irish autonomy was utterly unthinkable, the Irish were considered useful for acquiring knowledge but deficient analysts of their own customs, social mores, and political environment.[161] Asenath Nicholson was one of a few foreign correspondents to challenge this assumption: "Yes, the poor Irishman has a mind that can and does think; but, like the American slave, he is told by his master, and he is told by all the world, 'You do the working, and I'll do the thinking.'"[162] The persistent representation of indigenous absence and the near total erasure of local voices were constantly evoked to justify external intervention in Irish affairs.[163]

Second, I have sought to chart the development of a culture of travel able to enlarge and contract the space between the haves and the have-nots, the "satiated" and the "emaciated." On the one hand, Irish life was minutely surveyed and represented, while, on the other hand, what was intimately recorded was also profoundly abstracted and detached from the harsh realities of everyday life. In part this was due to the power of stereotypes (born from centuries of intercultural contact) that presented the Irish population as a curiosity to gaze at and ponder. Equally, if not more important, however, is the fact that intellectuals, travel writers, and government commissioners now came to Ireland to address poverty with a view to mobilising practical programmes for social improvement.[164] The racialisation of Irish poverty and theories of overpopulation are important illustrations of this process. These discursive regimes constructed "bare lives" that were in need of radical rehabilitation.[165] If racial characteristics explained Irish backwardness, then it was Irish nature that must be reconditioned.

If demographic patterns were the cause of Irish poverty, then population reform was required. In each case the tendency was to blame innate characteristics; it hardly occurred to these observers that these Irish characteristics might be the *result,* rather than the *cause,* of poverty.[166] As Lloyd has surmised, "every element of the colonized culture that cannot be translated and assimilated to the development of colonial capitalist modernity must either be erased or encoded as a symptom of underdevelopment."[167]

By the mid-nineteenth century, popular assumptions about native character—Irish mendacity, improvidence, domestic primitivism, agricultural backwardness, wicked obduracy, and habits of lassitude—powerfully shaped British attitudes toward Irish welfare and development. Instructive in this regard is a small handbook, entitled *A Farmer's Guide,* published in 1841. Written by George Nicholls, the guide was expressly dedicated to "the small farmers and cotter tenantry of Ireland." As well as providing practical advice on crop husbandry and livestock rearing, Nicholls dispensed advice on the consumption of wholesome foods, appropriate clothing, reordering "domestic arrangements," and avoiding "early and improvident marriage." The guide extols the virtues of honest exertion and the necessity of "moral training" to improve the habits of small farmers and cottiers. The latter groups were described in terms that are by now familiar:

> [F]or he still prefers a lounge or a saunter, with his pipe, and his long coat hanging about him, to taking up his spade, and opening a passage between his lazy beds for the water to escape, or bringing a few cartloads of clay or gravel to lay upon his mossy land; or in short doing any thing to make his home neat, his farm productive, and himself and his family comfortable. Such a man must always remain poor, and he not only brings poverty upon himself, but upon all belonging to or connected with him; and we place him here as a warning, that others may be corrected and stimulated to exertion by his example.[168]

Significantly, George Nicholls was also the author of the Irish Poor Law, which after 1847 bore the full burden of relieving the multitude of starving Irish. As we shall see, Nicholl's conviction that the Irish needed careful "moral training" was readily demonstrated in the way the Irish Poor Law sought to suture state relief to far wider socio-economic reforms. The Poor Law debate also established dangerous distinctions between productive and unproductive forms of life that are crucial for understanding the types of relief afforded during the Great Famine and how the disaster itself came to be thought of as an engine for social development. These policies would have been unthinkable without the social construction of Irish vice and deviancy and the growing perception that Irish poverty was a symptom of a deeper moral redundancy—the "inherent good-for-nothingness" of the Irish peasant.

CHAPTER THREE

ENGINEERING CIVILITY

Colonial Welfare and Irish Pauper Management

It was the English Government that invented paupers in Ireland when they imposed on us their Poor Law. Before that time there had been plenty of poor men in Ireland, but "no able-bodied paupers."
— John Mitchel, *The Last Conquest of Ireland (Perhaps)*

The literature on colonial development and European welfare has treated them as discrete topics, yet historically their objectives were never separate.
— James Vernon, *Hunger: A Modern History*

INSTITUTIONAL CARE AND POPULATION REFORM

The previous chapter explored how the Irish poor emerged as *objects* of calculation rather than acting *subjects*. This chapter moves the discussion forward by critically examining the Irish Poor Law system as it existed immediately prior to the Great Famine, situating its conception, organization, and implementation within an apparatus of colonial population management. Although earlier work on the Irish Poor Law underlines its centrality to the Great Famine, the debate focuses on the operations of the workhouse system, ignoring the fact that from its inception the Irish Poor Law was considered to be much more than a system for administering state welfare.[1] Contemporary discussion about Irish Poor Law legislation exposes an emerging consensus that economic restructuring, agricultural rationalisation, and population decline were essential to civilizing Irish society. This larger debate about modernising Irish society informed subsequent Famine policies, especially the callous decision in 1847 to place the full burden of famine relief on the Irish Poor Law system. In crucial respects British famine relief was simply an extension of *existing* developmentalist attitudes about revitalising Irish society. The fact that institutional correction was couched in a grammar of "development" and "improvement" reminds us that liberal colonial projects were routinely valorised as progressive and humanitarian—even though the supposed beneficiaries of political and economic intervention were rarely if ever asked for their opinion or consent. In investigating the origins of an Irish Poor Law, therefore, we are also tracing the refinement of a unique brand of colonial welfare, wherein the modes of political supervision always presuppose an extension of control over indigenous life.[2]

This last point is significant. It is still unproblematically asserted that Irish famine deaths resulted from a political commitment to the principles of laissez-faire, which is interpreted almost exclusively as a policy of nonintervention.[3] To be sure, in its most doctrinaire form, economic liberalism prohibits any formal interference by the state in food markets and it is certainly the case that several influential officials exhibited a "tender regard" for such principles; however, there exists an important and overlooked tension between economic liberalism and social interventionism.[4] It is often the case that state and institutional mechanisms are needed to promote market liberalisation, to quicken the reproduction of capital, and to keep populations docile and compliant. Thus, the "central paradox" observed in relation to colonial famines in North India holds equally true for nineteenth-century Ireland: "when the colonial regime was strenuously advocating noninterventionism and adopting a doctrine of strict laissez-faire . . . in actuality the famine situation contributed to a singular extension of the material power and the physical, statistical, and ideological infrastructure of the colonial state."[5] Likewise in Ireland, the difficulties of superintending a colonial population during an ecological crisis became the *raison d'être* to expand the "pastoral" role of the state, ultimately placing the Irish population at the centre of what Charles Trevelyan characterized as "extensive experiments in the science, if it may be so called, of relieving the destitute."[6]

Observers were noticeably struck by the magnitude of the "experiment" Trevelyan had in mind. Visiting his first Poor Law workhouse in 1849, S. G. Osborne (1808–89) compared the institution to a small town: "Food, clothing, shelter, education, medicine, religious teaching, industrial teaching, are to be found for this mass [of people]; grave-ground for a very large portion of it: the law has undertaken this monster task."[7] As Osborne insinuates, the machinery of the Irish Poor Law allowed the government to gradually manoeuvre itself into a powerful position vis-à-vis some of the most vulnerable members of Irish society. Government officials were also conscious of this rapid accrual of power. Trevelyan, in particular, was at pains to explain the scale of the administrative mission that befell his office and what one observer called his "tribes of superintendents."[8] In *The Irish Crisis* Trevelyan carefully itemized the full extent of the government's famine role:

> To advance the funds, to superintend the work; to pay the people weekly; to enforce proper performance of the labour; if the farm works were interrupted, to ascertain the quantity of labour required for them; to select and draft off the proper persons to perform it; to settle the wages to be paid to them by the farmers, and see that they were paid; to furnish food, not only for all the destitute out of doors, but in some measure for the paupers of the workhouses, [these] were the duties which the government and its officers were called upon to perform.[9]

These remarks suggest the process through which state-led biopolitical regulation became entwined with relief strategies meant to mitigate the suffering of the Irish poor. Another prominent British official recognised that the very terms of welfare provision—the strict superintendence of diet, the "task labour" system, and the principle of "less eligibility"—furnished the state with an extraordinary degree of power over the distribution of wages and food, and thus the entire means of subsistence, of a starving population.[10] As John Mitchel put it, "Government [was to] be all in all; omnipotent to give food or withhold it, to relieve or to starve, according to their own ideas of policy and of good behaviour in the people."[11] The politician and lawyer Isaac Butt (1813–79) passionately argued that this expansion of state power meant that aid depended on the munificence of the government and "the arbitrary power of those who [were] to carry its provisions into practice."[12] The shift from local to centralised management was a key factor enabling these developments and deserves some attention before we turn to the debates surrounding the implementation of the Irish Poor Law.

THE SOCIAL LABORATORY

Anthropologist Ann Stoler and historian Gyan Prakash have urged scholars of colonialism to examine Europe's colonies less as "sites of exploitation" than as "laboratories of modernity."[13] In the context of Irish Studies this approach has an impressive genealogy. In 1945 D. B. Quinn considered the confiscations and plantations of the sixteenth and seventeenth centuries as an "experiment" in English colonial praxis and theory.[14] Likewise, historians Nicholas Canny and Jane Ohlmeyer have found the "laboratory" model helpful for discussing the development of colonial government in early modern Ireland.[15] As early as 1948 W. L. Burn suggested that Victorian Ireland served as a "social laboratory, the scene of daring and ambitious experiments." "The most conventional of Englishmen," Burn averred, "were willing to experiment in Ireland on lines which they were not prepared to contemplate at home."[16] More recently, Oliver MacDonagh has developed this line of thought.[17] MacDonagh shows that between 1815 and 1840, local authorities in Ireland lost the bulk of their power:

> Thus, whereas the first stage of the administrative reform in English local government represented an attempt to broaden the relevant electorates, break the Anglican monopoly of power and recruit JPs [Justices of the Peace] from outside the ranks of the

traditional gentry, the equivalent phase in Ireland was marked by the passage of some of the old and almost all of the new functions of government from *local to central control.*[18]

This pronounced shift toward "central superintendence," to use Nassau Senior's term, was equally apparent in matters of urban government and public order.[19] In 1814 Robert Peel established a professional trained police force in Ireland (hence the nickname "peelers"), which predated the English metropolitan force by some fifteen years.[20] Law enforcement was reformed again in 1836 and the Irish Constabulary was born. The latter reforms introduced for the first time a standard system of management, uniform rules, and centralised control to the force.[21] According to MacDonagh, "Ireland possessed a coherent, stratified, paramilitary police at a time when the lonely, untrained village constable was still the instrument of law enforcement over most of rural England."[22] Contemporary observers were quick to grasp the sweeping nature of these reforms. "The legal instruments for the suppression of outrage," noted Senior, "are actually more powerful in Ireland than in England. The law is more stringent; there is a much larger army, and a much stronger police."[23] In the late 1820s, at the height of Catholic Emancipation, there was a regulatory infantry force of twenty-five thousand men stationed either in Ireland or on the west coast of England with a view to being dispatched to garrison the country if required. The size of the force is staggering when it is considered that the entire infantry for the rest of the United Kingdom was a mere thirty thousand.[24] By the time of the Great Famine, there were more troops stationed in Ireland than in all of India.[25] The fact that the Royal Irish Constabulary ("Royal" was added in 1867) served as a model for policing systems in other parts of the British Empire underscores the degree to which Ireland was a testing ground for managing troublesome colonial populations.

Other centralising developments were no less impressive. In 1836 the government refined the law to establish salaried magistrates who were expected to be resident in their localities. This was in contradistinction to England, where the amateur, unpaid magistrate was still very much the norm.[26] A national schools system, introduced in 1831,

established a state-supported system of elementary education in which
two-thirds of the cost of buildings, equipment, and salaries were gar-
nered from the public purse. The rest of Britain managed without
a system of elementary education until the 1870s.[27] For David Fitzpatrick this educational experiment was "a classic example of 'cultural
imperialism,' directed towards the moral and intellectual advancement
of a hitherto backward people."[28] During the final years of the Famine the government overhauled the entire dispensary system, establishing in its place a network of salaried part-time doctors and a centralised, national system of inspection. This development positioned
taxation and the machinery of the Poor Law in line with medical relief.[29] The act also assigned a medical practitioner to every district in
the country and established the practice of medical relief outside
the Irish workhouse system.[30] "In contrast to the British," MacDonagh concludes, "Irish government was remarkable for the extent to
which centralisation, uniformity, inspection and professionalism spread
throughout the system before 1850."[31] These ambitious reforms of the
state's roles and responsibilities involved nothing like the abnegation
of duties or retreat from social affairs that is frequently attributed to
classical liberalism.

For the most part, MacDonagh attributes these deviations to the
familiar tale of religious bigotry. "Any step to democratise Irish local
government," he writes, "would have admitted Catholics to a share
in power, and introduced factional struggles in the representative
institutions."[32] Allowing a Catholic educational system to develop was
tantamount to sanctioning and institutionalising "superstition" and
"sedition."[33] Although there is some truth to this claim, MacDonagh's
argument simplifies matters too much. In fact, from the beginning "the
laboratory" was much more than an experiment in sectarianism. Centralised political administration, a unified police force, paid magistrates, public dispensaries, a unified and regulated network of lunatic
asylums, and state-backed elementary schooling—this was a massive
undertaking requiring new regimes of calculation and surveillance.[34]
These developments position Ireland alongside other British colonies
where the meticulous management of indigenous life had become the
defining characteristic of colonial politics.[35] The popular question of

how to save the Irish from themselves was partly answered by increased institutional regulation, and it is in this principal sense that we need to frame the problems of poverty and development in the period after the introduction of the Irish Poor Law in 1838.[36]

THE POLITICAL ECONOMY OF "DIRECTIVE GOVERNMENT"

Notwithstanding these remarkable developments in nineteenth-century government, the Irish Poor Law has been described by Mac-Donagh as "the great exception to the rule that Irish government deviated increasingly from English until the close of the nineteenth century." The English Poor Law of 1834 was "simply translated across St George's channel fours years later."[37] Given the preceding discussion one might have expected the government to propose an experimental programme of reform to tackle Irish poverty, especially "in a country in which a great portion of the population are always bordering upon famine," as Isaac Butt stated; however, MacDonagh's characterisation of the Irish Poor Law ignores two significant points.[38]

First, from its inception the Irish Poor Law was conceptualised as a tool for accelerating socioeconomic transitions rather than simply as a measure for controlling mendicancy. In other words, the Poor Law specifically addressed a *degenerate public* as well as an indigent pauper class. Second, it is important to recognise the significant differences between the English and Irish Poor Laws, especially the degree to which the Irish variant was remodelled as the Famine unfolded. In crucial respects the Irish Poor Law of 1838 was remarkably different from the Irish Poor Law of 1852. This last point alone warrants a more careful consideration of the progressive transformations to the Poor Law system — transformations that were undertaken and defended as measures to *correct Irish behavior* rather than relieve deteriorating Famine conditions.

By the 1830s it was widely assumed that Irish poverty was indelibly tied to moral corruption, economic underdevelopment, and agrarian agitation. In 1833 the government established a Royal Commission to report on the condition of the poorer classes in Ireland with a view to practical legislation. The commission was to be chaired

by the archbishop of Dublin, Richard Whately. Holding the second
most senior office in the Church of Ireland, Whately's appointment
was bound to be controversial, although his professional credentials
were impressive. He previously held the chair of political economy at
Oxford (1829–31) and came on good recommendation from Nassau
Senior, a former student of Whately's and an influential economist in
his own right.[39]

From the present perspective, Whately's Irish commission seems
doomed to failure. For a start, he misread or possibly ignored the government's instructions and perceived his assignment in bold terms.
The great challenge, so he intuited, was to *prevent destitution* rather than
simply manage poverty:

> We feel that endeavouring to prevent destitution, we shall more
> strictly fulfil Your Majesty's Commission; than if we merely de-
> vised means for alleviating misery after it had arisen. We shall
> feel deep pain should we ultimately be compelled to leave to any
> portion of the Peasantry of Ireland a continuation of distress on
> the one hand, or a mere offer of charity on the other . . . Look-
> ing beyond the physical condition of the working classes, we are
> also desirous of guarding against the moral degradation which
> might follow in the train of measures benevolently intended, but
> ill-judged, when applied to a nation possessing the habits and
> being in a peculiar situation of the People of Ireland . . . An In-
> quiry as to whether any measures can improve the condition of
> the people, might and would include an investigation into the
> immediate and remote effects, both on morals and production,
> of every law and every usage. It must embrace every class of the
> community, in every district of the country.[40]

Investigating "immediate and remote effects"; "every law and every
usage"; "every class" and "every district" and preventing destitution
and alleviating poverty whilst not promoting moral degradation—
this was a broad canvas that not surprisingly produced the "most thorough survey of the condition of the Irish Poor yet attempted."[41] However, such thoroughness exacted a price. The considerable delay vexed
the government and forced the commission to publish its conclusions

in advance of the full report.[42] More seriously, while Whately and his commissioners were busily gathering evidence, a new report on the Poor Law was published in England.[43] This legislation deserves some attention as its provisions seriously impacted the definition of the Irish Poor Law.

Unlike Ireland, England had a Poor Law system that dated at least to the time of Elizabeth I.[44] By the 1830s, however, the system had been under attack for over a quarter of a century.[45] The rising burden of the Poor Rate, rural unrest (including the Swing riots of 1830–31), and electoral reform hastened calls for a thorough reassessment of the system. In response the British government sanctioned a high-profile Royal Commission to enquire into the administration and practical operation of the poor laws. Edwin Chadwick (1800–1890) and Nassau Senior led the commission, and they presented their multivolume report to Parliament in 1834. The English Poor Law report proposed grave changes based upon the broadly reformist principles of "definition" and "distinction."[46]

The object of reform was to "dispauperize" the poor by establishing an epistemological separation and legal distinction between poverty and indigence. The "indigent" or "able-bodied" pauper was defined as a person who could no longer guarantee his or her means of subsistence, whereas the "labouring poor" referred to all those who laboured to live hand to mouth. According to the terms of the new Poor Law, if an able-bodied pauper did not possess the means of support, he or she would no longer receive "outdoor relief" (that is, relief administered in money or in kind to parties outside the workhouse) from the parish but would have to relocate his or her entire family into the Poor Law workhouses. This became known as the *all-or-nothing* principle. A second principle, known as the principle of *less eligibility,* sought to make conditions in the workhouse less eligible (that is, less preferable) than the conditions of the lowest-paid labourer outside the workhouse system. It was assumed that if the poor were afforded anything more than was necessary to keep them alive, there would be no incentive to rehabilitate and return to society. This outcome could be deterred, however, by making the instrument of relief— the workhouse—also the test for relief.[47] Through the control of space and the conditions therein (including establishing a strict food regime, supervised labour, rigorous workhouse discipline, and human segregation) the principle of less eligibility would be enforced—"All by a simple idea in architecture," as Jeremy Bentham (1748–1832) famously remarked.[48] Under these utilitarian principles it was believed that the poor would be compelled to personal betterment in order to avoid the tedium and social stigma attached to workhouse life. The application of these two guiding principles became known as the *workhouse test*. The result of this legislation was inter alia to create a new status or category of person known as *pauper*.[49] In essence the Poor Law pauper was a second-class citizen who was to be cared for—and, crucially, corrected—by the state.

In theory the new legislation sought to exclude the poor from the Poor Law because it was the pauper class—not the labouring poor—that was thought to be in need of remedial attention. "Dispauperising" the poor meant (in the words of Nassau Senior) that a "marked line be drawn between the pauper and the independent labourer."[50] This, according to Gertrude Himmelfarb, might be grounds enough to speak of a "pauper law" rather than a Poor Law:

> One could argue that it was precisely to sharpen the distinction between pauper and poor, to give that distinction all the force of law, that the [English Poor Law] commission chose the course of reform rather than abolition. By providing for the pauper, even the able-bodied pauper, not outside the law (by private charity) but within it—within the framework of what would be, in effect, a pauper law—the commission proposed to legislate and institutionalize the distinction itself.[51]

Himmelfarb argues that what was being captured and established (that is, institutionalised and legalised) was neither the pauper nor the poor but the "line" that distinguished the two—the very "distinction itself." Himmelfarb concludes, "The whole of the [English Poor Law] report was, in effect, an exercise in definition and distinction, an attempt to establish that line theoretically and to maintain it institutionally."[52] "We do not believe," observed the English Poor Law commissioners, "that a country in which this line has been effaced, can retain its prosperity, or even its civilisation."[53] The Poor Law was, therefore, a *techné* for separating the "normal" from the "pathological" in such a way as to naturalise the violence of incarceration and correction. In fact, the distinction between the "pauper" (a social delinquent) and the "labouring poor" (those who struggled to make ends meet)— codified in law and spatialised in the workhouse—correlates precisely with Foucault's caesura distinguishing the "people" from the "population."[54]

Such iterations of inclusion and exclusion were to take on a profound role in Ireland, where famine conditions and government ideology encouraged a more disturbing reliance on human distinction and disaster triage. Nassau Senior in particular worried that an over-generous Poor Law might remove the "positive check" of starvation and disease, which acted as a restraint on idleness and improvidence. Only a rigid adherence to the scientific principles of the "workhouse test" would guard against this outcome in Ireland:

> Hunger and cold are the punishments by which she [nature] represses improvidence and sloth. If we remove those punishments, we must substitute other means of repression. The pauper must purchase by some other sacrifice his immunity from the ordinary obligations of life; or, in other words, we repeat it, his situation must be rendered less eligible than that of the independent labourer.[55]

Such statements confirm just how far political opinion in England had drifted while Whately and his commissioners laboured to produce their three-volume report. The new workhouse system was constructed to wage war on pauperism (depicted as a "disease") and not poverty. Any Irish commission that proposed an alternative solution to poverty was unlikely to find favour.[56] As it turned out, Whately's report played directly into the government's hands. His commission rejected the possibility of transplanting the English Poor Law system into Ireland on the grounds that the "poorer classes in Ireland may be considered as comprehending *nearly the whole population*," and high unemployment made it virtually impossible to distinguish the able-bodied pauper from the population of labouring poor.[57] Moreover, they reasoned, the Irish stood on a different scale of civilization and legislation ought to have "reference to circumstance as well as principles."[58] Instead of a Poor Law modelled on English lines, the commission recommended assisted emigration for "redundant labour," not as "the main relief for the evils of Ireland" but "for the present as an auxiliary essential to a commencing course of amelioration."[59] In addition, they proposed establishing a "Board of Improvement" to superintend various tasks ranging from drainage and fencing to more radical remedial measures, such as tearing down "cabins which may appear unwholesome, or calculated to generate or continue disease."[60]

True to its original objective, the Whately commission recommended sweeping (and costly) changes that must have seemed quaint in comparison to the utilitarian economy of the workhouse system proposed by the English commission. In response the British government solicited the opinions of Nassau Senior and George Cornewall Lewis on the substance of Whately's findings. Although the principal author of the English Poor Law, Senior was against legislating a Poor Law for Ireland for much the same reasons as Whately: Irish poverty was too pervasive for a Poor Law to work successfully. Senior had recommended Whately for the job, however, and although he ventured some disapproval, his criticisms were essentially minor.[61] In contrast, Lewis's report is a point-by-point rejection of Whately's recommendations.[62] Lewis concluded in favour of extending the English Poor Law to Ireland.[63] On the back of these contradictory assessments, Lord Russell instructed George Nicholls, also an English Poor Law commissioner, to proceed to Ireland to conduct a fresh enquiry into the applicability of extending the English system and, in particular, to ascertain "whether any kind of Workhouse can be established which shall not, in point of food, clothing, and warmth, give its inmates a superior degree of comfort to the common lot of the independent labourer."[64]

Nowhere in his report does Nicholls declare how long he spent in Ireland, but since we know he received his instructions from the government in August 1836, and he presented his first report to Lord Russell in November of that year, we can assume that his findings were gleaned *en passant*. We also know that as early as January 1836 (that is, before the final volume of Whately's report had even appeared) Nicholls had contacted the government to express his confidence that the new Poor Law system could be transplanted to Ireland with only minor amendments. Knowledge of Nicholls's legerdemain left Whately feeling bitter. He described Nicholls's terse deliberations in Ireland as no more than getting "one bottle of water out of the Liffey and one out of the Shannon" (figure 3.1).[65]

Nicholls's report became the foundation for the Poor Law Ireland Act that became law on July 31, 1838.[66] The aim, scope, and provisions of the act merit particular attention, bearing in mind that after June 1847 the Irish Poor Law became, to all intents and purposes, the principal means of state relief during the Famine.[67] In hindsight, Nicholls's short stay in Ireland did not affect the magnitude of his final proposals to the government, nor was he particularly daunted by the nature of the task at hand. Indeed, he frankly admitted that he did not collect new evidence (there was, he insisted, enough gathered by the late commissioners). His survey took him to a number of towns and villages where he enquired into the "conditions and habits" and "character and wants" of the people.[68] In marked difference to the English Poor Law, Nicholls favoured "practical conclusions, with a view to early legislation."[69] A central authority was to be the "responsible body" that would command "the machinery of the poor law." Such a machine required Herculean men at its helm—not just men, but exclusively Englishmen, because Nicholls doubted that experienced and responsible Irishmen could be found. The hired hands must be accustomed to "unceasing and excessive work." Indeed, their commitment and moral fibre was to be beyond reproach because "nothing but the hope of accomplishing a great public good" would render bearable the onerous duties of office.[70] If Ireland was trapped in a state of social and moral decay, what it needed most, Nicholls thought, were Englishmen of unimpeachable character committed to superintending its socioeconomic reconstruction.

In line with Malthusian reasoning, Nicholls criticized the "superabundant population," the extreme subdivision of land, and, above all, the presence of a tenacious cottier class "too often reduced to a

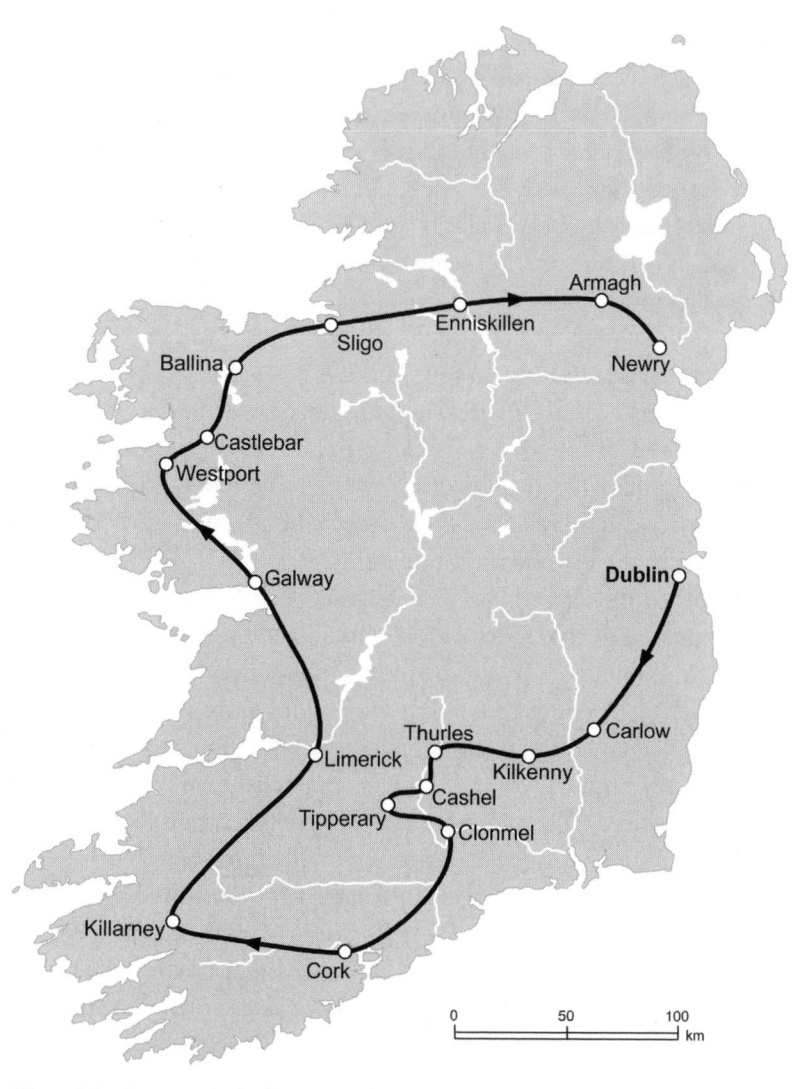

Figure 3.1. George Nicholls's tour of Ireland in 1836

level little above that of a mendicant." "The occupation of a plot of land," he wrote, "has now gotten to be considered by a great portion of the Irish people, as conferring an almost interminable right of possession."[71] This condition had to be broken: "labour, the only protection against actual want, the only means by which a man could procure food for his family, was by getting and retaining possession of land: for this he has struggled — for this the peasantry have combined, and burst through all the restraints of law and humanity."[72] Following classical economic thought, Nicholls believed that development occurred in decisive stages and that the Irish needed to be encouraged to "transition" from their barbarous system of farming to a more civilised agrarian economy. "By the term 'transition period,'" Nicholls clarified, "I mean to indicate that season of change from the system of small holdings, allotments, and subdivision of land, which now prevails in Ireland, to the better practice of day-labour for wages, and to that dependence on daily labour for support. This transition period is, I believe, generally beset with difficulty and suffering. It was so in England; and it is, and for a time will probably continue to be so, in Ireland."[73] Although Nicholls understood that "land is to them [Irish smallholders] the great necessary of life," and that the peasant "must get possession of a plot of land, on which to raise potatoes, or starve," he was impatient to have farms redrawn and resettled in more commercial ways — which is to say in less communal and less egalitarian ways.[74] Put simply, Nicholls was advocating the *proletarianisation of Irish farming*.

Scholars familiar with colonialism in other contexts will immediately recognise the customary appeal to the higher goals of the "civilising mission," as well as the strong impulse toward principles of rationality and social control. For Nicholls the "disencumbrance of land" and diffusion of agrarian capitalism were the obvious panacea to Irish underdevelopment.[75] Irish opinion was neither requested nor considered. There is, however, something else, arguably more profound, happening here. Notice how Nicholls's report seamlessly slips from discussing the control of pauperism to the regulation of the cottier class and from enthusing over the "machinery of the Poor Law" to speculating on much broader societal transformations. This was a powerful tool of association — linking as it did state welfare and social engineering — that did not begin with Nicholls but possibly gained a new orthodoxy from this point on. Crucially, this gave the Irish Poor Law a wide mandate to regulate society far more generally.[76] In other words, the slippage between pauper management and principles of agricultural improvement reflects the shifting boundary between *disciplinary measures* (undertaken through the Poor Law and directed at

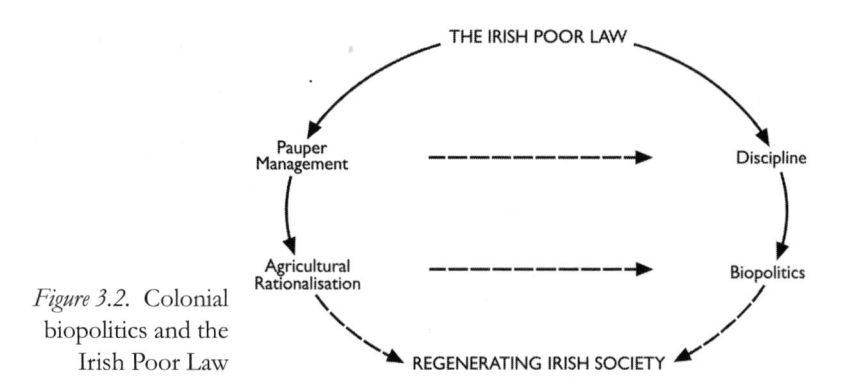

Figure 3.2. Colonial
biopolitics and the
Irish Poor Law

the pauper) and a new *biopolitics of regulatory functions,* directed beyond
these institutions and aimed at revitalising Irish society more generally. The factors that inform this shift (see figure 3.2) animate much
of the discussion that follows.[77]

Given these broad reformatory aims, it is no surprise that in
his final report Nicholls evokes a spiralling, seemingly endless vision
of vice:

> Ireland is now suffering under a circle of evils, producing and
> reproducing one another. Want of capital produces want of
> employment—want of employment, turbulence and misery—
> turbulence and misery, insecurity—insecurity prevents the intro-
> duction or accumulation of capital—and so on. Until this circle
> is broken, the evils must continue, and probably augment.[78]

That the originary sin is a "want of capital" is also unsurprising; Nicholls clearly associated capital with individual industry: "capital we are
told is the accumulation of savings, which are the fruits of industry,
which again is nourished and supported by its own progeny."[79] These
arguments certainly struck a chord because the same point (in virtually the same language) was made by Nassau Senior writing in the *Edinburgh Review* in 1843: "It is easy to show how insecurity occasions want
to capital—how want to capital occasions idleness and misery—and
idleness and misery lead to turbulence and insecurity, until the result
is a circle of calamities, each in turn creating, aggravating, and recre-

ating the others."[80] And like Nicholls, Senior viewed "*Material* evils" (such as want of capital) as indivisible from "*Moral* evils." "It is obvious," he confidently declared, "that it must be the Moral evils of Ireland which exclude the remedies for her material evils. And to these Moral evils, therefore, we now address ourselves."[81] Especially serious, Senior thought, were Irish "Ignorance" and "Indolence":

> Not only are the cabins, and even the farmhouses, deformed (within and without) by accumulations of filth which the least exertion would remove, but the land itself is suffered to waste a great proportion of its productive powers. We have ourselves seen field after field in which the weeds covered as much space as the crops. From the time that his crops are sown or planted until they are reaped, the peasant and his family are cowering over the fire, or smoking or lounging before the door—when an hour or two a day, employed in weeding their potatoes, or oats, or flax, would perhaps increase the produce by one third.[82]

The moral tone of Nicholls's Poor Law report is equally noteworthy, and like Senior's account it draws explicitly on the iconography of domestic degeneration discussed in chapter 2 of this volume. Of the peasant class Nicholls wrote, "They seem to feel no pride, no emulation; to be heedless of the present, and reckless of the future. . . . Their cabins still continue slovenly, smoky, filthy, almost without furniture or any article of convenience or decency."[83] Reflecting a common discursive trend, the peasantry—and not poverty—was considered to be the root cause of Irish misery. Nicholls described feeling assailed on all sides by the "desultory and idle habits of the Irish peasantry," and it is to these moral suspicions that his report continually turned:

> One of the circumstances that first arrests attention in Ireland, is the almost universal prevalence of mendicancy. It is not perhaps the actual amount of misery existing amongst the mendicant class, great as that may be, which is most to be deprecated; but the falsehood, the trickery, and fraud, which become a part of their profession, and spread by example.[84]

That Nicholls situates the Irish Poor Law within a more expansive discussion on social regeneration is surprisingly overlooked in the Famine literature, which tends to underscore the punitive nature of workhouse life. From the beginning, however, the Irish Poor Law was conceived partly as a conservative social institution (disciplinary) and partly as a radical transformational tool (biopolitical). This is readily demonstrated in two additional comparisons drawn by Nicholls. In the third and final report on the Irish Poor Law, Nicholls travelled in the company of Dr. Kay to Belgium and Holland, where he reported on the different systems of institutional relief for the poor.[85] In his written report, however, it quickly becomes clear that Nicholls did not travel to Belgium to examine only the *depôts de mendicité* (that is, provincial workhouses), nor to Holland to peruse only the schemes for the relief of indigence. In fact his report devotes careful attention to the condition of smallholders, especially the Belgian small farmers who, in contrast to the Irish, he found to be perfect examples of "scrupulous economy and cautious foresight."

> There was no tendency to the subdivision of the small holdings; I heard of none under five acres, held by the class of peasant farmers, and six, seven, or eight acres, is the more common size. The provident habits of these small farmers enable them to maintain a high standard of comfort, and are necessarily opposed to such subdivision. Their marriages are not contracted so early as in Ireland, and the consequent struggle for subsistence among their offspring does not exist.[86]

Nicholls concluded that "the first step in the improvement of this important class in Ireland [that is, small farmers] must be, I think, to endeavour to assimilate their farming operations, and agricultural and domestic management, to that of the same class in Belgium."[87] Nicholls also considered the Irish Poor Law to be the first stage in the development of a more intensive agrarian economy:

> This would, in fact, be beginning at the lowest point in the scale,— improved management in the small farms would bring increase of capital, and improved habits among the cottier tenants,— with

the increase of capital will come the desire to extend their holdings, and thus will arise a tendency to consolidate occupancies for the employment of increased capital which the vast extent of now waste, but reclaimable, land in Ireland, will greatly facilitate. An increase of agricultural produce will speedily act upon all the other sources of industry, and thus the demands of the home market for agricultural produce will be augmented, while, for all that is produced above that demand, the markets of England will be open.[88]

In short, the Poor Law would promote "general wellbeing, because it will be accompanied by an improvement in the habits of the whole class."[89]

It is little known, however, that Nicholls also designed and authored a small agricultural booklet to better publicize his opinions on Irish improvement. Published in 1841, *The Farmer's Guide: Compiled for the Use of the Small Farmers and Cotter Tenantry of Ireland* was designed to be "a small book of plain instruction, to which you may refer in your agricultural occupations and domestic economy."[90] The book is an extraordinary testament to colonial paternalism, offering worldly advice (ironically to a largely illiterate audience) on everything from cropping and livestock breeding to personal cleanliness and appropriate "domestic arrangements" (figure 3.3). It is Nicholls's remarks on the "cottager's diet," however, that make clear his belief that formal guidance and "moral training" are the key to rehabilitating slovenly habits. "Every man in good health may obtain a sufficiency of wholesome food, if he will make due exertion," Nicholls admonished, "and when we hear the complaints every year of the want of food, and observe the want of care and industry in making provision against the recurrence of evil one's commiseration is sometimes weakened by the blame which we cannot but see is too often deserved."[91] In Malthusian tones, he also urged moral restraint in the formation of "early and improvident marriages" and made clear his belief that depopulation was a cornerstone in regenerating Ireland:

We by no means deny, but on the contrary would wish to secure to the poorer classes, all those enjoyments which spring from

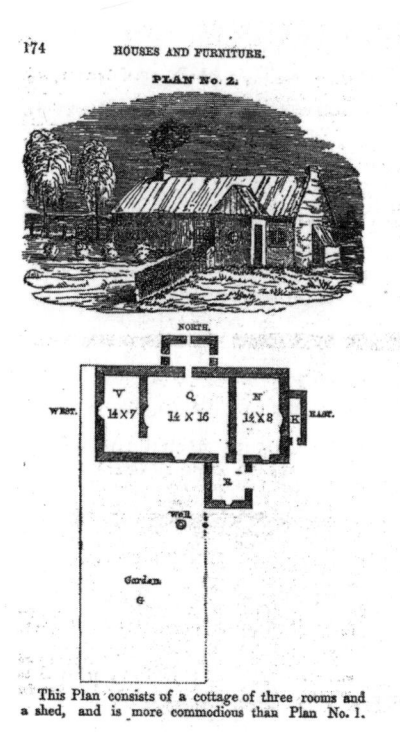

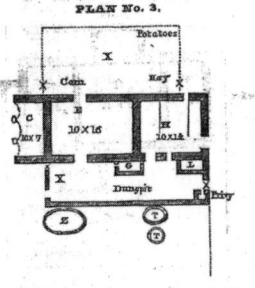

174   HOUSES AND FURNITURE.

PLAN No. 2.

NORTH.

WEST. 14 X 7 14 X 16 14 X 8 EAST.

Well

Garden
G

This Plan consists of a cottage of three rooms and
a shed, and is more commodious than Plan No. 1.

HOUSES AND FURNITURE.   175

R is the porch; Q the kitchen, entered from the porch;
D is the dairy, built as a lean-to at the back of the
house, having a northern aspect, and a window in each
of the three outer walls, to be opened or closed according to the weather—the entrance is from the kitchen;
V the bed-room, entering from kitchen, and warmed by a
thin back to the fire-place F, as in the first plan; N is
another bed-room, entering from the porch. If there be
a fire-place to bed-room N, it should be built at the
gable-end, which would afford an opportunity of warm-
ing the poultry-house K, which is built as a lean-to at
the end. G is the garden. One bed-room in this cottage might be plastered, and ceiled. The kitchen might
be paved with flags or flat tiles, and the walls should
certainly be built with mortar throughout.

PLAN No. 3.

Potatoes

Corn

14X7 10X16 10X14

Dung pit Piggery

This Plan shows the offices and out-buildings for
farming purposes, which would serve for, and might be
adapted to, either of the two preceding plans.
You will observe that the privy is in the same yard
with the dung-pit, and is so situated as not to be
immediately exposed, the wall being raised six feet, for

Figure 3.3. Domestic regeneration (Nicholls, *The Farmer's Guide,* 174–75)

the exercise of domestic and social feelings; but it must be borne
in mind that every one is bound both in a religious and moral
sense, to keep his animal impulses under the control of reason;
and not to wreck his own happiness, and that of others, by levelling them and himself with the brutes, and disregarding the
plainest dictates of prudence.[92]

On the inside cover of the booklet a note from the Poor Law Commission Office (dated December 10, 1841) describes the guide as contributing to "promoting Improvement in Agricultural Operations."
It also declares Nicholls's intention to form a "Union Agricultural
Society" that would comprise "an area co-extensive with the limits
of each Poor Law Union, as has been done in Ballinasloe and other

places." The explicit link between the guide and the Irish Poor Law system illustrates how closely debates about welfare and relief mapped onto designs to encourage socioeconomic transition.

The didactic nature of Nicholls's farming programme has striking parallels with seventeenth-century colonial practice whereby newly planted estates were purposefully designed "to stimulate a mimetic response . . . thereby acting as an agency for diffusing 'taste.'"[93] Indeed, a revision to the Poor Law in 1848, permitting auxiliary farmsteads (comprising up to twenty-five acres) to be cultivated and used for instructional purposes, turned pauper relief into lessons in political economy and domestic reform.[94] An observer of one such "Union agricultural school" remarked that "nothing domestic in all Ireland struck me more than the neatness and cleanliness of these houses. They looked as if they had been purposefully set up as patterns for imitation by the cottagers; and there seems little doubt that, among the other lessons learned in them by the more juvenile part of their inmates, that of domestic as well as of personal tidiness will be one."[95]

This belief in moral and social advancement through inducement and habitual training is strongly endorsed in Nicholls's final Poor Law report:

> The [Poor Law] Union established would thus become *like a colony, a kind of centre of civilization,* and the Unions collectively might be made *important engines for effecting improvements in the condition and habits of the Irish people,* in whose clothing, cottages, and domestic economy as well as in their agricultural and other management, there now appears a lamentable deficiency of the faculty happily so common in England.[96]

Here the colonial rhetoric complements the logic of biopolitical regulation. The union was supposed to function exactly like a colony—or more precisely, a colony *within* a colony—"a centre of civilization" correcting not just the lives of individual paupers but more general arrangements like habit and dress, rural life, and "domestic economy."[97] The workhouses were to be the showpiece in this "rational landscape," which sought to marry moral reform to government-led social welfare.[98]

In this way, the practices of peasants, subsistence farmers, and other economically marginal groups could be corrected through a colonial brand of welfare.

This was government designating what Foucault terms the "right disposition of things."[99] The ultimate aim was to rehabilitate backward practices by strengthening what Edward Lytton Bulwer (1803–73) described as *directive government:*

> I would wish that you should see the Government educating your children, and encouraging your science, and ameliorating the condition of your poor; I wish you to warm while you utter its very name, with a grateful and reverent sense of enlightenment and protection; I wish you to behold all your great Public Blessings repose beneath its shadow.[100]

Through Nicholls's initiatives, this mode of "directive government" was to be extended to include agrarian transition through welfare management. To attain these goals the final Poor Law report proposed a drastic reterritorialisation of the country into a series of administrative units, totalling 130 (later to be increased to 163), known as "poor law unions"[101] (figure 3.4). Each union was to have a workhouse administered by an elected Board of Guardians and financed by rates that were to be levied locally (in effect, a Poor Law tax). However, the Irish Poor Law Act differed in some crucial respects from its prototype in England.[102] First, Irish relief could only be provided to whole family units within the confines of the workhouse; there was to be no provision for outdoor relief. In England this clause was widely disregarded. In 1842, for example, an Outdoor Relief Act was passed to meet deteriorating conditions and local food shortages, evidence that the principle of "testing destitution" could be circumvented in certain situations.[103] Second, and crucially, a "right to relief" was to be studiously avoided in Ireland. Nicholls was very clear on this in his recommendations: "I do not propose to impart a *right* to relief, even to the destitute, but to place the ordering and directing of all relief in the hands of the central authority." According to Nicholls, "the claim to relief [is] to be founded on prescription" and not "legislative enactment."[104]

Poor law unions 1838 to 1849   Poor law unions 1850

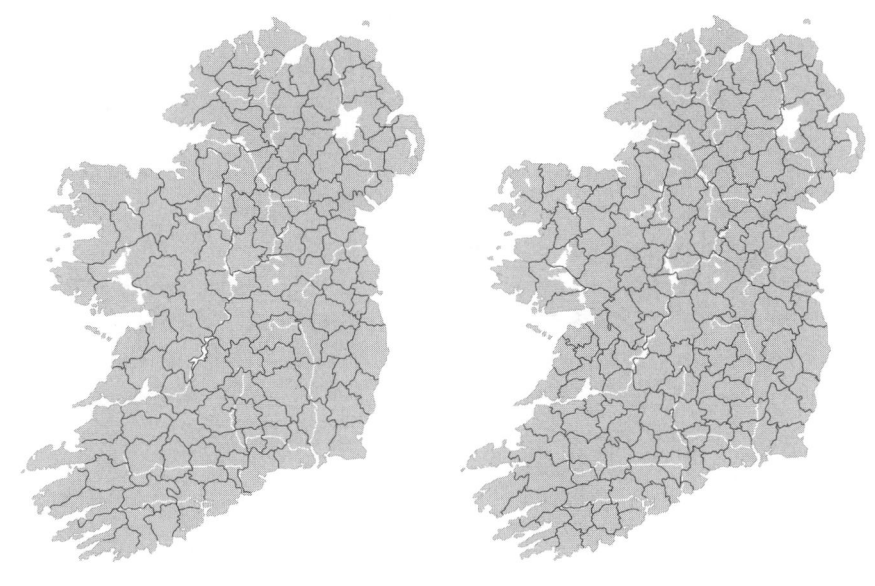

Figure 3.4. Irish Poor Law unions

These were subtle, but significant, departures from the English norm. Under the new Poor Law the English pauper could be granted outdoor relief, but if refused she or he always had the option to fall back on the workhouse. As Gustave de Beaumont astutely observed,

> Thus the English pauper has preserved the chance of being relieved according to the old form of English charity, and he has the certainty of being assisted according to the new. It is evident, therefore, that the condition of the English pauper is theoretically different from that of the Irish pauper, who can in no case obtain relief without losing his liberty, and who, though unable to obtain relief except in a kind of prison, has not the right, but merely the chance, of admission.[105]

These differences between the English and Irish Poor Laws illustrate the profound challenges facing liberal doctrines when applied to colonial environments. Were the methods of poor relief developed in

England, for instance, appropriate for dealing with considerably worse conditions of poverty in the colonies? Furthermore, if a right to relief was implicitly enshrined in the English Poor Law system, was this to be considered a universal right, equally applicable to colonial subjects? Even the most vocal supporters of liberal government wondered whether its principal tenets might be geographically circumscribed. These were critical questions asked of English liberal politics and classical economics in the nineteenth century, and it is difficult to overestimate the extent to which such problems exercised the minds of the most advanced political thinkers of this period.[106] Sympathetic commentators like George Poulett Scrope favoured a limited recognition of rights on humanitarian principles; others, such as Nassau Senior, deplored even a "discretionary power" to relieve Irish paupers: "We have seen that—unless accompanied by conditions which, whether capable or not of being enforced in England, are certainly inapplicable in Ireland—a right to relief depending simply on destitution must in time destroy the property and the civilisation of the community which has been blind enough to grant it."[107] Others, such as Robert Torrens (1780–1864), advocated extensive overseas colonization in place of an expensive system of Poor Law aid. His fellow economist John Wheatley agreed with "getting rid of a large proportion of the existing population"—which he described as a necessary system of "*euthanasia*"—though he also favoured free trade, population control, and legal prohibitions against subdivision.[108]

In this way the Irish Poor Law report became the very basis for subsequent debates on state provision and relief in times of distress. However—and this is crucial—when the state (particularly the *colonial* state) decides to institutionalise a "test of eligibility," and later reserves for itself the right to regulate relief wages (through public work schemes) and determine the conditions for the provision of food (through soup kitchens), it has actually agreed to function as a key *intermediary agent* in the "entitlements" network. By reserving to itself the right to test destitution, the state enshrines, codifies, and institutionalises the right to *govern access to provisions.* "Relief," wrote Nicholls, "is only to be administered by receiving the applicants into the [work]-house, and subjecting them to the regulations established for its government."[109] The command and control nature of the Poor Law—

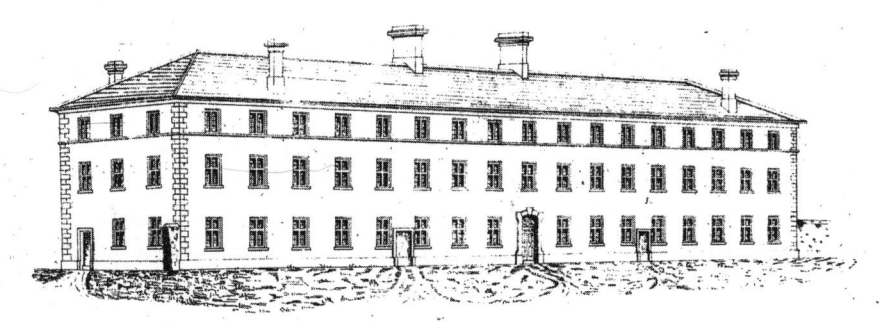

Figure 3.5. Elevation of main building of the new workhouses of Castletown and Dingle ("First Annual Report of the Commissioner for Administering Laws for the Relief of Poor in Ireland")

the "ordering and directing" of Irish life—therefore included the assumption of responsibility for managing entitlements to food.[110]

VITAL MACHINES

Given these broad objectives, Irish workhouses were designed to be austere and imposing structures (figure 3.5). Preferably, they were to be located in the centre of the district near a chief police station, with a school close by and a dispensary beside if not attached to it. German traveller J. G. Kohl provides a useful description:

> I have designated the workhouses as fortress-like, and for this reason—they are generally situated on elevated ground, outside the town, probably for the sake of the fresh air; they are built of a gray, firm stone, are surrounded by loft walls, and provided with small turrets and other little castellated appendages. They command an extensive prospect over the country, and are the terror of the beggars, who prefer the independence of a mendicant's life to confinement in one of these houses.[111]

Entrance into the workhouse involved an elaborate matrix of human segregation and classification, which in turn relied upon complex iterations of inclusion and exclusion. "Confinement of any kind," declared

Nicholls "is more irksome to an Irishman, than it is even to an Englishman."[112] From the moment an applicant and his or her family set foot
in the workhouse, they agreed to surrender control of their lives and
submit themselves to the Poor Law's edicts and norms.[113] In fact, the
entire "administration block" of the workhouse (furnished with a separate yard and sleeping quarters, comprising what one historian has
called a "workhouse within a workhouse"[114]) was devoted to the purpose of human isolation and categorization. Here male and female
members of an applicant's family were separated and transferred to discrete "receiving rooms" and "probationary wards" to await interview.
Gerard O'Brien describes in detail the subsequent "screening" process:

> In these rooms details were recorded of the identity, sex, age,
> status, employment or trade, and religion of the applicants, who
> would then be examined by the workhouse doctor . . . Medical
> examination was followed by "purification," during which the
> applicant's clothes were removed for cleansing and storage and
> the applicant washed under supervision before being clothed in
> a workhouse uniform. From this moment until his presentation
> before the board the applicant was subjected to the full rigours of
> workhouse life and discipline, but was not allowed any contact
> with inmates other than fellow applicants of the same sex.[115]

According to the testimony of one Poor Law inspector, any applicant
"eaten up with vermin" or affected with "cutaneous disease" was received in a special "probationary ward," where his or her head was
"closely cut" and a "thorough ablution" administered.[116] Arriving on
"admission day" at the Kilrush workhouse, Osborne found "ample
evidence" that the workhouse rules functioned as "a real test of destitution." The appearance of the applicants—"infants at the breast of
mothers, with the skin and visage of advanced, careworn childhood;
children whose sores and dirt and squalid famished looks, told of the
loss of all the elasticity of their age, of their premature acquisition of
that stolid care-blunted nature, which years in common suffering
alone can give"—made clear that the workhouses were indeed what
Donegal man Hugh Dorian called "the last game of all."[117]

Admitted paupers were classified into five categories: males above the age of fifteen years; boys aged two to fifteen; females above the age of fifteen; girls aged two to fifteen; and children under two years of age.[118] "Pauper lunatics" were typically transferred to a special "idiot ward," and women who had birthed children outside of wedlock were placed apart as well.[119] Each morning the pauper inmates were awakened at six o'clock by the ringing of a bell. Shortly thereafter they assembled in the dining area for prayer, where they were inspected to ensure all the resident paupers were in attendance and suitably clean. Adult inmates were fed two "marvellous scanty" meals per diem, consisting "exclusively of farinaceous food,—that is, of stirabout, bread, and a sort of gruel soup made of oatmeal and vegetables."[120] Breakfast was served at eight o'clock and eaten in silence. The dinner meal was typically served from two to four in the afternoon (an additional supper, reserved for infants, was provided at five, and women nursing were allowed an additional pint of gruel or soup and one glass of milk daily). During the day children were sent to the workhouse school; the able-bodied men worked at stone breaking, corn milling, oakum picking, pipe laying, and digging—tasks that were exceptionally hated—while the women pitted themselves and their energy to sewing, knitting, carding, or, in some cases, housework—washing, scrubbing, mending clothes—and tended to the sick.[121] The routine and monotony of this labour bore a striking resemblance to the work rhythms of modern industrial capitalism, even though the target of liberal improvement in this instance was the agricultural practices of the population.[122] The workhouses were designed to incorporate as best as possible the entire fabric of "everyday" living, including everything from vaccinations and industrial schooling to "useful auxiliaries [and] a well directed plan of emigration."[123] Nicholls oversaw the implementation and was impressed with the results: "little more can be done in the way of preparation than to send them forth imbued with habits of industry, their frames strengthened and inured to labour, their tempers and mental faculties duly cultivated, and above all their minds duly impressed with a sense of their moral and religious duties."[124]

If Irish workhouses were essentially punitive in nature, this was punishment administered in an entirely novel way.[125] Nicholls was deeply critical of the Houses of Industry (the semi-official relief institutions that predated the Irish Poor Law workhouses), stressing that the rules therein were so severe and "the privations so calculated" as to incite the inmates to acts of resistance. These methods were likened to seventeenth-century laws whereby "rogues," "vagabonds," and "sturdy beggars" were disciplined by "putting fetters or gyres upon them and by moderate whipping."[126] The administration of Irish workhouses was to be entirely different. According to Nicholls, the "excitable" Irish could be "easily governed, and easily led," if power could be wielded—above all—economically. As elsewhere, Nicholls was appealing to racial prejudices derived from pre-Famine depictions of Irish life. "Every one knows how easily a mob, especially an Irish mob, is reduced to obedience by the trifling display of firmness and force," Henry Inglis had confidently declared.[127] In a similar vein Nicholls called for "more enlightened benevolence": "the real friends of the people of Ireland are those who lead them, even where necessary by compulsory measures, to active, independent exertion, to a reliance upon themselves and their own efforts for support." The Irish Poor Laws therefore aimed "to restore, or create the feeling of self-confidence—to revive, or establish, the habit of reliance . . . [and] *compel them to acts of local self-government.*"[128] This was not simply another variant of the classic colonial ruse of coercion made over as gift; it was also legislation as moral navigation. Nicholls is articulating a new corporeal regime for regulating what Foucault termed the "conduct of conduct."[129]

In addition to enforced segregation and task labour, dietary regulation formed "the backbone" of workhouse discipline, suggesting forceful comparisons with other colonial contexts where dietetics was considered central to social engineering.[130] By the mid-nineteenth century it was widely assumed that potato cultivation and barbarity went hand in hand in Ireland. The social historian Thomas Carlyle was not unusual in mocking Ireland's "potato culture" and its "potato-phagus" population; as early as 1688 anti-Irish gangs carried emblems depicting a potato impaled on a stick.[131] In line with earlier accounts detailing Irish domestic degeneracy, Trevelyan professed "there is scarcely a woman of the peasant class in the west of Ireland, whose culinary

art exceeds the boiling of a potato."[132] "Provided they have had sufficient supplies of potatoes," remarked the Scottish economist J. R.
McCulloch (1789–1864), "they have been content to vegetate, for
they can hardly be said to live, in rags and wretchedness."[133] By Famine times the age-old adage "you are what you eat" had become a fully
fledged biopolitical mantra, a form of "dietary determinism" that was
deployed as justification for a succession of harsh reformatory measures.[134] Nassau Senior linked the Irish diet to overpopulation ("A labouring population eating meat must be more thinly scattered than
one eating corn; and a potato-fed community might be denser than
one eating wheat"), while Trevelyan made clear the connections between diet and the productivity of Irish labour: "In every way it is desirable to teach him the use of a more substantial diet, both to enable
him to give a proper amount of labour for his hire, and in order to
raise him to a higher standard as a social being."[135] Trevelyan justified
these remarks by appealing to superior conditions of Irish workers
overseas: "the Irishman works better out of Ireland than in it . . . when
he leaves his native country and obtains regular employment elsewhere he commences at the same time a more strengthening diet than
the potato."[136]

Dietary determinism was instrumental in shaping the institutional environment of the Irish workhouse. Analysing the management
of a workhouse in Cork, for example, Gerard O'Brien observed that
the pauper diet was interfered with no less than a dozen times within
a nineteen-month period—an impressive tally and timely reminder
that the "free market" anathema to social interventionism was principally a doctrine of convenience.[137] To strengthen the rule of "less
eligibility," meat was prohibited in rural workhouses, and by the first
year of the blight the potato diet had been replaced with frugal portions of rice, soup, bread, oatmeal, and corn in 69 out of 130 workhouses (figure 3.6).[138] Having travelled extensively around Ireland, the
Scotsman John Forbes discovered only one union workhouse where
potatoes formed part of the dietary system, and even then they were
only employed on alternate days for a fixed period of the year: "This
total absence of potatoes in the workhouse dietaries of Ireland has always struck me as very singular. Has it been adopted with any view of

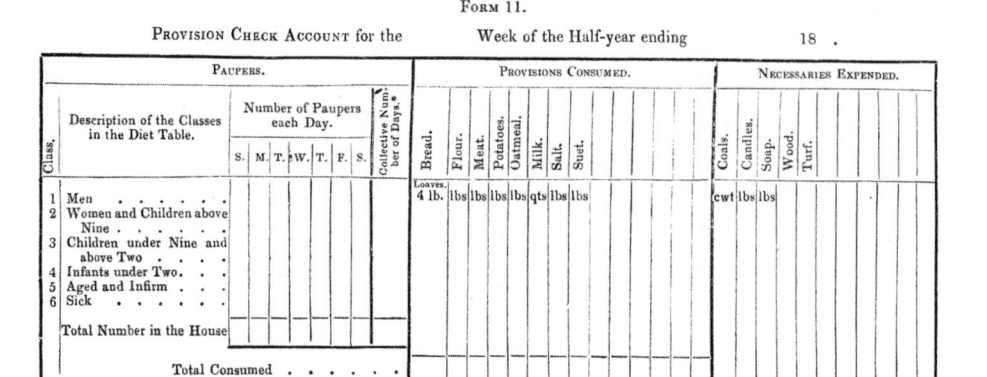

Figure 3.6. The Poor Law commissioners' dietary recommendations ("Sixth Annual Report of Commissioners of Inquiry into the Administration and Practical Operation of the Poor Laws," 257)

weaning the people from the taste of that root which has been so fatal to their country, both by its prosperous condition and by its failure? Or has it originated in purely economic views?" Forbes was willing to set aside these reasonable scruples, safe in the knowledge that the new dietary order would render "the people of Ireland . . . more attached to cereal food."[139] The transformation of the pauper diet was confirmation that certain Irish habits (especially those that seemed most recalcitrant to change) could be confronted and modified through dedicated institutional regulation (figure 3.7). The workhouses therefore became the first stage in a larger project of modernisation—quite literally a *vital* machine "for indoctrinating the rising generation in much that their fathers knew not," and thereby kick-starting a "social revolution" in the Irish national economy.[140]

AIDING CHANGE AND CHANGING AID

The extent to which the state was endeavouring to regulate the "bare life" of its subjects cannot be underestimated. For significant numbers of Irish people even the most mundane aspects of living, such as sleeping, eating, and moving about, were now subject to minute at-

TABLE I. (IRISH DIETARIES.)

WORKHOUSES.	No. of days in the week each form of food is supplied.	BREAKFAST.	No. of days in the week each form of food is supplied.	DINNER.	No. of days in the week each form of food is supplied.	SUPPER.
Skibbereen	7 {	9 oz. Indian meal / ½ pint of milk	7 {	14 oz. bread (brown) / 1½ oz. oatmeal (in gruel)	7	None
Killarney	7 {	16 oz. bread / 1 pt. milk or veg. soup	7 {	8 oz. Ind. meal (in stir.) / 1½ pt. milk	7	None
Enniskillen	7 {	8 or 9 oz. meal (mixed) / 1 pt. milk	7 {	9 or 10 oz. meal (mixed) / ½ pt. milk	7	None
Castlebar	7 {	8 oz. of Indian meal / ½ pt. milk	7 {	16 oz. brd. (compound) / 2 pt. gruel	7	None
Londonderry	7 {	7 oz. meal / ½ qt. of milk	7 {	12 oz. bread / 1 qt. vegetable soup	7 {	6 oz. meal (in stir.) / ½ qt. of milk
Ballycastle	7 {	6 oz. oatmeal / ½ qt. of buttermilk	3 {	6 oz. oatmeal (in stir.) / ½ qt. of buttermilk	7 {	5 oz. oatmeal (in stir.) / ½ qt. of milk
			4 {	6 oz. oatmeal (in soup) / 2 oz. meat (in soup) / 8 oz. bread		

TABLE II. (ENGLISH DIETARIES.)

UNION.	No. of days each form of diet is given.	BREAKFAST.	No. of days each form of diet is given.	DINNER.	No. of days each form of diet is given.	SUPPER.
Aylesbury (Bucks)	7 {	6 oz. bread / 1 pt. milk porridge	2 / 2 / 2 / 1	5 oz. meat, 4 oz. bread, 12 oz. potatoes / 4 oz. bacon, 12 oz. potatoes / 14 oz. suet or rice pudding / 8 oz. bread, 1½ oz. cheese	2 { / 5 {	6 oz. bread / 1 pt. rice broth / 6 oz. bread / 1 oz. cheese
Winslow (Bucks)	7 {	6 oz. bread / 1½ pt. gruel	3 / 2 / 1 / 1	12 oz. suet or rice pud., vegetables / 2 pts. soup, 6 oz. bread / 6 oz. meat, 3 oz. bread, vegetables / 12 oz. meat pudding, vegetables	7 {	7 oz. bread / 1½ oz. cheese
Westhampnett (Sussex)	7 {	6 oz. bread / 1½ pt. gruel	3 / 2 / 2	2 pts. soup, 4 oz. bread / 6 oz. bacon, vegetables / 12 oz. rice or suet pud., vegetables	7 {	6 oz. bread / 2 oz. cheese
Northampton	7 {	6 oz. bread / 1½ pt. gruel	3 / 3 / 1	5 oz. meat, 12 oz. potatoes, 2 oz. bread / 1½ pt. soup, 2 oz. bread / 14 oz. suet or rice pudding	7 {	7 oz. bread / 1½ oz. cheese
Thame (Oxford and Bucks)	7 {	6 oz. bread / 1½ pt. milk porridge	2 / 2 / 1	6 oz. meat, 4 oz. bread, 8 oz. potatoes / 1½ pt. soup, 4 oz. bread / 14 oz. suet or rice pud., 8 oz. potatoes / 7 oz. bread, 1½ oz. cheese	7 {	7 oz. bread / 1½ oz. cheese.

Figure 3.7. John Forbes's comparison of workhouse diets in Ireland and England, 1852 (Forbes, *Memorandums Made in Ireland,* 2:231–32)

tention and control. Seemingly marginal matters regarding the administration of workhouses achieved a general importance. Take, for instance, the controversial subject of classification and proximity in the workhouses. Guardians, commissioners, chaplains, and politicians alike were greatly concerned about the "moral contamination" spread from the "promiscuous mixing together of women of all characters."[141] As a strong opponent of the Irish workhouse system, Osborne was incensed by what he observed: "There is, and there must be, a constant wholesale process of female degradation going on, where married women and single women—girls of 16—women of 40, are associated in hundreds in idleness by day; lay down to rest—but too often in nakedness, by hundreds together in a room at night."[142] In Cork Archibald Stark was more optimistic that "the separation of the sexes is as nearly as possible complete." If during the hours of labour male and female paupers occasionally met, they did so, he enthused, "under the eye of a paid officer."[143]

The welfare concerns mentioned above should not be dismissed as merely Victorian prudishness. They give voice to more fundamental concerns directed toward disciplining the life of the body (anatomo-politics) and regulating the biological life of the species (biopolitics). As Stuart Elden perceptively notes, sexuality is "situated at the crossroads" of anatomo-politics and biopolitics, "a means of access both to the life of the body and the life of the species." It is arguably for this reason that it assumed such general importance in the running of Irish workhouses.[144] The dream of complete anatomical surveillance was thus part of a large experiment designed not only to chasten "notorious" women but also as general technology for reforming a backward race through institutional rigour.[145]

In *The History of Sexuality* Foucault described how the care of life came to be, more and more markedly, a prerogative of government.[146] Foucault's "metaphysics of power" aids my analysis of colonial welfare in two significant ways.[147] First, if biopolitics implies investing state power in the corporeal life of *citizens,* then the secondary status of colonial *subjects* becomes especially important.[148] Colonial welfare takes place in the context of a bare or depotentiated form of life, leaving greater room for systemic violence justified in the name of improvement. Second, the potential to use relief as a radical transformational tool (and an expression of sovereign power) remains implicit in the definition of the Irish Poor Law. This conclusion seems to run against the common understandings of laissez-faire principles and the presumed retrenchment of state power. As this chapter suggests, however, the commitment to colonial improvement demanded greater institutional guidance, which in turn required legislative action by the British government. Significantly, in his history of the Irish Poor Law, Nicholls anticipated the tension between doctrines advocating economic liberalism and the necessity of social intervention, citing with approval the comments in an earlier government report that noted "the unquestionable principle that legislative interference in the operation of human industry is as much as possible to be avoided." There were, however, important exceptions to this rule, "either when injurious impediments are to be removed, or when a branch of industry cannot at its commencement be carried on by individual exertion."[149] For Nicholls, the committee's conclusions were profoundly significant: "danger attends all interferences with industrial pursuits, which prosper best when left to their own natural development; but they consider that the state of Ireland constitutes an exception to the general rule, and that the aid of government in support of local effort is there absolutely necessary."[150]

Once it was admitted that Ireland was in fact an "exception" to established norms on state interference, Nicholls was free to conceptualise the Irish Poor Law as the first stage in the "rapid consolidation of small holdings." A visionary to be sure, Nicholls was also a pragmatist who recognised that in Ireland "the obstructions which arise from fixed habits and social arrangements generally render great organic changes impossible, excepting in the lapse of years."[151] Even accepting government interference, change was likely to be slow because of the recalcitrant nature of the Celt. No one writing in 1838 could have foreseen the coming of blight and the devastation caused to the Irish potato harvest; however, the arrival of such an "exceptional calamity" became the pretext for mobilising this preexisting ideology of biopolitical improvement. The potato failure was that extreme point where "great organic changes" became not only thinkable but also uniquely possible. For Senior, "nothing is more striking in the long and intricate history of Irish distress, than the intimate connection of much of that distress with carelessness, the inactivity, and the improvidence of the suffers."[152] As the Famine wore on—and the tendency to blame the victims became more entrenched—appeals to social engineering became more common and less controversial. The blight was thus renarrated as a great "providential act" and a means of revivifying postponed plans for anglicising Irish society. In this sense, as I will show in the next chapter, the modern association between disaster and opportunity was also a colonial project that drew sustenance from earlier attempts to civilise the Irish out of existence.[153]

CHAPTER FOUR

IMPOSING CIVILITY

The Administration of Hunger

Could you call it targeted genocide?

Well said "Dr. G.," we have got our Poor Law, and it is a great instrument for giving the victory to the landlords . . . No friend to Ireland can wish the war to be prolonged — still less, that it should end by victory of the tenants; for that would replunge Ireland into barbarism, worse than that of the last century. The sooner it is over — the sooner Ireland becomes a grazing country, with the comparatively thin population which a grazing country requires — the better for all classes.

—Nassau Senior, *Journals, Conversations and Essays Relating to Ireland*, Volume 2

No conceivable measure for relieving the poverty of Ireland can be effectual, until, by the operation of combined labour upon the land, a less proportion of the population shall be enabled to raise subsistence for the whole. But, during this transition, in what manner can that portion of the rural population, which must be displaced from their small holdings, be disposed of? This is a momentous question.

—Robert Torrens, *Colonization of South Australia*

IDEOLOGY AND STATE ASSISTANCE

In this chapter I critically review the politics of relief operations during the Irish Famine: how they came to be developed, organised, managed, and administered through mechanisms and at scales never before conceived. According to numerous observers, the famine relief schemes were profoundly implicated in the catastrophe they resolved to manage.[1] After visiting several workhouses Archibald Stark concluded that "the project of meeting the evil of poverty by confining the paupers in houses, built for the purpose, and feeding and clothing them in perfect idleness, was in theory as clumsy and expedient for encountering a difficulty as in practice it was revolting to humanity."[2] S. G. Osborne agreed, noting that "the evils encountered [there] are worse than the evils fled," while a correspondent for the *Times* witheringly characterised government relief as "a very expensive but rapid training for the grave."[3] These were not atypical charges, nor were they confined to the radical or nationalist press. Indeed, the uniformity and stability of this discourse raises important questions about the role of state assistance during catastrophes. In what follows I explore the ideological dimensions of state assistance, arguing that famine relief was grounded in a colonial project of regeneration that increasingly viewed population reform as a "sovereign remedy" to Irish underdevelopment.[4]

Although the damage to the potato crop was partial in 1845, the announcement of the arrival of blight in Ireland was deeply worrying for many officials. The dependency of the poor on the potato harvest was infamous, and although over nine million pounds were expended in building Irish workhouses, the initial target of 130 institutions had not been achieved when the blight struck.[5] The immense suffering in the wake of the first crop failure forced a serious reassessment of Poor Law provisions. By the time the worst of the horrors were over, Ireland had a total of 163 unions, each with its own workhouse, and a plethora of other relief programmes had been tried, tested, and abandoned. The context of these developments needs to be examined in detail.

In a note published amongst the British Parliamentary Papers, Father Theobald Mathew (1790–1856), the great temperance campaigner, famously recorded the fear that greeted the appearance of *Phytophthora infestans*:

> On the 27th of last month [July] I passed from Cork to Dublin, and this doomed plant bloomed in all the luxuriance of an abun-

dant harvest. Returning on the 3rd instant [August] I beheld with sorrow one wide waste of putrefying vegetation. In many places the wretched people were seated on the fences of their decaying gardens, wringing their hands and wailing bitterly the destruction that had left them foodless.[6]

We now know that the early part of the potato harvest mostly escaped the blight but the late—or what was commonly called the "people's crop," which was dug in late autumn—was heavily spoiled. Akin to the blighted potato leaves, early optimism quickly shrivelled as it emerged that nearly one-third of the Irish harvest was lost. The Irish press reflected "an atmosphere of terror and despair."[7] Given the severity of the situation it was felt that the government had to take measures to alleviate distress. Outdoor employment under the fledgling Poor Law system was initially proposed. This suggestion was deeply unpopular, however, with critics claiming that outdoor assistance implied a forfeiture of institutional control (especially the all-important "test of destitution") and ran counter to prevailing economic orthodoxies. It would, it was insisted, ultimately create more paupers in Ireland.[8] The prime minister, Robert Peel (1788–1850), was convinced that the potato failure was "qualitatively different and infinitely more serious" than previous periods of dearth, and as such it warranted a unique response.[9] These factors guided Peel's initial step to establish relief measures *outside* the parameters of the new Poor Law.

The prime minister's plans were threefold. First, the government would establish (in November 1845) an entirely "new administrative structure" named the "Temporary Relief Commission" for dealing with the crisis.[10] The immediate effect of this move was to create local relief committees responsible for fundraising and encouraging apparently indifferent Irish landlords to provide employment for the destitute. In addition, the government established a public works programme to stimulate the provision of employment. These early measures suggest that the government initially saw famine as far more complex than the standard Malthusian view of declining food availability. By their very nature employment schemes are designed to address household *purchasing power* rather than food scarcity per se. The government's public works typically included road improvements, rail and pier constructions, and arterial drainage schemes, half the cost of which was to be met by a government grant and the remainder to be repaid as a loan over twenty years. Under this scheme, local relief committees were responsible for distributing tickets to those "considered unable to provide food for their families."[11]

Second, as an *immediate* precaution the prime minister ordered £100,000–worth of maize—commonly called "Indian corn"—from North America. Peel conducted this transaction in secret, even concealing the matter from his own cabinet. In line with laissez-faire principles it was imperative that the government should not be *seen* to be intervening in Irish markets. Significantly, although in previous seasons Indian corn had been used to halt the effects of famine, the commodity was virtually unknown in Ireland. According to Trevelyan this last point justified government policy because private merchants "could not complain of interference with a trade that did not exist, nor could prices be raised against the home consumer on an article of which no stock was to be found in the home market."[12] To distribute the government's food supply, a chain of subdepots was established under the charge of the Irish Constabulary and the Coast Guard (see figure 4.1). When local markets were "deficient," the corn could be sold to relief committees for distribution.[13] However, this supply alone could not, nor was it ever meant to, replace the nutritional gap left by the failure of the potato harvest.

Third, and most controversially, on October 31, 1845, the prime minister called an emergency meeting of the cabinet where he proposed that the government would repeal the Corn Laws to hurry assistance to Ireland. The Corn Laws were a series of legislative measures that protected British farmers from cheap imported grain. In truth Peel had been gradually swayed by the logic of classical economy and the arguments of staunch proselytisers such as John Wheatley, who complained that "there is not a single branch of commerce that does not groan under the weight of some excessive impost, that is not fettered in irons for no fault of its own, and that may not be substantially improved by a more liberal and enlightened policy."[14] Until "commerce be as free as the air we breathe," Wheatley elsewhere

Figure 4.1. Government sale of Indian corn at Cork (*Illustrated London News,* April 4, 1846)

argued, "it is impossible that we can be raised to so high a state of prosperity as we otherwise might be."[15] The appearance of blight handed Peel an opportunity to argue that the difficulties in Ireland were the result of a shortfall in cheap grain rather than the more immediate failure of the potato harvest. Through Peel's intercession *Phytophthora infestans* was quickly turned into a "divine indictment" against protectionism.[16]

Government debate began in earnest in November, and the ensuing embroilments succeeded in turning Irish relief into a party question.[17] The "protectionists" accused the Peelites of embellishing the extent of the Famine, whilst the "free-traders" charged their opponents with ignorance of the laws of political economy. The lawyer, economist, and politician Isaac Butt captured the mood well: "The potato famine in Ireland was represented as the invitation of the agitators on either side of the water . . . Men's politics determined their belief. To profess belief in the fact of the existence of a formidable potato blight, was as sure a method of being branded as a radical, as to propose to destroy the Church."[18] Peel and the free-traders eventually won out, even though the issue dragged on until the summer of 1846, and it took a further three years for the Corn Laws to be entirely dismantled. Nevertheless, it would be difficult to exaggerate the influence of laissez-faire ideology on the political management of the Irish Famine.[19]

How did these initial relief measures perform? Both historians and contemporaries are mixed in their views. There is, on the one hand, the incontrovertible fact that starvation deaths were mostly avoided in the first season of famine. As Butt declared, "whatever estimate may be formed of his [Peel's] measures . . . provision was made with the most consummate skill."[20] To this sanguine view, however, I want to register several significant reservations.

Peel's programmes set the political stage for considering famine relief as a way of accelerating the reconstruction of Irish society, a policy that was to have a profound impact on the administration of hunger.[21] From an early stage it was clear that economic thinking would be the decisive force in shaping the direction of relief, even when the discipline of the market might *increase* the vulnerability of the Irish agricultural sector by *decreasing* the effectiveness of local economies. The prime minister himself was aware of such adverse consequences: "if there be any part of the United Kingdom which is to suffer by the withdrawal of protection, I have always felt that that part . . . is Ireland," Peel coldly declared.[22] Kinealy also points out that surpluses in European grain, resulting from the conclusion of the Napoleonic Wars, were exhausted by the 1840s, which meant that repealing the Corn Laws was an "ideologically attractive" option for England.[23]

The move toward laissez-faire economics — what one contemporary termed "an experiment in social economy" — deserves further qualification.[24] Although the government had now decided that the market would naturally supply food to Ireland, it failed to extend the policy of "free trade" to the Navigation Laws, which stipulated that merchandise could only be transported using British ships or ships belonging to the country that supplied the original products.

This outgrowth of British mercantilism (used in South Asia, Africa, and America to control supplies and regulate commodity markets) meant that the importation of corn was impeded by freight charges that eventually soared to nearly three times the normal rate during the Great Famine.[25] Despite public genuflections to "free trade," the importation of corn occurred under a *protective* umbrella that ensured healthy profits for traders able to monopolise shipments and dictate the terms of supply and demand.

Second, the government clearly saw corn relief as a vital element in the dietary reformation of Ireland:

> Leader after leader castigated the potato as a crop and those who exploited mass subsistence upon it. Diet [became] the benchmark of civilization, and those dependent on the potato were in a debased and savage state, equalling that of the "untutored Indian" and the "ocean islander." Providence intended that civilized man live on foodstuffs of a higher order—*defined less in terms of nutrition than of viability as a commercial good.*[26]

The use of food aid to encourage dietary reform and commercialisation recapitulates the debates leading to the formation of the Irish Poor Law, particularly the state's commitment to solving Ireland's agricultural malaise through remedial tutoring and intervention. As with the Poor Law, the aim of provoking "great organic changes" necessitated deeper levels of political regulation and a more ambitious grasp of social engineering.[27] In short, food aid policy became a cornerstone of colonial biopolitics.

The distribution of food was hampered by two additional factors, the first and most obvious being the absence of an existing food and provisions trade in Ireland. As Trevelyan patiently explained,

> A large proportion of the people of Ireland had been accustomed to grow the food they required, each for himself, on his own little plot of ground; and the social machinery by which, in other countries, the necessary supplies of food are collected, stored, and distributed, had no existence there. Suddenly, without preparation,

economic starvation

the people passed from a potato food, which they raised themselves, to grain food, which they had to purchase from others, and
which in great part, had to be imported from abroad; the country
was so entirely destitute of resources applicable to this new state
of things, that often, even in large villages, neither bread nor flour
was to be procured; and in country districts, the people had to
sometimes walk twenty miles before they could obtain a single
stone of meal.[28]

If in its initial response the government was guilty of organising Irish
Famine relief based on an "Indian model" (that is, presuming that distress would be "seasonal"), now it was distributing food as though
Irish towns were as commercialised as their English counterparts.[29]
The infrastructure for importing and distributing foodstuffs was largely
confined to the prosperous districts of Ulster and the larger towns in
the south, meaning that "where relief would be most needed, the
means by which it was to be supplied seldom existed."[30]

This disorganised state was compounded by the fact that Indian corn could not be treated like most grain. Maize is an exceptionally firm grain and ordinary mills proved completely inadequate. In
addition to the task of unloading and drying the supplies, the corn
had to be ground twice, which further delayed the process of food
provisioning.[31] These difficulties meant that maintaining sufficiently
stocked depots was especially problematic. The third significant problem, calamitously misunderstood by relief officials, was the fact that
the destruction of the potato crop involved a "double misery" for the
poor: "It destroyed their food, and at the same time it took from them
their income." "The poor man's store was altogether gone," continued
Butt, "a purchaser of his provisions he never had been—the means
of purchasing them he never had."[32] The poorest areas of Ireland did
not operate a "cash economy," meaning the poor had not the means
to purchase the provisions that were offered to them.

The public works, established under the Temporary Relief Commission, were also controversial and allegations of local abuse were
common. Writing shortly after the Great Famine, Hugh Dorian claimed
that local "committee men" enforced their own arbitrary laws to keep
their preferred candidates on the relief list.[33] Dorian also alleged that

tickets often were only obtainable through humiliating supplications: "The applicant for relief presented himself at the committee man's dwelling, got an hour or so at some job, then was supplied with the desired ticket drawn out of favour of some petty shopkeeper at some distance, and having reached that place, would have to wait his turn. All this circuitous way of doing good was more like hard labour or convict punishment."[34] Significantly, this method of aid was designed to be provisional. Once the "probationary season of distress" had ended, the works were expected to close because it was feared that Irish labourers, otherwise in regular employment, would abandon their farms *en masse* in favour of the government's schemes.[35] Thus began a long litany of claims of peasant deceit, simulation, and duplicity that gained wider currency as the Irish Famine wore on. Even so, by August 1846, ninety-seven thousand people were employed on the government works.

Just as it was becoming clear that the new harvest was more severely blighted than the previous year, Peel lost his ministry. The government did not fall over the contentious repeal of the Corn Laws but rather over the attempted imposition of another Irish Coercion Act designed to check the growing unrest in the Irish countryside. Assuming office on June 30, 1846, the new prime minister, Lord John Russell, decided to revamp the government's relief strategy. In August 1846 Trevelyan authorised the disbandment of the Temporary Relief Commission.[36] Henceforth, government efforts were to be concentrated on public works, a move sanctioned by the Labour-Rate Act.[37] In line with this revision, the government gave assurances that the supply of Ireland's food would be left to private enterprise and the food depots would no longer be used to counteract price inflations in local markets. It was thought that any "artificial" cheapening of food would have the effect of maintaining existing levels of consumption, thereby prolonging the period of government assistance.

Scholars tend to overemphasise the degree to which these changes represented a departure in policy, however. In ideological terms, the new relief strategies were entirely consistent with Peel's previous policies. After all, Peel had never intended government imports to meet the deficiencies caused by the partial failure of the potato harvest. The distribution of maize was permitted precisely because it was an unknown commodity in Ireland and the government could claim to have not interfered in the food market. Lord Russell's declaration that the government would no longer act as a trafficker in food was simply a restatement of old principles.[38] In the remote western parts of the island food depots remained operational, though they were now intended "to be a last resort to supply the deficiencies of trade and not to take the place of trade." This "noninterventionist" policy extended to exports as well as imports, and throughout the Famine food shipments left from Irish ports.[39] No longer a trafficker in food, Trevelyan proposed that the government should operate instead as "pioneers [in] trade, and lead the way to habits of commercial enterprise where before they had no existence."[40]

Isaac Butt provided a stinging condemnation of what he characterised as a "most miserable misapprehension" of Irish conditions:

> By what delusions could any man persuade himself, that by the natural operations of this [market] process, Indian corn could find its way to the wilds of Mayo, or the village of Carberry? There were neither retail dealers nor merchants in the article required. The people whose food was gone were, in fact, beyond the pale of mercantile enterprise. To supply a country so circumstanced, was to expect men suddenly to embark in the trade of supplying Ireland with food, not by any of the ordinary processes by which merchants are led into the affording of additional supplies, by orders coming in the usual way of trade, but upon some vague and uncertain speculation that a country of which they knew nothing would have a demand for corn, and the still more uncertain speculation that the pauper inhabitants of that country would have the means of paying for that demand.[41]

Although local relief committees continued to function, their powers were now curbed in favour of a centralised chain of command that consolidated the treasury's control over Irish famine relief.[42] In future employment projects would be determined by the Board of Works and paid by local taxation, a divergence summarised by the popular aphorism "Irish property should support Irish poverty."[43] This "monstrous system of centralisation" had the unfortunate effect of slowing relief procedures considerably.[44] It also stripped Irish rate-payers of any control over relief expenditure. Trevelyan continued to describe the new relief arrangements in panglossian terms: "The Board of Works became the centre of a colossal organization; 5,000 separate works had to be reported upon; 12,000 subordinate officers had to be superintended. Their letters averaged upwards of 800 a-day."[45] Under the watchful eye of the treasury, the government was now aligning famine relief with a centralised system of social regulation.

In general, however, the drudgery of unproductive public labour was preferred to the humiliation of workhouse rule. By December 1846, 440,000 people were employed on the government's public works.[46] This colossal congregation of paupers was considered to be morally harmful. "Huddled together in masses," complained George Nicholls, "they screened each other's idleness."[47] The poor selected public labour, Nicholls intuited, because of the attractions of "the Queen's pay" and the absence of an exacting deterrent test. This problem was partly remedied by the new Labour-Rate Act, which substituted the "task labour" or "piece work" system for the daily wages previously paid. In addition to making work less tolerable than ordinary employment, Irish labourers were now to be paid according to the amount of work they could complete. To reinforce the principle of "less eligibility," and as an incentive to "independent industry," it was directed that task work be paid below what was normally provided locally. Any amount above what was necessary to keep labourers alive would only encourage welfare dependence and unscrupulous conduct:

> The Indolence of the Irish artisan is sufficiently accounted for by the combinations which, by prohibiting piece-work, requiring all workmen to be paid by the day, and at the same rate, and prohibiting a good workman from exerting himself, have destroyed the motives of industry . . . The Irish occupier, working for a distant object, dependent in some measure on the seasons, and with no one to control, or even to advise him, puts off till tomorrow what need not necessarily be done to day—puts off till

next year what need not necessarily be done this year, and ultimately leaves much totally undone.[48]

So there's a view of [illegible]

Senior believed that careful invigilating was necessary to extract an
honest day's work from an Irish labourer.[49] "Working under the eye
of a master, or at piece-work," he declared, "produces habits of un-
remitted industry, which can not easily be acquired by the man who is
his own taskmaster."[50] British famine policy in India was similarly
preoccupied with "encouraging people to be self-reliant."[51] In each
case, relief policies were based on a *negative* deterrent test (to eliminate
presumed imposture) and a *positive* improving function (to inculcate
desirable behaviour). But again—and this is crucial—these schemes
actually *increased* government control over what George Nicholls diplo-
matically termed "sensitive points": that is, government was now managing the wages and food and hence the entire means of subsistence
of a starving population.[52] Trevelyan reported that the "government
has been brought into direct collision with the entire labour population of the country in the capacity of Employer, & to a great extent in
that of provision Merchant also."[53] Without the least sense of irony,
confirmed liberals like Trevelyan and Nassau Senior (who detested
"paternal government") were now endorsing the state-led regulation
of biological life.

According to Hugh Dorian, the destitute poor hated the gru-
elling task work system: "for if he [the Irish labourer] did not put in
an appearance on the ground in all kinds of weather, no matter what
the distance might be, or if he was not present at every roll call, his
pay, small as it was, was reduced one-half or one-fourth."[54] Dorian's
indictment minces no words:

> Here is where the government advisers dealt out the success-
> ful blow—and it would appear premeditated—the great blow
> for slowly taking away human life, getting rid of the population
> and nothing else, by forcing the hungry and the half-clad men
> to stand out in the cold and in the sleet and rain from morn till
> night for the paltry reward of nine pennies per day. Had the poor
> pitiful creatures got this allowance, small as it was, at their homes

it would have been relief, it would be charity, it would convey the impression that their benefactors meant to save life, but in the way thus given, on compulsory conditions, it meant next to slow murder.[55]

After questioning men working the roads, William Forster deduced that the wages earned could not have *averaged* "more than four shillings and sixpence per week per head: and this we confirmed by our enquiries in other districts . . . Four and sixpence per week, thus earned, the sole resource of a family of six; with Indian meal, their cheapest food, at 2s. 10d. to 4s. per stone! What is this but slow death."[56] Hungry, scantily clad, and poorly paid, many labourers were physically unable to perform the assigned work, and the grim scenes that inevitably ensued clearly unnerved some of the rank and file in Trevelyan's "tribes of superintendents." One official working for the Board of Works who witnessed "the emaciated condition of the labourers" protested to Trevelyan "that, as an engineer, he was ashamed of allotting so little task work for a day's wages, while, as a man, he was ashamed of requiring so much."[57] According to the logic of political economy, however, relief was to be "determined by the value of the workman's labour, not by his wants."[58] This cynical move was meant to check the widespread indolence that was popularly assumed. Even though food prices were steadily rising, labourers were typically remunerated from one-fifth to one-third less than the amount paid for "unmeasured work."[59] To some observers the conditions seemed prefeudal. Even vassals were "weaponed and fed, at the lord's expense," commented the American traveller W. M. S. Balch, whereas "they [the labourers] are sent into the field to work and starve."[60]

By this time endemic destitution and starvation were very much in evidence. In early December 1846 Captain Edmond Wynne expressed the horror before him:

I must again call your attention to the appalling state in which Clare Abbey is at present; I ventured through that parish this day, to ascertain the condition of the inhabitants, and although a man not easily moved, I confess myself unmanned by the extent and intensity of the suffering witnessed, more especially amongst the women and little children, crowds of whom were to be seen scattered over the turnip fields, like a flock of famished crows, devouring the raw turnips, mothers half naked, shivering in the snow and sleet, uttering exclamations of despair, whilst their children were screaming with hunger; I am a match for anything else I might meet here, but this I cannot stand.[61]

How are we to judge government policy in light of such appalling descriptions? It has been argued that the government simply underestimated the extremity of the situation and that the limited response to extreme want was a reflection of ignorance rather than callous design. Historian George Bernstein goes further, claiming that the "Irish mythology" of the Famine ignores "a basic fact": "the government's principal famine policy was a programme of public works, which at its peak, employed nearly 715,000 men and thus supported 3.5 million people, nearly half the population of Ireland."[62] Bernstein is simply repeating Trevelyan's grand claim that by March 1847, 734,000 people were employed on the Board of Works, "representing, at a moderate estimate of the average extent of each family, upwards of three millions of persons."[63] In both cases, however, to offer the figure of 3.5 million without critically engaging with all the known deficiencies of the public works—the late wages; the task labour system; deductions for broken days and illness; the escalating "famine price" for provisions; the jobbing and flagrant abuses that accompanied the selections; the complete exclusion of women regardless of how many mouths they were expected to feed—is deeply problematic.[64] In fact, the ideology behind the public works was entirely in keeping with the principles of the Irish Poor Law, particularly its emphasis on testing destitution (Trevelyan's insistence that the wages paid on the works be less than the lowest wages paid locally was in effect another means of deploying the principle of "less eligibility").[65]

Arguably, the public works *maintained* destitution as they took people away from other remunerative activities that could have served future needs and personal economic recovery. "Not only has misapplied labour left land uncultivated," charged the *Times*, "[it] has acted in aid of famine."[66] Hungry and weakened bodies were forced to la-

bour on purposefully futile work schemes because productive employment was thought to inhibit private investment and risked disturbing
the operation of an independent labour market.[67] Finally, according
to the prevailing view of political economy, public works were considered to be a central component of social engineering. As early as
1830 a Select Committee championed public works as a means of producing "extended cultivation, improved habits of industry, a better administration of justice, the re-establishment of peace and tranquillity
in disturbed districts, a domestic colonisation of a population in excess in certain districts, a diminution of illicit distillation, and a very
considerable increase to the revenue."[68] The Devon Commission cited
the opinions of the Commissioners of Public Works, who argued that
"the execution of such works leads to . . . the abandonment of the
rude and primitive implements in common use, and opens to the officers of justice and the local authorities, places which had been the secure haunt and impenetrable refuge of the outlaw and robber."[69] In
sum, public works were considered an important tool for correcting
errant populations, rather than merely a facility for delivering much-
needed famine relief.

The constant appeals to improvement underscore the extent to
which biopolitical regulation and colonial welfare were being extended
to include famine relief. "Temporary relief measures," mobilised to
alleviate "exceptional" circumstances, were now directed at the social
body (rather than the starving body), even though, as one exasperated
official protested, the problem was "one of food, not labour."[70] Individual requirements for food were increasingly superseded by ideological concerns regarding the "evils of leisure" and the improvidence
of Irish landowners, who were seen to be dependent on the British exchequer. Captain Arthur Kennedy (1810–83) wrote of "the great difficulty and danger in relieving a people who are not disposed to help
themselves; and the landlord and tenant class set them the example
of doing nothing."[71] This alleged complacency had to be redressed
through reformatory modes of discipline.

By early 1847 the government began to reel somewhat from its
previous policies of affording relief. With little in the way of options,
the poorest were now pouring onto the work schemes. By March the
government was employing over 700,000 persons. Critics described

this system of supervised labour as an "eleemosynary allowance, under the name of wages" and as a system that merely "indulged habits of indolence."[72] The chairman of the Board of Works, Lieutenant Harry David Jones, wrote to Trevelyan: "The fact is that the system . . . is no longer beneficial employment to many; their bodily strength being gone, and spirits depressed, they have not power to exert themselves sufficiently to earn the ordinary day's wages."[73] More worryingly, the public works were failing as a "test of destitution." As conditions deteriorated, the "idleness of the idle" could no longer "be distinguished from the feebleness of the weak and the infirm."[74] The obvious point that "hungry people make poor labourers" upset the system of "checks" and "tests" necessary for a programme of *qualified* relief.[75] The distinctions and exclusions—on which Victorian notions of relief depended—imploded in the face of widespread hunger and disease. Lord Dufferin (1826–1902) reported the case of one man who had been refused relief on account of his respectable appearance and was found dead near the workhouse door one quarter of an hour later.[76] The American philanthropist Elihu Burritt (1810–75) watched in horror as "once athletic labourers"—many with limbs now swollen from "dropsy" or oedema—tried to "eke out a few miserable days to their existence."[77] In a very real way the state was now exercising a murderous form of sovereign power, as labourers were being asked to exchange the product of their labour, not for another product, but for the "right to live."[78]

In response to mounting criticisms, on March 20, 1847, the government "took matters into its own hands" as Trevelyan directed that 20 percent of persons employed on public works should be summarily "struck from the [relief] lists."[79] The government now wished "to complete the system of relief by the distribution of food, to give it legal validity, and to place it more decidedly on the basis of the Poor Law."[80] The Temporary Relief Act (more commonly known as the "Soup Kitchen Act") was inspired by the Society of Friends, a religious organisation managed by the Quakers, which had been using public kitchens to distribute food relief for some time (see figure 4.2).[81] Trevelyan recognised distinct advantages to this mode of relief. "Stir-about," he enthused, "becomes sour by keeping, has no value in the market, and persons were therefore not likely to apply for

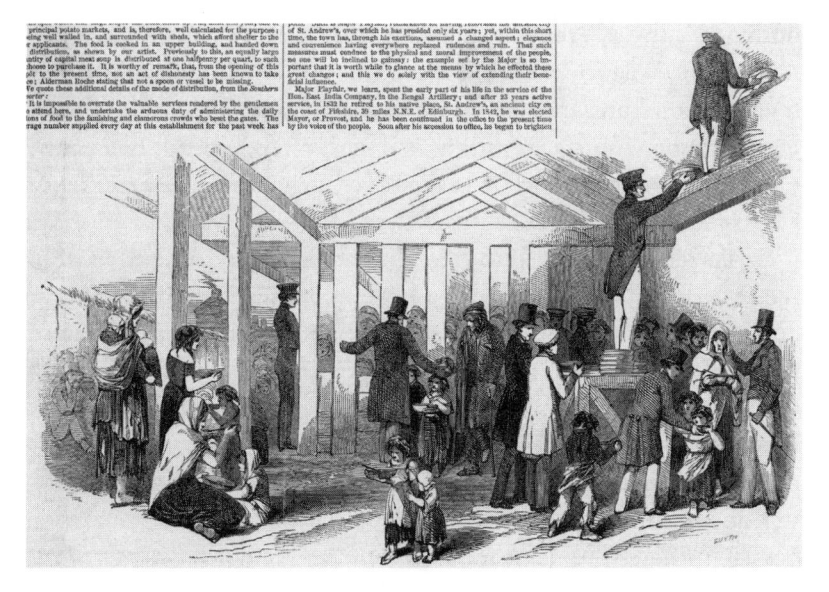

Figure 4.2. The central soup depot, Barrack Street, Cork (*Illustrated London News,* March 13, 1847)

it, who did not want it for their own consumption."[82] Put differently, cooked food doubled as yet another "test of destitution," because unlike seeds or grain, it was virtually impossible to resell. Secondly, as a "probationary measure" the soup kitchens bought the government invaluable time (and created significant savings) while the workhouses were prepared for their new function as an instrument of famine relief.[83] In fact, the soup kitchens were to last a mere seven months before being superseded by the provisions of the new Irish Poor Law Extension Act.[84]

The new strategy of direct food relief was not without its critics. Akin to other centralised systems of aid, the paper shuffling was enormous and the relief sluggish. As Donnelly points out, "the mere preparation, printing, and distribution of the forms and documents considered necessary—over 10,000 account books, 80,000 sheets, and 3,000,000 ration tickets—constituted a vast undertaking in itself, consuming valuable time."[85] The soup itself was also controversial, many insisting that it was not so much soup for the poor as poor soup.[86] Part of the problem was that "soup may be anything, everything, and nothing," as W. S. Trench explained; "it may be thin gruel or greasy water . . . or it may be the essence of meat, and very wholesome where there is some substantial food taken with it; but given to those who have nothing else to use with it, and who often expend, by coming miles for it, more strength than the soup restores, it is very inefficient for sustaining life."[87]

Trevelyan continued to extol the enormous effort on the part of the government: "Organised armies, amounting altogether to some hundreds of thousands, had been rationed before; but neither ancient nor modern history can furnish a parallel to the fact that upwards of three millions of persons were to be fed every day in the neighbour-hood of their own homes, and by administrative arrangements ema-nating from and controlled by one central office." In an apparent nod to Edmund Burke, Trevelyan warned that this was in fact the second occasion whereby so many millions were fed "out of the hands of the magistrate."[88] Notwithstanding this claim, these policies demonstrate once again the government's willingness to intervene in food mar-kets. The Soup Kitchen Act, as Butt dryly observed, "contemplates a complete departure from the policy of leaving the supply of food to the people to the ordinary operations of commerce, since it authorises the distribution, the sale, and even the culinary preparation of food under the direction of these committees."[89] The principles of laissez-faire were seemingly rescindable, so long as the government consid-ered it expedient.

Relief in the form of soup was not without its prescriptions and exclusion. Only the destitute were to be fed free of charge.[90] Those earning insufficient wages to purchase food at market prices could re-ceive provisions at low cost, while children aged nine and under were fed half portions.[91] Soup kitchen relief could also be refused if the workhouses were not entirely full.[92] But most importantly, the soup kitchens were pedalled as a *temporary* measure. Thus, between August and September 1847 the soup kitchens were closed and, in Trevel-yan's words, "the multitude was again gradually and peacefully thrown on its own resources."[93] From this point onward the machinery of the recently amended Poor Law, funded by Irish rate-payers, was to be the only form of famine relief.[94]

The Irish Poor Law Extension Act involved a complete re-organisation of the existing Poor Law.[95] Nicholls ceased to be a commissioner and became a permanent secretary, the Poor Law commission was relocated from London to Dublin, and Edward Twisleton (1809–74), an Englishman, was appointed chief commissioner. Perhaps the most significant change was the provision for outdoor relief through the new Poor Law. This was a contentious shift in policy.[96] In his original report Nicholls was adamant that outdoor relief should be restricted in Ireland, although it could be granted in exceptional situations under the provisions of the English Poor Law.[97] While outdoor relief was now permissible—and a right of relief was ipso facto recognised for specified groups of people—the act itself operated according to strict exclusions. Section 1 of the act declared that only three kinds of "destitute poor persons" (widows with two or more legitimate dependents, the maimed and the disabled, and those who were chronically ill) were entitled to relief outside the workhouse.[98] Everyone else who did not have the means to support themselves and their families had to apply to the workhouse. There was, however, one final exception. Outdoor relief for the "able-bodied" was authorised under section 2 of the Irish Poor Law Extension Act and was to be reserved for situations of "unusual distress."[99] In practical terms this meant that the "able-bodied" could receive relief in the form of cooked food only in the most desperate circumstances, for a period of not more than two months, provided that the local workhouse was full or infected with fever.

Nicholls explained the importance of these new provisions: "The concession made in the *1st and 2nd sections* [to provide outdoor relief] must however be regarded as exceptional, and as being intended to meet an exceptional case; for the necessity of workhouse relief being the established rule, never perhaps commanded more general assent, than at the time when a departure from it was thus sanctioned."[100] The exception explained the rule: workhouse relief was to be the new norm for famine assistance. Only the Poor Law commissioners had the authority to grant outdoor relief to the so-called able-bodied, although this neat distinction was fast becoming absurd as starvation and disease took its toll. In various circulars the government made clear that "indoor relief" was to be prioritised, and Poor Law guardians were instructed to expend every effort in finding accommodation within the workhouse, even if this involved emptying the buildings of the infirm, the sick, and the old.[101] The new regulations also authorised the dismissal of any noncompliant Board of Guardians, a power that was invoked on numerous occasions during the Great Famine.

To meet the burden of outdoor relief, five additional assistant commissioners were appointed, and the local boards were provided with extra staff. In a directive the commissioners outlined the duties of relieving officers:

> It will be his duty forthwith to examine into circumstances of every case by visiting the home of the applicant, by making all necessary inquiries into the state of health, the ability to work and the means of such applicant; and he will have to report the result of such inquiries, in a prescribed form, to the Board of Guardians at the next meeting. Under ordinary circumstances, the amount of relief to be granted in each case will be fixed by the Board of Guardians exclusively.[102]

Decisions were final. There was no apparatus for appeals—including the courts—and little effort was made to seek out those who were in serious need of assistance. With little or no "danger of riposte" this was an ideal situation for systemic abuse.[103] Even for successful applicants, outdoor relief was granted only as a probationary measure and the claimant's status was kept under permanent review.[104] Furthermore, the commissioners ordered a systematic "thinning" of outdoor relief lists (as they had previously done when the public works were closed) based on the ill-informed notion that employment could be readily obtained at harvest time.[105] In other words, relief was effectively defined by its *constant capacity to be revoked,* meaning that for those whose very lives depended upon it, nothing was so certain as uncertainty itself. The government's decision to publish and publicly display lists of all peoples receiving indoor and outdoor relief confirmed the feeling that relief was an "engine of degradation and oppression more than a means of material relief."[106]

Under such conditions one can scarcely imagine any destitute pauper holding the central authorities accountable for inappropriate treatment or specific injustices. "How is a pauper to prosecute?" wondered Osborne.[107] As the new norm was workhouse relief, those who were excluded from admission or too sick to travel were literally abandoned to their fate: "it does not appear to me that the responsibility of deaths from starvation outside the workhouse rests either with the Board of Guardians or the Commissioners."[108] Twisleton's words are an accurate assessment of relief protocol and its duties and obligations—but also, crucially, its derogations and exclusions. "Never was there an act passed," declared Butt, "the result of which so much depends on the administration, because every thing is left to the arbitrary power of those who are to carry its provisions into practice."[109] Gustave de Beaumont similarly warned that under the Poor Law all morality would be reduced "to the mere simple procedure of arbitrary selection."[110] It is precisely this noncoincidence between death and accountability that guarantees situations of structured, continuous violence.

Even when "able-bodied" persons were granted outdoor relief, the tasks (usually stone-breaking for ten hours per diem) were designed to be as "unattractive" and "useless" as possible, less they lead to the "paralysis of all ordinary industry."[111] Again it was thought that if relief was "attractive," Irish labourers would abandon normal employment, while if the labour was "productive" it would adversely affect the sanctity of private enterprise ("speculators would not have risked their capital to feed the people," explained one observer).[112] Accordingly, "ample work should be required in exchange for the means of livelihood."[113] These principles were valorised by a cynical reading of Irish behaviour. "The truth is that when useless and merely penal work is preferred as being 'unattractive,' what is meant is, that it is 'repulsive,'" declared Scrope.[114]

In a letter to Trevelyan, Twisleton indeed confirmed that relief operations were *designed* to be "as repulsive as possible consistent with humanity."[115] The "able-bodied" on outdoor relief were not entitled to fuel, clothing, or shelter.[116] Unsurprisingly, many labourers considered this mode of relief to be intensely degrading. In February 1848 applicants for outdoor assistance in Newcastle Union, County Limerick, stated that "they would rather die than break stones," a threat many undoubtedly fulfilled.[117] During his tour of Ireland, Osborne noted that "the so-called 'able-bodied,' were [the] most wretched samples of 'starved in' humanity" he had witnessed, adding that "it was clear they had fought the battle of life without the hated [workhouse] wall, until all power to contend had left them."[118] "My father's wonder and my own," declared William Forster, "is not that the people die, but that they live."[119] Despite such scenes, by July 1848 over 800,000 people were on outdoor relief, while the numbers being admitted into the workhouses continued to rise.[120] What explains this rush for institutional assistance at a time when the government had declared the Irish Famine officially over?

THE WAR ON DWELLING

As part of the revision of the Irish Poor Law, the government introduced the infamous "Gregory Clause," named after its author William Gregory and sometimes called the "Quarter Acre" or "Conacre Clause."[121] This provision precluded tenants holding more than a quarter acre of land from receiving relief without first conceding possession of their property. Previously, paupers were asked to exchange their liberty and the product of their labour for the right to live. Now Irish paupers were ordered to relinquish their holdings in exchange for government assistance. Dispossession thus became the latest in a long list of deterrent tests, even though a correspondent for the *Times* acknowledged that "[a test] must cease to be a test at all when there is no option but to accept it or die."[122] In his autobiography Gregory remained defiant: "though I got an evil reputation in consequence, those who really understood the condition of the country have always regarded this clause as its salvation."[123] Modern historians have been less charitable in their assessment, describing the clause as "a charter for land clearance and consolidation" that was clearly premeditated.[124]

The Gregory Clause itself needs to be understood alongside an 1843 amendment to the rating of the Poor Law that made landlords liable for paying half the poor-rate on tenements and holdings over £4 per annum and the *whole rate* for holdings under that annual rent.[125] By making smallholders an encumbrance on Irish landowners, the provision incentivised population clearances and land consolidation. The Devon Commission recorded the common refrain of Irish landlords: "There is no use me allowing you the poor-rate; as, if I do, I must raise your rent."[126] Trollope observed that "labour is suspended and cultivation is abandoned, as farmers declared it was impossible to pay both rates and wages" with little prospect of receiving any rent.[127] "Here is society dislocated at both ends," declared William Bennett.[128]

For many the coffers were stretched if not empty when the government produced two further pieces of legislation—the Encumbered Estates and Rate-in-Aid Acts—that decisively affected the fortune of landowners and their tenantry. Based on ideas first advanced by the Devon Commission and now pressed by Robert Peel in parliament, the Encumbered Estates Acts of 1848 and 1849 were designed to assist the sale of insolvent estates and force the eviction of profligate landlords.[129] According to Thomas Drummond's (1797–1840) well-known censure, Irish property must have "its duties as well as its rights."[130] Trevelyan was in favour of this legislative initiative, describing the sale of encumbered estates as the "master-key to unlock the field of industry in Ireland."[131] There are two significant points to note about this legislation. First, the 1849 legislation placed the duties of the act beyond the jurisdiction of the Court of Chancery and into the hands of three commissioners. The commissioners were authorised to craft their own rules of court and were answerable only to the sanction of the Irish Privy Council. The value of an estate and how it would be sold were internally decided, and there was no appeals process.[132] Evidently, "free trade in land" would require the same kinds of legislative interference that characterised the government's previous attempts to stimulate "great organic changes" in Irish society. As Peel reasoned,

> I believe, although the ordinary courts of law are admirably suited for the conduct of ordinary proceedings and for the

administration of justice between man and man, without extraordinary courts, yet I must say, when great social difficulties
have to be contended with, my belief is that you should step beyond the limit of those ordinary courts of justice and establish
some special tribunal, unfettered by reference to technical rules,
for the purpose of solving those difficulties.[133]

Significant also is the language Peel used in promoting the act, "suggesting a 'new plantation' of Connacht by British landowners and
capitalist farmers," and underscoring the parallels being drawn between relief policies and the colonial confiscations in early modern
Ireland.[134]

The Rate-in-Aid Act became law on May 24, 1849.[135] Properly
speaking it was part of a long-standing Whig policy to place the burden of relief squarely on the shoulders of the Irish. The legislation
made all Irish Poor Law Unions taxable for the relief of stricken western regions as well as for the loans dispensed by the government. Irish
indignation rose to new heights. The call for "Irish property to support Irish poverty" confirmed that the Act of Union was hardly worth
the paper it was written on. Several voices complained that it was
grossly unfair that the better-off districts should be dragged down to
the levels of destitution found in the south and west of Ireland, while
others argued that this policy amounted to a curious lesson in self-
reliance.[136] Indeed, if Ireland was truly an equal partner, why was not
the rest of British property proportionately taxed to lighten the Irish
burden? Even to speak of an *English* treasury, declared Butt, is to declare the Union void: "If the Union be not a mockery, there exists no
such thing as an English treasury. The exchequer is the exchequer of
the United Kingdom." With palpable anger Butt continued: "when
calamity falls upon us . . . we then recover our separate existence as a
nation, just so far as to disentitle us to the state assistance." "If Cornwall had been visited with the scenes that have desolated Cork," he
reasoned, "would similar arguments have been used?"[137] "If there be a
real Union between England and Ireland," protested John Mac Hale,
"it should have the reciprocal conditions of all such covenants —
mutual benefits and mutual burdens."[138] George Nicholls agreed that
the bill violated the civic principle of "one part of the empire coming

to the assistance of the other," but he thought the new policy was nonetheless necessary if the Irish were to be encouraged to relinquish old habits:

[T]he repeated failures [of the potato] caused apprehensions as to the perpetuity of the burden, and seemed to point to *the necessity of compelling the Irish to abandon the treacherous potato,* which it was thought they would hardly do, so long as they could turn to England for help whenever it failed them. The rate-in-aid was *calculated to effect this object,* by casting the consequences of the failure entirely upon Ireland itself, which in such case would be unable to persist in its reliance upon a crop so treacherous and uncertain as the potato.[139]

These laboured justifications ignored one obvious problem: How was a famine-stricken country to support these new taxes? The travel writer James Johnson satirised a certain mood well when he wondered if it would not be more prudent to collect the poor in place of the poor-rates and "drown them quietly in the Shannon."[140]

These legislative acts gave landlords clear *incentives* to turn the poor from their land. Indeed, according to John Forbes, a keen observer of Irish affairs and an avid supporter of agricultural reorganisation, the very presence of the Poor Law system meant that evictors could not be accused of "knowingly exposing" their tenants to fatal conditions. Irish landowners, he claimed, "were not merely legally but *morally justified* in carrying it [clearances] into effect." "The existence of the Poor Law system," Forbes continued, "with its Union Workhouses in every district, was an essential preliminary, not merely to render such an act justifiable, but to render it possible without incurring the responsibility of a most positive outrage on humanity, which no mere legal authority could either want or palliate."[141] In the absence of legal restraint, eviction and enclosure were turned into a righteous course of civic action.

Undoubtedly, for some landowners it was a case of "evict their debtors or be dispossessed by their creditors."[142] Sir John Benn-Walsh, a substantial landowner in Cork and Kerry, wrote in his journal in August 1849: "The fact is that the landed proprietors are now the mere

nominal possessors of the soil. All the surplus produce is levied by
the poor law commissioners."[143] In these circumstances many felt
that only eviction or death "would release them [the poor] from their
sufferings, and the landlord of his burden."[144] It would be wrong to
deduce from this, however, that Irish landlords found themselves in
an invidious position and acted only according to the political cards
they had been dealt. Several landowners welcomed the crisis as a way
of repatriating assets to their rightful owners—a process that has
been aptly characterised as "accumulation by dispossession."[145]

Moreover, if the landed gentry suffered we can be sure that the
position of the small farmer and cottier tenant was abysmal in the extreme. This is reflected in eyewitness accounts, many of them penned
by conscientious Englishmen. S. G. Osborne witnessed firsthand the
effects of this legislation, and he ardently condemned what he described as a state-sponsored "war on dwelling." Relating a scene of
eviction at Oranmore, Galway, he wrote that "the whole town seemed
like a hospital for dwellings, in which they had been kindly received
from some field of deadly war."[146] Travelling through Kilrush, County
Clare, at about the same time, G. P. Scrope reported the devastating
traces of the "levellers": "at times a whole street in a village had been
destroyed. I seemed to be tracking the course of an invading army"[147]
(see figure 4.3). At the fishing village of Kiel, another English visitor
observed more than 150 evicted persons: "A crowd of these miserable
ejected creatures collected around us, bewailing, with bitter lamenta-
tions, their hard fate. One old grey-headed man came tottering up
to us, bearing in his arms his bed-ridden wife, and putting her down
at our feet, pointed, in silent agony to her, and then to the roofless
dwelling, the charred timbers of which were scattered in all directions
around"[148] (see figure 4.4).

Where could the dispossessed and ejected go? For those who
were evicted, as well as others who "voluntarily" gave up their holdings to qualify for public assistance, emigration or the workhouse
were the principal options. Others began desperate efforts to convert
ditches and bogs into makeshift dwellings known as "scalpeens" (see
figures 4.5 and 4.6). Osborne offers a vivid description of this harrowing faminescape:

Figure 4.3. The village of Moveen, three miles west of Kilkee (*Illustrated London News,* December 22, 1849)

Figure 4.4. The ejectment of Irish tenantry—troops help evict tenants and their houses are "tumbled" (*Illustrated London News,* December 16, 1848)

Figure 4.5. "Scalpeen" of Tim Downs at Dunmore (*Illustrated London News,* December 22, 1849)

On our journey we had ample opportunity of seeing to what shifts the peasantry will resort before they will face the Union House, after they have been evicted, and seen their homes "tumbled." Their usual practice is, with thatch and some of the roof sticks to build up a dwelling called a "scalpeen," the most common form of this species of dwelling is, what I suppose the Englishman would call, "the lean to." The construction is simple; some of the roof-sticks, or beams, are placed, so that one end of them shall rest on the ground, while the other end of them rests against the side wall of one of the ruins, or failing this, against a bank on the road-side: on these beams, with the help of a few short sticks, the old thatch is heaped up; stones and more wood are laid on it, to keep it together; one end is closed up with a heap

Figure 4.6. An evicted family with their scalpeen in a ditch (*Illustrated London News,* December 16, 1848)

of thatch and stones, the other end left just open enough for the inmates to have egress; into this stye a whole family will crowd, and even take a lodger; and in a few hundreds of such, would often be found a population of many thousands.[149]

Whole families existed in bogs and ditches until they were discovered by the police and driven on. Osborne echoed what was well known since the formulation of an Irish Poor Law: "Eviction, as carried on in this part of Ireland, is very much the same as extermination."[150] The Quaker James Tuke agreed: "The loss of little plots

of land has been and still is a question of existence."[151] Exposure to
inclement weather carried off many already-weakened frames. Eyewitnesses described the winter roads as "charnel houses": "several
car and coach drivers have assured me that they rarely drove anywhere without seeing dead bodies strewn along the road side, and
that in the dark they had even gone over them." An inspector of roads
near Clifden had to remove and bury 140 bodies before he has able
to proceed.[152]

Much of the folklore evidence collected corroborates the perspectives of these foreign witnesses.[153] The Irishman Hugh Dorian
claimed a "war upon cottiers" was underway. It was, he said, "eviction on the plea of giving to other men their rights"—which is to
say, the elevation of the rights of property over and above the right
to food and life.[154] According to Dorian, the word "ejectment" was
the best understood word in the English language, understood by
"young and old who had not a second word of English."[155] Scrope
charged the government with a policy of "extermination" not by
direct design, but "by their deprivation of the means of living, of
shelter, clothing, and of sufficiency of food."[156] Mitchel claimed that
ejectment laws were used "to clear off the 'surplus population,'" while
Butt condemned them as "a measure of confiscation."[157] In one of
the first histories of the Great Famine, John O'Rourke insisted that
ejectments were "purely for the sake of clearing the soil of its human
incumbrances"—that is, life considered devoid of any utility or value.
According to James Fintan Lalor (1807–49), the thinly veiled assumption was "that the small occupier is a man who ought not to be
existing."[158]

The total number of evictions is controversial. The figures between 1846 and 1848 are extrapolated from courtroom proceedings.
Beginning in 1849, however, the local constabulary began to record
ejectments. The evidence is complicated further by the fact that removals continued well into the 1850s, police records do not account
for "voluntary" surrenders, and the complexity of the law pertaining
to ejectments may indeed obscure the true extent of the problem.[159]
Ó Gráda claims that 225,000 people were ejected between 1849 and
1854.[160] Donnelly agrees but adds that "if we are to guess at the equiva-

lent number for 1845–8 and to include the countless thousands pressured into voluntary surrenders during the whole period (1846–54), the resulting figure would almost certainly exceed half a million persons."[161] Tim O'Neill's revised figure is higher again.[162]

It is well established that "migration can be a crude form of disaster relief," and several witnesses bore testimony to the "truly affecting" tide of emigration during the Irish Famine.[163] Heartbreaking scenes of departure and the horrors endured on overcrowded "coffin ships" are frequent focal points in these narratives; other accounts prove to be variations on William Bennett's lament that "the obvious strength of the country is departing with those who go."[164] Although pre-Famine emigration was substantial—between 1815 and 1845 Ireland contributed one-third of all voluntary trans-Atlantic movements—the swelling of evictions and the resulting destitution forced many more to seek out a livelihood elsewhere.[165] Between 1845 and 1855, 2.1 million Irish left the country, mainly for America, Britain, Canada, and Australia. Indeed, from the point of view of numbers, "more people left Ireland in just eleven years than during the proceeding two and one-half centuries," making Irish emigration the most significant outflow from any European country during this period.[166] Landlords who were able (and willing) helped their stricken tenants to emigrate; others were "assisted" through the Poor Law, but many more were cast adrift and left to fend for themselves.[167]

A deadly synergy of colonial dogma and classical political economy valorised the violence of "depeasantisation" and severely attenuated the sorts of humanitarian sentiments expressed above.[168] It is well established that smallholdings had lost favour in contemporary economic opinion, and several persuasive voices had concluded that Ireland was "overpopulated." If "the wealth of Ireland was almost entirely territorial," as Trollope remarked, then a radical restructuring of Irish property was necessary to maximise economic utility.[169] Some politicians were willing to contemplate significant sacrifices in order to "civilise" Irish society. The foreign secretary, Lord Palmerston (1784–1865), who engaged in clearances on his own Irish estate, informed the cabinet on March 31, 1848: "It is useless to disguise the truth that any great improvement in the social system in Ireland must be founded upon an extensive change in the present state of agrarian occupation, and that this change necessarily implies a long continued and systematic ejectment of Small Holders and of Squatting Cottiers."[170] The chancellor of the exchequer, Charles Wood (1800–1885), wrote, "Except through a purgatory of misery and starvation, I cannot see how Ireland is to emerge into a state of anything approaching to quiet or prosperity."[171] Upon reflection Trevelyan viewed the Irish Famine as "a salutary revolution in the habits of a nation." Surveying the scene in 1848, he declared, "Supreme Wisdom has educed permanent good out of transient evil."[172]

These calculations mark the rise of a form of "disaster capitalism" that used catastrophes to engage in radical social and economic engineering.[173] Evidently, senior statesmen and relief officials were not only thinking about delivering aid and saving lives; their statements and policies were concerned with restructuring the very fabric of Irish society and aligning Irish behaviour with Enlightenment norms of rationality and human progress. These policy choices percolated to the grassroots of society. The Englishman John Ashworth, who came to Ireland in a bid to resettle his family in 1850, voiced the conviction that the smallholders of Ireland were impeding the modernisation of the Irish economy: "The small sub-divisions of land which have caused so much misery and moral degradation in Ireland are on all hands condemned, and better were it that the present *race of occupants* should emigrate and leave the whole country to be re-colonised, than such a scandalous and demoralising system should be continued."[174] The *Times* linked destruction with renewal through the colonial image of *terra nullis:* "In a few years," one editorial rejoiced, "a Celtic Irishman will be as rare in Connemara as Red Indian on the shores of Manhattan."[175]

Agrarian improvement increasingly appealed to the colonial logic of native exodus and commercial resettlement, but the striking feature about these land policies is that they occurred under the protection of legal enactment, giving substance to the claim that under biopolitical norms the originary relation of law to life is abandonment.[176] Thus, in a stinging letter to the prime minister the Catholic archbishop of Tuam, John MacHale, protested that "the people received only the chilling assurance that in those deaths, however numerous, there was nothing illegal or unconstitutional! It is, then, it seems, no matter what may be the amount of the people's sufferings, or what may be the number of those who fall victims to the Famine, provided that nothing illegal or unconstitutional is done in vindicating the rights of property."[177] Scrope subjected the legislature to a stinging indictment: "'Public indignation' has little or no effect on the authors of these atrocities. I want to direct the public indignation against the state of law which permits them. They are murders in the common sense of the term; but they are murders sanctioned by law. Then, it is the law that is responsible for the crime, and that should fall before the just indignation of the public."[178] Hugh Dorian thought much the same: "Murder though it was in reality, but sanctioned under the name of law."[179] Osborne was equally horrified by the complicity of the law in driving the peasantry from the land, realising too well that ejectment laws overruled the possibility of legal redress for those who were thrown from the land: "Rats might as well hope for the conviction of ferrets by a jury of rat-catchers, as the peasantry to obtain redress for manslaughter against drivers, from juries, many of whom daily employ them." For these observers, it was an extreme condition of rightlessness that ensured that thousands of Irish men, women, and children were "doomed to the workhouse, to banishment, or to death."[180]

Juridical power in colonial contexts has been described as a series of inclusions (extending the rule of law) that are simultaneously exclusions (the denial of basic civic protections).[181] This same configuration applies to the administration of hunger, which brought huge numbers of Irish under the control of government whilst at the same time radically excluding them. The use of juridical power thus served a double function: on the one hand, it enabled the remaking of agrarian relations and the cannibalisation of Irish smallholders, while, on the other hand, the rule of law worked to normalise political violence by rendering all opposition *illegal*. The intimate connection between the state and capital was therefore an important precondition for the Famine-era clearances and the subsequent reterritorialisation of Irish society.[182] It is estimated that in less than one decade (1849–58) approximately

one-tenth of the total acreage of Ireland was placed under new ownership; the success of this programme "was a matter of almost unani-
mous acknowledgement in Parliament and outside."[183] Using the annual agricultural returns, the editors of the book *Mapping the Great
Irish Famine* observe an extensive process of reterritorialisation occurring between 1845 and 1851. The number of plots under or equal to
one acre declined by 75 percent. A reduction on a similar scale took
place among holdings between one and five acres. Farms in the category of five to fifteen acres fell by 25 percent, while the number of
farms between fifteen and thirty acres increased by 80 percent. Farms
larger than thirty acres increased threefold.[184]

The core of agrarian modernisation lay in the imposition of a
tripartite division of labour among landlords, capitalist tenant farmers, and (landless) wage labourers.[185] For quite some time the elimination of "cotterism" through *forced proletarianisation* had been considered the "master key" to unlocking Irish industry. Trevelyan berated
the "old barbarous Irish tenure called *Rundale* . . . which stops short
of the institution of individual property, and by making the industrious and thriving responsible for the short-comings of the idle
and improvident, effectively destroys the springs of improvement."[186]
Captain Arthur Kennedy similarly complained about regressive Irish
agrarian habits: "Their mode of scratching the land does not deserve
the name of cultivation. Their attempts are inferior to what I have seen
among North-American Indians."[187] Kennedy went on to describe the
common Irish peasant as "ignorant of the use of land, labour, or capital; in their appearance, clothing and mode of living hardly human"—
a description that was reprinted with approval by Nassau Senior.[188]
Like her fellow economists, Harriet Martineau considered the proletarianisation of Irish farming to be a sovereign remedy for Irish backwardness, although she wondered whether this could occur without
the aid of mass removals:

> Up to a very recent time—probably up to this hour—there
> has been discussion among English political economists as to
> whether, in consideration of the Irishman's passion for land,
> there might not be, in his case, some relaxation of established

rules, some suspension of scientific maxims, about small holdings of land; whether the indolence, improvidence, and turbulent character of the Irish peasantry might not be changed into the opposite characteristics of the Flemish and Saxon countryman, by putting them in the same position. We have borne this question in mind throughout our survey of the country. We presently saw that the habits of slovenly cultivation, of the dependences on the potato, and of consequent idleness for the greater part of the year, were too firmly associated in the peasant mind with the possession of land to allow the peasant to be a safe proprietor at present. A course of discipline was obviously necessary to fit him, in any degree, for the possession of the land: and this discipline he could never have while on the land.[189]

Although this "visionary geography" recalls the framing of the Irish Poor Law (especially the explicit desire to abolish cottierism and reorder colonial property relations), its ideological roots stretch back to early modern Ireland and the initial attempts to anglicise Irish society.[190] It had long been assumed that Ireland required radical reform, but the arrival of potato blight provided the pretext necessary to justify further socioeconomic engineering, especially at a time when nonmarket adjustments were officially condemned. As famine aid became more tightly intertwined with projects of structural adjustment, relief strategies became increasingly biopolitical in nature and intent (see tables 4.1 and 4.2). To better understand the nature of this development, we turn once more to the spaces of the Irish workhouse, where the mass production of "bare life" was most pronounced and vivid.

Breaking into Jail and the Production of Bare Life

All outside relief for the able-bodied was suspended in 1849, which led to a massive influx of pauper inmates to the workhouses (see table 4.3).[191] By January 1849, two years after Trevelyan declared that the Famine had been "stayed," over one million people were being afforded relief in the workhouses. "Before it was go to hell. Now, it is

Table 4.1. The Ideological Dimensions of State Assistance: Relief and Improvement

Spaces of Relief	Checks and Tests	Social Engineering
Poor Law Workhouse	Less eligibility (enacted through separation, confinement, institutional supervision, labour test, dietary regimes)	Moral reform Dietary transition Agrarian reform
Food Depots	Discriminate distribution Use of Indian corn	Normalising laissez-faire policies Dietary transition
Public Works	Local taxation Labour test (enacted through "piece" or "task" work, unproductive projects, constant superintendence) Wage test	Habits of self-reliance Moral reform Work ethic
Soup Kitchens	Cooked food test Dietary regime	Dietary transition
Irish Poor Law Extension Act	Gregory Clause	Dispossession and depopulation Proletarianisation Agrarian reform (from tillage to pastoral farming) Emigration
Outdoor Relief	Publicly displayed lists of people receiving relief Home inspections Temporal limitation	Habits of self-reliance Moral reform Work ethic

Table 4.2. The Ideological Dimensions of State Assistance:
Disciplining Irish Landlords

Legislation	Social Engineering
Rate in Aid	Habits of self-reliance Dispossession and depopulation
Encumbered Estates	Eviction of insolvent landlords Dispossession and depopulation "Free trade" in land Agrarian reform

Table 4.3. Workhouse and Outdoor Relief

Year	Number of Workhouses in Operation	Expenditure (£)	Total Number of Persons Relieved in the Workhouses	Total Number of Persons Receiving Outdoor Relief
1840[a]	4	37,057	10,910	—
1841	37	110,278	31,108	—
1842	92	281,233	87,604	—
1843	106	244,374	87,898	—
1844	113	271,334	105,358	—
1845	123	316,026	114,205	—
1846	130	435,001	243,933	—
1847[b]	130	803,684	417,139	—
1848	131	1,732,597	610,463	1,433,042
1849	131	2,177,651	932,284	1,210,482
1850	163	1,430,108	805,702	368,565
1851	163	1,141,647	707,443	47,914
1852	163	883,267	504,864	14,911
1853	163	785,718	396,436	13,232

Source: Adapted from Nicholls, *A History of the Irish Poor Law,* 323, 395.
[a] Year ending December 31.
[b] Year ending September 29.

Figure 4.7. Starving peasants at a workhouse gate (*Illustrated London News,*
September 12, 1847)

go to the poorhouse," recalled Séamus O'Riordan (figure 4.7).[192] Numerous accounts point to the sheer wretchedness of Irish existence.
"They have already reached the lowest point in the descending scale,
and there is nothing beyond but starvation or beggary," wrote Trevelyan.[193] Two points are immediately striking about commentaries
concerning the workhouses, however. The first relates to the complex
intertwinings that bind pauperism and criminalisation; the second
point concerns the pattern of language used to portray workhouse
existence.

On May 3, 1849, Michael O'Shaughnessy, an assistant barrister
in County Mayo, was called before a Select Committee of the House of
Commons to present his opinion on the operation of the Irish Poor
Law. When asked if there were any circumstances that might illustrate
the "extreme distress of the people," O'Shaughnessy produced evidence from local court proceedings that showed paupers "desiring" a
conviction and using the penal system as an emergency form of fam -
ine relief:

Dominick Ginnelly was indicted for larceny of hempen ropes, and convicted. The police man who arrested him said, that the prisoner told him that he wanted to rob and get into gaol. He had been convicted twice before, and had been only just discharged from gaol. I asked him if he wanted to be transported, and he said "Yes;" he should do the same thing again if let go . . . John, Austin, and Charles Ruddy, three boys, whose ages were stated to be 8, 12 and 15 years, brothers, pleaded guilty of stealing sheep. Mr. Walsh, the police inspector, said they were starving, and would not have done it if they had not been starving. They were the children of the honestest [*sic*] people in Clare Island; they were imprisoned. Mr Walsh also stated that he took the census of that island from January 1847 to January 1849, which showed that there were 576 deaths out of a population of 1,700 . . . Michael Gavan pleaded guilty to sheep-stealing; he had been convicted before; he wished to be transported; he said he should do the same thing again if let out: he was transported . . . Martin McGunty, John McGreene, and John English were indicted for stealing a quantity of hemp, and were convicted; they were about 17 years of age; they requested to be transported, as they had no means of living . . . Michael Eady pleaded guilty to stealing a shawl; he had been convicted before, and had been only just out of gaol; he said he should do the same thing again, as he had no means of living, and wished to be transported . . . Owen Eady, his brother, pleaded guilty to stealing linen; he was about 18 years old, and wished to be transported; he said he should rob again if let out. I asked him if he knew what transportation was; he said he knew he would be kept at work for seven years, and that at the end he would have liberty in another country, which would be better than starving, and sleeping out at night; he was told he might have chains on his legs; "If I have," he said, "I will have something to eat:" he was transported for seven years . . .[194]

Similar incidents were noted across the country.[195] At an assize court in County Kerry, two men who were discharged due to insufficient evidence refused to leave custody. The judge observed that "*to them their acquittal was a punishment.*"[196] Travelling through Newcastle, in the county of Limerick, the American W. M. S. Balch noted "that during the recent quarter sessions, there were over 1,200 prisoners to be tried, and it occupied the court but three days to try them all. And why? Simply because they all plead guilty, in the hope of being detained in prison; and two who were discharged were the next day accused of riot in an attempt to break into gaol."[197] An official working for the Galway union reported that 92 paupers were caught begging, which they had done in the hope of being sent to prison.[198] Amongst the substantial Irish emigrant population in England, crime was often undertaken with the same intention. In 1847, 888 Irish were committed to Liverpool borough prison, an increase of nearly 125 percent of committals in 1846. "Previously to this," admitted one official, "there was very little crime among these poor people, not even in petty thefts; but it soon appeared that they preferred being sent to prison to being sent back to Ireland."[199] How are we to make sense of the peculiar fact that a prison sentence was eagerly sought by large numbers of Irish men and women?[200]

The political philosopher Hannah Arendt has written that "the best criterion by which to decide whether someone has been forced outside the pale of law is to ask if he would benefit by committing a crime."[201] Entry into the workhouse deprived an inmate of very basic rights, and even a "right to relief" was carefully evaded in the drafting of the Irish Poor Law. For the hundreds of thousands of Irish reclassified as "paupers," however, the jails held conceivable advantages: first, there was no arbitrary test of destitution; second, prisoners received equal if not better meals and shelter as a matter of course; and third, deportation to the colonies was the likely result of repeated offence.[202] Indeed, under exceptional circumstances being labelled a "criminal" actually meant recapturing certain rights that were otherwise denied to subaltern groups—after all, even the petty criminal could claim a right to ample sustenance independent of any "test of destitution."[203] Thus, what Amartya Sen terms "extra-entitlement transfers" (stealing, looting, brigandage, etc.) gave back to Irish paupers certain rights that had been gradually withdrawn by the state; in the harrowing testimony recalled above, the poor connived to break the law if only to be included under its protections.[204] This suggests that the Irish workhouses were not, in the final analysis, spaces of confinement but in fact *spaces of exception,* to use Agamben's terminology.[205]

Despite their panoptical nature, Irish workhouses maintained a highly ambiguous relationship with the law. Paupers could be punished for minor offences, including playing cards ("or other games of chance") and not properly cleaning themselves. Punishment for "disorderly" or "refractory" behaviour often involved being forced to go without rations, severe floggings, or solitary confinement in the "Black Hole." According to Gerard O'Brien, it was deemed far "more desirable to settle serious offences within the confines of the workhouse rather than in the courts."[206] This created ideal conditions for abuse, and complaints of excessive cruelty were not uncommon. O'Brien documents the death of a heavily pregnant "pauper" in the "Black Hole" who, contrary to regulations, had been locked in without bedding. The woman's death was accepted without official enquiry. The last words on the matter were that of the workhouse guardian who pithily claimed "the woman was a most infamous character" and that the child was in any case already dead.[207] In male-dominated workhouses women were particularly vulnerable (figure 4.8). Sexual assault was often excused as a momentary lapse in the master's code of conduct, "a breach in his position of trust rather than an act of criminal violence."[208] No doubt the increased bureaucratisation of relief helped convert poor law officials into what Scrope characterised as "passive instruments of law."[209] Insofar as workhouses managed human conduct, ill treatment itself became a symptom of mere "mismanagement." What Trevelyan called "the preservation of life" had become a matter of *bureaucratic discretion,* something with which rights apparently had very little to do.

This much is clear from contemporary accounts of the workhouses, which repeatedly stress the wanton neglect of those supposedly receiving relief. At a meeting of the Society of Friends, the situation under the Poor Law was summed up in the following words:

> The paupers are *merely kept alive,* either in the crowded workhouses, or in alarming numbers dependent on out-door relief. *But their health is not maintained. Their physical strength is weakened; their*

Figure 4.8. Woman begging at Clonakilty (*Illustrated London News,* February 13, 1847)

mental capacity is lowered; their moral character degraded. They are hopeless themselves, and they offer no hope to their country, except in the prospect, so abhorrent to humanity and Christian feeling, of their gradual extinction by DEATH![210]

Osborne penned the following description after visiting one of the "Leviathan workhouses" in Limerick:

I have no words with which I can give any real idea of the sad condition of the inmates of two large yards at the parent house, in which were a very large number of young female children; many of them were clothed in the merest dirty rags, and of these they wore a very scanty allowance; they were in dirt collected on their persons for many weeks; there was not about them the slightest evidence of any least care being taken of them; as they filed before me, two and two, they were a spectacle to fill any human heart with indignation: sore feet, sore hands, sore heads; ophthalmia [a famine-related disease that affects the victims' eyesight] evident in the case of the great portion of them; some of them were suffering from it in its very worst stage; they were evidently eat up [*sic*] with vermin—very many were mere skeletons: I know well what the appearance of a really famine-stricken child is; there were, it is true, some here who had brought their death-like appearance into the house with them; but the majority were as the type in which the word *neglect* was printed, in no mistakeable characters—the neglect of their latter state, not the consequence of their former state.[211]

After reciting a panoply of abuses—unchanged bed linen, lack of clothing, dangerous overcrowding, inadequate diets, physical punishments (including the use of hunting whips on paupers)—Osborne concluded that "no human ingenuity could contrive more powerful machinery to degrade human nature than that now contained." He described the Irish pauper class as "mere 'wrecks' of life," human beings at the very "last stage of existence." Like other eyewitnesses, Osborne resorted to zoomorphisms to convey the depth of human degradation: "Dogs would have had more attention paid to them," he declared. All around him he observed humans "living as beasts" and bodily frames that were now a "mere anatomy of a human being."[212] Osborne concludes in frightening language: "it is mere animal vegetation, it is not human life, in any common accepted sense of the term."[213] This condition is the same "barely protracted existence" that haunted Scrope and what Twisleton coldly referred to as "the minimum capable of sustaining life in health."[214] In each of these descriptions we are confronted with "neither an animal life nor a human life, but only a life that is separated and excluded from itself—only *bare life.*"[215]

SOVEREIGN REMEDIES

Reflecting on the government's relief efforts during the Irish Famine, Trevelyan declared: "The day has gone for letting things take their course."[216] This comment suggests that mass famine was no longer considered an inexorable "act of nature." On Trevelyan's watch famine emerged as an event that could be controlled and managed—in a word, governed—through appropriate scientific and economic principles. During the Irish Famine "things" did take their course—which is far from saying its development was inevitable. State and municipal power continually grappled with the exigencies of famine conditions, regulating and refashioning relief operations to meet the ideological currents of colonial improvement. The difficulties of superintending a "backward race" during an ecological crisis became a powerful reason to *expand* "the social laboratory," placing the Irish population at the centre of what Trevelyan characterised as "extensive experiments in the science, if it may be so called, of relieving the destitute."[217]

This "monster task" required a monster laboratory where the law and the state assumed control over the management of social life.[218] In other words, over the course of the Irish Famine the state had manoeuvred itself into a very powerful position vis-à-vis the famished. The famine relief programmes (the workhouses, soup kitchens, public works, and outdoor relief schemes) ultimately permitted institutions, laws, and disciplines to target the starving body. Through the strict regulation of diets, the "task labour" system, and the principle of "less eligibility," the state virtually monopolised the means of subsistence for vast numbers of people, thus producing—and assuming control over—a radically depotentiated form of life. In this way the machinery of relief became an important technology of biopower. The productive force of this biopolitical project also ought to be underlined. Famine relief mobilised a reterritorialising project that involved the shift from tillage to pastoral farming, the ejectment of Irish smallholders, the realignment of colonial class and property relations, as well as the reconstitution of Irish labour and diets. As instances of "outright interventionism," to use K. T. Hoppen's term, confiscatory policies like the Gregory Clause and the Encumbered Estates and Rate-in-Aid Acts prove the lie that it is "simply anachronistic" to believe the government could interfere with private markets.[219]

Above all, this chapter has traced what Slavoj Žižek calls the "constitutive limit" that marks the "ultimate traumatic point of biopolitics," where the regulation of life manages to combine administrative surveillance and moral certitude with an array of injunctions, prohibitions, and exceptions.[220] At this "constitutive limit" biopolitics becomes *necropolitics,* and a vast body of people appear, to all intents and purposes, perfectly superfluous.[221] In a colonial environment, the administration of famine involved authoritarian expressions of sovereignty, famously defined by Bataille as power wielded over life deemed "beyond utility."[222] For Agamben a "state of exception" is a precondition for such extraordinary violence. The Great Famine served as such an exception, the terminal point for what one English witness characterised as "a very ugly page in the history of the exercise of man's power, over those who are themselves powerless."[223]

CHAPTER FIVE

THE "*UNGOVERNED MILLIONS*"

Thomas Carlyle and the Irish Question

> *The destructive character knows only one watchword: make room; only one activity: clearing away . . . But what contributes most of all to this Apollonian image of the destroyer is the realization of how immensely the world is simplified when tested for its worthiness of destruction.*
>
> —Walter Benjamin, *Reflections*

> *All his [Carlyle] methods included a good deal of killing . . .*
> —Letter from Ralph Waldo Emerson to Lidian Emerson,
> March 23, 1848, *Letters of Ralph Waldo Emerson*

DEHUMANISED GEOGRAPHIES

In recent years much of the discussion on the Irish Famine has focused on the political motivations behind *present* reconstructions of the Irish past. Especially important are the revisionist and postrevisionist claims that have sparked so much debate in Irish Studies, much of it focusing on the Famine period; however, far less attention has been devoted to how the Famine was sanitised and naturalised as the event unfolded.[1] It is interesting, therefore, to think further about what it is that representations actually *do,* as well as what sorts of political roles representations are made to play.

The postcolonial scholar Achille Mbembe recently described a modern form of rationality that produces dehumanised subjects through its very terms of description.[2] Mbembe's argument might be usefully applied to specific administrative accounts of the Great Famine. Trevelyan's meticulous descriptions of the famine relief efforts, for instance, were meant to inspire thoughtless approval of the government's conduct and discourage any questioning of the the political and economic dominance these same structures imposed. Referring to Trevelyan's official narrative, Scrope charged that "a stranger to the real events . . . might read through the whole hundred pages without ever finding out that during the 'Irish Crisis' several hundred thousand souls perished in Ireland of want, through the inefficiency of those 'colossal' relief measures."[3] In a short footnote Trevelyan explained that his account does not extend beyond 1847: "progress of events after that date will form the subject of a separate article."[4] Thus, one of the greatest demographic tragedies in European history is scripted as a short-lived "crisis," while events after 1847—when excess mortality was highest—are consigned to a paratextual footnote promising a discussion never to be articulated. As Derek Gregory has said, narratives are almost always "double spaces of articulation . . . in which connections are elaborated in some registers even as they are disavowed in others."[5] In this sense, this small note at the foot of Trevelyan's account might be read as a vivid *mise-en-scène* of colonial relations. The capacity to make acts of violence invisible or remote is itself a powerful political tool. One faminescape can bury a thousand others.

A similar criticism might be levelled at George Nicholls's *History of the Irish Poor Law,* which nevertheless is far more comprehensive than Trevelyan's brief narrative. Given that the very institutions Nicholls helped establish turned into citadels of death and disease, it is unsurprising that he might want to minimise the extent of Irish suffering. Only toward the end of his long narrative, however, does Nicholls begin to focus specifically on the Famine period. When the issue of famine mortality can no longer be deferred, the author directs the reader to two tables (printed on the final page of his *History*) that summarise the numbers relieved in and out of the workhouse, the total relief expenditure, and the extent of mortality under these aid programmes (figure 5.1). Nicholls explains that these two tables are designed to

Numbers relieved in the workhouses in each of the weeks ending on the dates in the first column respectively; together with the number and the rate per 1,000 of the deaths.

Number of destitute persons relieved out of the workhouses under the 1st and 2nd sections of the Extension Act (10th and 11th Vict., cap. 31) respectively, in each of the weeks ending on the dates in the first column; together with the weekly cost of such relief.

Weeks ending	Total number in the workhouses	Deaths in the week	Rate per 1,000.
1846.			
4 April	50,861	159	3·0
4 July	50,693	146	2·9
7 Nov.	74,175	312	4·2
1847.			
2 Jan.	98,762	1,206	12·2
6 Mar.	115,645	2,590	22·0
3 July	101,439	1,239	12·2
4 Sept.	75,376	589	7·8
13 Nov.	102,776	523	5·1
1848.			
1 Jan.	117,568	1,362	11·6
12 Feb.	135,467	1,316	9·7
1 July	139,397	620	4·5
9 Sept.	107,320	350	3·3
2 Dec.	172,980	787	4·5
1849.			
13 Jan.	191,445	1,477	7·7
3 Mar.	196,523	1,846	9·4
5 May	220,401	2,730	12·4
16 June	227,329	2,009	8·8
6 Oct.	140,266	488	3·5
1 Dec.	180,641	471	2·7
1850.			
5 Jan.	203,320	792	3·9
2 Feb.	230,348	994	4·3
2 Mar.	237,939	1,150	4·8
4 May	243,224	1,247	5·1
22 June	264,048	1,126	4·3
3 Aug.	219,231	808	3·7
28 Sept.	155,173	526	3·4
7 Dec.	191,341	501	2·6
1851.			
4 Jan.	206,468	654	3·2
22 Feb.	251,836	1,201	4·8
22 Mar.	248,501	1,512	6·1
7 June	263,397	1,264	4·8
2 Aug.	222,038	789	3·6
27 Sept.	140,458	386	2·8
1852.			
3 Jan.	168,248	407	2·4
21 Feb.	196,966	594	3·0
5 June	187,003	541	2·9
18 Sept.	111,117	261	2·3
25 Dec.	134,476	281	2·1
1853.			
19 Feb.	160,774	627	3·9
30 July	113,099	272	2·4
1 Oct.	79,410	202	2·5

Weeks ending	Numbers relieved under Section 1 of Extension Act.	Numbers relieved under Section 2 of Extension Act.	Total.	Weekly cost of relief.
				£. s. d.
1848.				
5 Feb.	337,665	107,811	445,476	12,788 9 0
4 Mar.	425,949	228,763	654,712	17,564 18 2
1 April	408,923	235,076	643,999	17,092 6 6
6 May	485,364	266,430	751,794	18,786 18 5
1 July	490,902	342,987	833,889	21,800 14 10
2 Sept.	279,567	96,523	376,090	10,335 14 5
7 Oct.	192,401	7,202	199,603	5,925 4 2
2 Dec.	246,125	31,859	277,984	7,845 12 10
1849.				
6 Jan.	327,733	75,622	423,355	11,170 7 5
3 Mar.	422,693	170,012	592,705	15,051 14 3
2 June	402,184	239,229	642,413	19,263 7 1
7 July	492,503	291,864	784,367	21,757 8 3
1 Sept.	425,197	50,796	276,793	6,493 13 11
13 Oct.	114,316	1,647	115,963	2,653 7 2
3 Nov	102,247	13	102,260	2,336 11 11
1850.				
5 Jan.	104,305	345	104,650	2,159 0 3
23 Feb.	148,909	..	148,909	3,216 8 8
1 June	127,727	128	127,855	2,805 9 2
3 Aug	73,129	40	73,169	1,617 7 5
14 Sept.	3,794	..	3,794	96 14 2
19 Oct.	2,249	..	2,249	63 13 6
1851.				
4 Jan.	2,713	6	2,719	76 14 0
22 Feb.	9,103	20	9,123	229 4 6
3 May	11,145	7	11,153	268 17 9
5 July	19,454	28	19,482	486 4 11
4 Oct.	3,084	..	3,084	75 10 4
1852.				
3 Jan.	3,170	..	3,170	88 6 3
6 Mar.	3,396	..	3,396	100 0 10
3 July	3,579	..	3,579	102 19 0
9 Oct.	2,491	1	2,492	74 1 3
25 Dec.	2,998	..	2,998	87 12 10
1853.				
26 Feb.	4,152	..	4,152	116 16 10
30 July	3,092	..	3,092	96 5 2
8 Oct.	1,977	..	1,977	61 16 10

Figure 5.1. Nicholls's tables detailing Famine relief efforts (*A History of the Irish Poor Law,* 404)

condense "the character of the period—the waxing and waning of distress . . . so that the state of the country at several periods is as it were mapped out before the reader, and can be taken in at one glance, requiring nothing further in the way of explanation."[6] Nicholls's own book would scarcely be needed if we took what he said at face value. Nevertheless, these tabulations—abstract, clinical, and concise—remind us that a critical study of the Famine needs to consider not only the reasons for violence but also the violence of reason.

These sorts of considerations frame my discussion of Thomas Carlyle's visits to Ireland and his subsequent comments on these journeys. In 1846 and again in 1849 the Scottish-born historian and social critic travelled around famine-stricken Ireland. Both journeys are important because of the different faminescapes Carlyle bore witness to. More importantly, however, Carlyle engaged the Irish Question—placing himself *in* Ireland for this very purpose—because Irish conditions appeared to him to reflect a deeper crisis of authority between the liberal idea of freedom and what Carlyle saw as a moral injunction to govern weaker races.[7] Taking inspiration from recent theoretical approaches to what Stuart Elden calls "the politics of calculation," I want to place Carlyle's behaviour within a much broader debate on the geopolitics of travel.[8] To many of his contemporaries Carlyle appeared to be a vociferous defender of the rights of labour and one of the most gifted critics of free market fundamentalism.[9] The young Friedrich Engels (1820–95), for instance, was impressed with the political philosophy of the "Chelsea sage" (the famous "cash nexus" phrase that appears in the *Communist Manifesto* was appropriated from Carlyle), and many of the Young Irelanders—including the prominent Irish nationalist Charles Gavan Duffy (1816–1903), who provided help, advice, and companionship and who wrote his own account of their travels, offering a vivid counterpoint to Carlyle's perspective—considered Carlyle to be the true voice of revolution.[10] Yet when faced with Ireland, Carlyle shifted from being a severe critic of laissez-faireism to being a staunch defender of property. The problem of how to transform the cottier farmer into a self-motivated independent labourer was readily apprehended by Carlyle and forcefully filtered through his earlier concern with social order and modes of political governance.

The drive to establish capitalist modes of production brought into sharp relief the tensions between liberal ethics (proposing "social autonomy and self-sovereignty") and market values (requiring a rational and disciplined labour force).[11] For Carlyle the danger of embracing liberal reforms was manifest when dealing with subaltern populations such as the Irish, whom he judged to be slovenly and ill-equipped for self-improvement. To embrace the noninterventionism of economic liberalism was absurd, Carlyle reasoned, because social betterment *required* institutional arrangements capable of disciplining errant behaviour. To teach individuals the self-autonomy necessary for a commercialised society would require statecraft, political judgement, and institutional reform.

These tensions between politics and economics, between "directive government" and the free market, haunt Carlyle's discourse on Ireland as well as his related ruminations on the West Indies. His final solution to this conundrum was to combine the two, forming an *authoritarian mode of political economy*—what Morrow usefully calls a "moralized capitalism"—capable of responding to specific Irish conditions.[12] Although Carlyle prided himself on being the voice of reason as well as one of the few public intellectuals willing to challenge orthodox political thinking, his ideas on Ireland are simply a reworking of colonial opinion on how to force labour from reluctant bodies.[13] In fact, Carlyle's conclusions on the Irish Question can be read as an attempt to legitimise the disciplinary apparatus of the state as it faced an indigenous population seemingly unwilling to fulfil their end of the "capitalist symbolic contract."[14]

Defining the Irish Question

It has been said of the Irish Question that each time Britain moved to solve it the Irish changed the problem. Whatever the truth of this popular aphorism, it certainly captures the level of frustration felt on both sides of the Irish Sea. By the time Carlyle turned his attention to Ireland, it had become increasingly obvious that a political resolution was needed—and needed urgently. The swell in the rank and

confidence of the Young Irelanders at the expense of Daniel O'Connell's Repeal Association—and at a time when revolution seemed
rife in Europe—added a new set of anxieties to the British government's already long list of problems with rule in Ireland.[15] If Britain
could not safeguard its interests in Ireland, "her oldest possession,"
how could order be maintained in the rest of the empire?[16] The will
to solve the Irish Question was matched by an abiding passion to preserve the empire.

In an exceptional reading of Carlyle's literary career, Chris Vanden Bossche argues that Carlyle's growing interest in Irish affairs
should not be read alongside his long-standing interest in the nature
of political power. Carlyle's treatise on *The French Revolution* (1837)
and, even more significantly, his massive tome *Oliver Cromwell's Letters
and Speeches* (1845) were different attempts to come to terms with one
problem: what *form of authority* was needed to curb the widespread destruction of values and social cohesion that seemed to encompass the
new industrial order of the nineteenth-century.[17] In *The French Revolution* insurrection served to "recover rather than destroy authority,"
whereas in the *Letters and Speeches* Carlyle visualized the salvation of
England through the advent of an enlightened theocratic figurehead.[18]
Carlyle felt that both works were deeply misunderstood, however, and
his disappointment reached a new nadir when his attempts to mould
Robert Peel into a modern theocratic "prophet" were dashed when
Peel lost his ministry (Carlyle had sent Peel a copy of *Letters and Speeches*
stapled with practical advice and encouragement). In the light of Peel's
failure, Carlyle was forced to espouse the role of the righteous prophet
for himself.[19] These events crystallize in Carlyle's rhetorical shift from
a more "formal poetics of persuasion" to a language of "coercion and
attack."[20] It is from within this political and intellectual bandwidth that
Carlyle turned his attention to Ireland.

Perhaps as early as *Sartor Resartus* (1833–34), in which he depicted
the poor masses as Irish peasants, Carlyle had considered Ireland a
key to understanding the state of England, which he believed was on
the cusp of terminal decline. This theme was carried over into *Past and
Present* (1843), in which Carlyle depicted "the unforgettable story of
the Irishwoman":

A poor Irish widow, her husband having died in one of the Lanes of Edinburgh, went forth with her three children, bare of all resource, to solicit help from the charitable Establishments of that City. At this charitable establishment and then at that she was refused; referred from one to the other, helped by none;— till she had exhausted them all; till her strength and heart had failed her: she sank down in typhus fever; died, and infected her Lane with fever, so that seventeen other persons died of fever there in consequence. The humane Physician asks therefore, as with a heart too full for speaking, Would it not have been *economy* to help this poor Widow? She took typhus fever, and killed seventeen of you!—Very curious. The forlorn Irish Widow applies to her fellow creatures, as if saying "Behold I am sinking, bare of help; Ye must help me! I am your sister, bone of your bone; one God made us: ye must help me!" They answer, "No impossible; thou art no sister of ours." But she proves her sisterhood; her typhus fever kills *them:* they actually were her brothers though denying it! Had human creature ever to go lower for a proof?[21]

Such passages attained for Carlyle the status of a "champion of labour" and an honest voice on the evils of laissez-faireism. However, the new political economy—later to be derided as the "*dismal science*"—is never the sole target of Carlyle's allegory.[22] The fear of contagion and the suggestion that the Irish are a mortal threat to the life and security of Britain is a persistent theme in Carlyle's writing and a recurring feature in Victorian literature.[23] In *Latter-Day Pamphlets* (1850) Carlyle warns of the ruinous effects of the Irish on British metropolitan life: "The Irish Giant, named of Despair, [who] is advancing upon London itself, laying waste all English cities, towns and villages . . . I noticed him in Piccadilly . . . thatched in rags, a blue child on each arm; hunger-driven, wide eye-mouthed, seeking whom he may devour . . . prophecy of him there has long been; but now by the rot of the potato . . . he is here in person!"[24] The Irish, he subsequently recorded, "unfortunately speak a partially intelligible dialect of the English language, and having a white skin and European features, cannot be prevented from circulating among us at discretion, and to all manner and lengths."[25] Carlyle had not failed to notice that the Famine and mass emigration meant that contagion was no longer a metaphor of impending social collapse but rather physical evidence of the very crisis he had warned of since the publication of *Sartor Resartus*. Indeed, between the publication of *Sartor* and *Pamphlets*, Carlyle had travelled to Ireland twice to examine the scenes of disease and starvation that were then being reported with astonishing regularity. These experiences profoundly shaped his ideas about the problems of free labour, the nature of political government, and the place of Ireland within the empire at large.

MEETING YOUNG IRELAND

In April 1845 Frederick Lucas (then editor of the *Tablet*) introduced Carlyle to three young Irish law students and enthusiastic Irish nationalists. Charles Gavan Duffy, one of the three youths, forged an immediate and, for the most part, cordial relationship with Carlyle and his wife Jane that spanned a lifetime.[26] Carlyle described his first impressions of these Young Irelanders to his mother:

> On Saturday Night I had three redhot Irish Repealers here; one of them Duffy, a fellow Prisoner of O'Connell—a really interesting young man. Full of zeal, of talent and affection; almost *weeping* as he spoke of his country,—and taking *this* plan for relief of it, poor fellow! They are all sworn disciples of *mine* they say; which astonished me beyond measure. They came to complain of my unfairness to Ireland; I had called them all "liars and thieves," which was hard talking!—I liked this poor Duffy very much. They are all ready for "insurrection," for "death" &c&c I strongly advised them to make a general insurrection *against the Devil* first of all, and see what came of that!"[27]

Carlyle was sufficiently charmed to send Duffy a brief letter in early September 1846 stating that he would be en route to Ireland forthwith and politely requesting an "intelligent monitor" to instruct him on what to observe. Duffy duly obliged and ensured that Carlyle met with "most of the writers and orators on whom their contemporaries bestowed the soubriquet of Young Ireland."[28] Arriving in Belfast, Carlyle made haste southward to join Duffy and John Mitchel (who also, incidentally, revered Carlyle), noticing in passing the "poisoned air" and "fateful smell" of rotting potatoes that came to mark the familiar dearth of famine.[29] His letters during this time demonstrate a budding abhorrence for pretence and "Irish balderdash," which was to incense him upon his second tour.[30] He considered Daniel O'Connell, whom he heard orate at Conciliation Hall, to be the "the Prince of Humbugs," a "chief quack," and a hideous incarnation of Irish "bulls" and platitudes.[31] Otherwise Carlyle appeared to enjoy his visit and spoke very highly of both Duffy and Mitchel.

On the face of it, Carlyle's brisk visit—lasting a mere four days—seems ad hoc, even capricious.[32] This stay was, nevertheless, instrumental in nurturing his interest in the condition of Ireland and its people. In a letter written to the American poet and essayist Ralph Emerson (1803–82), some months after his return, Carlyle elaborated on the significance of his voyage:

> I saw Ireland too on my return; saw the black potatoe-fields, a ragged noisy population, that has long in a headlong baleful manner followed the *Devil's* leading, listening namely to blustering shallow-violent Imposters and children of darkness, saying, "Yes, we know *you,* you are Children of Light!"—and so has fallen all out of elbows in body and soul; and now having lost its *potatoes* is come as it were to a crisis; all its windy nonsense cracking suddenly to pieces under its feet: a very pregnant crisis indeed! A country cast suddenly into the melting pot,—say into the Medea's-Cauldron; to be boiled into horrid *dissolution;* whether into new *youth,* into sound healthy life, or into eternal death and annihilation, one does not yet know![33]

Evidently the Irish Question revived a similar crisis of authority that freighted Carlyle's earlier work on Cromwell and the French Revolution.[34] In a letter to Duffy, Carlyle admitted that "[t]he aspect of Ireland is beyond words at present. The most thoughtless here is struck into momentary *silence* in looking at it; the wisest among us cannot guess what the end of these things is to be."[35] More importantly, however, these letters are the first rumblings of Carlyle's resolve to arrange human beings into groups and subgroups ("ragged noisy population" and "blustering shallow-violent Imposters"), the function of which is to allow judgements on what forms of life deserve "eternal death and annihilation."

After his brief excursion, and in the wake of the European revolutions and an unspectacular uprising in Ireland, Carlyle quickly set to writing up his impressions.[36] In April and May of 1848 he produced a series of articles that appalled many of his Irish acquaintances and prompted Henry M'Cormac, a philologist and physician from Belfast, to write a sharp letter in response.[37] In these essays Carlyle asserts that repeal of the union between England and Ireland would be yet another instance of the British government shirking its "divine" responsibility to govern. Continuing the theme of his earlier writings, these works conveyed a deep apprehension regarding the thousands of starving Irish now arriving in Britain. In his reply to M'Cormac, Carlyle appealed to what he considered to be a mutual problem: "We are getting into fearful conditions on this side of the water, too, if nothing be done. The streets of London itself are getting studded with Irish beggars more thickly every day, presenting the 'Irish Problem,' which no legislator will take up to the British community at large with intimation that they must either solve it or sink along with it to worse than death."[38] Later Duffy recalled Carlyle arguing more stringently: "Carlyle said, if there was dislike [for the Irish], it arose from the way Irish men conducted themselves in England. They often entitled themselves to disfavour by their private performances. Irishmen who knew better must teach these persons to live quite differently, and they ought not to feel the slightest necessity for championing blackguards because they happened to be Irishmen." Duffy was quick to admonish, reminding Carlyle that he had only ever observed a population "resembling a famished crew just escaped from a shipwreck."[39]

Perhaps Duffy was also aware that Carlyle's recourse to metaphors of dirt, disease, and contagion drew on a long tradition of colonial thought that depicted Ireland as a diseased society bringing ruin in its wake. In *A View of the State of Ireland,* for example, Edmund Spenser spoke of a "secret scourge which shall by her come unto England," while the character Eudox declares, "For were it not the part of a desperate phisitian to wish his diseased patient dead, rather then to apply the best indevour of his skill for his recovery?"[40] In *Chartism* Carlyle made full use of this trope: "Such a people circulates not order but disorder, through every vein of it;—and the cure, if it is to be a cure, must begin at the heart; not in his condition only but in himself must the Patient be all changed."[41] To prevent Ireland's disease from becoming England's debility, radical therapy was needed.[42]

"Eternity's Commissioner"

Carlyle's hopes for a new social order were set back with the news that the 1848 revolutions in Europe had failed. In Paris a new government was reinstated after the dethronement of Louis Philippe, while in Britain the crisis had not even been sufficient to unseat Lord Russell let alone provide an opening for Peel. Across the channel, the Young Irelanders were suppressed and Carlyle's new confidant, Duffy, was imprisoned. To add to matters the potato blight, which had been absent in 1847, reappeared and famine stalked the land with renewed vigour. Undeterred, Carlyle decided that his ideas "might perhaps get nearer to some way of utterance if [he] were looking face to face upon the ruin and wretchedness that [is] prevalent" in Ireland.[43] For some time he had thought about writing a book on the condition of Ireland: "Alas! a *book* is sticking in my Heart, which cannot get itself written at all; and till that be written there is no hope for peace or benefit for me anywhere."[44] He wrote the following in his journal on May 17, 1849:

> Am thinking of a tour of Ireland: unhappily have no call of desire that way, or any way, but am driven out somewhither (just now) as by the point of bayonets on my back. Ireland really *is* my problem; the breaking point of the huge suppuration which all British and European society now is. Set down in Ireland, one might at least feel, "*Here* is thy problem: In God's name what wilt thou do with it?"[45]

Initially the Irish Question did not seem too perplexing to the Scotsman. "Ireland is, this long while past, pretty satisfactorily intelligible to me," he professed to Duffy; "no phenomenon that comes across from it requiring too much explanation; but it seems worth while to *look* a little at the unutterable *Curtius Gulf* of British, and indeed European, things, which has visible broken there: in that respect, if not in another, Ireland seems to me the noblest of all spots in the world at present."[46] For Carlyle the starving Irish embodied a more general social malaise that had to be addressed.

After a protracted flurry of dispatches, careful revision, and preparatory reading, Carlyle began to define his second tour in Ireland (see figure 5.2).[47] His correspondence with Duffy, who acted as his personal tour guide for most of the journey, suggests his growing eagerness to begin his expedition. "Day after day," he wrote, "the project is assuming a more practical form. Probably something really *may* come of it."[48] Carlyle had already decided to visit the "famished Unions" of Glendalough, Ferns, Enniscorthy, Doneraile, and Wexford, and he later added Dublin, Kildare, Maynooth, and the "famine districts" to his must-see list.[49] He was keen to assure Duffy of his necessary inclusion: "I mean that *you* shall initiate me into the methods of Irish travel, and keep me company so far as our routes, once fixed upon will go together. Your friendly cheerfulness, your knowledge of Ireland, all your goodness to me, I must make available. Define to yourself what it is you specially aim towards in travelling, that I may see how far without straining I can draw upon you."[50] Carlyle was right to anticipate a degree of "straining" with Duffy, who was an equally determined, confident, and articulate character but did not share Carlyle's politics.[51]

Carlyle set sail for Dublin Bay on the last day of June 1849. Never a content traveller ("Travelling suits me very ill, only the fruit of travelling is of some worth to me. Heaven, I think, among other things, will be a place where one has leave to sit still"), he was deeply unsuited for the physical nature of the journey.[52] His well-known bouts of dyspepsia exacerbated the situation and often led to fickle and sharp mood swings.[53] He described himself as setting out from Scotland in "sad health and sad humour," a condition that moved Duffy to absolve Carlyle of the harsh conclusions contained in his memoirs.

Figure 5.2. Thomas Carlyle's second tour of Ireland, 1849

A few words are needed on the style, format, and context surrounding the publication of the travelogue. Carlyle did not begin to write *Reminiscences of My Irish Journey in 1849* until he had returned safely to his Chelsea home. His early hopes for an extensive treatise on the condition of Ireland were soon dashed. Instead, aided only by hastily scribbled notes, a trove of correspondence, and the selective art of memory, Carlyle laboured hard between October 4 and 16 to bring to life the "ugly spectacle" he had encountered on his voyage.[54] Carlyle countenanced this erratic method of work early in his tour. In a letter to his wife Jane dated July 8, Carlyle instructed her to forward the letter to his brother Jack: "[y]es send it;—only bid Jack send it back to you, that it be not lost; for I cannot get the smallest leisure to jot a word on paper; and if this go on, all memorials of me on this expedit*n* [*sic*] may be useful one day."[55] The letters were to be preserved and organised for his return. To this suggestion Jane laconically remarked, "Mr Carlyle . . . is making *me* his human *note-book* for the moment."[56]

The circumstances surrounding the manuscript's eventual publication are complicated. At some point Carlyle seems to have given the manuscript to Joseph Neumberg (a friend whom Duffy describes as Carlyle's "amanuensis"), who gave it to Thomas Ballantyne, who later sold it to an unidentified Mr. Anderson, from whom it eventually came to the publishers Sampson Low and Company.[57] Carlyle died in 1881, and his memoir was published posthumously the following year. Duffy was adamant that Carlyle would never have sanctioned its publication without serious revision, and therefore it should have been suppressed.[58] Whatever Duffy's reservations about publication (guided, to be sure, by his fear for the posthumous reputation of his friend), it appears that the text was released as an anticipated "boost" for Gladstone's 1881 Irish Coercion Bill, a story that certainly prolongs the geopolitical significance of the manuscript.[59]

The textual pattern of the document—particularly Carlyle's habit of excessive emphasis and exaggeration of speech, his highly idiosyncratic use of style (italics and capitalisation, in particular) and frequent punctuation (commas, hyphens, and semicolons), his trenchant moralising and inappropriate humour—seems to incorporate the fitful physical nature of the expedition. Carlyle regularly complained of insomnia, the failure to procure "good food," fervent arguments with Duffy, and his own inability to articulate the "wretchedness" of Irish life. Above all the document literally enacts the burden of a man who has recognised the stakes in the task he has assigned himself. Before he left for Ireland, Carlyle wrote to Duffy: "In short, why shouldn't I go and look at Ireland, and be my own (*Eternity's*) commissioner there?"[60] In a conflation that stands in line with his earlier writings (in

particular his failed solicitation of Peel and his earlier faith in theocratic government), Carlyle identifies himself with state power, which
was then in the throes of managing conditions of starvation, endemic
disease, and mass emigration. Life and death were issues Carlyle condemned himself to decide.

GOVERNING STARVATION

Ireland's fortunes had changed for the worse since Carlyle's first
visit. The potato crop failed in 1846 and recovered in 1847, only to fail
again in 1848 and 1849. Like most travellers, Carlyle arrived in Ireland
during the summer months, which were the traditional season of distress. With the failure of the potato the scenes must have been awful
in the extreme. Two days before Carlyle arrival in Ireland, the government was administering outdoor relief to 784,367 destitute persons.[61]
The policy overhaul under the new Whig administration meant that
the greater cost of famine relief would henceforth be met by local
taxation. Both sides spoke of unsurpassed treachery. To Irish nationalists the call for "Irish property to support Irish poverty" nullified
the Act of Union and made the depopulation of rural Ireland a *fait
accompli*. On the other hand, the bungled Irish uprising in 1848 and
the continued evacuation of a diseased and starving population made
it relatively easy for the British press to depict the Irish as inherently
treacherous, improvident, and ungrateful (see figures 5.3, 5.4, and
5.5).[62] If "'do unto others as you would they do unto you,' was forgotten on one side," remarked one Irish landlord, "we cannot wonder that 'Love your neighbour as yourself,' was not remembered on
the other."[63]

Addressing the House of Commons on March 5, 1849, the ousted
leader Robert Peel gave voice to the popular view that Ireland's food
problem was really a labour problem: "The true lesson to teach a man
who is able to work, and particularly an Irish man who is able to work,"
declared Peel, "is that it is much better for him to rely upon his own
exertions for his support, than to be dependent upon charity for the
means of subsistence."[64] Carlyle had already begun to formulate his
own version of this doctrine:

Figure 5.3. The Irish "Old Man of the Mountain" and his £50,000 of relief
(*Punch,* February 24, 1849)

Evidently there is nothing wanted but a just and good discern-
ment as to this; for if the land and the people *could* be brought
into true relation to one another, it seems admitted that there are
ample resources then for them all; that there need not be, at this
hour, one idle man in Ireland who could not handle his spade or
hoe, and was willing to work. It is a tremendous reflexion that

Figure 5.4. The impudent Irishman asks John Bull for a "thrifle" to buy a blunderbuss; note the simianised features (*Punch,* December 19, 1846)

this should be the horrible fact, and that the actual one is what we see![65]

Carlyle's long-standing belief in salvation through earnest labour was now wedded to the conviction that the Irish were incapable of securing the natural advantages of the soil.[66] Carlyle's "true relation" between nature (represented under the sign of "ample resources") and culture (represented under the sign of honest labour) was firmly entrenched in a colonial discourse that symbolically conflated a wild nature with an untamed people (early modern terms such as "bog-Irish"

MR. BARNEY FINNIGAN AND FAMILY AS THEY LANDED IN LIVERPOOL, MARCH 30TH, 1847.

MR. BARNEY FINNIGAN AND FAMILY AS THEY DEPARTED FOR IRELAND, AT THE EXPENSE OF THE AUTHORITIES.

Figure 5.5. Sketch of a famished family landing in Liverpool and later departing for Ireland looking considerably plumper having been maintained "at the expense of the authorities" (*Liverpool Lion,* July 1847)

and "wood-kerne" are classic examples).[67] From the upper deck of his ship en route to Dublin Bay, Carlyle was still unusually optimistic, noting that "if the Irish faculty be good, you *can* breed it, put it among conditions which *are* fair or at least fairer."[68] By the end of his travels, however, Carlyle was convinced that the Irish were *unwilling* to work and only compulsion would free them from their lethargy and establish a "true relation" between land and labour.[69] Like Peel, Carlyle feared that government relief encouraged habits of lassitude by artificially shielding the population from the worst effects of extreme want. The Irish Question thus becomes a question about racial improvement that gets worked out during his second tour of Ireland.

Once in Dublin Carlyle quickly sought Duffy's assistance and together they travelled throughout July and August, almost always *tête-à-tête,* according to Duffy's testimony.[70] In Kilkenny Carlyle was afforded his first opportunity to examine the workhouses—those vast "citadels of mendicancy"—which he had so eagerly anticipated:

> Workhouse; huge chaos, *ordered* "as one could;" . . . Huge arrangements for eating, baking, stacks of Indian meal stirabout; 1000 or 2000 great hulks of men lying piled up within brick walls, in such a country, in such a day! Did a *greater* violence to the law of nature ever before present itself to sight, if one *had* an eye to *see* it? Schools, for the girls, rather goodish; for the boys, clearly bad; forward, impudent *routine*—scholar, one boy, with strong Irish physiognomy,—getting bred to be an impudent superficial pretender. So; or else sit altogether stagnant, and so far as you can, *rot*. Hospital: haggard ghastliness of some looks,—literally, their eyes grown "colorless" (as Mahomet describes the horror of the Day of Judgement); "take me home!" one half-mad was urging; a deaf-man; ghastly *flattery* of us by another, (*his* were the eyes): ah me! boys drilling, men still piled within their walls: no hope but of stirabout; swine's meat, swine's *destiny* (I gradually saw): right glad to get *away*.[71]

Later in their tour they visited Westport workhouse (located in an area more severely affected by famine), where Carlyle provides another extended commentary (figure 5.6):

> Human swinery has here reached its *acme,* happily: 30,000 paupers in this union, population supposed to be 60,000. Workhouse proper (I suppose) cannot hold more than 3 or 4,000 of them, subsidiary workhouses, and outdoor relief the others. Abomination of desolation; what *can* you make of it! Outdoor quasi-*work:* 3 or 400 big hulks of fellows tumbling about with shares, picks and barrows, "levelling" the end of their workhouse hill; at first glance you would think them all working; look nearer, in each shovel there is some ounce or two of mould, and

Figure 5.6. The workhouse at Clifden, Galway, which Carlyle visited in late July 1849 (*Illustrated London News,* January 5, 1850)

> it is all make-believe; 5 or 600 boys and lads, pretending to break stones. Can it be charity to keep men alive on these terms? In face of all the twaddle of the earth, shoot a man rather than train him (with heavy expense to his neighbours) to be a deceptive human *swine.*[72]

Duffy recalled Carlyle's fierce indignation. The latter could not fathom "a *greater* violence to the law of nature" than a workhouse where no one seemed to work. Duffy countered that Carlyle's recriminations betrayed a serious misunderstanding of the social and economic position of Ireland at this time.[73] In the first place, those "big hulks of fellows" were generally humiliated by the menial tasks they were forced to perform in order to stay alive, and there were plausible reasons besides laziness to explain why the Irish poor took to the workhouses, including the closing of the soup kitchens and the substantial ejectments that followed the imposition of the Gregory Clause. Carlyle ignored or dismissed this sort of social analysis—a practice that tested Duffy's patience though never his loyalty—and he remained convinced that the Irish character thwarted all attempts toward improvement.

As they appprached Lord Kenmare's estate in Kerry, Duffy invited Carlyle to take leave of their car and enter some hovels:

> Bare, *blue,* bog without limit, ragged people in small force working languidly at their scantlings or peats, no other work at all; look hungry in their rags; hopeless, air as of creatures sunk beyond hope, look into one of their huts under pretence of asking for draught of water; dark, narrow, *two* women nursing, other young woman on foot as if for work; but it is narrow dark, as if the people and their life were covered under the tub, or "tied in a sack"; all things smeared over too with liquid *green;*—the cow (I find) has her habitation here withal. No water; the poor young woman produces butter-milk; in real pity I give her a shilling. Duffy had done the like in the adjoining cottage, ditto, ditto in Charcuter, with the addition that a man lay in fever there. These were the wretchedest population I saw in Ireland. "Live, sir? The Lord knows; what we can beg, and rob," (rob means scrape up; I suppose?): Lord Kinmare's [*sic*] people, he never looks after them, leases worthless bog, and I know not what. Bog all reclaimable, lime everywhere in it: swift exit to Lord Kinmare and the leases, or whatever the accursed *incubus* is![74]

Although the sight of the hovels visibly moved Carlyle, his harsh solution involved "laying a hearty horsewhip over that back of your's [the Irish]."[75] Carlyle's fondness for equine metaphors dates back to the 1830s. In *Sartor Resartus* Teufelsdröckh is described as a "colt" that has broken off the "neck-halter," and in *The French Revolution* the people are described as "gin-horses" who rear up when threatened with the "whip."[76] In Ireland this metaphor found full service. After visiting another residence in Kerry, Carlyle informed Duffy that he often felt how alike the Irish were to his horse "Larry" that he kept at Craigenputtock in Scotland. Larry, too, he opined, routinely was insubordinate but was on the whole "generous, kindly, and affectionate." Carlyle was insisting that the Irish required firm masters. Duffy

was having none of it, and quickly retorted that like Larry an Irishman knew "when he was well treated, and had a decided objection to
the perpetual whip and the spur."[77]

For Carlyle the Irish were slaves of indolence rather than, as
Duffy insisted, "serfs of a Parliament."[78] In December 1849—five
months after his second visit—Carlyle sent Duffy an essay entitled
"Trees of Liberty," which we may take as an accurate sample of his
philosophy at this time.[79] With much satire, Carlyle beseeched all pa-
triotic persons to plant one tree in the hope that Ireland would again
be replete in woodland and industry. Thus, "each man's tree of industry will be, of a surety, *his* tree of liberty."[80] It would have been clear to
many contemporaries that Carlyle was deliberately inverting an age-
old association between nature and freedom:

> What is that in your hand? It is a branch.
> Of what? Of the Tree of Liberty.
> Where did it first grow? In America.
> Where does it bloom? In France.
> Where did its seeds fall? In Ireland.[81]

This sort of windy rhetoric ("terrible solecisms") was, according to
Carlyle, a blatant contravention of "the everlasting Acts of Heaven's
Parliament!" that had decreed that some men be master of others.[82]
Again Duffy pointed out that Carlyle's position betrayed his poor
acquaintance with Irish affairs. It was hopeless, Duffy said, to refor-
est a country where, if a tenant planted a sapling and tended it to
maturity, the law declared it to be the property of the landlord. Carlyle remained unmoved. During his visit to Donegal, Carlyle told
the renowned landlord Lord George Hill there was "No hope for
the men as *masters;* their one *true* station in the universe is *servants,*
'slaves' if you will; and never can they know a right day till they attain that."[83]

After visiting Killaloe in County Clare, Carlyle wrote, "everywhere in Ireland one finds that the 'Government,' far from stinginess
in public money towards Ireland, has erred rather on the other side;
making, in all seasons, extensive *hives* for which the *bees* are not yet
found."[84] For Carlyle the problem was one of genes, not geography:

Ireland for the present is not to be accounted a pleasant land-scape. Vigorous corn, but thistles and docks equally vigorous; ulcers of reclaimable bog-land lying black, miry and abominable at intervals of a few miles: no tree shading you, nor fence that avails to turn cattle—most fences merely, as it were, soliciting the cattle to be so good as to come through—by no means a beau-tiful country just now! . . . Alas, it carries on it, as the surface of this earth ever does ineffaceably legible, the physiognomy of the people that have inhabited it: a people of holed breeches, dirty faces, ill-roofed huts—people of impetuosity and of levity—of vehemence, impatience, imperfect, fitful industry, imperfect fitful *veracity*. Oh, Heaven! there lies the woe of woes, which is the root of all.[85]

These sorts of comments were common to other racialised accounts of Irish conditions, such as that from Thomas Campbell Foster—the "*Times* Commissioner": "I have been over every part of Great Britain . . . I have traversed the 'Land's end,' in Cornwall, to 'John-o'-Groat's,' in Caithness; but in no part of it have I seen the natural capa-bilities surpass those of Ireland, and in no part of it have I seen those natural capabilities more neglected, less cultivated, more wasted, than in Ireland."[86] Like Carlyle, Foster concluded that "the people must be taught, and led and encouraged—nay, forced on to do that which will benefit themselves."[87] Carlyle also concluded that methods of com-pulsion were necessary:

There can *nothing* be done, then, for the poor Irish people at present? Nothing by express enactment or arrangement; but they must follow the *dumb* law of their positions and sink, sink, till they do come upon a rock? I rather judge so . . . Well, there is no help; we must all get down to the *rocks;* we are in a place equivalent to *Hell* . . . Five-and-thirty years of parliamentary stump oratory, all ending in less than nothing; now let us try drill-sergeantry a little even under these sad terms![88]

The contrast Carlyle draws between "stump oratory" and "*dumb* law" is suggestive in light of the fact that he failed to produce the extensive book on Ireland he had planned. Indeed, by his own admission he concluded his journey "farther from speech on any subject than ever."[89] Carlyle did, however, develop his racial opinions in a series of pamphlet publications. "The Negro Question" and *Latter-Day Pamphlets* draw upon Carlyle's experiences in Ireland and his renewed faith in the necessity of slavery.[90] Many of Carlyle's close friends (including Mill, Emerson, and Mazzini) were horrified by the tone and sentiment of his arguments in these commentaries.[91] Carlyle was unapologetic, and in typical fashion he responded by republishing "The Negro Question" under the revised and purposefully more provocative title, "The Nigger Question." The tenor of the arguments to be presented in the pamphlets was discernible in his letters to Emerson after returning home from Ireland:

> What is to be done? Asks everyone; incapable of *hearing* an answer, were there even one ready for imparting to him. "*Blacklead* those two million idle beggars," I sometimes advised, "and sell them to Brazil as Niggers,—perhaps parliament, on constraint, will allow you to advance them as Niggers!"—In fact the Emancipation Societies should send over a deputation or two to look at *these* immortal Irish "Free men," the *ne-plus-ultrà* of their class: it would perhaps moderate the windpipe of much eloquence one hears on that subject! Is not the most illustrious of all "ages"; making progress of the species at a grand rate indeed?[92]

Talk of freedom and "philanthropic liberalism" was inexcusable because it promoted sympathy ("rosepink sentimentalism"), the very qualities that had allowed places like the West Indies to drift "free" into barbarism: "really is there any such *totally* accursed *sin* as that (with no redeeming side *at all*): or even such general, nay universal one, in this illustrious thrice-hopeful epoch of Free Press, Emancipation, Toleration, Uncle Tom's cabin, and the rest of it?"[93] The "Divine Drill-Sergeant" and "steel whips" could only "teach poor canting slaves to *do* a little of the things they eloquently say (and even *know*) everywhere, and leave *un*done."[94] In "The Nigger Question" Carlyle returns to the trope of "wasteland," invoking the image of a freed slave lounging with "rum bottle in his hand, no breeches on his body, pumpkin at discretion, and the fruitfullest region of the earth going back to jungle around him." If the government intends "to retain human colonies, and not Black Irelands," Carlyle warned, they must be willing to "induce" slaves to work. "[B]ut if your nigger will not be induced? In that case, it is full certain, he must be compelled."[95] Like the emancipated slaves in the West Indies, the Irish would need to be reconditioned into an ordered and modern labour force.[96]

In this context it is interesting to speculate a bit more on the cause of Carlyle's "silence" on Ireland. Undoubtedly, the old problems of political economy—the *"dismal science"* of supply and demand that "reduces the duties of human governors to that of letting men alone"—continued to frustrate Carlyle.[97] "Talk again *England versus Ireland,*" wrote Carlyle after another "vinaigrous" argument with Duffy, "a sad unreasonable humour pervading all the Irish population on this matter—'England does not hate you at all, nor love you at all; merely values and will pay you according to the work you can do!'"[98] In the same way that Malthus viewed hunger as a check on improvidence, Carlyle increasingly saw the free market as a means to discipline the intractable for the rigours of honest labour. "[L]et the disconsolate Malthusian fling his 'geometric series' into the corner," he later professed, "[and] assist wisely in the 'free trade movement;' and dry up his tears." Whereas *political liberalism* stood for "rosepink sentimentalism," *economic liberalism* could force social order by threatening the ruination of those who defied market logics. As a substitute for slavery that would "save the precious thing in it," Carlyle came to see laissez-faire as a way of rendering governable the *"un*governed millions," overcoming Irish inertia, and extending the blessings of civilisation to those who seemed most impervious to change.[99] By this reading Carlyle, the former "champion of labour," had in fact worded himself into a corner.

This development should not be too surprising.[100] As early as *Chartism*—and thus before his visits to Ireland—Carlyle had argued that "A people [the Irish] that knows not to speak the truth, and to act the truth, such people has departed from even the possibility of well-being. Such people works no longer on Nature and Reality; works now on Phantasm, Simulation, Nonentity; the result it arrives at is naturally not a thing but no-thing,—defect even of potatoes."[101] Here

the famished Irish body—a "nonentity," "not a thing but no-thing"—
is discursively stripped down to "bare life." For Agamben "bare life"
marks the site of an "incessant decision on value and non-value"—
and it is exactly these kinds of distinctions that Carlyle drew on in
his tours of Ireland and in his subsequent writings.[102] This debate on
human worth marks Carlyle's passage into the domain of biopower
and capitalist political economy, two of the more powerful forces directing the course of the Irish Famine.[103] Clearly, this is also the domain of geopolitics, and for this reason Melissa Fegan is surely correct in maintaining that certain travel writings are in fact "the literary
equivalent of an estate clearance."[104]

THE LANGUAGE OF LEGITIMATION

In her treatise *On Violence* Hannah Arendt warned of the immense dangers of talking in nonpolitical, organic terms. These dangers are particularly great, she says, when racial issues are invoked: "So long as
we talk in non-political, biological terms, the glorifiers of violence can
appeal to the undeniable fact that . . . destruction and creation are but
two sides of the natural process, so that collective, violent action . . .
may appear as natural a prerequisite for the collective life of mankind
as the struggle for survival and violent death for continuing life in the
animal kingdom."[105] "Racism," she concludes, "is fraught with violence
by definition because it objects to natural organic facts—a white or
black skin—which no persuasion or power could change; all one can
do, when the chips are down, is to exterminate their bearers."[106] In
Carlyle's thinking the notion of the diseased body, a "sick society,"
and the concept of social regeneration are all powerfully present—as
is the promotion of violent political action. "The time has come," he
declared, "when the Irish population must either be improved a little,
or else exterminated . . . In a state of perennial ultra-savage famine, in
the midst of civilization, they cannot continue."[107] The literal force of
this argument may help explain why his writings invariably took the
form of preaching rather than presentation. In fact, his discursive
strategy corresponds exactly to David Scott's model of "colonial governmentality," whereby reason is given an explicitly "prescriptive and

programmatic mission" that entails "striking uncompromisingly at the presumed foundation of [human] error."[108]

Driven by the imperatives of social regeneration, Carlyle is asserting what sort of place Ireland *ought* to become and how Irish men and women *ought* to behave. We have moved from description to normative concerns, and to this end Carlyle's ideas find their most explicit appeal and expression in the delegation of state power focused on reforming subjectivities and reterritorialising social space.[109] Carlyle's language stifles the economic and sociopolitical context of Irish suffering by paring it back to functional, limiting categories, such as "deserving life," on which judgments are made. It was on exactly these points that Duffy and Carlyle argued so vociferously. By Carlyle's logic, sacrifices are necessary because what are destroyed are not human beings but human encumbrances that no longer retain any economic value. Carlyle was developing the political syntax for what Fiona Mackenzie calls "the language of legitimation."[110]

In *Chartism* Carlyle spoke of "extermination" *or* "improvement," but by the end of his tour in Ireland he saw both positions as virtually indistinguishable. Perhaps in some sense this also contributed to Carlyle's "silence." After discovering that the Irish should be "let die" in order to commence the regeneration of Irish society, what else was there to say? After all, as Cormac Ó Gráda has astutely noted, "the rhetoric of fatalism is silence."[111] Although Carlyle can hardly be considered a "typical" traveller to Ireland in the mid-nineteenth century, his way of thinking does express a more general and advanced mode of racialising the Irish Question.[112] One sees these calculations in the "*Times* Commissioner's" reports, which were available to a large audience as the Famine unfolded. The author endorses the same biological metaphors, the same preaching tone, and above all an identical faith in the logic of violence when dealing with the Irish. "For the greater part of the severity of this unhappy calamity," he professed, "*the people of Ireland have themselves to blame,* and their own disgraceful apathy and laziness. But the Government *ought to know* this is their character, and ought to have taken measures to *drive them on,* if they were too lazy and apathetic to follow when led."[113] In designating himself "(*Eternity's*) commissioner," Carlyle was merely taking this logic to its rational limit.

CHAPTER SIX

THE ANGEL OF PROGRESS

Visionary Geographies and Disaster Triage

This is how one pictures the angel of history. His face is turned toward the past. Where we perceive a chain of events, he sees one single catastrophe which keeps piling wreckage upon wreckage and hurls it in front of his feet. The angel would like to stay, awaken the dead, and make whole what has been smashed. But a storm is blowing from Paradise; it has got caught in his wings with such violence that the angel can no longer close them. This storm irresistibly propels him into the future to which his back is turned, while the pile of debris before him grows skyward. This storm is what we call progress.

—Walter Benjamin, *Illuminations*

Society is not founded or reconstructed without agonies and throes proportioned to the work to be done. But whatever the future, the present is nothing less than a dissolution of the Irish social state and common weal.

—*Times,* July 5, 1849

The land was all held under the Rundale System; that is to say, a Man's Holding of Five Acres was probably in Twenty different Divisions of the Farm. A Townland was occupied by Sixty or Eighty different Families, the whole of whom lived in One Village, and the land, although it might be of great Extent, was held by them in separate Sub-divisions. It became necessary to root this System out thoroughly.

—"Report of the Select Committee of House of Lords on Colonization from Ireland," 1847

THE LONG HAEMORRHAGE

That the Great Famine had an enormous impact on Irish life is hardly in doubt. Besides the devastating loss of life, there was the sustained socioeconomic haemorrhage of mass emigration. Between 1846 and 1850 one million people left the country, and this figure nearly doubled over the next four years. In 1866 Ireland's population was roughly equivalent to its 1801 figure of 5.5 million.[1] By 1891 almost two out of every five persons born in Ireland were living outside the country.[2] Today, with 6 million people, the island of Ireland remains a "demographic exception": it is the only country in Europe whose population is less than it was 160 years ago.

Although pre-Famine emigration was significant (an estimated 300,000–500,000 people left Ireland between 1600 and 1800), the suffering during the 1840s established emigration "as part of the lifecycle of nineteenth-century Ireland"—what Ó Gráda referred to as the "new normality."[3] By far the largest group of emigrants was composed of the rural smallholders, cottiers, and labourers, leading Kerby Miller to conclude that "catastrophes such as the Great Famine of 1845–55 and the near-famine of 1879–81 were necessary to discredit [peasant] culture and expose its adherents to the full force of commercialization."[4] The depopulation of the Irish countryside reconfigured the dynamics of agrarian reform. In the absence of those individuals and groups most recalcitrant to political and cultural transformation, larger farmers could "expand and consolidate their holdings with less fear of retaliatory violence from the land poor and the landless."[5] One should therefore consider ensuing patterns of emigration—assisted and otherwise—as broadly fitting the disaster paradigm of social improvement and biopolitical regulation. Consideration of the scale and cultural impact of this exodus has led at least one scholar to characterize emigration as a "distinctive act of disciplining that differentiates the Irish colonial experience from most others."[6]

The culture and language of the Irish people were also victims of this massive dislocation. The majority of emigrants came from rural, Irish-speaking areas of Ireland. By 1851 the number of Irish speakers had already halved.[7] This trend continued unabated. In 1800 half the population conversed in Irish; at the turn of the twentieth century that figure was reduced to 14 percent.[8] By the end of the twentieth century the number of native Irish speakers had dwindled to a mere 600,000. To address the loss of the Irish language is to deal with the "death of the signifier" far more seriously than postmodernists usually allow.[9] In Connemara William Wilde, father of the famous playwright, observed the operation of the "tally-stick," a brutal system used to enforce the adoption of English.[10] The English language became associated with socioeconomic mobility (literally a way of *expressing* one's modernity) while Irish increasingly symbolised backwardness, illiteracy, and impoverishment. Miller describes post-Famine Ireland as "culturally orphaned" and refers to "the demoralization of men who have lost a past without gaining a future."[11] The Republic of Ireland remains the only European state to have gained its independence without revivifying its hereditary language.

The assault on the Irish diet, particularly the potato, was also partially successful. By the late 1850s potato output was down 75 percent relative to its pre-Famine level.[12] These results were part of a larger transformation from labour-intensive tillage to pastoral production. By the end of the nineteenth century the acreage of potatoes and grain had halved as cattle, sheep, and poultry played an increased role in Ireland's agrarian economy.[13] In the two decades after 1841, owners of more than thirty acres increased their share of the country's valuable livestock from 50 to 67 percent, whereas "the number of pigs—once the sole possessions of cottiers and smallholders—declined with their owners by 22 per cent."[14] In 1850 livestock amounted to £11.2 million of Irish agricultural output. By 1870 the share had risen to almost £29 million, or 71 percent of the total agricultural production.[15]

We have already remarked that the Irish Famine substantially transformed the landholding system, noting also that the most immediate and severe losses were dealt to the smallest holdings.[16] An estimated one in every four agricultural holdings disappeared in the immediate aftermath of the Famine, most of them being less than fifteen acres.[17] It gratified Nassau Senior to note that the failure of the potato harvest had "destroyed much of what was best established in Irish rural economy; above all, it has destroyed three acre, five acre, or even eight acre farms."[18] The dispersal of clachan and rundale farming—collective patterns of living emblematic of the traditional agrarian order— was the clear objective of "improving" landlords such as Lord Hill of Donegal. The two estate maps (see figure 6.1) accompanying Hill's exemplary pamphlet, *Facts from Gweedore,* neatly illustrate Whelan's point about "the spread of a logical lattice of ladder farms over the west of Ireland."[19] The decimation of Irish smallholders was in fact the precondition for the "transition" to commercial farming.[20] Mitchel's account of the Great Famine ends by evoking Jonathan Swift's (1667–1745) image of sheep replacing people, and Marx likewise saw Ireland fulfilling its "true destiny, that of an English sheep-walk and cattle pasture."[21] Many displaced tenants certainly sympathised with this interpretation. In response to population clearances in north Donegal, for example, hundreds of sheep were savagely attacked by displaced tenants and labourers.[22] In an appeal mailed to Westminster, ten local priests complained that "this fine old Celtic race is about being crushed to make room for Scotch and English sheep."[23] The rise in agrarian crime—the maiming of livestock, attacks on officials serving eviction notices, death threats, and the destruction of household property—reflected a gritty "moral economy" at war with the new science of political economy.[24] Indeed, Scrope characterised the "agrarian code of terrorism" as a *legitimate* nonlegal strategy for securing the means of subsistence. "Its object," he concluded, "is to afford that *right* which the law denies."[25] "If the rights of property are to be exercised for the extinction of the people," cautioned another observer, "we must wonder if the people begin to think that their only hope of safety lies in the extinction of all rights of property in land."[26]

The clearances described above occurred on Lord Hill's estate in Gweedore immediately prior to the Great Famine. However, Hill's own account made clear his belief that the failure of the potato represented a unique opportunity to reorganise Irish society: "The Irish people have profited much by the famine, the lesson was severe; but so rooted were they in their old prejudices and old ways, that no teacher could have induced them to make the changes which this visitation of Divine Providence has brought about, both in their habits of life and in their mode of agriculture."[27] Hill's "improvements" won him considerable praise and admiration. The Devon Commission reprinted the

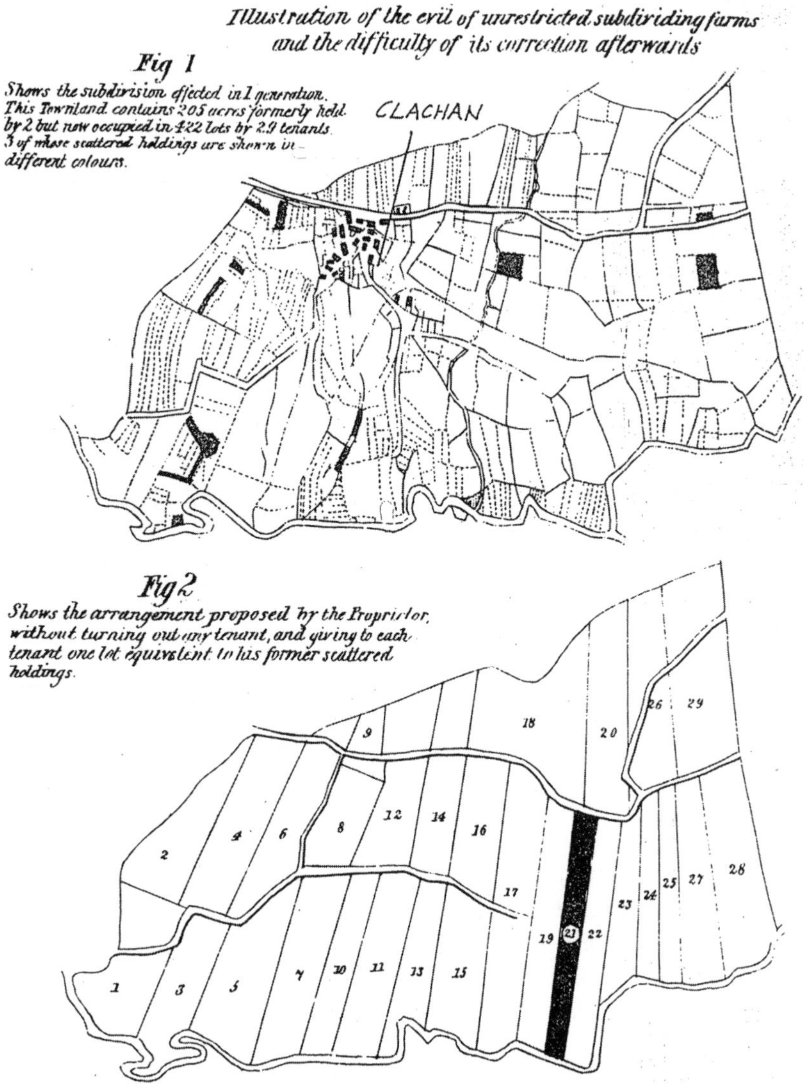
Illustration of the evil of unrestricted subdividing farms and the difficulty of its correction afterwards
Fig 1
Shows the subdivision effected in 1 generation.
This Townland contains 205 acres formerly held by 2 but now occupied in 422 lots by 29 tenants.
3 of whose scattered holdings are shown in different colours.
CLACHAN
Fig 2
Shows the arrangement proposed by the Proprietor, without turning out any tenant, and giving to each tenant one lot equivalent to his former scattered holdings.
1
2
3
4
5
6
7
8
9
10
11
12
13
14
15
16
17
18
19
20
21
22
23
24
25
26
27
28
29

Figure 6.1. The visionary geography of an improving landlord (Hill, *Facts from Gweedore,* appendix)

estate maps accompanying Hill's pamphlet, contrasting the new rationalised landscape with the inefficient system it replaced.[28] When Carlyle visited Hill's estate in 1849, he read the ensuing tensions as a *racial
struggle* for social advancement: "Lord George and his Aberdeens versus Celtic nature and Celtic art."[29] The influential "*Times* Commissioner" also visited Gweedore and praised how "this former desert
and bleak wilderness—this example of barbarism and starvation"
was transformed into "fertile corn fields, the seat of industry and content, and into a humanized abode." Like Carlyle, he attributed social
progress to the influence of the "Saxonizing" gentry, who are not "for
the most part Celtic." Senior characterised rural Ireland as a "warren
of yahoos" but cited Hill's "account of the district of Guidore [*sic*]" as
an exemplary lesson in social progress.[30]

Although not directly influenced by the experiment in Gweedore, other writers like the Scotsman John Forbes borrowed the modernising teleology of Hill's pamphlet. Travelling through post-Famine
Connemara, Forbes commended the work of "planted" Englishmen
who "converted this wild spot, if not to a paradise, certainly to a cultivated, fertile-seeming, English-looking homestead,—a green smiling
island amid the dark desert of moors and bogs around it." For Forbes
this act of "enterprising philanthropy" was proof that "social and intellectual refinement" was best spread through colonial instruction.[31]
At the Earl of Lucan's estate in County Mayo, Forbes contemplated
the massive clearances that had turned their owner into "the most extensive farmer in the three kingdoms." He directly questions whether
Lucan's exploitation of famine conditions was compatible with a concept of justice:

> Whether it was wrong in doing what he done, or whether he may
> not, in reality, rather claim . . . the merit of conferring on his
> country the greatest boons, is a question which will be answered
> differently by different individuals . . . I will venture to say this
> much—that though there are many good and wise men who
> would have shrunk from doing, or even from witnessing, such
> things, there is no patriotic Irishman who must not rejoice that
> they have been done. The thunder-storm and the hurricane are

felt and deplored as terrible inflictions, but we are told by philosophers that they are wise and benevolent provisions in the economy of nature.[32]

Removals on other estates—by Colonel Wyndham in Clare, Lord Palmerston in Sligo, Mr. Spaight in Tipperary, Major Mahon in Roscommon, and C. B. Wandesford in Kilkenny—attracted the attention of several officials, with one report commenting on the "increased Productiveness, Obedience to the Law, and general contentment" to be found in these districts.[33] The human consequences of these removals are given little or no place in these official records, which tend to extol the "benevolent provisions" of nature and the future prospects of Irish farming.

Given the candour of these opinions on the reconstitution of Irish labour and property, it should not surprise us that similar opinions were openly endorsed in certain circles of government. Trevelyan believed that "posterity will trace up to that famine the commencement of a salutary revolution in the habits of a nation."[34] Shortly after the overhaul of the Irish Poor Law, he wrote to the *Times* to garner support for the replanting of Irish society:

> That the change from an idle, barbarous, isolated potato cultivation, to corn cultivation, which enforces industry, binds together employer and employed in mutually beneficial relations, and requiring capital and skill for its successful prosecution, supposes the existence of a class of substantial yeomanry who have an interest in preserving the good order of society, is proceeding as fast as can reasonably be expected under the circumstances.[35]

Thereafter similar sentiments appeared with some frequency in the *Times*:

> There is a glimmer of regeneration and a tendency to a better state of things is perceptible. Thus the small holdings of 1l. a year are disappearing fast, and large farms of 30l. and 40l. are being formed owing to the practical instructions sent out by

Lord Clarendon, a more careful mode of husbandry is pursued, and a better treatment of the green crops and cereals applied; there is also a greater extent of land under cultivation this year than last. Then, the appearance of strangers from Ulster and Scotland, disposed to become settlers, either as tenants or purchasers of farms, forms a new and cheering feature of Mayo. Not less is the favourable change which has taken place in the minds of the Catholic clergy as regards the value of the Poor Law and the English connexion, and their horror of Repeal or so-called Irish Independence; and, lastly, the recovery of the masses themselves from that bewilderment, frenzy, stupor, and superstitious despondency into which I saw them plunged in 1847.[36]

The link between catastrophe and regeneration also found intellectual support in utilitarian political economy, which, in its most stringent form, regarded famines as a "natural" purge of "supernumerary hands." Observers of Irish affairs were not immune to thinking along classical Malthusian lines. James Johnson believed that emigration functioned as "a safety valve to allow the redundant population to flow through," while Whately's Poor Law Commission thought it "extremely advantageous to draw off the redundant population."[37] The report concluded that this "drawing off" would always be difficult (one witness lamented the "foolish attachment to home" among the Irish) but nonetheless "essential to commencing a course in amelioration."[38] Contrary to facts, Benjamin Disraeli (1804–81) asserted that Ireland was the most densely populated country in Europe. On arable land, he declared, the population was denser than that of China.[39] Published the year the potato blight appeared, the report of the Devon Commission expressed its own "conviction that a well organized system of emigration may be of great service, as one amongst the measures which the situation of the occupiers of land in Ireland at present call for."[40] The frequency and frankness of such remarks convinced Mitchel that the discourse of redundancy had metastasized into a policy of removal. Mitchel sternly criticised the Devon report, citing in particular the commissioners' "Digest of Evidence," which claimed that the consolidation of the smallholdings (up to eight acres) would "require the removal of about 192,386 families."[41] "That interposed, "the removal of about one million of persons"— chillingly close to the "drawing off" by starvation and diseases that occurred during the Famine.[42] Although several English officials declared these policies inhumane, many more felt that benign development was impossible when dealing with the Irish. Benjamin Jowett (1817–93) is said to have lost his respect for economists when he overheard Nassau Senior declare that the Irish Famine, "would not kill more than one million people, and that would scarcely be enough to do any good."[43]

Indeed, ideas about "improving" Irish society infiltrated a diverse spectrum of British politics, influencing advocates of overseas colonial settlement, such as Robert Torrens and John Wheatley, as well as economists like John Stuart Mill and William Thornton, who promoted the "internal colonization" of Ireland by removing and replacing some 200,000 families and constructing a substantial class of "yeomanry."[44] Mill discussed his hopes for the "general introduction throughout Ireland of English farming" and consequentially of "getting rid of cottierism."[45] The renowned agriculturalist and writer James Caird (1816–92) backed Peel's proposal for a new "Plantation Scheme" modelled on "high farming" principles, the free transfer of land, and the general commercialisation of Irish farming. His revealing account, *The Plantation Scheme, or, the West of Ireland as a Field for Investment,* replayed many of the themes addressed by Nicholls in his formulation of the Irish Poor Law, including plans for a "model farm" suitable for progressive methods of cultivation (figure 6.2).[46]

While the distinctions between these theories of modernisation were sometimes significant, it is important to stress their common lineage in a politics of improvement that drew from the wellsprings of colonial history and the benefits of *la mission civilisatrice*. By measures, theories tagged as "ameliorative" were later wielded as tools to reconstitute Irish society. Before the appearance of potato blight the Devon Commission complained that "The smallness of the farms, as they are usually let . . . render the introduction of the English system extremely difficult, and in many cases impractical."[47] Only by removing the "human encumbrances" from the soil could the "English system"

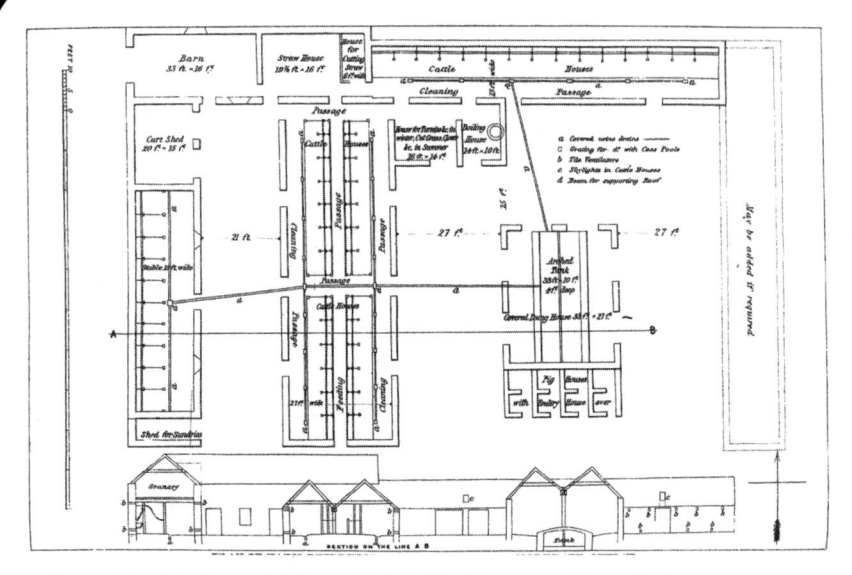

Figure 6.2. Caird's model farm (Caird, *The Plantation Scheme,* 171)

be successfully implanted. Once this was accomplished, so the theory went, Irish society would finally be anglicised.

The transformation of nonmarket social formations into market economies—or, at least, the *acceleration* of this historical process—had the added advantage of forcing the more general shift to pastoral farming, as Irish livestock was increasingly directed toward feeding the booming industrial cities of Britain. As early as 1800 the Irish economy was supplying British cities with 83 percent of its beef, 79 percent of its butter, and 86 percent of its pork.[48] Engels put in stark terms the market logic driving these violent structural transformations: "Today England needs grain quickly and dependably—Ireland is just perfect for wheat-growing. Tomorrow England needs meat—Ireland is only fit for cattle pastures."[49] For Mitchel the subordination of Irish agriculture "with a view to British interests" was one of the defining principles of government policy:

> One hundred years ago, Ireland imported much corn from England; *because* it then suited the purpose of the other island to promote Irish sheep-farming in order to provide wool for York-

shire weavers. Tillage and cattle-feeding were discouraged; therefore the Irish were forbidden to export black-cattle to England. Sheep then became the more profitable stock, and the port of Barnstaple was open to receive all their fleeces. But soon after, when England had full possession of the woollen manufacture, and that of Ireland was utterly ruined, it became apparent to the prudent British, that the best use they could make of Ireland would be to turn it into a general store-farm for all sorts of agricultural produce.

The belief that underdevelopment was a consequence of colonial impositions carried over into Mitchel's analysis of the Irish Famine. "[T]he exact complement of a comfortable dinner in England," he declared, "is a coroner's inquest in Ireland."[50]

This process of accumulation by confiscation left behind a tense landscape of "winners" and "losers" that was burned deep into the psychic world of those who survived. Evidence collected in the Irish folk archive alludes to the disruption of rural social relations and an ethic of care that was thought to characterise pre-Famine life.[51] Hugh Dorian described his native Donegal as a place where "Friendship was forgotten [and] men lived as if they dreaded each other."[52] Fears of contagion (in particular "famine fever" and later cholera) led to cruel instances of stigmatisation and social outcasting. Communal attachments could be forged or mired around the fortunes of relief, and the shunning of stricken relatives and friends—the micropolitics of triage—was a brutal debasement not easily forgotten.[53] Certain episodes recorded in folk memories—especially the "moral lore" suggesting that cruel acts brought a curse on the wrongdoer—suggest that communal affections shuddered in the wake of the disaster.[54] William J. Smyth argues that the Great Famine forged a society where "extreme caution in property transfers" led to the deliberate deferral of marital relations.[55] One contemporary ballad refers to young couples preferring to spend their dowries on a passage to America.[56] These kinds of anecdotes, of which there are many more examples, convey the impression that famines not only destroy life but often whole *ways of life*. Those who considered the Irish Famine as a shortcut to modernity would scarcely have lamented this fact.

Religious and political life in Ireland were also profoundly fractured by the disaster. The decrease in population led to a higher proportion of priests to people, resulting in greater clerical control.[57] Allegations of "souperism" (making religious conversion a condition of famine aid), now regarded as widely embellished, ignited ancient prejudices and contributed to acute devotional cleavages.[58] Irish rural life was increasingly polarised, and this divide spilled over into politics. The Repeal movement, led by the Catholic landlord Daniel O'Connell, dominated the pre-Famine political scene. It is sometimes forgotten, however, that the movement also attracted powerful and talented figures from various religious creeds. Prominent leaders included the Protestant poet Thomas Davis and the Catholics James Fintan Lalor, Charles Gavan Duffy, and Thomas Francis Meagher (1823–67), who were later joined by the Presbyterian republican John Mitchel and the Protestant landowner William Smith O'Brien (1803–64).[59] There is a danger of painting a consensus where religious and political distinctions were more important, and it goes without saying that there were real and significant differences between the physical force tradition of the Young Irelanders and the "moral force" of O'Connell's Repeal agitation.[60] Nonetheless, the wane of the Repeal movement, marked by the death of O'Connell, and the transportation of many of the most influential leaders of the Young Irelanders created a political void that was filled along more overtly sectarian lines.[61] The contrast between the regional economy of the northeast (where the linen and shipbuilding industries propelled growth) and the impoverished south and west of the island seemed to confirm the cultural distinctions that were often drawn between the two poles of the country.[62] Increasingly, Irish unionists looked to British civic institutions to guarantee their freedoms, whereas Irish nationalists demanded greater political autonomy. Both ideologies were coloured by devotional creeds, but they were also defined through *different imaginings of the traumas of the Irish past*. In this respect the Great Famine became, amongst other things, a vital resource for political manoeuvring.[63]

This is especially evident in the post-Famine progression of Irish nationalism. Some of the most important political personalities of the following half-century were profoundly shaped by the catastrophe.

Isaac Butt played a major role in the Home Rule movement, while Michael Davitt, who was born in 1846 and remembered his family being evicted from their home in County Mayo, was later a key leader in the Irish Land War. Although Davitt was just four years old, he never forgot the humiliation of ejectment and frequently made reference to his personal experience of hunger throughout his political career.[64] "Exile" is also a particularly potent theme in Irish nationalism, especially evident among the Irish in America, where militant republicanism was endemic. "The Irishman, banished by sheep and ox," as Marx recorded, "re-appears on the other side of the ocean as a Fenian."[65] The diasporic dimensions of Irish republicanism are unimaginable without the exodus during the Famine years and the social meaning conferred on these events.

On a wider level, the Great Famine catapulted the "land question" into British politics. The demand for the so-called three Fs — fair rent, fixity of tenure, and free sale — became the popular platform for politics as Parnellite nationalism mobilised a "rhetoric that equated the cause of the tenant farmer with that of the Irish people."[66] It is fascinating to trace how members of the Irish Land League mobilised the memory of the Famine and how in the process the demands of agrarian radicals like Lalor, Davitt, and Mitchel were mainstreamed and ownership of the soil was made a national cause.[67] Again, these developments are inconceivable without the devastation of the Great Famine.

The precise number of Famine deaths has also played a significant role in nationalist historiography from the first histories of the Great Famine to the present day. Here we need to begin with Mitchel, who accused the government's census commissioners of underestimating the number of Irish who died during the Famine. Mitchel showed how the census commissioners placed the emigration of ten years (computed from data collected in 1841 and 1851) against the population loss of five years (1846–51), thereby failing to account for the births that would have taken place between 1841 and 1851. Mitchel estimated that 1.5 million people perished (for one of the first estimates, this is fairly accurate), adding that "this is without computing those who were born in the five famine years, whom we may leave to be

balanced by the deaths from *natural* causes in the same period."[68] Joel
Mokyr has circumvented one aspect of this controversy by presenting
two sets of mortality estimates. According to Mokyr excess mortality
for the period 1846–51 amounted to 1,082,000 persons if "averted
births" are excluded and 1,498,000 if the latter are included as part of
the calculation.[69]

It is all too easy to get bogged down in this sort of analysis, and it
is worth emphasising that it was not the issue of "averted births," or
the vicissitudes of subtracting emigrants from population estimates,
that outraged contemporary critics of the government's performance.
On record are the strong protestations from members of parliament
who highlighted the fact that the administration was making no effort
to file returns on the number of Irish perishing from famine and
famine-related illnesses.[70] In the House of Commons the leader of the
opposition, George Bentinck (1802–48), repeatedly challenged the
government on the exact extent of Irish mortality, and his close ally
Disraeli suggested that if a return had been requested on pig and poultry supplies, it would have been furnished with greater alacrity.[71] Butt
echoed this sentiment from the other side of the channel: "How is it
that the GRAND INQUEST of the nation has made no inquiry as to
the death of thousands of the people?"[72] In parliament the critics might
have lost the argument but not without registering a crucial point: it
was increasingly difficult to avoid the conclusion that Irish deaths literally did not count.[73]

The response to the crisis of famine was clearly conflicting and
divergent. Perhaps unsurprisingly, those who played a positive role in
determining state policy usually found less fault in the government's
position. Trevelyan's account is an obvious case in point. Not only is
the government's handling of the "crisis" celebrated; the suffering of
the lower classes is coldly embraced as a necessary outcome of socioeconomic progress.[74] Although Trevelyan's providential reading of
the "Irish crisis" was deeply influential, it is important not to lose sight
of the fact that these policies and ideologies also generated vociferous opposition. When the government announced its new Rate-in-
Aid policy, for example, the Irish Poor Law commissioner Edward
Twisleton resigned in protest. The Lord Lieutenant privately explained

Twisleton's embarrassing resignation: "He thinks that the destitution here is so horrible, and the indifference of the House of Commons to it so manifest, that he is an unfit agent of a policy that must be one of extermination . . . Twisleton feels that as Chief Commissioner he is placed in a position . . . which no man of honour and humanity can endure."[75] Urged to account for his resignation before a public Select Committee, Twisleton left his assessment of the government's performance and his own moral scruples in little doubt: "I wish to leave distinctly on record that, from want of sufficient food, many persons in these unions are at present dying or wasting away; and, at the same time, it is quite possible for this country to prevent the occurrence there of any death from starvation, by the advance of a few hundred pounds."[76]

Eyewitnesses were also profoundly affected by the extent of Irish suffering. Between Cratloe and Six-Mile-Bridge in County Clare, Spenser Hall met and spoke to a group of starving men:

> They told me that they were almost unable to dig for want of food; that when the land was dug they would still be in the great difficulty of not knowing how to get seed to put into it; that it was quite certain they would not be able to afford potatoes; but that, as a greater breadth of parsnips than potatoes could be sown for the same money, they were doing their best to prepare the ground, on the forlorn hope that something unforeseen might occur to enable them at last to get a little parsnip seed.[77]

Hall was obviously moved by their plight:

> That evening, to the family I was visiting, my conduct must have seemed unaccountable. It was not merely what I had seen, but what was indicated by it as prevailing over a great part of the country, that was present to my feelings; and I sat at the table quite dumb, for had I attempted expression at all, it could only have been in compulsive weeping; and from that hour I resolved to return and plead in England, however humbly, the cause of Ireland among my countrymen.[78]

The Quaker accounts of the Famine are strikingly similar, with pity often making way for incomprehension, anger, and disgust. "Ten thousand people within forty-eight hours journey of the metropolis of the world," observed Tuke, "living or rather starving upon turnip-tops, sand-eels, and sea-weed, a diet which no one in England would consider fit for the meanest animal which he keeps."[79] Other accounts clearly censure government conduct. Osborne believed that there was a "tacit determination to let things take their course, at any cost," while another witness remarked, "How unfortunate, that those who legislate for hunger should be unable to understand without really enduring it! I wonder what would be the act of parliament if it were kept for three days without food and with no prospect of any for the fourth!"[80]

Others such as Charles Le Quesne (1811–56) confronted the economic logic driving state policy. Le Quesne berated "the tendency of political economists," such as J. R. McCulloch, to omit "all moral considerations" and see "man [only] . . . as a mere bundle of goods, or a mere productive machine."[81] He also attacked the intellectual foundations of Malthusian reasoning and its violent application to Ireland:

> What is the proper method to check a population? It is certainly not to be found in the doctrine, that the destruction of human life in a variety of ways, from epidemics, from want, from starvation, and misery, must follow its geometrical increase — a doctrine, which, if followed to its legitimate conclusions would lead to hardness of heart and cruelty. We cannot find, that, to keep the population within bounds, the excess perish by natural causes or inevitable circumstances; for it is a well ascertained fact, that an increase of births follows that of deaths; that where mortality is greatest there the number of births increases.[82]

Based on his knowledge of land tenure arrangements in the Channel Islands, Le Quesne argued in favour of peasant proprietorship and against consolidation, which he believed "would be productive of the most dreadful consequences."[83] The popular essayist Lieutenant-Colonel William Blacker (1777–1855) shared some of Le Quesne's suspicions regarding classical economics and Malthusianism in particular. He pointed out that the assessment of population ought to register the "unequal distribution" and not merely the "aggregate amount" of people. Furthermore, he noted that some of the most populous counties, for example, Down, Armagh, and Antrim, were also the most prosperous.[84] Blacker pointed to the productivity of smallholdings—arguing that cottier farmers ought to be given legislative support—and he also was quite clear in his opposition to land clearances in the name of agricultural rationalization:

> The consolidation of farms I understand to mean, the conversion of sundry small holdings into others of larger dimensions. In this I have some experience, and my opinion is decidedly against it, in all cases, where the object can only be accomplished by turning out the unfortunate occupants without making provision for their future support. In Ireland, I apprehend, we are too apt to be carried away by the ideas and practice of our English fellow-subjects, without considering the difference of circumstance between the two countries."[85]

Similar views on the advantages of smallholdings and the significance of peasant proprietorship were echoed by Lord Dufferin, James Hack Tuke, and William Thornton.

The English MP G. P. Scrope wrote dozens of searing epistles condemning the government's Irish policies, a practice that earned him the unfortunate moniker "Pamphlet Scrope." In one important account he asked whether the Irish poor might be justified in resisting the machinations of "sovereign power":

> And who will say that the peasantry ought not, in such a state of the law, to combine for their mutual protection? Is there no point of oppression at which resistance to the law becomes a duty? . . . [A]llegiance is only due where protection is afforded, and that where the law refuses its protection it cannot claim allegiance . . . It [the law] does not protect him from being thrust out from his home and little holding into absolute destitution, to perish on

the highways of famine, or to waste away in those abodes of filth, misery, and disease, in the suburbs of the towns . . . the ordinary refuge and dying place of the ejected cottier and his family . . . Hundreds are at present exposed. Millions know they are liable to it. Can the law justly require their allegiance? Can we expect them willing to pay it? No! the peasantry of Ireland feel that the law places their lives at the mercy of the few whom it invests with sovereign power over the land of their native country— with power to sweep them at will off its surface.[86]

It would be difficult to uncover a harsher review of the government's famine policy even in the more extreme nationalist literature. A horrified Nassau Senior labelled Scrope's opinions "anarchical." "Doctrines more subversive of property," he declared, "and therefore more subversive of government, of civilisation, and of human morality and happiness, were never proclaimed by Fourier or by Owen, by Robespierre or by Babeuf."[87]

Opposition to government policy was therefore perilous but not impossible. Indeed the protestations of Scrope, Blacker, Le Quesne, Thornton, Lord Dufferin, and many others remind us that colonial doctrines were always contested in the centre as well as resisted in the periphery; they also go some way toward challenging the positivistic belief that the Irish Famine was "unavoidable."[88] Clearly many observers did not subscribe to this fatalistic view because their reasoning and values led them to different conclusions about the causes of destitution and the appropriate political response to those conditions. The crucial point about ideology, therefore, is not whether it is true or false but rather "how it comes to be believed in, to be lived out."[89] The fact that more progressive voices were silenced, marginalised, or wilfully ignored should only deepen our attention to the "strategies of moral avoidance" that enabled government officials, bureaucrats, and economists to view Irish poverty as the result of Irish conduct and to seal themselves from the implications of their own involvement in Irish affairs.[90] When evaluating the Great Irish Famine, we need to take seriously the fact that the "rights of the poor" and the "rights of property" were not accorded the same value. This fundamental distinction shaped a social world in which rulers and elites were able to ignore the deeper injustices that expose populations to calamities (making disasters like famine more likely to occur in the first place) and to leave untouched the political and economic arrangements from which they clearly benefited. The different evaluations of poverty and property reflected the social rules of classical liberalism, colonial norms and values, and competing class interests — factors that lead us away from the "economy of nature" to the political realm of human affairs.

FAMINESCAPES

In the final analysis famines are acutely corporal: they are violence assigned to the body, or "stomach torture," as Alexander Somerville preferred.[91] However, famines are also rooted in and through spaces that are at once material, imagined, and techno-political.[92] In charting the "imaginative spaces" of famine, I have shown how discourses have the ability to produce the very objects they describe — a *performative* trait that conceals the potential for language to function as a political weapon. Rhetorical constructions played a crucial role in determining the course of institutional regulation during the Great Famine. The label "pauper," for example, called into being a new institutional space dedicated to population management and agrarian reform, while depictions of Irish degeneracy lent support to the view that human sacrifices were warranted. Moreover, the assumption that the Irish were objects, rather than autonomous subjects, legitimised the centralisation of state power and direct government interposition in the fabric of Irish life. In this sense, the colonial iconography of famine, by which famine victims are reduced to "the demeaning status of the begging bowl," is pivotal to the process of deprivation.[93]

Famines are also products of spatial management. In chapter 4 I highlighted how the organisation of material space served as a strategy for biopolitical management. The workhouses, food depots, soup kitchens, public works operations, and outdoor relief schemes allowed the state to target and manage Irish destitution. A deeper consideration of the material spaces of famine would also include wards and fever

THE GOVERNMENT INSPECTOR'S OFFICE

Figure 6.3. Emigrants at the government medical inspector's office (*Illustrated London News,* July 6, 1850)

hospitals, shipping ports, "coffin ships," and quarantine facilities as sites of biosocial regulation (figure 6.3). In the Irish case, famine was assuredly a transnational phenomenon. Trevelyan firmly believed the government's "war against famine and pestilence" should be conducted on *both sides* of the Atlantic.[94] In his opinion, state-assisted emigration schemes ought to facilitate colonial resettlement programmes, thus converting "paupers into Backwoodsmen by administrative measures."[95] In evidence presented to the House of Lords, Stephen De Vere (1812–1904) echoed Trevelyan's view: "I shall not regret the Disasters of the last Two years, if their warning Voice shall have stimulated and enabled us to effect a System of emigration, *leading to future colonization,* which shall gradually heal the diseased and otherwise incurable State of Society at home, and at the same Time infuse a Spirit into the Colonies which shall render them the Ornament, Wealth, and Bulwark of the Parent Company." If resettlement was organised systematically, he concluded, "the Locusts of the Old World will become the Honey

Bees of the New."[96] In England, by contrast, Removal Laws were used to *expel* the newly arrived Irish, a further example of how famine management strategies where determined by wider political considerations and geographical contexts.[97] Whereas the colonies might be "improved" through regulated resettlement schemes, it was feared that unregulated pauper transfers might lead to the "Wheat-fed Population of Great Britain" being "supplanted by the Potato-fed Population of Ireland."[98] There were, in other words, multitudinous spaces—and baroque circuits—through which the famished were subjected to "administrative measures." These policies and programmes *spatialised* the project of "pauper management" and, at the same time, afforded the state a leading role in "improving" the Irish population.[99]

Finally, I have emphasised the techno-political and juridical spaces of famine. The volume of legislation passed to facilitate government relief was truly staggering. These legal statutes were influenced by visionary geographies of social reform, and the legislation enacted invariably summoned into being new institutional mechanisms, which in turn stimulated additional imaginaries of improvement. For this very reason, it is rather difficult to disentangle the discursive, institutional, and techno-political (see table 6.1) apparatuses of power. A Poor Law workhouse, for example, is clearly an assemblage of all three practices. In focusing on the politico-juridical, however, I aim to draw attention to three points. First, I want to emphasise the tremendous efforts involved in regulating and directing the Great Famine. It is simply misleading to characterise famine relief after 1847 as a policy of nonintervention. The government continued to involve itself in the relief process, even when the endgame of these interventions was a policy of limited assistance for the Irish poor.

I have also emphasised the production of "bare life." The pre-Famine production of poverty through capitalist-colonial relations is central, not incidental, to the Great Famine. In chapters 3 and 4 I developed this enquiry, suggesting that relief measures enabled the state to virtually monopolise the means of subsistence. From the government's perspective, the Irish Famine was to be *financed locally* but *administered centrally*. The designer of the Irish Poor Law, George Nicholls, realised that this arrangement allowed the government to control the

Table 6.1. Faminescapes

Concept	Modality	Expression
Making up people	Discursive	Objects of calculation
Administration of hunger	Institutional	Pauper management
Production of bare life	Politico-Juridical	Radical rightlessness

wages and food—and hence the entire means of subsistence—of a starving population.[100] According to Mitchel, the state was now "omnipotent to give food or withhold it, to relieve or to starve, according to their own ideas of policy and of good behaviour in the people."[101] Beyond the colonial famines of the third world, we have to turn to "socialist-totalitarian famines" of the twentieth century to find a comparable assertion of state control, including the gradual "assumption of responsibility for managing entitlements to food."[102] In such situations the survival of the people depended on the maintenance of extraneous aid.

The redoubled efforts to supervise and direct the Irish Famine paralleled the move toward government by administrative norms rather than civic rights. This is evident in the state's continual departure from the ordinary rule of law when superintending the Irish. During the half century after the Act of Union, Ireland was governed under "ordinary" law for only five years.[103] *Fraser's Magazine* claimed that constitutional rights and trial by jury were "as little suited to the actual conditions of the Irish people as they are to the condition of a horde of Bedouin Arabs or a tribe of Red Indians."[104] The recourse to "packing" Irish juries overcame the tribulations of due process, though not without admitting that British law lacked popular legitimacy in Ireland. In addition, the recognition of a right to relief was purposefully avoided in Ireland, lest it encourage widespread simulation and duplicity. Although a right to relief was implicitly recognised in the Poor Law Extension Act in 1847, the illusion of benevolence receded as subsequent measures—including the Gregory Clause, the strict exclusions on outdoor relief, the thinning of the relief list, and so on—made a mockery of this supposed concession.

Table 6.2. Inside-Outside Dialectics

	Inside	*Outside*
Colonialism	Colonial centre	Colonised periphery
Biopolitics	Politically qualified life	Bare life
Capitalism	The market	Noncapitalist social formations

HUMAN ENCUMBRANCES

In the preceding chapters I have highlighted the transformative forces of colonialism, capitalism, and biopolitics. These modalities of power are no doubt different, but they arguably gather and converge around common distinctions between value and nonvalue, master and slave, core and periphery (table 6.2). In each case the target of power—life itself—is captured and included in a "space of exclusion [that] is now rigidly regimented and controlled."[105] Important conclusions can be drawn from this. The colonial dimensions to the Great Famine are still too often ignored. The idea of Irish "regeneration" has a long genealogy that stretches far beyond Nicholls's drafting of the Irish Poor Law (which codified the idea of cultivating a new class of yeomanry through institutional measures) to earlier moments when the Crown attempted to anglicise Irish territory by establishing English law, promoting the English language, revitalising central government, and disposing the country on a more commercial footing.[106] There is also, I believe, a compelling case to be made for repositioning Irish Famine historiography vis-à-vis the devastating practices of proletarianisation at work in other nineteenth-century colonial famines. Mike Davis has powerfully argued that "devastating drought provided an environmental stage" in which commodity markets, price speculation, and the "will of the state" shaped vulnerability to famine "and determined who, in the last instance, died."[107] Davis's emphasis is on the late Victorian period, but his thoughtful extension of Michael Watts's "political ecology of famine," as well as his suggestive invocation of India and Ireland as a "Utilitarian laboratory," offer compelling ways to think about the violence of hunger.[108]

In light of these comments, how are we to respond to Mitchel's claim that British policy amounted to a calculated act of extermination? As we have seen, contemporaries in England and Ireland adopted language every bit as fiery as Mitchel's. Other Irish voices were more wary, however. Butt strongly condemned the government's "tender regard" for commercial interests, which meant that "upon an experiment of social economy [are placed] the lives of thousands of Irishmen."[109] On a compact of "wilful murder," however, Butt concluded, "we acquit the ministers."[110]

In one sense this debate proves just how polarised the study of the Famine has become. Clearly, one does not need to agree with the use of the term "genocide" to accept that certain government decisions contributed to increases in famine mortality. Peter Gray articulates this "conscious choice" position very well:

> The charge of culpable neglect of the consequences of policies leading to mass starvation is indisputable. That a conscious choice to pursue moral or economic objectives at the expense of human life was made by several ministers is also demonstrable. Russell's government can thus be held responsible for the failure to honour its own pledge to use "the whole credit of the Treasury and the means of the country . . . as is our bounden duty to use them . . . to avert famine, and to maintain the people of Ireland."[111]

This is one of the strongest denunciations of recent years; however, since Gray introduces the language of responsibility—"culpable neglect"—but rejects the nationalist charge of genocide, we ought to ask in what sense he uses the term "culpable."

Here the arguments of Giorgio Agamben are quite useful. He suggests that the concept of responsibility has been "irredeemably contaminated" by juridical procedures—to the point that today when someone declares that they "did nothing wrong" they usually mean that the *law decrees* that their actions do not constitute a crime. Agamben's concern is that this confusion between criminality and ethics opens up a "grey zone" in which law and fact, right and wrong seem to constantly blur. The substance behind this charge has been reiterated in the recent literature on "famine crimes." David Marcus, for instance, helpfully identifies what he calls four degrees of *faminogenic behaviour* responsible for creating and promoting famine. The fourth degree he describes as the least deliberate. It usually involves "incompetent or hopelessly corrupt governments" who are faced with an endemic food shortage, which they are unable to respond to effectively. Third-degree faminogenic behaviour is characterised as benign indifference: "Authoritarian governments, impervious to the fate of their populations even though arguably possessing the means to respond to crises, turn blind eyes to mass hunger." Second-degree faminogenic behaviour is defined as overt recklessness; governments either enforce or continue to pursue policies that engender famine. Finally, first-degree faminogenic behaviour is intentional: "Governments deliberately use hunger as a tool of extermination to annihilate troublesome populations."[112]

Marcus proceeds to analyse this typology of faminogenic behaviour in relation to the jurisprudence of "crimes against humanity"; however, he purposefully excludes third- and fourth-degree faminogenic behaviour from his analysis.[113] The reason offered is that while this behaviour is "deplorable," it is not criminal.[114] Or put differently, third- and fourth-degree faminogenic behaviour constitutes a form of "famine crime" that is *demonstrably legal*. Furthermore, while Marcus holds on to the possibility of formally criminalising first- and second-degree faminogenic behaviour, he also recognises that the international community has never called for criminal trials for government officials responsible for "creating, inflicting, or prolonging famine."[115] These conclusions are deeply troubling. On the one hand, we are confronted with behaviour that aids and abets famines but does *not* constitute a criminal act; on the other hand, we are presented with "starvation crimes" that are all but unenforceable as such.

It is interesting to consider how the British government's relief policies fare on Marcus's scale of accountability.[116] At one point or another, the British government has been charged with the entire range of faminogenic behaviour; revisionist historians tend to emphasise incompetence, whereas scholars influenced by nationalist accounts are inclined to see the Famine as an act of intentional exterminatic

might be argued, however, that this debate is polarised by an uncon-
scious equation of responsibility with legal culpability. As Marcus surprisingly finds, to allow hundreds of thousands of people to starve is
perfectly permissible—legally speaking—so long as one can demonstrate that something as benign as "political indifference" was the
ultimate cause.

In this sense the present has much to teach us about our past.
"Never has an age been so inclined to put up with anything while finding everything intolerable," writes Agamben, "only that when someone
actually risks giving a definition, one realizes that what is intolerable in
the end is only that human bodies be tortured and hacked to pieces,
and hence that, apart from that, one can put up with just about anything."[117] Agamben's work is an attempt to find the political terms for
the fact that some of the worst human atrocities occur "precisely in
the most profane and banal ways."[118] Genocidal interpretations do *not*
apply to the British handling of the Irish Famine; however, it is also
true that genocidal interpretations apply to only a very small proportion of modern famines. The fact that nationalists "maximise" government culpability whereas revisionists tend to "minimise" blame
(emphasising the "lesser crimes" of incompetence and indifference)
suggests that nothing short of deliberate design is worthy of censure.

It might be argued that this unfortunate polarisation is an expression of a deeper inability to find the terms for awful acts of violence that happen—and continue to happen—"under the colour of
law" and with total impunity.[119] "It would be, particularly, a mistake,"
as Jean Drèze and Amartya Sen suggest, "to relate the *causation* of famines to violations of legality . . . the millions that die in a famine typically die in an astonishingly 'legal' and 'orderly' way."[120] These distinctions were recognised by contemporaries such as James Warren Doyle
(1786–1834) who questioned the violence of the law and reminded
readers that the failure to take action, or to suppress conduct that pro-
motes mass hunger, amounted to an avoidable policy of letting die.
"He who sees a man perish whom he could save by a sacrifice of property," Doyle declared, "is guilty of the loss of that life."[121] For Doyle
the decision to place "the laws of property in competition with those
of life" was based on a rigid adherence to "theorems on the 'transition' of society" that was morally inexcusable.[122]

The government's decision to implement certain forms of famine relief—and *not others*—should therefore be assessed alongside the modernising visions of key officials and related decisions as to the utility and value of particular social groups. Progressive "anti-scarcity" programmes—including embargoes on the exportation of food, proscriptions against the use of grain for distilling alcohol, the slaughter of livestock for home consumption, wage adjustments to meet the rising cost of provisions, and the duty free import of rations—could have been implemented and would doubtlessly have spared many lives. Those measure that were put into operation—such as the use of food depots, direct distribution of food, price support schemes (in the form of public works), and the sourcing of provisions in foreign markets—could have been extended or conducted with greater magnanimity. Unquestionably, more could have been done had those in power attached more significance to the human consequences of their actions.

This is not the end of the matter, however. As Thomas Pogge persuasively argues, our analysis of poverty must go beyond the remedies designed to "help the poor" to consider the routine violence that sustains the status quo and makes those corrective interventions necessary in the first place. This distinction invites a deeper consideration of the "stable background factors" (including official conduct over an extended period of time) that make crises more probable.[123] In the Irish case, the violence of conquest and plantation settlement, backed by the administrative and legal reorganization of indigenous society, contributed to acute poverty and rural stagnation and made subsistence crises a recurrent feature of Irish life. A similar example of official wrongdoing can be found in the British government's attempt to use the Famine as a lever to accelerate socioeconomic change. This policy arose from a dogmatic insistence on the laws of political economy and an equally firm belief, fostered through centuries of colonial contact, that the Irish were slovenly, improvident, and uncivilised, and therefore in need of external disciplining. This discipline would be delivered in various ways. By enforcing a rigid programme of qualified famine relief, based on a Benthamite system of "checks" and "tests" (meant to distinguish the "deserving" from the "undeserving" poor), government officials could eliminate imposture, stimulate positive behaviour, and force labour from reluctant bodies. Furthermore, the establishment of free markets was openly theorised as a tool to teach poor cottier farmers the social autonomy and industry necessary to become independent labourers. The shift from a potato diet to cereal foods would force households to abandon "barbarous" subsistence practices and accelerate the "transition" to a more civilised brand of agrarian capitalism. And through the implementation of policies like the Rate-in-Aid Act and the Gregory Clause, officials felt that they had finally uncovered the "master-key" to unlock industry and disencumber Irish property. In the context of colonisation (and other situations of structural abuse), the assignation of "culpability" should to be based, above all, on the presence or absence of intention. Judged on those terms the Great Famine was a "crime of commission" as much as a "sin of omission," even if the crime in question implied no violation of legality.

To suggest that famines are regulated, and that they have *functions* as well as causes, is not to condone the radical nationalist view of a calculated genocide. What needs emphasis is the ideological view that the Irish could be *improved out of existence* and, moreover, that relief strategies could be used as a tool to accelerate the transition to a more civilised market economy. E. M. Wood has shown how in England "the history of early agrarian capitalism—the process of domestic 'colonization,' the removal of land from the 'waste,' its 'improvement,' enclosure and new conceptions of property rights—was reproduced in the theory and practice of empire."[124] In Ireland during the 1840s "the theory and practice of empire" was most clearly expressed in the competing tensions between capital accumulation and extra-economic modes of colonial expropriation. As the Famine wore on—and the tendency to blame the victims became more pronounced—we find parallel claims regarding the effects of racial degeneracy, the acceptability of biological management, and, finally, the necessity of sovereign violence in order to clear the land for improvement. In terms of government calculus, there appears to be a steady move from care to regulation to correction, but it is only in this final remedial stage—in the drawing off of unproductive life and redundant labour—that the colonial state exercises its sovereignty over those lives it now considers to be waste.[125] In this sense the Great Irish Famine can be seen as an integral part of what Foucault interpreted as a revolution in the ancient practices of sovereign states, when "to *take* life and *let* live was replaced by a power to *foster* life or *disallow* it to the point of death."[126] Here sovereignty is no longer the power to "dispense fear and death" but rather the ability to distribute "the living in the domain of *value and utility*."[127]

For those holding political and economic power, "improvement" has always been both a promise and an experiment—part of a collective endeavour to realise unbridled opportunities and overcome the supposed poverty of others. For those less fortunate, "the angel of progress" unleashes a storm that leaves individual lives and whole communities shuddering in its wake.[128] That the past is a nightmare from which we are trying to awake begs the further question, a question that continues to resonate today and that demands urgent attention: How are catastrophic famines to be prevented? One possible answer is provided by those who resisted famine policies in the 1840s: stop creating them.

1. Arendt, *On Violence,* 82, 47, 50.

2. Farmer, "An Anthropology of Structural Violence," 305–25. Slavoj Žižek makes a useful distinction between "subjective" and "systemic violence" that is apposite to this discussion. Žižek, *Violence,* 1–2.

3. Spitz, "Livelihood and the Food Squeeze," 27–30.

4. As Louise Tilly perceptively notes, "Understanding hunger and starvation as consequences of shifting social and political relationships does not deny their reality. Rather, it examines the context of these phenomena in search of an explanation in structural terms, of class, mode of production, political power, or change in these relationships" ("Food Entitlement," 334).

5. Roberts, *The End of Food,* 321–22.

6. Spenser, *A View of the State of Ireland,* 11.

7. Scrope, *How Is Ireland to Be Governed?* 27–28.

8. Davis, *Late Victorian Holocausts*; Watts, *Silent Violence.*

9. Trevelyan, "The Great Irish Famine."

10. Trevelyan, "The Threatened Famine in Bengal."

11. Ibid.

12. See Bender, "The Imperial Politics of Famine"; C. Boylan, "Victorian Ideologies of Improvement"; Brennan, "The Development of the Indian Famine Code"; Gray, "Famine and Land in Ireland and India, 1845–1880."

13. Devereux, *Theories of Famine.*

14. Sen, "Starvation and Exchange Entitlements," 33–59.

15. George O'Brien, *The Economic History of Ireland from the Union to the Famine,* 23. See also Lee, "The Famine as History"

16. For example, O'Sullivan and Lucking, "The Famine World Wide."

17. Johnson, *A Tour in Ireland,* 9.

18. Arnold, *Famine,* 41. Arnold also points out that too many people is often shorthand for declaring that there are too many of the *wrong sorts of people.*

19. Thompson, *The Making of the English Working Class,* 12.

20. S. G. Osborne, *Gleanings,* 201; Stark, *The South of Ireland,* 85.

21. C. Nash, "Cultural Geography," 221.

22. In the same vein David Lloyd urges scholars to "dispense with the satisfactions of hindsight," which tend to promote the view that the Famine was

inevitable. "For the materialist cultural historian," he writes, "the actual outcome of multiple social vectors is less important than the swirling eddies of possibility out of which that outcome emerged" ("The Political Economy of the Potato," 315). See also Eagleton, *After Theory*, 7.

INTRODUCTION

1. Póirtéir, Introduction to *The Great Irish Famine*, 10; Solar, "The Potato Famine in Europe."

2. Bourke, *"The Visitation of God."*

3. Devine, *The Great Highland Famine*.

4. L. M. Cullen has expressed the view that "the Famine was less a national disaster than a social and regional one." If by "social and regional" Cullen means that morbidity and mortality rates were determined by factors such as gender, occupation, age, literacy, relative poverty, etc., then there is nothing novel in this assertion. As Sen points out, it is by no means clear that there has ever been a famine where all sections of the population are *equally* affected. Clearly, Cullen's remark needs to be placed in the context of his overall assessment of the disaster, which tends to lessen the significance of the Famine and emphasise the extent of British relief. Cullen, *An Economic History of Ireland*, 132; see also Solar, "The Great Famine"; Sen, "The Right Not to Be Hungry."

5. Gray, "Famine Relief Policy in Comparative Perspective," 86; Sen, *Identity and Violence*, 105; Eric Hobsbawm describes the Irish Famine "as the greatest human catastrophe of the nineteenth century anywhere in the world" (*Industry and Empire*, 93).

6. Post, *The Last Great Subsistence Crisis*.

7. Kinealy, "Was Ireland a Colony?" 62; Ó Gráda, *The Great Irish Famine*, 9–10.

8. Ambirajan, "Malthusian Population Theory"; George, *How the Other Half Dies*; Sen, *Poverty and Famines*; Sen, *Development as Freedom*, 160–88; Watts, *Silent Violence*; Rangasami, "'Failure of Exchange Entitlements' Theory"; Devereux, "The Malawi Famine," 70; Devereux, *Theories of Famine*.

9. Arnold, *Famine*, 29.

10. Ó Gráda, *Ireland Before and After the Famine*, 99–100. See Ambirajan, *Classical Political Economy*; Sen, *Poverty and Famines*.

11. Arnold, *Famine*, 2.

12. The best example of this thesis is Connell, *The Population of Ireland*. Joel Mokyr makes the significant point that the most vociferous challenge to Malthusianism was "expounded by a large number of contemporary writers, pamphleteers, and Irish political economists" (*Why Ireland Starved*, 39). I draw on a wide range of those contemporary writers in the discussion that follows, but see especially chapter 6.

13. In his classic account of famines in India (first published in 1963), B. M. Bhatia dismissed the view that famines are natural catastrophes: "This description of the calamity is valid only under primitive and mediaeval [*sic*] conditions of famine" (Bhatia, *Famines in India,* 1).

14. Ó Gráda, *The Great Irish Famine,* 76. To be fair, Ó Gráda's comments seem anomalous in the context of his other writings on the Famine. See especially Ó Gráda, *Black '47 and Beyond.*

15. Dickson, "The Other Great Irish Famine," 51.

16. See Eagleton, *Heathcliff and the Great Hunger,* 12; Dunlop, "The Famine Crisis"; Gray, "'Potatoes and Providence.'"

17. Crawford, "Food and Famine," 64; Daly, *The Famine in Ireland,* 113.

18. R. F. Foster, *Modern Ireland,* 325; emphasis added.

19. Woodham-Smith, *The Great Hunger,* 405; Haines, *Charles Trevelyan,* 5.

20. Gray, "Ideology and the Famine," 87.

21. Here I am indebted to the astute comments of Eagleton in *Heathcliff and the Great Hunger.*

22. Arendt, *Responsibility and Judgement.*

23. Quoted in Smyth, "Introduction," 7.

24. Johnson, *A Tour in Ireland,* 9.

25. Society of Friends, *Transactions of the Central Relief Committee,* 168.

26. Hughes, *A Lecture on the Antecedent Causes of the Irish Famine in 1847,* 18.

27. Ibid., 17. "The fault that I impute to it [political economy]," continued Hughes, "is that it values wealth too much, and man too little; and that it does not take a large and comprehensive view of self-interest; that it does not embrace within its protective sphere, the whole entire people, weak and strong, rich and poor, and see as its first primary care, that no member of the social body, no man shall be allowed to suffer or perish from want" (19–20).

28. Ibid., 5. See, for example, Devereux, Howe, and Deng, "The 'New Famines'"; P. Howe, "Reconsidering 'Famine.'"

29. Mac Hale, *The Letters of the Most Reverend John Mac Hale,* 614, 621.

30. Wheatley, *A Letter to Lord Grenville,* 3–4. Wheatley rebuked politicians and economists for failing to grasp the anthropogenic causes of the food crisis: "Like Indians, at the firing of a gun, they have looked on with stupid astonishment, wondering why the bird fell" (9).

31. Scrope, *A Plea for the Rights of Industry in Ireland,* 49; emphasis added.

32. Foucault, *Security, Territory, Population,* 45–46.

33. See Fred Block's introduction to Polanyi, *The Great Transformation,* xxvii.

34. Foucault, *Security, Territory, Population,* 32.

35. Devine, *The Great Highland Famine,* 120.

36. Ó Gráda, *Famine,* 69–89; Watts, "The Demise of the Moral Economy"; J. Scott, *The Moral Economy of the Peasant*; Thompson, "The Moral Economy of the English Crowd"; Spitz, "The Right to Food in Historical Perspective."

37. Physiocratic thinkers included François Quesnay (1694–1774), Anne-Robert-Jacques Turgot (1727–81), and Jean Claude Marie Vincent de Gournay (1712–59). See Roncaglia, *The Wealth of Ideas,* 96–102.

38. Foucault, *Security, Territory, Population,* 34.

39. E. Burke, *Thoughts and Details on Scarcity,* 251. Tellingly, Burke drew on the history of the Roman Empire to highlight the dangers faced in relation to the indiscriminate feeding of the population: "This example of Rome which has been derived from the most ancient times, and the most flourishing period of the Roman empire (but not of the Roman agriculture) may serve as a great caution to all Governments, not to attempt to feed the people out of the hands of the magistrates. If once they are habituated to it, though but for one half-year, they will never be satisfied to have it otherwise. And, having looked to Government for bread, on the very first scarcity they will turn and bite the hand that fed them. To avoid that *evil,* Government will redouble the causes of it; and then it will become inveterate and incurable" (269).

40. Smith, *An Inquiry into the Nature and Causes of the Wealth of Nations,* book 4, chapter 5.44.

41. See Abraham, *Food and Development.*

42. Mill, *Principles of Political Economy,* 549.

43. See the evidence compiled by Cullen, *An Economic History of Ireland,* 73–74.

44. Rashid, "The Policy of Laissez-Faire."

45. Kinealy, *A Death-Dealing Famine,* 43; George O'Brien, *The Economic History of Ireland in the Eighteenth Century,* 105.

46. Post, *The Last Great Subsistence Crisis.*

47. See the discussion in Davis, *Late Victorian Holocausts.*

48. Shenton and Watts, "Capitalism and Hunger."

49. Ambirajan, *Classical Political Economy,* 63. See also Spitz, "Right to Food for Peoples"; Spitz, "The Public Granary."

50. Parnell, *The Tale of the Land League,* 60–61. Referring to the subsistence crisis in 1879–80, Anna Parnell described the Irish Land League as a "government *de facto*" precisely because they set about establishing measures to ensure local food entitlements. Parnell's claims were anticipated by James Fintan Lalor. According to Lalor, when the social contract failed to secure life, it was, ipso facto, dissolved: "We owe no obedience to laws enacted by another nation without our assent; nor respect to assumed rights of property which are starving and exterminating our people." Elsewhere he wrote, "I acknowledge no right to property which takes away the food of millions, and gives them a famine — which denies to the peasant the right of a home, and concedes, in exchange, the right of a workhouse" (*Collected Writings,* 65, 85).

51. This argument was recently highlighted by Drèze and Sen in *The Amartya Sen and Jean Drèze Omnibus.* See especially the comments in *Hunger and Public Action.*

52. As Arnold contends, "The triumph of *laissez faire* signalled a profound revolution in state responsibilities. For centuries the state or monarch had been viewed as the ultimate provider of the people in times of direst need, and though this expectation had often passed unfulfilled, it had never been emphatically denied as it was in the early nineteenth century. This reversal was all the more remarkable in that ideas of *laissez faire* ... gained ascendency at a time when the state in Britain in particular was taking responsibility for many other aspects of public welfare from sanitation to factory hours and working conditions and, latterly, even education and provision for the aged and sick. Seen in this light, the denial of government responsibility for food provisioning stands out as an extraordinary anomaly" (*Famine,* 109). For a different perspective on the relationship between free markets and famines, see Ó Gráda and Chevet, "Famine and Markets."

53. Mokyr points out that shortly after the Great Famine, Britain spent no less than £69.3 million on an "utterly futile adventure in the Crimea." See Mokyr, *Why Ireland Starved,* 292. This and the £20 million spent compensating West Indian slave owners make British famine relief—a combined total of £7 million—seem paltry. Donnelly has drawn attention to the fact that "the British government contribution was considerably less than what was raised in Ireland itself ... Altogether, expenditures under the [Irish] poor laws from 30 September 1846 to 29 September 1851 amounted to almost £7.3 million." To this, Donnelly reckons, "should be added about £300,000 incurred for poor law expenses in the first nine months of 1846" ("The Administration of Relief, 1847–51," 328–29). Significantly, these figures ignore the private subscriptions raised in Ireland as well as the employment created by Irish landlords to relieve distress. The operations of various philanthropic societies are also important and certainly complicate matters. In 1846, after the second successive failure of the potato crop, money, food, and clothing were shipped to Ireland. Private aid continued to grow throughout 1847, after which it slowly petered out. In terms of excess mortality, however, this was also the worst period of famine, a serious reminder of the horrors that would have attended without this life-saving support. Kinealy estimates that private donations probably amounted to two million pounds during the Irish Famine (*The Great Irish Famine,* 63, 89). The Whig government was generally quite supportive of these relief efforts, a fact that reflects another very real situation on the ground—namely, that Irish Famine aid was ultimately considered to be a charity and not a right. See also Mac Hale, *The Letters of the Most Reverend John Mac Hale,* 614; Ó Gráda, *The Great Irish Famine,* 57.

54. Mitchel, *The Last Conquest of Ireland,* 112; Smith O'Brien, quoted in Kinealy, *The Great Irish Famine,* 95.

55. Ó Gráda, *Black '47 and Beyond,* 123–24.

56. Ibid., 124.

57. Kinealy, *The Great Irish Famine,* 90–91. Kinealy asserts that "Ireland was producing enough food to feed its people after 1846" (116). See also

Kinealy, "Food Exports from Ireland, 1846–47"; Kinealy, "Peel, Rotten Potatoes and Providence."

58. Kinealy, *The Great Irish Famine,* 105, 110; Kinealy, *A Death-Dealing Famine,* 33.

59. Kinealy, *The Great Irish Famine,* 98, 115. Daniel O'Connell had called on the British government to prohibit the distillation of alcohol during the Great Famine; ban food exports; allow the free importation of rations; and extend loans to Ireland. For O'Connell's relief proposals in 1845 and the government's reaction, see Davitt, *The Fall of Feudalism,* 52–53; Woodham-Smith, *The Great Hunger,* 43–44.

60. In 1848 the figure was 5,737,687. These statistics include only spirits on which duty was paid, and it should be borne in mind that the illegal distillation of alcohol was rife in Ireland. Between 1811 and 1813, for example, the government destroyed 19,067 illicit stills. George O'Brien, *The Economic History of Ireland from the Union to the Famine,* 346, 360.

61. Kinealy, *The Great Irish Famine,* 103, 106.

62. George O'Brien, *The Economic History of Ireland from the Union to the Famine,* 266.

63. Keen, *The Benefits of Famine.* See also Brass, "The Political Uses of Crisis"; Misra, "Productivity of Crises"; Giroux, *Stormy Weather.*

64. Devereux, "Sen's Entitlement Approach," 246. See also Derrida, "Force of Law."

65. Sen, *Poverty and Famines,* 166.

66. Scrope, *Some Notes of a Tour,* 27. On modern echoes of this point, see in particular the criticisms made by Pierre Spitz regarding food justice and redistribution in "The Right to Food in Historical Perspective."

67. For an exemplary treatment on the violence of law, see Townshend, *Political Violence in Ireland.*

68. Butt, *A Voice for Ireland,* 12.

69. Trevelyan, *The Irish Crisis,* 199.

70. Foucault, *The History of Sexuality,* 140.

71. Ibid.

72. Ibid., 135.

73. Ibid., 136.

74. From Foucault's earlier studies (see especially *Discipline and Punish*) we know that the regulation of the individual bodies (what he later called "anatomo-politics") operates in and through "disciplinary spaces" such as the prison, the asylum, the schoolhouse, the army barracks, and so forth; discipline works at the somatic level, through distribution, separation, and surveillance, using techniques like inspections, bookkeeping, reporting, and drilling, which are carefully arranged and deployed in order to seize, manage, and exert influence over individual lives. Unlike anatomo-politics, which is localised on the human body, biopower is applied "not to man-as-body but to the living man, to man-as-living

being . . . to man-as-species" (Foucault, *Society Must Be Defended,* 243). Thus, we no longer have simply an anatomo-politics of the human body but a biopolitics of the human race (the distinction between anatamo-politics and biopolitics is elaborated in *The History of Sexuality,* 139). For further discussion, see Foucault, *Security, Territory, Population*; Lemke, "'The Birth of Bio-Politics.'"

75. Foucault, *The History of Sexuality,* 140; Li, *The Will to Improve,* 13. See also Duncan, *In the Shadows of the Tropics.*

76. Roberts, "Sovereignty, Biopower and the State of Exception," 35; Elden, "The War of Race"; Legg, "Foucault's Population Geographies"; Neilson, "Potenza Nuda?"

77. More recently the Italian philosopher Giorgio Agamben has extended Foucault's thoughts on sovereignty and biopolitics. Whereas Foucault appears to oppose a "death-dealing" sovereign power to a "life-administering" biopower, in Agamben's judgement the two converge in the Western state. For Agamben "the first foundation of political life is a life that may be killed, which is politicized through its very capacity to be killed." This twist on Foucault's definition of sovereignty suggests that the power of the modern state is not based on the constitution of a social contract but rather on the latent power to "untie" all juridical obligations, leaving a "bare life" radically exposed to death. The paradigmatic example of "bare life"—the life that is incorporated in the political order through its capacity to be abandoned—is the ancient Roman figure of *homo sacer* (meaning sacred man), who can be killed without committing any crime. See Giorgio Agamben, *Homo Sacer,* 89, 29, 9. Although I have serious problems with Agamben's rereading of Foucault (especially the ahistorical suggestion that biopolitics is the ontological core defining Western politics), his analysis of sovereignty as the production of "bare life" seems suggestive of particular modalities of colonial rule. Persuasive critiques of Agamben are to be found in Duarte, "Hannah Arendt, Biopolitics, and the Problem of Violence"; J. M. Bernstein, "Bare Life, Bearing Witness"; Ojakangas, "Impossible Dialogue."

78. Foucault, *Security, Territory, Population,* 42; emphasis added. In an interview Agamben draws on Foucault to suggest that famines and other disasters will no longer be prevented but rather allowed to happen so as to be "able to orientate them in a profitable direction" (Raulff, "An Interview with Giorgio Agamben," 611). For further discussion, see Nally, "Biopolitics."

79. Foucault, *Security, Territory, Population,* 44; Foucault, *Society Must Be Defended,* 256; Foucault, *Abnormal.* For discussion see Elden, "The Constitution of the Normal," 91–105.

80. Foucault, *Society Must Be Defended,* 256.

81. Ibid. The spectre of the disposable subject is also present, for example, in warfare in the figure of the "civilian casualty" whose killing or maiming is frequently depicted as inconsequential. See Gregory, *The Colonial Present,* 70; M. Curtis, *Unpeople.*

82. Li, *The Will to Improve*, 68. Li goes on to suggest that "the use of the sovereign's right to kill and command was necessary to set the conditions of [indigenous] improvement" (75).

83. Stokes, *The English Utilitarians*; Davis, "The Origins of the Third World," 1–36; Davis, *Late Victorian Holocausts*. Davis specifically excludes the Irish experience from his study (hence the "Late" in his title), although there are striking parallels in terms of the personalities involved, the administration of famine relief, and the use of normative economic theories to guide and justify draconian policies.

84. Quoted in de Waal, *Famine That Kills*, xii.

85. Bhatia, *Famines in India*, 110; Escobar, *Encountering Development*.

86. Farmer, "An Anthropology of Structural Violence," 305–25.

87. See Edkins, *Whose Hunger?*

88. Vernon, *Hunger*, 8.

89. Mokyr, *Why Ireland Starved*.

90. Sen, *Poverty and Famines*, 175.

91. W. T. Murphy, quoted in P. Fitzpatrick, "'These Mad Abandon'd Times,'" 267.

92. Agamben, *Homo Sacer*.

93. Nicholls, *Poor Laws, Ireland*, 168.

94. Lebow, *White Britain and Black Ireland*, 111.

95. Mary Louise Pratt coined the phrase "contact zone" to signify "social spaces where disparate cultures meet, clash, and grapple with each other, often in highly asymmetrical relations of domination and subordination" (Pratt, *Imperial Eyes*, 4).

96. Compelling alternatives to the use of violence are explored in Kurlansky, *Non-Violence*. See also Kearns's elaboration of a "progressive geopolitics" in *Geopolitics and Empire*.

CHAPTER ONE. FATAL CIRCUMSTANCES

1. The major exceptions are Miller, *Emigrants and Exiles*; Mokyr, *Why Ireland Starved*; Ó Gráda, *Ireland Before and After the Famine*; and Ó Tuathaigh, *Ireland Before the Famine*.

2. Gibbon, "Colonialism and the Great Starvation," 139.

3. Whelan, "Pre- and Post-Famine Landscape Change," 33.

4. Vincent, "A Political Orchestration"; Waters, "The Great Irish Famine"; Gray, "Famine and Land in Ireland and India"; Bender, "The Imperial Politics of Famine."

5. Ambirajan, "Malthusian Population Theory"; Currie, "British Colonial Policy and Famines"; Davis, *Late Victorian Holocausts*; Hall-Matthews,

"Colonial Ideologies of the Market and Famine Policy"; Hill, "Philosophy and Reality in Riparian South Asia."

6. "Most historians would concur that the history of modern Ireland has been intimately associated with that of the British Empire," Stephen Howe has argued, but beyond this basic agreement, "there is wide, often deep, sometimes bitter dispute" (quoted in Kenny, "Ireland and the British Empire," 2). For a critique of postcolonial readings, see Howe, *Ireland and Empire*; Jeffery, *An Irish Empire*; Kennedy, *Colonialism, Religion, and Nationalism.* Strong counterpoints can be found in Kearns, "Ireland after Theory"; Carroll and King, *Ireland and Postcolonial Theory*; McDonough, *Was Ireland a Colony?*

7. Kennedy urges us to consider the Irish experience within a *European* historical context that was just as "brutal, bloody and oppressive." Significantly, Kennedy hardly mentions the Great Famine (it is not listed in the author's subject index), and his chapter on the "Union of Ireland and Britain, 1801–1921" virtually skips over the disaster. Kennedy, *Colonialism, Religion, and Nationalism,* 217, 222.

8. Notoriously, in 1963 undergraduate students in the Department of History at University College Dublin were assigned the question "*The Great Hunger* is a great novel. Discuss" (Ó Gráda, *The Great Irish Famine,* 11). There is a very large body of literature covering the so-called revisionist debate, from which a "post-revisionist" school has emerged. See R. F. Foster, "'We Are All Revisionists Now.'" For a critique see Whelan, "'Come All You Staunch Revisionists.'"

9. Boyce, *Nineteenth-Century Ireland,* 122–23. In fact, Woodham-Smith explicitly rejects the "genocide-race murder" interpretation of the Famine (*The Great Hunger,* 405).

10. Kinealy, *A Death-Dealing Famine*; Kinealy, "Was Ireland a Colony?"

11. *A Death-Dealing Famine* did not entirely escape invective, however. L. A. Clarkson penned an extremely negative review, to which Kinealy responded in kind. See Clarkson, "Review of *A Death-Dealing Famine.*"

12. Kinealy, "'The Historian Is a Haunted Man.'"

13. R. Young, *Postcolonialism.*

14. Mbembe, "Necropolitics," 25–26.

15. Rangasami, "'Failure of Exchange Entitlements' Theory"; Watts, "Entitlements or Empowerment?" 17.

16. Mokyr, *Why Ireland Starved,* 2, 286–87; Smyth, *Map-Making, Landscapes and Memory,* 462.

17. For a helpful discussion of these distinctions, see Tribe, *Genealogies of Capitalism,* 59.

18. Li, *The Will to Improve,* 97. See also E. Wood, "The Agrarian Origins of Capitalism"; and Habib, "Capitalism in History," 16. The term "forced markets" comes from Keen, *The Benefits of Famine,* 111.

19. Mamdani, "Karamoja," 68.

20. Duncan, *In the Shadows of the Tropics,* 35, 40.

21. Eagleton's insistence that we make room for understanding the "different levels or dimensions to colonialisation" is perfectly congruent with my argument. See Eagleton, "Afterword," 328.

22. Whelan, "The Modern Landscape," 68.

23. Graham, "The High Middle Ages."

24. "A Statute of the Fortieth Year of King Edward III, Enacted in a Parliament held in Kilkenny, A.D. 1367, before Lionel Duke of Clarence, Lord Lieutenant of Ireland."

25. Ibid.

26. Referring to a series of "rigorous and uncompromising government directives" in the late medieval period, John Morrissey thinks that they "may merely suggest the ineffectiveness of [the English] administration" ("Contours of Colonialism," 95). Similarly, on the Penal Laws Declan Kiberd has written: "The verbal harshness of the statutes was the reflection of their inoperability in a country lacking a comprehensive police force or a system of prisons" (*Inventing Ireland,* 16).

27. Herein lies the suggestive power of John Lynch's famous epigram that the early settlers steadily became *Hiberniores Hibernicis ipsis* (more Irish than the Irish themselves). The biographer, critic, and author Sean O'Faoláin took this argument to the limit when he characterised the early Norman settlers as Ireland's first Home Rulers (*The Irish,* 63–64). "The gaelicisation of the Anglo-Norman colony" is discussed by Nichols in *Gaelic and Gaelicised Ireland.* For a critical review of these issues, see Morrissey, "Cultural Geographies of the Contact Zone," 561.

28. Canny, "The Permissive Frontier"; see also R. F. Foster, *Modern Ireland,* 9; Morrissey, "Cultural Geographies of the Contact Zone," 560–61.

29. MacCarthy-Morrogh quoted in Morrissey, "Geography Militant," 169; see also R. F. Foster, *Modern Ireland,* 9.

30. Quoted in Bhabha, *The Location of Culture,* 1

31. Edwards and Hourican, *An Atlas of Irish History,* 156–57.

32. S. Duffy, *The Concise History,* 97.

33. Ohlmeyer, "'Civilizinge of Those Rude Parts,'" 137.

34. Edwards and Hourican, *An Atlas of Irish History,* 157.

35. Ohlmeyer, "'Civilizinge of Those Rude Parts,'" 137. See also McDonough and Slater, "Colonialism, Feudalism and the Mode of Production," 28–29; Canny, *The Elizabethan Conquest.*

36. R. F. Foster, *Modern Ireland,* 13. It was reported that many inhabitants "now wore shoes (rather than brogues), English caps, stockings, breeches, and jerkins, while an ever-increasing number of people spoke English" (Ohlmeyer, "'Civilizinge of Those Rude Parts,'" 137–38). Ohlmeyer is drawing on MacCarthy-Morrogh, "The English Presence," 188.

37. Half the money Elizabeth spent on foreign wars was paid for by the subjugation of Ireland. T. McLoughlin, *Contesting Ireland,* 21.

38. Edwards and Hourican, *An Atlas of Irish History,* 159.

39. S. Duffy, *The Concise History,* 109.

40. Edwards and Hourican, *An Atlas of Irish History,* 159.

41. Kennedy discusses the Longford settlements, focusing on how the Protestant community fared between 1660 and 1921 (*Colonialism, Religion, and Nationalism,* 1–34).

42. Ohlmeyer, "'Civilizinge of Those Rude Parts,'" 139.

43. Miller, *Emigrants and Exiles,* 18.

44. Barnard, *The Kingdom of Ireland,* 25–32; Corish, *The Irish Catholic Experience,* 123; Edwards and Hourican, *An Atlas of Irish History,* 163; Kinealy, *A Death-Dealing Famine,* 18.

45. S. J. Connolly, *Divided Kingdom,* 381.

46. Arthur Bennett told how "certain parts of the province did not contain 'wood enough to hang, water enough to drown, or earth enough to bury a man'" (*John Bull and His Other Island,* 1:59–60).

47. Barber, "Settlement, Transplantation and Expulsion"; Smyth, *Map-Making, Landscapes and Memory.* T. M. Healy (1855–1931) said that so complete was Cromwell's removals to Connaught, and so lost were old Gaelic traditions and ways of life, that new planters were compelled to bring back the expelled for a short time just to point out their lands (*Why There Is an Irish Tenant Land Question,* 10).

48. O'Hearn, "Ireland in the Atlantic Economy," 8. Barnard suggests that Catholic resilience in the face of "losses and sufferings" reflected their numerical advantage over newcomers as well as the "difficulty of ensuring compliance" with new orders (*Improving Ireland,* 46).

49. The Treaty of Limerick, which ended the Jacobite rebellion in Ireland, resulted in another exodus of the native aristocracy, later referred to as the "Flight of the Wild Geese" (a term first used in 1722). It is estimated that a further one million acres of land were confiscated. S. J. Connolly, *Divided Kingdom,* 289.

50. Barnard, *The Kingdom of Ireland,* 51–54; Corish, *The Irish Catholic Experience,* 123–24; Woodham-Smith, *The Great Hunger,* 22. The law school at the University of Minnesota provides a concise summary and full text of the penal legislation between the years 1691 and 1759. The material may be searched in chronological order or by subject matter. See http://www.law.umn.edu/irishlaw/index.html (accessed April 22, 2010).

51. Miller, *Emigrants and Exiles,* 21–22.

52. Quoted in Harrington, *The English Traveller,* 121. "Why should they breed cattle," continued Petty, "since 'tis penal to import them into England? . . . how should merchants have stock, since trade is prohibited and fettered by the statutes of England? And why should men endeavour to get estates, where the legislative power is not agreed upon; and where tricks and words destroy natural right and property?" (127).

53. T. Campbell, *A Philosophical Survey*, 250. Campbell's remedy for Irish poverty would be repeated ad nauseum over the following two centuries: "no great improvement of this country can be rationally expected, when the body of the people derive no advantage from that improvement . . . Even the best laws cannot operate in favour of agriculture, when five to one of those who should be employed in it, can have no interest in the ground they till. Property, stable property, is what alone can make the *sleep of a labouring man sweet*" (253).

54. "Royal Commission of Inquiry into State of Law and Practice in Respect to Occupation of Land in Ireland," 7.

55. Miller, *Emigrants and Exiles*.

56. O'Hearn, "Ireland in the Atlantic Economy," 5. See also Frank, "The Development of Underdevelopment."

57. O'Hearn, "Ireland in the Atlantic Economy," 8–9.

58. S. J. Connolly, *Divided Kingdom*, 353.

59. Quoted in Harrington, *The English Traveller*, 122.

60. Kinealy, *A Death-Dealing Famine*, 20; O'Hearn, "Ireland in the Atlantic Economy," 8–11.

61. O'Hearn, "Ireland in the Atlantic Economy," 10. Although the Cattle Acts were passed by an English Parliament, L. M. Cullen believes that "they did not spring from English policy toward Ireland." Cullen is at pains to point out that the policy was the result of the lobbying power of English breeders, who regarded Irish cattle as competition. However, the same point could be made about virtually every act of economic reform. The repeal of the Corn Laws and the introduction of laissez-faire markets, for instance, reflected the triumph of English industrial interests over English agricultural interests. But surely the key point is that *Irish interests* hardly figured at all in these "prolonged and sharp" debates. See Cullen, *An Economic History of Ireland*, 16–17. Drawing on Cullen's work, Roy Foster takes this point even further. "The importance of cattle export as a profit-making sector," he writes, "has been exaggerated at the best of times," concluding that there "was no specific government policy of keeping the Irish subservient and benefiting the English" (*Modern Ireland*, 127–29).

62. O'Hearn, "Ireland in the Atlantic Economy," 10–11.

63. S. J. Connolly, *Divided Kingdom*, 346.

64. O'Hearn, "Ireland in the Atlantic Economy," 9.

65. The "subsistence ethic" is defined by three basic principles: (1) the *safety first* principle, whereby risk aversion becomes the default position in peasant societies; (2) a tendency toward *mutual support*—what has also been called the "norm of reciprocity"; and (3) communal patterns of social provision, the so-called moral economy. See J. Scott, *The Moral Economy of the Peasant*.

66. Miller, *Emigrants and Exiles*, 32.

67. Nicholls, *A History of the Irish Poor Law*, 41.

68. "We are always writing the history of the same war," Foucault declared, "even when we are writing the history of peace and its institutions" (*Society Must Be Defended,* 15–16).

69. Kearns, "Bare Life."

70. Arendt, *On Violence,* 53. Although Arendt is making a general claim, she was acutely aware of the significance of the colonial and imperial violence, as her exemplary work on totalitarianism makes clear.

71. Harvey, *The New Imperialism.* See also Kearns, "Making Space for Marx"; Lloyd, *Irish Times,* 47–49.

72. Luxemburg, *The Accumulation of Capital,* 371.

73. The following colourful remark, attributed to an English juror, gets to the heart of the matter: "*You may track Ireland through the statute book, as you'd follow a wounded man through a crowd—BY BLOOD*" (quoted in Balch, *Ireland as I Saw It,* 303).

74. Smyth, *Map-Making, Landscapes and Memory,* 425; Carroll, *Circe's Cup,* 12; Brady, *The Chief Governors.*

75. Mokyr, *Why Ireland Starved,* 6.

76. J. Connolly, *Labour in Ireland,* 58.

77. Ó Tuathaigh, *Ireland Before the Famine,* 29. For a perspective on the Union at odds with the claims made here, see Kennedy, *Colonialism, Religion, and Nationalism.*

78. Hadfield and McVeagh, *Strangers to That Land,* 19.

79. Woodham-Smith, *The Great Hunger,* 10.

80. Harrington, *The English Traveller,* 18.

81. The point about the grammar of the Union is taken from Martin, "'Becoming a Race Apart,'" 190.

82. Greenblatt, *Marvelous Possessions*; Keogh and Whelan, *Acts of Union.* Brian Friel's play *Translations* dramatises the idea that naming is a central act of Othering.

83. Ryan, *The Irish Labour Movement,* 30–31.

84. At this time Ireland constituted 40 percent of the population of the United Kingdom. Mitchel, *The Last Conquest of Ireland*; S. J. Connolly, "The Great Famine and Irish Politics"; Kinealy, *A Death-Dealing Famine,* 25.

85. The relaxation of the Penal Laws began in 1771, when Roman Catholics were entitled to take a lease of sixty-one years for ten and fifty acres of land. However, Catholic-owned land could not be situated within a mile of a town. In 1777 Roman Catholics were allowed to lease land for any term under one thousand years, and in 1782 they were entitled to acquire freehold premises for lives or by inheritance. "Royal Commission of Inquiry into State of Law and Practice in Respect to Occupation of Land in Ireland," 7.

86. The full repeal of the Penal Laws and the granting of Catholic emancipation had been promised as a condition of Union; however, within weeks of

the Act the government reneged on its promise, following sustained pressure from King George III.

87. Healy cites Lord Normanby: "In Ireland the landlord has a monopoly of the means of existence, and has a power for enforcing his bargains which does not exist elsewhere — the power of starvation" (Healy, *Why There Is an Irish Tenant Land Question,* 47).

88. C. G. Duffy, "Ungrateful Ireland," 1017.

89. Ryan, *The Irish Labour Movement,* 19–20. See also Healy, *Why There Is an Irish Tenant Land Question,* 39.

90. Marx, *Capital,* 1:664.

91. "Royal Commission of Inquiry into State of Law and Practice in Respect to Occupation of Land in Ireland," 8.

92. S. J. Connolly, "The Great Famine and Irish Politics," 35.

93. These concessions came on the back of the mobilisation of the Irish Volunteers and American independence. Kinealy, *A Death-Dealing Famine,* 21.

94. Mitchel, *The Last Conquest of Ireland,* 29.

95. J. Connolly, *Labour in Ireland,* 146.

96. D. Fitzpatrick, "Ireland and the Empire," 496.

97. J. Connolly, *Labour in Ireland,* 146.

98. See the *Oxford Dictionary of National Biography* entry on Richard Whately (1787–1863).

99. J. Connolly, *Labour in Ireland,* 145. See also Butler, *South Tipperary,* 230; Davitt, *The Fall of Feudalism,* 36.

100. Edwards and Hourican, *An Atlas of Irish History,* 186.

101. McDowell, "Ireland on the Eve of the Famine," 30–32.

102. These biases have enjoyed a long shelf life. Raymond Crotty cites Black's "quasi-racial" account for industrial progress in the north: "Why Ulster has so much growth when the rest of Ireland had so little . . . it seems to me in most instances personal initiative overcame comparative lack of natural advantage" (Crotty, *Ireland in Crisis,* 15). Black's later work — which I employ in this study — seems to me to be far more sociologically based.

103. Mokyr, *Why Ireland Starved,* 14.

104. Inglis, *Ireland in 1834,* 6.

105. John O'Rourke also notes that the potato was first seen as a means of famine prevention and protection against scarcity. He records a letter by "Mr. Buckland, a Somersetshire gentleman" to the Royal Society in 1662, "recommending the planting of potatoes in all parts of the kingdom, *to prevent famine,* for which he received the thanks of that learned body; and Evelyn, the well-known author of 'The Sylva,' was requested to mention the proposal at the end of that work" (O'Rourke, *The History of the Great Irish Famine,* 31).

106. Mokyr, *Why Ireland Starved,* 11; Dowley, "The Potato and the Late Blight"; Dickson, "The Potato and Diet"; Daly, "Farming and the Famine."

107. At Youghal in County Cork, for example, Inglis observed that the exports—corn, cattle, pigs, and butter—far exceeded the imports for the year 1833 (Inglis, *Ireland in 1834,* 102–3).

108. Dowley, "The Potato and the Late Blight," 53. Ireland is certainly not unusual in placing so much stock in one crop. Still today complex carbohydrates in the form of rice, bread, and cassava form a large part of the diets of the world's poor. Again, the *reasons* for this dependence deserve scrutiny. See Patel, *Stuffed and Starved.*

109. S. J. Connolly, *Divided Kingdom,* 361.

110. Crawford, "Food and Famine," 60. [Wilde], "The Food of the Irish."

111. O'Donoghue, *Sir Walter Scott's Tour in Ireland,* 92. Over time the Irish perfected an indigenous means of cultivation, which was rather unfortunately referred to as the "lazy bed" system. "Efficient" rather than "lazy" might have been a more fitting epithet, for the system had distinct advantages in wet, poorly drained soil, where all the labour was completed by hand using a spade called a "loy" or "fack." The Englishwoman Charlotte Elizabeth Tonna was struck by the ingenuity and quaintness of the system: "With us a potato field is a very homely affair: our straggling ridges, the single rows of plants placed length-wise, and the flat confusion of the whole thing defy all idea of the ornamental. But paddy knows better: he separates a rising ground into parcels of about two or three yards in width: digging between them a very deep trench, say two feet over, running in as straight a line as the eye of mathematical precision could desire. Across the bed thus divided, he sets the root; so that the ridges do not appear on a front view; and thus a long, wide, highly raised bed of very rich plants stretches from the road-side to the hill, well defined by the spreading trenches." Employing this agro-system, the potato quickly became "the staff of life" for the Irish poor (Tonna, *Letters from Ireland,* 223–24). See also Dowley, "The Potato and the Late Blight," 24–25.

112. See my discussion on indirect exports in the introduction. An Irish acre is larger than the statute acre, one Irish acre being equal to 1.619835 statute acres. Mokyr, *Why Ireland Starved,* 7.

113. Inglis saw evidence that the abrogation of salt duties adversely affected the Irish bacon industry by lessening the expense of English curing (*Ireland in 1834,* 75).

114. Mokyr cites Jonathan Pim's testimony that there were eight thousand landlords, whereas both Hoppen and Black cite the higher figure of ten thousand. Mokyr, *Why Ireland Starved,* 16; Hoppen, *Ireland since 1800,* 39; Black, *Economic Thought,* 5n2.

115. Black, *Economic Thought,* 6. "The true source of the calamities of the country," declared Anne Plumptre in 1817, "is in the principal landholders absenting themselves from it, spending in foreign climes (for even England is in

this respect a *foreign clime*) the fortunes which ought to be participated with the poor, from the *sweat of whose brows* they are derived" (Plumptre, *Narrative of a Residence,* 338). See also the evidence of two subsequent Select Committees on the occurrence of absenteeism. "Second Report of the Select Committee on State of Disease, and Condition of Labouring Poor in Ireland," 461, 464; "Select Committee on Condition of Labouring Poor in Ireland and on Application of Funds for Their Employment," 337.

116. Miller, *Emigrants and Exiles,* 44.

117. Black, *Economic Thought,* 5–6. Arthur Young described the middleman as "the most oppressive species of tyrant that ever lent assistance to the destruction of a country" (*Arthur Young's Tour,* 2:26).

118. Black, *Economic Thought,* 6. Notwithstanding this legislation, as late as 1844 one witness declared that "although there are thousands of landlords who are without direct tenants, there is not a single tenant without a landlord of some kind" (Johnson, *A Tour in Ireland,* 212).

119. See Darby, "The Age of the Improver"; Wilmot, *"The Business of Improvement"*; Proudfoot, "Spatial Transformation"; Proudfoot, "Landownership and Improvement"; Busteed, "The Practice of Improvement."

120. C. G. Duffy, "Ungrateful Ireland." As a Select Committee reported in 1823, "Many of the evils of Ireland, moral and political, as well as the depressed state of the Peasantry, may, in the judgement of Your Committee, be traced to the mischievous and frequently fraudulent multiplication of the elective franchise. The subject is highly deserving of notice, if not the interposition of legislature." "Select Committee on Condition of Labouring Poor in Ireland and on Application of Funds for their Employment," *Parliamentary Papers,* 1823 (561) vi:337. Mokyr challenges the centrality of Catholic Emancipation and the raising of the franchise (*Why Ireland Starved,* 83).

121. Ibid.

122. Quoted in "Royal Commission of Inquiry into State of Law and Practice in Respect to Occupation of Land in Ireland," 19.

123. Ibid., 22.

124. Griscom, *A Year Comprising a Journal,* 2:424. Marx called emigration "one of the most lucrative branches" of the Irish export trade. Referring to the importance of remittances from abroad, he wrote, "For every troop that emigrates one year, draws another after it the next" (Marx, *Capital,* 1:658–59).

125. Inglis, *Ireland in 1834,* 103.

126. Engels is referring to housing provision for the poor in urban areas, but the claim applies to the de-peasantisation of the countryside. Quoted in Harvey, *Spaces of Hope,* 154.

127. "Royal Commission of Inquiry into State of Law and Practice in Respect to Occupation of Land in Ireland," 16.

128. Johnson, *A Tour in Ireland,* 207.

129. Cullen, *An Economic History of Ireland,* 10; Plumptre, *Narrative of a Residence,* 342; "Royal Commission of Inquiry into State of Law and Practice in Respect to Occupation of Land in Ireland," 16.

130. Black, *Economic Thought,* 5. For G. P. Scrope the system whereby the landlord could confiscate the improvements of the tenant "imposes a special penalty on the investment of capital and labour" and therefore restricts the "very foundation and germ of all material wealth." He advocated full tenant "compensation" for improvements. To not recognise this right, moreover, was robbery "sanctioned by law . . . robbery of the poor by the rich, of the industrious by the idle!" (Scrope, *A Plea for the Rights of Industry in Ireland,* 54, 56).

131. Woodham-Smith, *The Great Hunger,* 17.

132. Quoted in ibid., 17.

133. D. Mitchell, "Dead Labor and Political Economy," 233–48.

134. "Royal Commission of Inquiry into State of Law and Practice in Respect to Occupation of Land in Ireland," 14.

135. There is some anecdotal evidence to suggest that when tenants felt secure improvements soon followed. En route to Dublin, for instance, N. H. Carter was perplexed by the sight of a number of exceptionally clean cabins. A gentleman travelling on the same coach explained that the tenants were all freeholders "feeling the pride and ambition of citizens" (Carter, *Letters from Europe,* 45). The difficulty, of course, is how to define and measure the security of tenure. Mokyr has provided the best systematic analysis (*Why Ireland Starved,* 81–111).

136. "Royal Commission of Inquiry into State of Law and Practice in Respect to Occupation of Land in Ireland," 15.

137. Mokyr, *Why Ireland Starved,* 8, 16. Mervyn Busteed has written that "the groups which occupy a hegemonic position in society will make the deepest impact on a landscape, since they have direct control over the land and they alone are capable of accumulating the necessary resources of human, artistic and engineering skill, capital and labour" ("Identity and Economy," 175).

138. It was not until the Land Acts in the later part of the nineteenth century that there was "any serious attempt made to give by law to all tenants those protections that were available in Ulster by custom" (Edwards and Hourican, *An Atlas of Irish History,* 156, 161).

139. Kohl, *Ireland,* 20–21. See also Davitt, *The Fall of Feudalism.*

140. Quoted in Mokyr, *Why Ireland Starved,* 18. See also Freeman, "Land and People."

141. Mokyr, *Why Ireland Starved,* 18.

142. Thornton, *Over-Population and Its Remedy,* 94.

143. See Black, *Economic Thought,* 7–8. "In these transactions money often played the role of a unit of account but not of a means of exchange, the labour services being valued at a pre-determined rate and subtracted from the rent" (Mokyr, *Why Ireland Starved,* 21).

144. Ryan, *The Irish Labour Movement,* 17.

145. Thornton, *Over-Population and Its Remedy,* 94. Rental exactions (which increased tenfold between 1600 and 1800) were not the only drain on the scarce resources of the peasant. O'Brien argues that tithes, the grand jury cess, county rates, parochial rates, tolls in corporate towns, support for Catholic clergy, and, after 1838, the Poor Rate, significantly depleted the little capital that was available. George O'Brien, *The Economic History of Ireland from the Union to the Famine,* 95–96, 122; Whelan, "The Modern Landscape," 68.

146. Anon., "Famine in the South of Ireland," 403. George O'Brien points to the different regional names for conacre: "mock ground" in Clare, "dairy land" in southeastern counties, "stang" in Wexford, and "quarter land" and "rood land" in other districts (*The Economic History of Ireland from the Union to the Famine,* 11). See also "Royal Commission of Inquiry into State of Law and Practice in Respect to Occupation of Land in Ireland," 34–35; Mokyr, *Why Ireland Starved,* 21; Beames, "Cottiers and Conacre."

147. W. Bennett, *Narrative of a Recent Journey,* 8. See also Gibbon, "Colonialism and the Great Starvation," 136.

148. "Royal Commission of Inquiry into State of Law and Practice in Respect to Occupation of Land in Ireland," 35. See also Rogers, *The Potato Truck System.*

149. Miller, *Emigrants and Exiles,* 53.

150. Scrope, "Poor Laws for Ireland," 513.

151. Mokyr, *Why Ireland Starved,* 9.

152. Thornton, *Over-Population and Its Remedy,* 92.

153. "Select Committee on Condition of Labouring Poor in Ireland and on Application of Funds for Their Employment," 336.

154. Thornton, *Over-Population and Its Remedy,* 92.

155. Ibid., 93, 102. See also Miller, *Emigrants and Exiles,* 53.

156. Thornton, *Over-Population and Its Remedy,* 93. For further descriptions of pre-Famine poverty, see Murphy, *Before the Famine Struck.*

157. See Mokyr, *Why Ireland Starved,* 20–21. "[A]gricultural Ireland presented the aspect of two violent extremes—irresponsible wealth and helpless semi-pauperism" (Anon., "Famine in the South of Ireland," 492).

158. Mokyr, *Why Ireland Starved,* 21. "For a poor society," S. J. Connolly observed, "Ireland was exceptionally commercialized" (*Divided Kingdom,* 349).

159. I take this term from the Marxist economist Ray Bush (*Poverty and Neoliberalism,* 153).

160. Balch, *Ireland as I Saw It,* 231.

161. Kinealy, *A Death-Dealing Famine,* 33.

162. Marx, *Capital,* 1:657.

163. "Second Report of the Select Committee on State of Disease, and Condition of Labouring Poor in Ireland," 462. Such debates bring to mind accusations of colonial resource extraction in India. As in Ireland, the improved transportation infrastructure facilitated the greater penetration of English

commodities, which destroyed home industries and left the indigenous poor dependent on market conditions. See Hall-Matthews, "Colonial Ideologies of the Market and Famine Policy."

164. "Select Committee on Condition of Labouring Poor in Ireland and on Application of Funds for Their Employment," 335.

165. Ibid. A very different perspective to the commissioners is offered by an anonymous observer of events in 1822: "The horrible system of finding out upon *how little* a human being can be kept in existence, has reduced the Irish to potatoes and oatmeal; and if it were discovered that they could be kept alive upon the '*wild vegetables*,' even the potatoes would be seized and exported. In this view, a *commercial tyranny*, a *despotism of property*, is still worse than the evils of an absolute Monarchy" ([Anon.], "Famine in Ireland!" 684).

166. Sen, "Starvation and Exchange Entitlements," 33–59.

167. Miller, *Emigrants and Exiles*, 35.

168. "Select Committee on Condition of Labouring Poor in Ireland and on Application of Funds for Their Employment," 335. The Devon Commission similarly applauded the restraint of the Irish poor: "we cannot forbear expressing our strong sense of the patient endurance which the labouring classes have generally exhibited under sufferings greater, we believe, than the people of any other country in Europe have to sustain." "Royal Commission of Inquiry into State of Law and Practice in Respect to Occupation of Land in Ireland," 12.

169. "Select Committee on Condition of Labouring Poor in Ireland and on Application of Funds for Their Employment," 339; emphasis added. The quotation is from Malthus, *An Essay on the Principle of Population*, 2:42.

170. Lalor, *Collected Writings*, 85. Elsewhere he wrote: "I acknowledge no right to property which takes away the food of millions, and gives them a famine—which denies to the peasant the right of a home, and concedes, in exchange, the right of a workhouse" (65).

171. Mitchel quoted in J. Connolly, *Labour in Ireland*, 179–80. See also Morash, "Mitchel's Hunger," 114–24.

172. "Select Committee on State of Poor in Ireland, and Means of Improving Their Condition," 9. On "transitionality," see Lloyd, "The Political Economy of the Potato," 311–35, and chapter 3 in this volume.

173. "Select Committee on State of Poor in Ireland, and Means of Improving Their Condition," 9. See also Bicheno, *Ireland and Its Economy*, 237–38. The American visitor Balch also underscored Ireland's "peculiar position": "It [Ireland] is intimately connected with the ancient and the modern. It properly belongs to neither. The ravages of time have demolished the Old, but the spirit of progress has not constructed the New. Nor can it be ranked in the transition series. It is in a state of social and political abnegation" (Balch, *Ireland as I Saw It*, 9). See also Barnard, *The Kingdom of Ireland*, 12.

174. Fabian, *Time and the Other*. See also Whelan's discussion of the "politics of stadial ethnography" in "Writing Ireland."

175. Li, *The Will to Improve.*

176. "Royal Commission of Inquiry into State of Law and Practice in Respect to Occupation of Land in Ireland," 13.

177. Wood, *Empire of Capital.*

178. Davitt, *The Fall of Feudalism,* xvii. See also Ryan, *The Irish Labour Movement,* 13.

179. Mokyr, *Why Ireland Starved,* 15.

180. Dickson, *Arctic Ireland.* See also George O'Brien, *The Economic History of Ireland in the Eighteenth Century,* 102–6; Post, "Nutritional Status"; S. J. Connolly, *Divided Kingdom,* 359; R. F. Foster, *Modern Ireland,* 320.

181. George O'Brien, *The Economic History of Ireland in the Eighteenth Century,* 102. O'Farrell's comments are also apposite. "Crises of any magnitude," he writes, "are usually the culminating points of periods of degenerative historical development" (*England and Ireland,* 10).

182. Smyth, *Map-Making, Landscapes and Memory,* 377, 196.

183. Ibid., 4.

184. Lloyd, "The Political Economy of the Potato."

Chapter Two. Defining Civility

1. Hacking, "Making up People."

2. Gregory, "Edward Said's Imaginative Geographies."

3. Sen, *Development as Freedom,* 160–88.

4. Dorian, *The Outer Edge of Ulster,* 223.

5. I have found the following anthologies of travel writing on Ireland helpful: Glenn Hooper, *The Tourist's Gaze*; Harrington, *The English Traveller*; O'Muirithe, *A Seat Behind the Coachman*; Ryle, *Journeys in Ireland.* By far the best is Hadfield and McVeagh, *Strangers to That Land.* For an indispensable bibliography, see McVeagh, *Irish Travel Writing.*

6. "If printer's ink could have solved the problems of Ireland," proclaimed geographer T. W. Freeman, "it would have become an earthly paradise long ago" ("Land and People," 242).

7. I see no problem in considering "official" narratives alongside what Edward Said (*Culture and Imperialism,* xxi) described as the "aesthetic investments" that dominate the "cultural archive" of empire. In his brilliant study of political violence in nineteenth-century Ireland, Charles Townshend reminds us that no state has ever held anything like a complete monopoly over the abstractions of politics, and therefore the study of power must always move beyond the tidy world of politicians and state papers (and the privileged walls of Whitehall and Westminster) to include the more obscure world of local determinants, popular opinion, and so forth. Getting to the grassroots of government power (its "microphysics," if you like) means understanding that the modern state's

most compelling characteristic — and perhaps its greatest weapon — is its ability to circulate and insinuate itself into the knife-and-fork realities of everyday life. See Townshend, *Political Violence in Ireland,* ix.

8.   Cited in Nicholls, *A History of the Irish Poor Law,* 61.

9.   A. Bennett, *John Bull and His Other Island,* 1:vi–vii.

10.   Woodham-Smith, *The Great Hunger,* 36.

11.   "Royal Commission of Inquiry into State of Law and Practice in Respect to Occupation of Land in Ireland," 5, 228.

12.   Mokyr, *Why Ireland Starved,* 88.

13.   Thomas, *Colonialism's Culture,* 111.

14.   Scott, *Seeing Like a State,* 51; emphasis added. See also Hacking, "How Should We Do the History of Statistics?"; Hacking, "Biopower."

15.   Thomas, *Colonialism's Culture,* 205n66. Thomas's approach to the social construction of difference complements Timothy Mitchell's caveat on Derridian methods of deconstruction: "Derrida's work is usually employed to demonstrate, in the reading of a particular text, how [the] effect of meaning can be made to collapse . . . Despite the ease with which such feats of deconstruction seem to be accomplished, *what needs explaining is not why meaning collapses but why it does not*" (*Colonising Egypt,* 149; emphasis added).

16.   Greenblatt, *Marvellous Possessions,* 13.

17.   Inglis, *Ireland in 1834,* 1:iii–iv.

18.   Plumptre, *Narrative of a Residence,* vi.

19.   Self-characterisations of innocence and objectivity were a common feature in other arenas of colonial travel writing. M. L. Pratt discusses what she terms a discourse of "anti-conquest": "strategies of representation whereby European bourgeois subjects seek to secure their innocence in the same moment as they assert their hegemony" (*Imperial Eyes,* 7). See also James Buzard's account of the "anti-tourist" — the cultural practices that distinguished the true "traveller" from the "vulgar tourist" (*The Beaten Track,* 18–79).

20.   T. C. Foster, *Letters,* 8. For discussion see Frankel, "Blue Books."

21.   Gray, *Famine, Land and Politics,* 76–78.

22.   Venedey, *Ireland and the Irish,* 1.

23.   Anne Plumptre fared worse. Her journey to Ireland in 1814–15 began with a twenty-four-hour trip from Liverpool to Holyhead, in North Wales. Although by dawn the following day she could see the Hill of Howth, it was not until six in the evening that she could step ashore, for a total of fifty-seven hours of travel. Hadfield and McVeagh, *Strangers to That Land,* 139.

24.   Ibid., 135; O'Muirithe, *A Seat Behind the Coachman,* 21.

25.   Freeman, "Land and People," 256; "First Report from the Select Committee of the House of Lords, on Colonization from Ireland; Together with the Minutes of Evidence," 187.

26.   Harvey, *Spaces of Hope,* 62; Harvey, *The Conditions of Postmodernity;* Smith, *Moving Lives,* 1–28.

27. Ashworth, *The Rambles of an Englishman,* 115.

28. The "culture of travel" I am invoking here differs greatly from the routes and routines of the Grand Tour, which, according to Bruce Redford, "drew and formed [Europe's] impressionable young aristocracy-in-training" (*Venice and the Grand Tour,* 7). The latter can be described as travel conducted under the sign of *pleasure:* the thrill of modern art, politics, and sexual awakening beyond the constraints of Victorian society. The heyday of the Grand Tour was the eighteenth and early nineteenth centuries, and its gradual demise was precipitated by the Napoleonic Wars, which effectively closed Europe to British travellers and undoubtedly heightened interest in Ireland. But this interest was of a very different order. Philip Luckombe's declaration in 1779 that Ireland ought to be known "next to Great Britain" (cited in Hadfield and McVeagh, *Strangers to That Land,* 20) suggests not only a decline in the importance of the Grand Tour but also the increased pursuance of travel under the sign of *science and utility.* Gradually political and economic concerns were infiltrating the realm of aesthetic travel. Although the repositioning of travel under the sign of science and utility was never unambiguous, it does partly explain the growing interest in domestic social order, and deviancy in particular. This was an age in which the traveller's gaze turned toward life in the manufacturing districts in Britain and the wretchedness of the new urban industrial class—in other words, the spaces where the forces shaping society were most clearly evident, and this included Europe's overseas colonies. The industrial slums and impoverished colonies were liminal spaces reflecting the Romantics' concern with the collapse of organic society and the seemingly endless upheavals unleashed by capitalism. Exploring these liminal sites allowed travel writers and social commentators to consider "how modernity itself might be characterised and confronted" (Buzard, *The Beaten Track,* 19). See especially Gregory, "Cultures of Travel."

29. Inglis, *Ireland in 1834,* 50.

30. A. Bennett, *John Bull and His Other Island,* 13.

31. Cited in C. G. Duffy, "Conversations and Correspondence," 135.

32. T. C. Foster, *Letters.* The *Times* was not unique in employing "commissioners." Alexander Somerville, for example, was dispatched to Ireland by the proprietors of the *Manchester Examiner.* Somerville, *Letters from Ireland,* 13.

33. This fact also renders problematic any uncritical acceptance of these narratives as "source material." See C. J. Woods, "Review Article."

34. Inglis, *Ireland in 1834,* 396.

35. Ibid., 2.

36. Ibid., 13.

37. Hadfield and McVeagh, *Strangers to That Land,* 135.

38. Inglis, *Ireland in 1834,* 13. The trails of these introductory epistles are just as important as the construction of roads, canals, and railways. They also produced routes and routines, making certain peoples and places accessible (and visible) and particular representations possible. See Ogborn, "Writing Travels."

At least two contemporaries—G. F. G. Mathieson and James Johnson—criticised Inglis's reliance on letters of introduction, with Johnson complaining that the only notes he found useful for procuring information were of a monetary kind (Johnson, *A Tour in Ireland,* 2). Mathieson thought that places receiving public monies ought to be open to public inspection, regardless of any introductions. He did admit, however, that Inglis "was not a party man, and he has always been quoted as an impartial authority" (*Journal of a Tour in Ireland,* 186). The American philanthropist Asenath Nicholson greatly disliked letters of introduction because she had no wish to be "peddled about as a second-hand article" (*The Bible in Ireland,* 6–7).

39. "First Report of the Royal Commission on Condition of Poorer Classes in Ireland."

40. Inglis, *Ireland in 1834,* 175.

41. Ibid., 364–65.

42. Ibid., 364.

43. Ibid., 365.

44. Ibid., 366.

45. Thackeray, *The Irish Sketch Book,* 364. Thackeray also found it difficult to converse with the Irish peasantry: "the people are suspicious of the stranger within their wretched gates, and are shy, sly, and silent."

46. Inglis, *Ireland in 1834,* 364.

47. Greenblatt is reflecting on the important question "can the subaltern speak?" "The responses of the natives to the fatal advent of the Europeans survive only in the most fragmentary and problematical form," he writes; "much of what I would like to learn is lost forever, and much of what is not lost exists only through the mediation of those Europeans who for one reason or another—missionary, commercial, military, literary, historical, or philosophical—saw fit to register the voices of the other" (*Marvelous Possessions,* 145–46). Greenblatt omits those unmediated moments when the other writes back—although this tactic of "speaking back" is also problematic because of what Leerssen describes as auto-exoticism: "a mode of seeing, presenting and representing oneself in one's otherness" (Leerssen, *Remembrance and Imagination,* 37). In *Imperial Eyes* Mary Louise Pratt offers another approach. Her book is an effort to decolonize knowledge and "revindicate" the lifeways of the oppressed and their struggles with Euroimperialism, androcentrism, and white supremacy: "The effort must be, among other things, an exercise in humility. For one of the things it brings forcefully into play are contestatory expressions from the site of imperial intervention, long ignored in the metropolis; the critiques of empire coded ongoingly on the spot, in ceremony, dance, parody, philosophy, counterknowledge and counterhistory, in texts unwitnessed, suppressed, lost, or simply overlain with repetition and unreality" (*Imperial Eyes,* 2). See also Barnett, "'Sing Along with the Common People.'"

48. Inglis, *Ireland in 1834,* 58.

49. Ibid., 73.

50. Ibid., 53, 38.

51. Ibid., 166. According to Inglis, excessive litigation was due to "an inherent defect of character; and competition for land" (361). Interestingly, Duncan notes similar patterns of perjury in the Ceylon courts. To the British this was a clear case of "moral failure and a justification of British rule" (*In the Shadows of the Tropics,* 163).

52. Inglis, *Ireland in 1834,* 295, 292.

53. Ibid., 212.

54. Ibid., 92.

55. Cronin, *Translating Ireland,* 47–90.

56. Plumptre, *Narrative of a Residence,* v.

57. Gray, *Famine, Land and Politics,* 2.

58. Tonna, *Letters from Ireland,* 300.

59. Ibid., 415.

60. See chapter 5 for further discussion of Carlyle's writings about Ireland.

61. Quoted in Kinealy, *A Death-Dealing Famine,* 36.

62. Anonymous, *Ireland in 1804,* 24.

63. Ibid., 20.

64. Ibid., 36.

65. Ibid., 66.

66. Plumptre, *Narrative of a Residence,* v.

67. Ibid., 255.

68. Griscom, *A Year Comprising a Journal,* 2:422, 449.

69. O'Donoghue, *Sir Walter Scott's Tour in Ireland,* 92.

70. Thackeray, *The Irish Sketch Book,* 8. Thackeray found it immensely difficult to sketch while in Ireland: "[b]ut it is impossible for the pencil to give due raggedness to the rags, or to convey a certain picturesque mellowness of colour that the garments assume" (208).

71. Forbes, *Memorandums Made in Ireland,* 2:99–100.

72. Venedey, *Ireland and the Irish,* 291.

73. Bigelow, *Leaves from a Journal,* 86. For a vivid, detailed, and comparative description of the miserliness of the peasants' habiliments, see Kohl, *Ireland,* 47–48.

74. During the Great Famine eyewitnesses also resorted to the trope of fear to describe the decrepit and wasted state of starvation. The miserable attire of the peasantry was described by Carlyle in 1849: "Scarecrow figures all busy among their peats, ragged all, old straw hats, old grey loose coats in tatters, vernacular aspect all" (Carlyle, *Reminiscences,* 72). Later Carlyle gave the metaphor added flavour: "Scarecrow boatman, his clothes or rags hung on him like a *tapestry,* when the wind blew he expanded like a tulip: *first* of many such conditions of dress" (77).

75. Mignola, *The Darker Side of the Renaissance.*

76. Osborne, *Gleanings,* 51.

77. Out of a population of 230,000, 170,000 were reported to be destitute. "Select Committee on State of Poor in Ireland, and Means of Improving Their Condition," 17. An earlier committee described the condition of fishermen on the coast as miserable in the extreme. "Second Report of the Select Committee on State of Disease, and Condition of Labouring Poor in Ireland," 463.

78. "Select Committee on State of Poor in Ireland, and Means of Improving Their Condition," 16. A century later shipwrecks were still a means of subsistence for poor people on the western seaboard. See Ó Criomhthain, *The Islandman.*

79. Nicholson, *The Bible in Ireland,* 217.

80. "Select Committee on State of Poor in Ireland, and Means of Improving Their Condition," 16.

81. Woodham-Smith, *The Great Hunger,* 14; Keating, *Irish Famine Facts,* 11–12.

82. W. Bennett, *Narrative of a Recent Journey,* 25. By the mid-nineteenth century, the image of the decrepit peasant hovel was firmly fixed in the Victorian imaginary, as William Thackeray's comments make clear: "One fancies that the chairs and the tables inside are broken, and that the teapot on the breakfast-table has no spout, and the tablecloth is ragged and sloppy, and the lady of the house is in dubious curl-papers, and the gentleman with an imperial to his chin, and a flaring dressing-gown all ragged at the elbows. To be sure, a traveller who in ten minutes can see not only the outsides of houses but the interiors of the same, must have remarkably keen sight; and it is early yet to speculate" (*The Irish Sketch Book,* 8). The German Kohl declared that he could see into the interior of Irish cabins without having to leave his coach seat owing to the gaping holes in the roof (*Ireland,* 20).

83. S. G. Osborne, *Gleanings,* 68.

84. Thackeray, *The Irish Sketch Book,* 136.

85. Nicholson, *The Bible in Ireland,* 22. James Johnson noted an important irony lost on nearly every other Victorian traveller: "Wherever there is an afflux of strangers, there will be an afflux of beggars" (*A Tour in Ireland,* 102).

86. Pückler-Muskau, *Tour in England, Ireland, and France,* 207. Unlike most travellers, the prince found this practice endearing: "They are the best brought-up and most cheerful street boys in the world." He felt the Irish "have others to thank for their faults, but for their virtues, only themselves" (221). Catherine O'Connell also reversed the charge, blaming "carelessly-generous Englishmen" for teaching Irish beggars how to earn a quick shilling (*Excursions in Ireland,* 9).

87. Somerville, *Letters from Ireland,* 7.

88. A. Stark, *The South of Ireland in 1850,* 117.

89. Ibid., 117. Thackeray's account was well known. He was quoted with approval by James Johnson and Harriet Martineau, among others. Pete Mc-

Carthy's recent—and massively successful—travelogue makes frequent use of Thackeray. See McCarthy, *McCarthy's Bar.*

90. Thackeray, *The Irish Sketch Book,* 86–87.

91. Ibid., 363, 312. Thackeray met Charles Lever in Dublin while doing research for *The Irish Sketchbook,* which he later dedicated to Lever. Although Lever defended Thackeray's book in the journal *Dublin Review*—and was criticised for doing so—he later caricatured Thackeray as Elias Howle in his novel *Roland Cashel* (1850). For discussion see MacCarthy, "Thackeray in Ireland"; Rone, "Thackeray and Ireland."

92. Thackeray, *The Irish Sketch Book,* 86.

93. Griscom, *A Year Comprising a Journal,* 2:449–50.

94. Johnson, *A Tour in Ireland,* 278; Plumptre, *Narrative of a Residence,* 342.

95. For Johnson hospitality was no proof of civilization: "It is rather the contrary; for we often see it burn with a brighter flame in the hut of the peasant than in the palace of the prince" (*A Tour in Ireland,* 183).

96. Venedey, *Ireland and the Irish,* vii.

97. Griscom, *A Year Comprising a Journal,* 2:456.

98. Mitchel, *The Last Conquest of Ireland,* 107.

99. Johnson, *A Tour in Ireland,* 169.

100. Thackeray, *The Irish Sketch Book,* 83.

101. Ibid., 232.

102. A. Stark, *The South of Ireland in 1850,* 1.

103. Anon., *Ireland in 1804,* 66, 64.

104. Quoted in in Black, *Economic Thought,* 82. According to Foucault, "whenever information is required concerning the population (sexual behaviour, demography, consumption, and so on), it must be obtained through the family" ("Governmentality," 216).

105. Wiggins, *The "Monster" Misery of Ireland,* 230, 218.

106. Johnson, *A Tour in Ireland,* 50.

107. For an account of American responses to Irish poverty, see Kincheloe, "Two Visions of Fairyland"; C. Woods, "American Travellers in Ireland." The English traveller Ashworth observed how the "half-naked, half-starved" peasants "throng the door; while the pig, fat and sleek, and reserved, I suppose, for the rent day, pushes his nose out of the same portal, as if asserting an equal right to be there" (*The Rambles of an Englishman,* 12).

108. W. S. Gilly, quoted in Lengel, *Ireland through British Eyes,* 107.

109. Martineau, *Letters from Ireland,* 16.

110. Forbes, *Memorandums Made in Ireland,* 2:100.

111. W. Bennett, *Narrative of a Recent Journey,* 73.

112. Plumptre, *Narrative of a Residence,* 342.

113. While local responses are difficult to estimate, James Hack Tuke noted the peasant's timidity on being approached, while various other travellers agreed with Thackeray's conclusion that the Irish feel "a peevish and puerile

suspiciousness" toward all things English (*The Irish Sketch Book,* 95). Furthermore, in other colonial contexts it has been shown how travel writers very often eviscerate the local knowledges they rely on, turning compound relations between peoples, places, and cultures into "a thing depicted or described . . . immediately subject to [the traveller's] gaze" (Thomas, *Colonialism's Culture,* 112).

114. Nicholson, *The Bible in Ireland,* 241. Balch also criticised the popular, prejudicial accounts of the Irish poor. "From the pores of his skin," he wrote of the Irish peasant, "oozes out the sweat which circulates life and fashion up to the nobleman who sits in the House of Lords, figures at the exchequer, bears the trail of Mrs. Victoria Guelph, or loiters, with his family, about the cities and watering places of the continent. He supports the petty aristocracy, so abundant in all Irish towns, in addition, and then is called *lazy, indolent, and worthless,* and sneered at as unfit to live in such a bountiful and beautiful country" (Balch, *Ireland as I Saw It,* 231). Leitch Ritchie (1800–1865) gives an extended account of a conversation with a "small farmer" that includes the following remark: "A man may submit to being starved; but can you wonder that he should feel chafed, if you insult him to the bargain?" (*Ireland,* 106).

115. "Royal Commission of Inquiry into State of Law and Practice in Respect to Occupation of Land in Ireland, Digest of Evidence, Part I," 7, 8, 12.

116. Tonna, *Letters from Ireland,* 301. Hall made this remark after talking to a young Irish woman who travelled nine to ten miles daily to sell milk at a measly profit: "There is one question which all those who charge the Irish with idleness ought to solve or be silent,—viz.— *how is it that they work so hard everywhere else but at home?*" (Hall, *Life and Death in Ireland,* 301).

117. Tonna, *Letters from Ireland,* 315.

118. See Gibbons, *Transformations in Irish Culture,* 149–63; Leerssen, *Mere Irish, Fíor Gael*; Martin, "Blood Transfusions."

119. Martin, "'Becoming a Race Apart,'" 191.

120. Tonna, *Letters from Ireland,* 138. This was not an isolated comment from Tonna: "We are bound to commiserate the priests; we are bound to seek every means of enlightening them; but till that be effected, we are also imperatively bound to disarm them" (55). Not all remarks were as irrational as Tonna's or as biting as Thackeray's, but it was commonly assumed that the priests lorded over the peasantry in dangerous ways. Jacob Venedey related the "habit of the priest interfering in all matters—in extending his views from the church to the forum, and from the forum to the fire-side, until at last he is engaged not only with political affairs, but also with domestic concerns, and thus may be induced to think more of his dominion than his doctrine" (*Ireland and the Irish,* 164). The celebrated economist Nassau Senior complained, "They [the priests] have always encouraged early marriages, and their consequence, the subdivision of the land into occupancies incapable of affording rent or even decent subsistence. They are the natural enemies of good Poor-law administration" (*Journals, Conversations and Essays,* 1:239).

121. Quoted in Miller, *Emigrants and Exiles,* 122.

122. Anon., *Ireland in 1804,* 41.

123. Johnson, *A Tour in Ireland,* 351, 328.

124. Inglis, *Ireland in 1834,* 305.

125. Ibid., 306; emphasis added.

126. Ibid., 343.

127. Quoted in Miller, *Emigrants and Exiles,* 108.

128. Venedey, *Ireland and the Irish,* 285.

129. McClintock, *Imperial Leather,* 53.

130. Ibid.

131. G. P. Scrope, quoted in George O'Brien, *The Economic History of Ireland from the Union to the Famine,* 24.

132. A. Stark, *The South of Ireland in 1850,* 59.

133. Johnson, *A Tour in Ireland,* 105, 181. Irish murders reminded Johnson of "the most gloomy wilds of the most savage tribes that ever roamed in Asia, Africa, or America" (144). Later he expressed the obduracy of the Celt in explicitly racial terms: "An Hibernian, like a Mahomedan Cadi, seldom contemplates more than one side of the question—and that will naturally be his own side. Hence it is, that, even now, when sober, he is much attached to the Courthouse as he used to be the pot-house, and would, though poor and naked, prefer a suit of law to a suit of frieze" (283).

134. Hall, *Life and Death in Ireland,* 59.

135. Thackeray, *The Irish Sketch Book,* 103–4.

136. Asenath Nicholson noted the frequent comparisons between the Irish and American slaves and declared, "What but oppression could produce this similitude" (*The Bible in Ireland,* 271). It is also notable that the American abolitionist and ex-slave Frederick Douglass compared the degradations of Irish poverty to the servitude of the black American slave (Douglass, "Thoughts and Recollections"). These interpolations remind us that racial comparisons can be radically and subversively inverted. See Ferreira, "All but 'a Black Skin and Wolly Hair.'" Significant too is the Orientalisation of the Irish. William Bennett observed a "considerable mixture of the old Spanish blood—transmitted likewise in the name of many of the places—all along the western coast of Ireland," while Plumptre declared, "here was the country where the Milesians from Spain, according to all traditions, both written and oral, were first established. Now the dark complexions, eyes and hair, have ever been, and still are, the distinguishing characteristics of all the Southern nations of Europe; as fair complexion, blue eyes, and light hair, sometimes deviating into red, were, and are still, of the Northern" (W. Bennett, *Narrative of a Recent Journey,* 122; Plumptre, *Narrative of a Residence,* 345). These authors were articulating the popular view that the "Celtics or Milesians had first colonized Ireland via Spain and Egypt and were related to various 'ancient' eastern cultures: Egyptian, Carthaginian, Etruscan, Phoenician, Armenian, Hebrew, Chinese, Indian and others" (Lennon, "Irish Orientalism," 130).

137. W. Bennett, *Narrative of a Recent Journey,* 122.

138. Gibbons, *Transformations in Irish Culture,* 153.

139. Said, "Representing the Colonized."

140. Thomas, *Colonialism's Culture,* 79.

141. Knox's *The Races of Men* and its relationship to British perceptions of Ireland are brilliantly discussed in Lengel, *Ireland through British Eyes.*

142. Knox, *The Races of Men,* v.

143. Ibid., 26–27.

144. For discussion see Richards, "The 'Moral Anatomy' of Robert Knox."

145. Quoted in Edkins, *Whose Hunger?* 29.

146. Quoted in Mokyr, *Why Ireland Starved,* 38.

147. Malthus, *An Essay on the Principle of Population,* 2:350. Ever since Malthus first claimed that famine is a necessary check for overpopulation, debate on Ireland's population and its influence on the outcome of the Famine has loomed large in Irish historical scholarship. Earlier studies tended to affirm the Malthusian logic that Ireland was seriously "overpopulated" and that a population cull through famine was unavoidable. Malthusianism has always had its fair share of critics, however. Susan George cautions that whenever you hear the word "overpopulation" you should reach, "if not for your revolver, at least for your calculator" (quoted in T. Mitchell, *Rule of Experts,* 212). Mokyr's own landmark study, *Why Ireland Starved?* takes this injunction seriously, and after a detailed quantitative analysis he concludes that "The burden of proof has now been shifted to those who still consider the history of Ireland in the nineteenth century to be a classical case of Malthusian disaster" (51).

148. Cited in Arnold, *Famine,* 39.

149. Following Malthus, Jeremy Bentham proclaimed, "the more people there, the poorer they will be: the fewer, the richer" (W. Stark, *Jeremy Bentham's Economic Writings,* 1:273).

150. Quoted in Harrington, *The English Traveller,* 127.

151. See, for example, Glassford, *Notes on Three Tours in Ireland,* 241–46. Glassford discussed the "great complaints of the theoretical politician and economist" and rejected the panacea of emigration (because "it would need to recur without ceasing"), favouring instead "moral remedies" directed at the population.

152. Johnson, *A Tour in Ireland,* 273, 282.

153. Wheatley, *An Essay on the Theory of Money,* 2:32, 36.

154. Lewis also stated "that the poorer classes in Ireland seem moreover at the same time to have been in that precise state which is the most favourable to the growth of population; namely, where the moral checks on increase scarcely operate at all, and the physical checks operate but feebly" (*On Local Disturbances in Ireland,* 55–56). I discuss some of the oppositional voices to Malthusian doctrines in chapter 6.

155. William Bennett described how the "population is nurtured, treading constantly on the borders of starvation; checked only by a crisis like the present, to which it inevitably leads, and almost verifying the worst Malthusian doctrines" (*Narrative of a Recent Journey,* 25).

156. Agamben, *Means without Ends,* 11.

157. Said, *Orientalism,* epigraph.

158. Leerssen, *Remembrance and Imagination,* 35.

159. Martineau, *Illustrations of Political Economy,* 178.

160. "First Report of the Royal Commission on Condition of Poorer Classes in Ireland," 7.

161. The fact that a hugely popular Repeal movement was consistently scoffed at exemplifies this point. Johnson's thoughts on the matter were not atypical: "A repeal of the Union resembles a divorce between man and wife. A separation would be the inevitable consequence, in both cases. A repeal of the Union would effectually divorce Hibernia from John Bull 'a mensa et thoro'— and that without alimony or maintenance . . . When England wishes to be dismembered, and reduced to an appendage to France, it will consent to a disunion and separation from Ireland" (*A Tour in Ireland,* 132). Economist J. R. McCulloch argued that the Act of Union was "fundamental and inviolable" (*A Descriptive and Statistical Account of the British Empire,* 2:238).

162. Nicholson, *The Bible in Ireland,* 121. For a good discussion of this account, see Kelleher, "The Female Gaze," 119–30; Kelleher, *The Feminization of Famine.*

163. Kleinman and Kleinman, "The Appeal of Experience," 1–23.

164. In contrast to previous centuries, nineteenth-century travellers came to Ireland "because of its misery rather than despite it" (Harrington, *The English Traveller,* 20).

165. Agamben, *Homo Sacer.*

166. Lebow, *White Britain and Black Ireland,* 40.

167. Lloyd, "Colonial Trauma/Postcolonial Recovery," 219.

168. Nicholls, *The Farmer's Guide,* 4.

Chapter Three. Engineering Civility

1. Kinealy, *This Great Calamity*; O'Connor, *The Workhouses of Ireland.*

2. Duncan, *In the Shadows of the Tropics*; Legg, "Foucault's Population Geographies"; Legg, *Spaces of Colonialism.*

3. For example, see Daly, *The Famine in Ireland*; G. Bernstein, "Liberals, the Irish Famine and the Role of the State."

4. The quoted phrase is from Butt, *A Voice for Ireland,* 10.

5. Sharma, *Famine, Philanthropy and the Colonial State,* ix–x.

6. Trevelyan, *The Irish Crisis,* 185.

7. S. G. Osborne, *Gleanings,* 120. It was clearly difficult for Victorian readers to grasp the scale of these "Leviathan" workhouses and Poor Law Unions. Here, for example, is the Quaker James Tuke trying to impress upon his readers the enormity of a union in the extreme west of Ireland: "The union of Ballina, (County Mayo,) is about 60 miles in width by 30 in breadth, or nearly three times the size of Middlesex, containing an area of 509,154 acres, with a population of 120,797 persons, and a net annual value of £95,774. Let us suppose a union stretching from London to Buckingham or Oxford in one direction, and from London to Basingstoke in another, with a poor-house at St. Albans, and we shall have a good idea of the extent of the Ballina union" (*A Visit to Connaught,* 19).

8. Trollope, *The Irish Famine,* 15.

9. Trevelyan, *The Irish Crisis,* 58.

10. Nicholls, *A History of the Irish Poor Law,* 314. The Labour-Rate Act (9th and 10th Vict., cap. 107, "An Act to Facilitate the Employment of the Labouring Poor for the Limited Period in the Distressed Districts in Ireland") substituted a system of task work for the daily wages previously paid. It was advised that payment should be *below* what was normally provided in the district. "Less eligibility" meant that relief conditions should be less preferable than the conditions of the lowest-paid labourer. The goal was to mandate a deterrent test in order to guarantee that only the "deserving poor" received assistance.

11. Mitchel, *The Last Conquest of Ireland,* 108.

12. Butt, *A Voice for Ireland,* 25.

13. Stoler, *Race and the Education of Desire,* 15; Prakash, *Another Reason,* 13.

14. D. B. Quinn, "Sir Thomas Smith"; Gillingham, "Images of Ireland."

15. Nicholas Canny, *The Elizabethan Conquest*; Ohlmeyer, "A Laboratory for Empire?" A more explicit connection between the Old and the New World colonies is drawn in Canny, "The Permissive Frontier"; Smyth, *Map-Making, Landscapes and Memory.* For a challenge to this historiographical trend, see Morgan, "Mid-Atlantic Blues"; and the response in Hadfield, "Rocking the Boat."

16. Burn, "Free Trade in Land," 68.

17. MacDonagh, *Early Victorian Government,* 181.

18. MacDonagh, *Ireland,* 27–28; emphasis added. See also Crossman, *Politics, Law and Order.*

19. Senior, *Journals, Conversations and Essays,* 1:194.

20. Kinealy, *A Death-Dealing Famine,* 25.

21. Griffin, "'Such Varmint.'" In relation to the Irish Famine, see Lowe, "Policing Famine Ireland."

22. MacDonagh, *Ireland,* 29. See also Deane, "Civilians and Barbarians."

23. Senior, *Journals, Conversations and Essays,* 1:237–38.

24. Kinealy, *The Great Irish Famine,* 119. "In 1842, whilst in Britain the ratio of the police to population was one to 1161, in Ireland it was one to 791, and by 1851 had risen to one to 480" (ibid., 144).

25. Russell, *Hunger,* 220.

26. MacDonagh, *Ireland,* 29.

27. Hobsbawm, *Industry and Empire,* 62.

28. D. Fitzpatrick, "Ireland and the Empire," 503.

29. 14th and 15th Vict., cap. 68, "An Act to Provide for Better Distribution, Support, and Management of Medical Charities in Ireland; and to Amend an Act of the Eleventh Year of Her Majesty, to Provide for the Execution of the Laws for the Relief of the Poor in Ireland"; Nicholls, *A History of the Irish Poor Law,* 383.

30. H. Burke, *The People and the Poor Law,* 154.

31. MacDonagh, *Ireland,* 37.

32. Ibid., 30.

33. Ibid., 35.

34. Massive advances were also made in the science of cartography with the establishment of an Ordnance Survey Office in 1824. By 1846, the entire island had been surveyed at a scale of six inches to one mile, making Ireland the first country in the world to be entirely mapped with such detail. See Andrews, *A Paper Landscape;* B. Klein, *Maps and the Writing of Space.* My reading has been influenced by Rose, *Powers of Freedom,* esp. chaps. 1 and 2.

35. D. Scott, "Colonial Governmentality"; Kalpagam, "Colonial Governmentality and the Public Sphere"; Duncan, *In the Shadows of the Tropics;* Legg, *Spaces of Colonialism;* Howell, *Geographies of Regulation.*

36. The issues of "policing" and "security" were clearly paramount, and many of these reforms were mobilised and advanced under the rubric of *threat.* In his Poor Law report, George Nicholls depicted the repression of vagrancy and mendicancy "as a measure of police," while Nassau Senior described the management of paupers as "not a law of charity or of economy, but of police." Nicholls, *A History of the Irish Poor Law,* 255; "Report of George Nicholls on Poor Laws, Ireland," 207, 232; Senior, *Journals, Conversations and Essays,* 1:139.

37. MacDonagh, *Ireland,* 33.

38. Butt, *A Voice for Ireland,* 19.

39. Whately has been appropriately described as the "great evangelist of political economy in nineteenth-century Ireland." See Boylan and Foley, *Political Economy and Colonial Ireland,* xii, 17–43.

40. "First Report of the Royal Commission on Condition of Poorer Classes in Ireland," 12–13.

41. Black, *Economic Thought,* 107.

42. The first volume was published in 1835; the third report, containing the conclusions and recommendations, appeared in 1836 and the second report in 1837.

43. By far the most extensive treatment of Whately's Irish Poor Law commission can be found in Gray, *The Making of the Irish Poor Law,* 92–129.

Although Gray presents an exceptionally detailed account of the origins of the Irish Poor Law system, he rejects—without discussion—the explanatory validity of "Foucauldian governmentalism" and "colonial modernity." These "problematic categories" are thought to be "theoretically-driven," a charge that presumably does not apply to his own use of the "Brundage approach." One is reminded of Eagleton's quip that "hostility to theory usually means an opposition to other people's theories and an oblivion to one's own" (Eagleton, *Literary Theory,* x).

44. Horden and Smith, *The Locus of Care.*

45. Himmelfarb, *The Idea of Poverty,* 153.

46. Arendt has written that "all our definitions are distinctions, [which is] why we are unable to say what anything is without distinguishing it from something else" (*The Human Condition,* 176).

47. Himmelfarb, *The Idea of Poverty,* 165.

48. Bowring, *The Works of Jeremy Bentham,* 4:66. Bentham proposed that human nature is driven by two all-encompassing prerogatives: the pursuit of pleasure and the avoidance of pain. From this simple observation he derived his science of liberal government, for which the goal is to facilitate self-motivated individuals to conduct themselves as they ought to do to ensure "the greatest happiness for the greatest number." Thus, according to Benthamite principles, a "deterrent test" is always future-oriented. Bentham, *A Fragment on Government,* xviii, 3. For pioneering treatments on the liberal regulation of pauperism, see Dean, *The Constitution of Poverty*; Driver, *Power and Pauperism.*

49. H. Burke, *The People and the Poor,* 18–22.

50. Senior, *Journals, Conversations and Essays,* 1:162. The phrase "dispauperising" belongs to George Nicholls, "Report of George Nicholls on Poor Laws, Ireland," 215–16.

51. Himmelfarb, *The Idea of Poverty,* 161.

52. Ibid., 163.

53. Quoted in Senior, *Journals, Conversations and Essays,* 1:162.

54. See the discussion of Foucault's concept of biopolitics in the introduction.

55. Senior, *Journals, Conversations and Essays,* 1:178.

56. Whately later recalled "receiving a pretty broad hint, once or twice while the inquiry was going on, what the government expected us to report . . . there was a very great desire among many persons in England, to assimilate the two countries, as far as regarded poor laws" (quoted in Black, *Economic Thought,* 108n5).

57. "First Report of the Royal Commission on Condition of Poorer Classes in Ireland," 7; emphasis added.

58. "Third Report of the Royal Commission on Condition of Poorer Classes in Ireland," 4. The commission did, however, recommend providing re-

lief for "the aged and infirm, orphans, helpless widows with young children, and destitute persons in general."

59. Ibid., 17.

60. Ibid., 21.

61. "Letter from Nassau W. Senior to His Majesty's Principal Secretary of State for the Home Department on the Third Report from the Commissioners for the Inquiring into the Condition of the Poor Law in Ireland"; Black, *Economic Thought,* 108; Himmelfarb, *The Idea of Poverty,* 157. Robert Torrens agreed with Senior's conclusion that the workhouse system could not be transplanted to Ireland. Estimating a family consisting only of a wife and two children, Irish workhouses would have to accommodate—by Torrens's estimate—at least 5,014,400 persons (this figure included 2,300,000 vagrants to which he "added three-fifths of the 1,131,000 labourers who now work upon the land, but who would be displaced from their small holdings by the consolidation of farms"). This required the building of 6,268 workhouses (each holding 800 inmates), costing a staggering £43,876,000, to which should be added an annual expenditure of £19,556,160 for the maintenance of this pauper army. Torrens, *The Budget,* 119–20.

62. "Remarks on the Third Report of the Royal Commissioners on the Condition of the Poor in Ireland, by G. C. Lewis."

63. H. Burke, *The People and the Poor Law,* 38.

64. "Report of George Nicholls on Poor Laws, Ireland," 201.

65. Quoted in McDowell, *The Irish Administration,* 227. In a letter to the Earl of Roden, Isaac Butt described the failures of "a system which was imposed upon us because an ignorant charlatan drove six weeks through our country," while an anonymous author charged that Nicholls "seems to have resolved to see nothing but what he had previously, made up his mind to see" (Butt, *"The Rate in Aid,"* 19; Anon., *Strictures on the Proposed Poor Law,* 4).

66. 1st and 2nd Vict., cap. 56, "An Act for the More Effectual Relief of the Destitute Poor in Ireland."

67. Individuals around the world also donated considerable sums of money for Irish Famine relief, and the Quakers and the Catholic Church also raised large sums of money. The role of religious organisations in the relief process is complex and vexed; there are claims and counterclaims of proselytism. Where monies were donated to the government, however, the government also determined their *use.* Moreover, the administration took charitable grain and refused to allow those groups that had donated it to oversee its release from the government's provision stores. For further discussion see Newsinger, "The Great Irish Famine." My thanks to Gerry Kearns for this last point.

68. In his report Nicholls stated that he visited Dublin, Carlow, Kilkenny, Thurles, Cashell [*sic*], Tipperary, Clonmell [*sic*], Cork, Killarney, Limerick, Galway, Connemara, Westport, Castlebar, Ballina, Sligo, Enniskillen, Armagh, and Newry. "Report of George Nicholls on Poor Laws, Ireland," 205.

69. Ibid., 214. On the English Poor Law Gertrude Himmelfarb has said, "It is difficult to think of any comparable legislative act in recent English history that was so long and so thorough in its preparation" (*The Idea of Poverty,* 154).

70. "Report of George Nicholls on Poor Laws, Ireland," 236.

71. Ibid., 206.

72. Ibid., 207.

73. Nicholls, *Poor Laws, Ireland,* 16. As Lalor witheringly noted, "The small landholdings are to be 'consolidated' into large farmers, the small landholders 'converted' into 'independent labourers'; those labourers are, of course, to be paupers—those paupers to be supported by a Poor Law—that poor law is to be in your hands to manage and administer. Thus to be got rid of the surplus of population beyond what the landowners require" (*Collected Writings,* 22). See also Lloyd, "The Political Economy of the Potato."

74. "Report of George Nicholls on Poor Laws, Ireland," 207.

75. The cited phrase is taken from Naper, *An Appeal to Irishmen,* 15.

76. Leitch Ritchie similarly described the Poor Law as the first step in civilising Ireland: "[T]he benefit I expect from a Poor Law will consist of the change it will produce on the surface of society . . . I will give the lower orders the habit of attending to, and thinking about, their own wants, instead of looking as thitherto, with more than childish helplessness, for some political miracle. It will afford, as it were, numerous tangible points for laying hold of the minds of men, who are at present moved only in great masses, stirred by the views of religious or political enthusiasts. Civilization never comes in the lump. It works its way in detail; and, until Irish society is broken into the small *selfish* circles of England, it will be impossible to operate upon it with advantage" (Ritchie, *Ireland,* 32).

77. See also Nally, "'That Coming Storm.'"

78. "Report of George Nicholls on Poor Laws, Ireland," 214, 211.

79. Nicholls, *A History of the Irish Poor Law,* 91.

80. Senior, *Journals, Conversations and Essays,* 1:49–50.

81. Ibid., 1:31.

82. Ibid., 1:22, 44.

83. "Report of George Nicholls on Poor Laws, Ireland," 208.

84. Ibid., 207, 208. In his first report Nicholls claimed "at the moment that they [the Irish] are complaining of poverty, that they take the most certain steps to increase it" (*A History of the Irish Poor Law,* 163).

85. Akin to their commission in Ireland, their European enquiries were "necessarily short, and our investigations were hurried and imperfect" (Nicholls, *Poor Laws, Ireland,* 153).

86. Ibid., 167.

87. Ibid., 168.

88. Ibid., 168–69.

89. Ibid., 168.

90. Nicholls, *The Farmer's Guide,* 1.

91. Ibid., 167.

92. Ibid., 181.

93. Whelan, "The Modern Landscape," 69; Barnard, *Improving Ireland,* 13–40. See also Tarlow, *The Archaeology of Improvement.*

94. 11th and 12th Vict., cap. 25, "The Poor Relief (Ireland) Act, 1848." By close of the year 1851, sixteen union agricultural schools were in operation. See Forbes, *Memorandums Made in Ireland,* 1:22–5, 2:357.

95. Forbes, *Memorandums Made in Ireland,* 1:279.

96. "Report of George Nicholls on Poor Laws, Ireland," 220; emphasis added.

97. Indeed, Nicholls explicitly linked Irish conditions to the *incompleteness* of English conquest and colonisation. "If Cromwell had remained longer in Ireland," he reasoned, "it is probable that he would with his usual vigour have crushed the seeds of many existing evils, and laid the foundation for future quiet; but this was not permitted, and the elements for disorder remained, repressed and weakened it is true, but still ready to burst forth whenever circumstances should give vent to the explosion" (*A History of the Irish Poor Law,* 10).

98. Driver, *Power and Pauperism.*

99. Foucault, "Governmentality," 209. On disciplinary guidance, see also Lloyd, "The Political Economy of the Potato," 324.

100. Quoted in Himmelfarb, *The Idea of Poverty,* 173.

101. Nicholls rationalised the changes as follows: "In forming the country into unions, it will I think be necessary to observe the civil rather than the ecclesiastical boundaries of parishes, but cases will arise in which it may be requisite to disregard all such boundaries — it being obviously more important that the district to be united should be compact, convenient and accessible, and be naturally connected with its centre" ("Report of George Nicholls on Poor Laws, Ireland," 224).

102. A Scottish Poor Law Act was formulated in 1845. Gerard O'Brien, "A Question of Attitude," 161.

103. Kinealy, *A Death-Dealing Famine,* 8. Furthermore, during the first quarter of 1839 approximately 100,000 people were granted outdoor assistance in England and Wales. See H. Burke, *The People and the Poor Law,* 99.

104. "Report of George Nicholls on Poor Laws, Ireland," 223.

105. Beaumont, *Ireland,* 286.

106. Mehta, *Liberalism and Empire*; Pitts, *A Turn to Empire.*

107. Senior, *Journals, Conversations and Essays,* 1:175–76, 188–89. See also Scrope, *How Is Ireland to Be Governed?*

108. Torrens argued for "the removal to South Australia of such a portion of the cottier tenantry of Ireland, as may render it practicable to consolidate

farms, and introduce improved modes of cultivation." Torrens, *Plan of an Association,* 23. Wheatley, *A Letter to His Grace the Duke of Devonshire,* 3, 4; Wheatley, *An Essay on the Theory of Money,* 2:26–32.

109. "Report of George Nicholls on Poor Laws, Ireland," 223. One commentator has argued that "George Nicholls' rejection of the Scottish system was founded less on its unsuitability to Irish conditions than on the more fundamental point that recipients of such relief came to regard it as a right rather than as a gift" (Gerard O'Brien, "A Question of Attitude," 161).

110. Haggard and Noland's contention that "socialist famines" occur in the context in which the state assumes responsibility for resource allocation is remarkably suggestive of nineteenth-century colonial famines whereby the survival of indigenous populations was dependent on maintenance of extraneous aid. See Haggard and Noland, *Famine in North Korea.*

111. Kohl, *Ireland,* 225. "The workhouses are as handsome in their outward elevation, as their contents are the contrary," commented another tourist (S. G. Osborne, *Gleanings,* 51).

112. Nicholls understood that the application of the "workhouse test" presented problems in Ireland where the standard of living was already so low that the establishment of still lower conditions would be almost impossible, or in Nicholls's words, "inexpedient." Hence strict confinement and segregation acted as an important surrogate for the "workhouse test" as applied in England. "Report of George Nicholls on Poor Laws, Ireland," 216.

113. Power is never unidirectional, of course, and in certain situations individual and collective agency can distort, reverse, or oppose these edicts and norms. As Dymphna McLoughlin reminds us, "In practice the amount of control functionaries had over their inmates varied considerably" ("Workhouses," 723). Others have written with considerable insight on resistance within Poor Law workhouses. See Clark, "Wild Workhouse Girls"; Edsall, *The Anti-Poor Law Movement*; Green, "Pauper Protests."

114. Gerard O'Brien, "Workhouse Management," 114.

115. Ibid.

116. See Colonel William Clarke's testimony in "Correspondence between Poor Law Commissioners of Ireland and Inspectors Relative to the Statements in Extract from Book, Entitled, *Gleanings in the West of Ireland,*" xlix.

117. S. G. Osborne, *Gleanings,* 14–15; Dorian, *The Outer Edge of Ulster,* 223. The Poor Law commissioners took Osborne's account very seriously. See also "Correspondence between Poor Law Commissioners of Ireland and Inspectors Relative to the Statements in Extract from Book, Entitled, *Gleanings in the West of Ireland,*" 209.

118. "Orders of Poor Law Commissioners to Unions in Ireland," 606. These classifications are slightly different to those presented in the "Sixth Annual Report of Commissioners of Inquiry into the Administration and Practi-

cal Operation of the Poor Laws." See also Gerard O'Brien, "Workhouse Management," 115.

119. Nicholls, *A History of the Irish Poor Law,* 286–87.

120. Forbes visited workhouses all over Ireland, but only in the northern unions did he observe inmates receiving a third meal. He assured his readers that although the diet of two meals a day sounded incapable of sustaining healthy life, it must be remembered that the Irish were accustomed to potatoes, "an article of diet much less nutritive than any of the kinds of meal which constitute the workhouse fare" (*Memorandums Made in Ireland,* 1:85, 2:116, 228).

121. Ibid., 1:293; Nicholls, *A History of the Irish Poor Law,* 274; "Sixth Annual Report of Commissioners of Inquiry into the Administration and Practical Operation of the Poor Laws"; H. Burke, *The People and the Poor Law,* 64. Apprenticeships were sometimes used to relieve the "problem" of orphaned children and to ensure that they became "useful members of the community." "Report of George Nicholls on Poor Laws, Ireland," 231. At a workhouse in Ennis, County Clare, S. G. Osborne found that every article of clothing had been made from raw materials spun at the workhouse (*Gleanings,* 38–39).

122. See Thompson, "Time."

123. Nicholls, *A History of the Irish Poor Law,* 287.

124. Ibid., 254.

125. McLoughlin, "Workhouses," 722.

126. "Report of George Nicholls on Poor Laws, Ireland," 215. See also Nicholls, *A History of the Irish Poor Law,* 28. In 1804 an anonymous traveller described a Dublin House of Industry as a "horrid scene of filth, profaneness, and obscenity . . . a great seminary of prostitution, thieves, plunderers, and rebels" (Anon., *Ireland in 1804,* 25–26).

127. Inglis, *Ireland in 1834,* 163.

128. "Report of George Nicholls on Poor Laws, Ireland," 215, 230, 235; emphasis added.

129. For an excellent discussion of this colonial ruse in another nineteenth-century setting, see Olund, "From Savage Space to Governable Space." Significantly, Foucault discusses the production of "docile bodies" as a technique for realising "mildness-production-profit" (*Discipline and Punish,* 219).

130. Gerard O'Brien, "Workhouse Management," 117.

131. Carlyle, *Reminiscences,* 73. "[T]hank Heaven," Carlyle elsewhere wrote, "that the potato has been so kind as [to] die" ("Indian Meal," 561). See also R. F. Foster, *Modern Ireland,* 132; Martin, "Blood Transfusions."

132. Trevelyan, *The Irish Crisis,* 7–8. Noting Trevelyan's disparaging comments on the Irish diet, Amartya Sen responded: "it is rather rare for an Englishman to find a suitable occasion for making international criticism of culinary art." Furthermore, Sen said, the "pointing of an accusing finger at the meagreness of the diet of the Irish poor well illustrates the tendency to blame the victim"

(*Development as Freedom,* 175). Trevelyan's comments are early examples of the "patronising insults" from those who blamed "the ignorance of the average working-class housewife in regard to food values and in the art of cooking." See Vernon, *Hunger,* 133, 199.

133. McCulloch. *The Principles of Political Economy,* 322.

134. Eagleton, *Heathcliff and the Great Hunger,* 16.

135. Senior, *Journals, Conversations and Essays,* 1:143; Trevelyan, *The Irish Crisis,* 195–96. In his retrospective account Nicholls also blamed the potato for Ireland's ills: "The universal and almost exclusive use of the potato as an article of subsistence, led to a rapid increase of the population—its failure led to a still more rapid decrease, accompanied by an amount of suffering and privation for which it would be difficult to find a parallel in the history of any people" (*A History of the Irish Poor Law,* 387). An anonymous author described the Irish potato economy as "the wretched husbandry of planting squatters and reaping rack-rents" (Anon., *Ireland's Hour,* 2). For the commissioners' dietary recommendations, see "Second Annual Report of Commissioners of Inquiry into the Administration and Practical Operation of the Poor Laws," 63–66.

136. Trevelyan, *The Irish Crisis,* 195.

137. Gerard O'Brien, "The Poor Law," 47.

138. Gerard O'Brien, "Workhouse Management," 120; Kinealy, "The Role of the Poor Law," 110; Kinealy, "The Poor Law During the Great Famine," 160.

139. Forbes, *Memorandums Made in Ireland,* 1:95, 2:236.

140. Ibid., 2:227; Anon., "Famine in the South of Ireland," 491.

141. Scrope, *The Irish Poor Law,* 23–24.

142. S. G. Osborne, *Gleanings,* 56.

143. A. Stark, *The South of Ireland in 1850,* 111.

144. Elden, "The War of Race," 146. See also Stoler, *Race and the Education of Desire*; Howell, "Foucault, Sexuality, Geography."

145. Clark, "Wild Workhouse Girls"; McLoughlin, "Women and Sexuality"; McLoughlin, "Workhouses and the Irish Female Paupers."

146. For Giorgio Agamben the seizure of "bare life"—the natural life of a person—is the ultimate expression of sovereign power and nothing less than the hidden matrix of modern politics: "The *puissance absolue et perpétuelle,* which defines state power, is not founded—in the last instance—on political will but rather on naked life, which is kept safe and protected only to the degree to which it submits itself to the sovereign's (or the law's) right to life and death" (Agamben, *Means without Ends,* 5; see also Agamben, *Homo Sacer,* 3, 5). This "paradox of sovereignty" is played out in what Agamben calls the "space of the exception": a temporary suspension of the rule of law that is revealed to constitute the fundamental structure of the legal system itself. Trading on the political philosophy of Carl Schmitt, Agamben writes, "Sovereign is he who decides

on the state of the exception" (Agamben, *Homo Sacer*, 11), leading him to sur-mise that the law appears to be "in force in the figure . . . of its own dissolu-tion" (*Homo Sacer*, 38). If Agamben's thesis is correct, and "the originary rela-tion of law to life is not application but Abandonment" (Agamben, *Homo Sacer*, 29), then right and wrong, law and violence, the exception and the rule become the effect of sovereign definitions and distinctions—or, in other words, the ability to include and exclude certain people from customary legal protections. See also Agamben, *Means without Ends*, ix, 32. My misgivings about Agamben's claims are outlined in the introduction, note 77.

147. The phrase belongs to Gregory, *The Colonial Present*, 63.

148. Rancière, "Who Is the Subject of the Rights of Man?" 303.

149. Nicholls, *A History of the Irish Poor Law*, 87–88.

150. Ibid., 95.

151. Nicholls, *Poor Laws, Ireland*, 168.

152. Senior, *Journals, Conversations and Essays*, 1:215.

153. For contemporary parallels see N. Klein, *The Shock Doctrine*; Nally, "Considering the Political Utility of Disasters."

CHAPTER FOUR. IMPOSING CIVILITY

1. For a modern perspective see Vaux, *The Selfish Altruist*; Duffield, "Governing the Borderlands"; Duffield, "Humanitarian Intervention."

2. A. Stark, *The South of Ireland*, 121.

3. S. G. Osborne, *Gleanings*, 204; Anon., "The Working of the Irish Poor Law." Reverend Peter Daly went so far as to say "that more would scarcely have died if there had been no relief afforded. And I am quite convinced there would have been less of human misery. They would have died more quickly" (quoted in Scrope, *The Irish Poor Law*, 30).

4. Hoppen, *Ireland since 1800*, 61.

5. By 1845, 123 workhouses were operational.

6. Quoted in J. O'Rourke, *The History of the Great Irish Famine*, 152.

7. Bourke, *"The Visitation of God,"* 171.

8. Nicholls made this allegation in his second report. Nicholls, *A History of the Irish Poor Law*, 197.

9. Gray, "'Potatoes and Providence,'" 78.

10. 9th and 10th Vict., cap. 1, "An Act for the Further Amendment of the Acts for the Extension and Promotion of Public Works in Ireland." H. Burke, *The People and the Poor Law*, 106.

11. Quoted in H. Burke, *The People and the Poor Law*, 108.

12. Trevelyan, *The Irish Crisis*, 46.

13. Ibid., 47.

14. Wheatley, *A Letter to the Lord Grenville,* 79.

15. Wheatley, *An Essay on the Theory of Money,* 2:198–99.

16. These arguments are brilliantly developed in Gray, *Famine, Land and Politics,* 80; and Hilton, *The Age of Atonement.* For the providentialist view, see Acraeus, *God's Laws Versus Corn Laws.*

17. Mintz described the Corn Law debate as "a parliamentary high-water mark for disingenuousness" (*Sweetness and Power,* 62). For further discussion see Kinealy, "Peel, Rotten Potatoes and Providence," 44 ff.

18. Butt, *A Voice for Ireland,* 3.

19. Woodham-Smith, *The Great Hunger,* 49.

20. Butt, *A Voice for Ireland,* 4. For a more positive assessment of Peel's famine policy, see R. F. Foster, *Modern Ireland,* 325–26.

21. Gray, "'Potatoes and Providence,'" 78.

22. Peel, *The Speeches,* 599. See also Kinealy, *A Death-Dealing Famine,* 58.

23. Ibid.

24. Butt, *A Voice for Ireland,* 8.

25. Cullen, *An Economic History of Ireland,* 12; J. O'Rourke, *The History of the Great Irish Famine,* 336; Beaud, *A History of Capitalism,* 28. See also Ogborn, *Global Lives.*

26. Gray, "'Potatoes and Providence,'" 81; emphasis added.

27. The use of "food aid" to pursue ulterior economic agendas is a persistent feature of modern geopolitics. To take one example, the U.S. "Food for Peace Program" (PL 480) also acts as a convenient means to dispose of food surpluses. See Millman et al., "Organization, Information, and Entitlement," 315.

28. Trevelyan, *The Irish Crisis,* 55.

29. For this reason, Archbishop Mac Hale warned Lord Russell that "Visitations, such as that we are passing through, are not always confined to one season. Nay, they sometimes continue for two or three successive years" (Mac Hale, *The Letters of the Most Reverend John Mac Hale,* 610).

30. Woodham-Smith, *The Great Hunger,* 49.

31. Ibid., 59.

32. Butt, *A Voice for Ireland,* 7. Jonathan Pim declared: "Potatoes were not merely the food of the people, but in many places they supplied the place of capital and of a circulating medium" (quoted in Crawford, "William Wilde's Table," 24). See also Rogers, *The Potato Truck System.*

33. "There were private laws made by the 'committee' men and those who had the distribution of relief; amongst their law acts was one that any man possessing a four-footed animal—not dog or cat—one which could be sold at fair or market, was in consequence debarred from government aid as long as he had such" (Dorian, *The Outer Edge of Ulster,* 217).

34. Ibid., 222.

35. Trevelyan, *The Irish Crisis,* 49. The same fears were expressed in India. See Bhatia, *Famines in India,* 107.

36. H. Burke, *The People and the Poor Law*, 114.

37. 9th and 10th Vict., cap. 107, "An Act to Facilitate the Employment of the Labouring Poor for the Limited Period in the Distressed Districts in Ireland."

38. In a letter to Lord Russell, Archbishop John Mac Hale condemned the government for "leaving the providing of food to mercantile speculations. This would be just in the ordinary circumstances of society; but, when the price of provisions rapidly rises, as it is doing now, to famine height, not to provide the government depots, would be to abandon the people to the merciless exactions of the commercial cupidity" (Mac Hale, *The Letters of the Most Reverend John Mac Hale*, 616).

39. This policy is particularly emphasised in nationalist historiography. Mitchel certainly exaggerates the extent of exportation, but work by Kinealy has called into question the conviction that food exportation was miniscule or negligible. Kinealy makes three relevant points. First, she contends that the figures are problematic. After the Act of Union Irish exports to Britain were considered to be *interregional* rather than international. As such, precise figures were not recorded. Second, the fact that Ireland also exported outside the United Kingdom has been unduly ignored when assessing the extent of exportation. Third, the historical debate has focused on grain, ignoring exports in other foodstuffs (and, one might add, "indirect exports" through the fattening of livestock and the distilling of alcohol). Kinealy, "Food Exports from Ireland," 32–36; Kinealy, *A Death-Dealing Famine*, 79. I discuss some of these issues in the introduction to this volume.

40. Trevelyan, *The Irish Crisis*, 78.

41. Butt, *A Voice for Ireland*, 9. In relation to India it has been suggested that "The Free Traders' argument based on the existence of free competition had hardly any validity in a country where the grain trade in small towns and villages was monopolized in the hands of one or two dealers who often combined, withheld supplies from the market, and raised prices" (Bhatia, *Famines in India*, 106).

42. H. Burke, *The People and the Poor Law*, 114.

43. "Though the treasury would advance the money for public works in the first instance, the county cess [a local tax levied on "plowlands"] was to be used to repay these loans in full" (Donnelly, "The Administration of Relief, 1846–7," 299).

44. Trevelyan, *The Irish Crisis*, 59.

45. Ibid. See also Anon., "Famine in the South of Ireland," 403.

46. Trevelyan, *The Irish Crisis*, 61.

47. Nicholls, *A History of the Irish Poor Law*, 314. Nicholls is almost certainly drawing on Trevelyan's account. The latter complained: "Huddled together in masses, they contributed to each other's idleness, and there were no means of knowing who did a fair proportion of work and who did not" (Trevelyan, *The Irish Crisis*, 61).

48. Senior, *Journals, Conversations and Essays,* 1:43. Significantly, Senior felt that Irish indolence *could* be corrected because "the Irishman does not belong to the races that are by nature averse to toil. In England and Scotland, or America, he can work hard. He is said, indeed, to require more overlooking than the natives of any of these countries; and to be less capable, or (to speak more correctly) to be less willing, to surmount difficulties by patient intellectual exertion; but no danger deters, no disagreeableness disgusts, no bodily fatigue discourages him" (1:44–45).

49. Scrope was quick to point out that "the principle by which hundreds of thousands of labourers were last year employed in spoiling the thoroughfares, at the expense of the British tax-payer," directly contradicted the laws of political economy and the stubborn refusal to interfere with the rights of private property (*A Plea for the Rights of Industry in Ireland,* 14).

50. Senior, *Journals, Conversations and Essays,* 1:207.

51. Ambirajan, *Classical Political Economy,* 88.

52. Nicholls, *A History of the Irish Poor Law,* 314.

53. Quoted in Haines, *Charles Trevelyan,* 5.

54. Dorian, *The Outer Edge of Ulster,* 216. Trevelyan wrote: "The opposition to task-work was general, and the enforcement of it became a trial of strength between the Government and the multitude" (*The Irish Crisis,* 59).

55. Dorian, *The Outer Edge of Ulster,* 216–17.

56. Society of Friends, *Transactions of the Central Relief Committee,* 154.

57. Trevelyan, *The Irish Crisis,* 63.

58. Scrope, *The Irish Poor Law,* 41.

59. In 1846 it was reported that the price of Indian corn flour rose from £9 a ton at the beginning of the year to £19 a ton at the close of the year. The price of cereal produce rose in the same proportion. Anon., "Famine in the South of Ireland," 494; Donnelly, "The Administration of Relief, 1846–7," 300.

60. Balch, *Ireland as I Saw It,* 59.

61. Quoted in H. Burke, *The People and the Poor Law,* 115.

62. G. Bernstein, "Liberals, the Irish Famine and the Role of the State," 513. Bernstein explains that his figure of 3.5 million comes from a multiplier suggested by James Donnelly in "Famine and Government Response," 284.

63. Trevelyan, *The Irish Crisis,* 64–65.

64. Lord Dufferin's stirring account details the exorbitant famine prices and explains some of the deficiencies of the public works. See Dufferin and Boyle, *Narrative of a Journey.*

65. H. Burke, *The People and the Poor Law,* 116; Ó Gráda, *The Great Irish Famine,* 54.

66. Anon., "Untitled," *Times* (London), July 5, 1849.

67. Trevelyan, *The Irish Crisis,* 5; Scrope, *A Plea for the Rights of Industry Part III,* 6.

68. "Royal Commission of Inquiry into State of Law and Practice in Respect to Occupation of Land in Ireland," 31.

69. Ibid., 30.

70. Ó Gráda, *The Great Irish Famine,* 54.

71. Quoted in Senior, *Journals, Conversations and Essays,* 1:218.

72. Ibid., 1:180.

73. Quoted in Donnelly, "The Administration of Relief, 1846–7," 305.

74. Ibid., 306. Nicholls also observed that the differences between the smallholders and "the destitute is often so little perceptible, that Ireland seems to constitute an exception to the general rule [that all property should contribute to the Poor Rate] in this respect" (*A History of the Irish Poor Law,* 290).

75. Russell, *Hunger,* 224.

76. Dufferin and Boyle, *Narrative of a Journey,* 12.

77. Burritt, *A Journal,* 11.

78. I am building on Elden's excellent discussion of Foucault. He points out that for Foucault, it is economic man as the "exchanger of rights" that founds society and determines the conditions of sovereignty. Elden, "The War of Race," 139–40.

79. Trevelyan, *The Irish Crisis,* 65.

80. Ibid., 84.

81. 10th and 11th Vict., cap. 7, "An Act for the Temporary Relief of the Destitute Persons in Ireland."

82. Trevelyan, *The Irish Crisis,* 86.

83. Gray, "Ideology and the Famine," 97.

84. H. Burke, *The People and the Poor Law,* 116.

85. Donnelly, "The Soup Kitchens," 308. Kevin Whelan accurately characterised this system as a vast "paper panopticon." Whelan, "The Other Within," 24.

86. Donnelly, "The Soup Kitchens," 313.

87. Trench, *Realities of Irish Life,* 400. The *Lancet* complained that the broth was nutritionally incapable of sustaining the "manufactory of blood, bone, and muscle which constitutes 'the strong healthy man'" (quoted in Crawford, "Food and Famine," 69). Others alleged that the Irish were being "indiscriminately fed in idleness," not soup. Scrope, *The Irish Poor Law,* 9.

88. Trevelyan, *The Irish Crisis,* 89–90. Edmund Burke had famously cautioned "all Governments, not to attempt to feed the people out of the hands of the magistrates" (*Thoughts and Details on Scarcity,* 267). Significantly, when challenged on the government's laissez-faire famine policy, Trevelyan responded with excerpts from Adam Smith's *Wealth of Nations* and Edmund Burke's *Thoughts and Details on Scarcity* (Gray, *Famine, Land and Politics,* 254). Moreover, Robin Haines suggests that "It was Adam Smith who awakened Trevelyan's earnest belief in the universal application of free trade, his repugnance for complicated systems of

taxation, and his enthusiasm for lean, efficient, and financially responsible government" (*Charles Trevelyan,* 33). Compare Ambirajan, *Classical Political Economy,* 71–72, which cites examples of officials in India similarly justifying government policy by invoking the claims of Smith and Burke.

89. Butt, *A Voice for Ireland,* 26.

90. Specifically, four categories of person were entitled to relief: (a) the destitute, the helpless, or the impotent; (b) the destitute and the able-bodied not holding land; (c) the destitute, the able-bodied, and holders of small tracts of land; and (d) earners of very small wages.

91. Crawford, "Food and Famine," 67.

92. Kinealy, "The Role of the Poor Law," 111.

93. Trevelyan, *The Irish Crisis,* 88.

94. In an extraordinary piece of revisionism, Trevelyan declared that the Famine was not only "stayed" but now over: "The 'affecting and heart-rending crowds of destitutes' disappeared from the streets; the cadaverous, hunger-stricken countenances of the people gave place to looks of health; deaths from starvation ceased; and cattle-stealing, plundering provisions, and other crimes prompted by want of food, were diminished by half in the course of a single month" (*The Irish Crisis,* 89).

95. 10th and 11th Vict., cap. 31, "An Act to Make Further Provision for the Relief of the Destitute Poor in Ireland."

96. 10th and 11th Vict., cap. 90, "An Act to Provide for the Execution of the Laws for Relief of the Poor in Ireland." H. Burke, *The People and the Poor Law,* 127.

97. Nicholls felt that allowing outdoor relief would mean forfeiting control and creating permanent paupers. Nicholls, *A History of the Irish Poor Law,* 197.

98. Ibid., 130; H. Burke, *The People and the Poor Law,* 131.

99. H. Burke, *The People and the Poor Law,* 131.

100. Nicholls, *A History of the Irish Poor Law,* 335–36.

101. Kinealy, *This Great Calamity,* 183.

102. Quoted in H. Burke, *The People and the Poor Law,* 132–33.

103. Guy Debord, quoted in Boal et al., "Afflicted Powers," 10.

104. H. Burke, *The People and the Poor Law,* 135.

105. Scrope, *Some Notes of a Tour,* 30.

106. Hobsbawm, *Industry and Empire,* 88.

107. S. G. Osborne, *Gleanings,* 145. In Scotland a pauper could complain directly to the central authority about inappropriate treatment. See Gerard O'Brien, "A Question of Attitude," 168.

108. Quoted in Kinealy, "The Role of the Poor Law," 111.

109. Butt, *A Voice for Ireland,* 25.

110. Beaumont, *Ireland,* 285.

111. Scrope, *A Plea for the Rights of Industry Part III,* 5. This work was often completed in terrible conditions with little or no shelter. S. G. Osborne described the scenes he witnessed in Balinasloe: "I went into the yard where about 140 men were employed in stone breaking; the state of all their clothing was bad enough to be quite disgraceful, one in particular, was in a condition of the grossest indecency. I ascertained from one of these men, *that for nine days past, not one of them had had one drop of water either to wash with, or to drink, day or night"* (*Gleanings,* 45).

112. Trollope, *The Irish Famine,* 8.

113. Ibid., 15.

114. Scrope, *A Plea for the Rights of Industry Part III,* 9; see also Scrope, *The Irish Poor Law,* 47.

115. Quoted in Kinealy, "The Role of the Poor Law," 115–16.

116. See the evidence given by Edward Twisleton: "When you relieve them out of the workhouse, have you any means of affording them shelter, or fuel, or clothing?—No, not able-bodied men. Not their families?—No" (quoted in Scrope, *The Irish Poor Law,* 30).

117. Quoted in Donnelly, "The Administration of Relief, 1847–51," 323. Compare Trollope, *The Irish Famine,* 6.

118. S. G. Osborne, *Gleanings,* 53–54.

119. Quoted in Reid, *Life of the Right Honourable William Edward Forster,* 192.

120. H. Burke, *The People and the Poor Law,* 136.

121. 10th and 11th Vict., cap. 31, "An Act to Make Further Provision for the Relief of the Destitute Poor in Ireland."

122. Anon., "The Working of the Irish Poor Law."

123. Gregory, *Sir William Gregory,* 136. Significantly, Gregory drew on his Irish experiences while he served as governor of Ceylon. Duncan, *In the Shadows of the Tropics,* 156–57.

124. Gray, "Ideology and the Famine," 98. "The drawbacks [of these policies]," Donnelly concludes, "were quite serious even from the administrative viewpoint and . . . they were no less than murderous from a humanitarian perspective" ("The Administration of Relief, 1847–51," 323–24).

125. 6th and 7th Vict., cap. 92, "An Act for the Further Amendment of an Act for the More Effectual Relief of the Destitute Poor in Ireland." There seems to be some confusion in the secondary literature about these changes to the poor-rate. For instance, Tyler Anbinder claims that this new form of rating was introduced in 1847 under the Poor Law Extension Act, while John O'Rourke argues that the rating was part of the Labour Rate Act (1846). Anbinder, "Lord Palmerston," 455; J. O'Rourke, *The History of the Great Irish Famine,* 168. However, Desmond Norton—in a critical article on Anbinder's claims—rightly argues that the new rating was introduced in 1843 as an amendment to the Poor Law. Norton, "On Lord Palmerston," 4, 6.

126. "Royal Commission of Inquiry into State of Law and Practice in Respect to Occupation of Land in Ireland," 36.

127. Trollope, *The Irish Famine*, 19.

128. W. Bennett, *Narrative of a Recent Journey*, 24. "Famine is creeping up in society," remarked Butt, "men who had some little money stored have been living on their stores, and one by one they will drop into the class of paupers, and become victims of famine" (*A Voice for Ireland*, 29).

129. 11th and 12th Vict., cap. 48, "An Act to Facilitate the Sale of Incumbered Estates in Ireland." 12th and 13th Vict., cap. 77, "An Act to Further Facilitate the Sale and Transfer of Incumbered Estates in Ireland."

130. Trevelyan, *The Irish Crisis*, 158; see also Senior, *Journals, Conversations and Essays*, 1:144. The widespread reporting of evictions in the Irish and British press reflected poorly on Irish landlords, who were fast losing favour with the British political elite. In pre-Famine narratives travellers politely inserted ellipses to disguise the identity of the landed gentry; now most commentators adopted a policy of "name and shame" to highlight the recurrent cruelties they witnessed. Irish landlords were increasingly depicted as "improvident." Their improvidence, however, concerned an apparent propensity to live beyond their means and neglect their tenantry (that is, improvidence toward idle luxury), whereas the peasants were accused of indolence and a lack of "moral restraint" (that is, improvidence toward idle misery). Accordingly, relief policies were now targeted to squeeze the landed class, although it is worth remembering James Donnelly's point that for landlords it was a portion of their incomes and not their lives that was at stake. No landlord is known to have starved to death during the Great Famine, a fact that reveals the poverty profile of famine-related mortality. See Scrope, *Some Notes of a Tour*, 33; Donnelly, "Landlords and Tenants," 332.

131. Trevelyan, *The Irish Crisis*, 31. An anonymous editorial in the *Times* (written by a "person distinguished for his services in the administration of Irish relief") concluded in language strikingly similar to Trevelyan's: "I cannot conclude without mentioning the hopes which are excited throughout the country by the prospects of the next harvest, and by those particularly which the operation of the Encumbered Estates bill is promising. The measure is looked upon generally here as the right key to unlock the hitherto hidden treasures of the west, and open the long looked-for market for a steady and remunerative employment of the peasantry" (Anon., "Untitled," *Times* (London), July 5, 1849, 5).

132. Burn, "Free Trade in Land," 70. Through the Encumbered Estates court Irish properties worth £20,000,000 were redistributed. R. F. Foster, *Modern Ireland*, 336.

133. Quoted in Burn, "Free Trade in Land," 70.

134. Gray, "Ideology and the Famine," 102. See also Gray, *Famine, Land and Politics*, 202n313; Gray, "'Shovelling Out Your Paupers,'" 48.

135. 12th and 13th Vict., cap. 24, "An Act to Make Provision, until the Thirty-First Day of December One Thousand Eight Hundred and Fifty for the General Rate in Aid of Certain Distressed Unions and Electoral Divisions in Ireland."

136. Black, *Economic Thought,* 128.

137. Butt, *A Voice for Ireland,* 21. Mitchel echoed these criticisms: "Assuming that Ireland and England are two integral parts of an 'United Kingdom,' (as we are assured they are), it seems hard to understand why a district in Leinster should be rated to relieve a pauper territory in Mayo—and a district in Yorkshire not" (*The Last Conquest of Ireland,* 212). See also Donnelly, "'Irish Property Must Pay for Irish Poverty,'" 60–76.

138. Mac Hale, *The Letters of the Most Reverend John Mac Hale,* 614. Again, it must be insisted that these charges did not emanate only from the nationalist press. The Irish Poor Law commissioner, Edward Twisleton, resigned over Rate-in-Aid for much the same reasons. Before a Select Committee he declared: "If Ireland is not taxed to the amount that it ought fairly to be taxed, then introduce a separate measure to tax Ireland accordingly; but what I object to is, taking money merely from Leinster and Ulster to assist the distressed unions in Connaught and Munster" ("Fifth Report of Select Committee on Poor Laws; Together with the Minutes of Evidence," 333).

139. Nicholls, *A History of the Irish Poor Law,* 356–57; emphasis added. See also Kinealy, *This Great Calamity,* 262.

140. Johnson, *A Tour in Ireland,* 98. These reflections bring to mind Swift's famous "Modest Proposal" (inspired by famine conditions in 1728–29) and anticipate Thomas Carlyle's harsh conclusions.

141. Forbes, *Memorandums Made in Ireland,* 1:297, 299–300; emphasis added.

142. Donnelly, "Landlords and Tenants," 336.

143. Quoted in Donnelly, "The Journals of Sir John Benn-Walsh," 106; see also Donnelly, "Landlords and Tenants," 334.

144. Tuke, *A Visit to Connaught,* 12.

145. Harvey, *The New Imperialism.* "I wish there was not a tenant in Baltiboys," declared Elizabeth Smith, wife of a Wicklow landowner, "there will not be many by and by, no small holders at any rate . . . What a revolution for good will this failure of cheap food cause" (Thomson and McGusty, *The Irish Journals of Elizabeth Smith,* 102).

146. S. G. Osborne, *Gleanings,* 36, 47.

147. Scrope, *Some Notes of a Tour,* 28–29.

148. Tuke, *A Visit to Connaught,* 11.

149. Osborne adds: "It is a rare thing to find any males at these scenes of desolation; and in the majority of cases, I fear, they desert their families, go seek work at a distance, perhaps in England; very often they start for America as soon as they find they are to be ejected. A very large proportion of the families

in the workhouses are deserted families" (*Gleanings,* 31–32). See also Tuke's description of scalpeen huts at Erris (*A Visit to Connaught,* 21–23).

150. S. G. Osborne, *Gleanings,* 155.

151. Tuke, *A Visit to Connaught,* 27.

152. Ibid., 8.

153. Póirtéir, *Famine Echoes.*

154. Dorian, *The Outer Edge of Ulster,* 237–38.

155. Ibid., 252.

156. Scrope, *Some Notes of a Tour,* 26.

157. Mitchel, *The Last Conquest of Ireland,* 66; Butt, *A Voice for Ireland,* 30.

158. J. O'Rourke, *The History of the Great Irish Famine,* 245; Lalor, *Collected Writings,* 34.

159. O'Neill explains that the Irish laws pertaining to evictions differed substantially from the laws in England. In Ireland the summons had to notify not just the tenant in possession but all persons who had a claim, right, title, or interest in the property (significantly, however, cottiers were excluded from the protections afforded to other categories of tenants). This leads O'Neill to suggest that one writ of *habere* could lead to many more evictions. Since most scholars base their figures on the processes entered rather than on the numbers served, they may underestimate the quantity of people affected. O'Neill, "Famine Evictions."

160. Ó Gráda, *Ireland Before and After the Famine,* 115; Ó Gráda, *Black '47 and Beyond,* 44–45.

161. Donnelly, "Mass Eviction and the Great Famine," 156; Donnelly, "Landlords and Tenants," 337.

162. O'Neill suggests a figure of 144,759 families or 723,795 persons who had decrees of *habere* against them. This revised number is offered with various qualifications. O'Neill, "Famine Evictions," 42.

163. Ó Gráda, *Famine,* 82.

164. W. Bennett, *Narrative of a Recent Journey,* 53. In contrast, Harriet Martineau was disgusted by the emotional scenes of farewell: "When we saw the wringing of hands and heard the wailings, we became aware, for the first time perhaps, of the full dignity of that civilization which induces control over the expression of emotions. All the while that this lamentation was giving a headache to all who looked on, there could not but be a feeling that these people, thus giving vent to their instincts, were as children, and would command themselves better if they were wiser" (*Letters from Ireland,* 140).

165. Ó Gráda, *The Great Irish Famine,* 14–15. For the figures between 1845 and 1855 that follow, see Donnelly, "Excess Mortality," 353.

166. Miller, *Emigrants and Exiles,* 291. See also Mokyr, *Why Ireland Starved,* 230.

167. The Rate-in-Aid Act included a clause to apply money toward assisted emigration, but since most unions were so hard-pressed it was little

availed of. Black, *Economic Thought,* 129. This system of assisted emigration was a continuation of earlier relief policies. For example, on June 24, 1823, the government gave £15,000 to "facilitate emigration from the south of Ireland to the Cape of Good Hope" (Trevelyan, *The Irish Crisis,* 15).

168. Edward Maginn lampooned the landlords who asked him to support projects for "removing the carrion people from before our eyes beyond the seas, or anywhere, that we may forget the misery that we created" (*The Great Letter,* 8–9). See also Araghi, "The Great Global Enclosure."

169. Trollope, *The Irish Famine,* 10.

170. Quoted in Gray, *Famine, Land and Politics,* 192. See also Anbinder, "Lord Palmerston."

171. Quoted in Whelan, "Pre- and Post-Famine Landscape Change," 29.

172. Trevelyan, *The Irish Crisis,* 1.

173. N. Klein, *The Shock Doctrine.*

174. Ashworth, *The Rambles of an Englishman,* 221; emphasis added.

175. Quoted in Kevin Whelan, "Pre- and Post-Famine Landscape Change," 32. This charge is resuscitated by James Joyce in *Ulysses* when the Citizen says, "They were driven out of house and home in the black 47. Their mudcabins and their shielings by the roadside were laid low by the batteringram and the *Times* rubbed its hands and told the whitelivered Saxons there would soon be as few Irish in Ireland as redskins in America" (427–28).

176. Agamben, *Homo Sacer,* 29; Margaroni, "Care and Abandonment."

177. Quoted in Donnelly, "Mass Eviction and the Great Famine," 163.

178. Scrope, *Some Notes of a Tour,* 25.

179. Dorian, *The Outer Edge of Ulster,* 242.

180. S. G. Osborne, *Gleanings,* 257, 204.

181. Hussain, *The Jurisprudence of Emergency.*

182. Liz Young has compared government policy with clearances in the Scottish Highlands in the late eighteenth and early nineteenth centuries ("Spaces of Famine," 666–80). This same comparison was made much earlier in the pages of the *New York Daily Tribune* by Karl Marx. On the logic of expropriation, Marx wrote, "The process of clearing estates which, in Scotland, we have just now described, was carried out in England in the 16th, 17th and 18th centuries. Thomas Morus already complains of it in the beginning of the 16th century. It was performed in Scotland in the beginning of the 19th, and in Ireland it is now in full progress" (quoted in Marx and Engels, *Ireland,* 53). See also Rodden, "'The Lever Must Be Applied in Ireland.'"

183. Burn, "Free Trade in Land," 71, 73.

184. The figures are based on Kennedy et al., *Mapping the Great Irish Famine,* 162 ff. The authors point out three important caveats regarding the figures. First, before the Famine many of the small plots had been measured in Irish acres, whereas from 1847 sizes were recorded in statute acres (one Irish acre

being equal to 1.619835 statute acres). Second, the earlier assessments excluded so-called wastelands, which was not the case after 1847. Third, the figures for 1845 refer to the number of *persons* holding land, while the figures for 1847 and 1851 refer to the number of *holdings*. These facts make exact computations extremely difficult, though it is quite probable that the real number of farmlands and families affected is significantly higher.

185. E. Wood, *Empire of Capital,* 76; Marx, *Capital,* 1:659; Gray, *Famine, Land and Politics,* 9–10.

186. Trevelyan, *The Irish Crisis,* 25. The term *rundale* refers to the system of collectivised farming—common in rural Ireland and Scotland—consisting of small strips of land dispersed over a wide area, in addition to common lands that were cultivated for grazing. This agrarian system was typically organised around a small nucleated settlement known as *clachan.* See Anderson, "Rundale, Rural Economy and Agrarian Revolution"; Whelan, "Pre- and Post-Famine Landscape Change."

187. Quoted in Senior, *Journals, Conversations and Essays,* 1:227.

188. Ibid., 255.

189. Martineau, *Letters from Ireland,* 216–17.

190. Nash, "Visionary Geographies," 49–78.

191. Nicholls, *A History of the Irish Poor Law,* 365; H. Burke, *The People and the Poor Law,* 136.

192. Quoted in Póirtéir, *Famine Echoes,* 200.

193. Trevelyan, *The Irish Crisis,* 9.

194. The court evidence can be found in "Eighth Report from the Select Committee on Poor Laws (Ireland); Together with Minutes of Evidence," 590–91. Some of this testimony is quoted in Scrope, *The Irish Poor Law,* 14–15.

195. The government made the commission of a crime especially easy when it included a Vagrancy Act as part of the amended Irish Poor Law (10th and 11th Vict., cap. 84, "An Act to Make Provision for the Punishment of Vagrants, and Persons Offending against the Laws in Force for the Relief of the Destitute Poor in Ireland"). The English Poor Law commissioners recognised the double standards implied in this legislation: "To refuse relief, and at the same time to punish mendacity, when it cannot be proved that the offender could have obtained subsistence by labour, is repugnant to the common sentiments of mankind" (quoted in Senior, *Journals, Conversations and Essays,* 1:162). Despite such scruples the Vagrancy Act proved popular. Nicholls had pushed for legislation prohibiting vagrancy in his Poor Law report of 1837: "The suppression of mendicancy," he declared, "is necessary for the protection of the peasantry against themselves" (*A History of the Irish Poor Law,* 206). James Johnson thought a Vagrancy Act "absolutely necessary": "Open and unchecked mendicancy does infinite mischief in Ireland. These peripatetics are active agents in the dissemination of lies, sedition, and misrepresentation, as well as the contagion of typhus, and the more fatal and poisonous example of laziness and dirt!" Furthermore,

"To erect asylums for mendicants [that is, workhouses] without prohibiting mendicancy itself, is not merely ridiculous but injurious. It gives the beggar two strings in his bow—private and parochial charity—on the *former* of which he will be sure to play till it breaks, when he will have recourse to the *latter*" (Johnson, *A Tour in Ireland*, 167). Senior endorsed an Irish Vagrancy Act even though this (once again) contradicted his disapproval of "paternal government": "To check mendicancy is, therefore, one of the most anxious tasks of a government, which strives to improve the condition of its people. One expedient is to punish vagrancy; for vagrancy, as we have remarked, is the most profitable form of mendicancy" (Senior, *Journals, Conversations and Essays,* 1:187).

196. Quoted in Kinealy, *The Great Irish Famine,* 137. In his account of colonial Ceylon, Duncan notes that "It was hunger that lay behind a spike in crime" (*In the Shadows of the Tropics,* 183).

197. Balch, *Ireland as I Saw It,* 84. At the village of Bansha, Archibald Stark observed that "The shooting of landlords and in-coming tenants has given place to acts of petty larceny, undertaken by the perpetrators to mitigate the horrors of starvation, or with the undisguised intention of getting transported" (*The South of Ireland,* 43).

198. Kinealy, *The Great Irish Famine,* 138.

199. Trevelyan, *The Irish Crisis,* 139. In 1847, 15,008 Irish were removed from Liverpool to Ireland. As Kinealy correctly points out, the Removal Laws—which were part of the English, Welsh, and Scottish Poor Laws—demonstrate that Irish "immigrants" in Britain "were there under sufferance rather than right" ("Was Ireland a Colony?" 59).

200. Incidences of petty robbery and burglary quintupled during the late 1840s. Ó Gráda, *Famine,* 52.

201. Arendt, *The Origins of Totalitarianism,* 286.

202. The German traveller Kohl noted of the period before the Famine, "without exaggeration, that for the commission of a wicked crime, an Irishman is removed from a hole to a palace. His diet is also, in general, very much improved; for while he remained at home, with unimpeached honour, he had only watery potatoes; but as an offender in prison, he receives daily two pounds of bread and an allowance of milk along with it. It would, indeed, be difficult to make Paddy more uncomfortable in gaol than he is at home" (*Ireland,* 171–72). S. G. Osborne observed a man out of jail who "proved in how superior a condition the criminal is kept, to that of the pauper" (*Gleanings,* 74). Touring Ireland in 1843, James Johnson observed a Galway jail—a "large operative Pantechnicon"—in which the diet "is nearly the same as that in the workhouses." For Johnson the provisions were "quite sufficient for people accustomed to a low scale nutriment from infancy" (*A Tour in Ireland,* 173).

203. One enquirer was told how an inmate had purposefully applied an irritating substance to his eyes in order to obtain the superior diets in Irish hospitals. Forbes, *Memorandums Made in Ireland,* 2:239.

204. Sen, *Poverty and Famines,* 49. It is important to note that Sen uses the word "entitlement" in a very particular way and this should not be confused with a "right" (which it often is). In his original formulation, Sen's main point was to attack Malthusian food supply arguments. He points out that resources can be used in many different ways to obtain other goods and services, including food. Therefore, analysing an "entitlement set" is much broader than looking only at, say, income, trade, or food supply as the determining factor in commanding food. Sen argues that people starve when either their "endowments" (that is, their resources) or "entitlement set" (that is, the bundle of goods and services that a person can command) shift to such a degree that they can no longer obtain sufficient sustenance. Note that this initial formulation is incredibly legalistic. Endowments are defined as resources "legally owned," and the "entitlement set" takes as its framework the structure of ownership in a market economy. For these reasons, "extra-entitlement transfers" are mostly disregarded (nor does Sen consider intra-household entitlements, which appear to be excluded as a nonownership issue). This formulation rules out the multitude of illegal strategies used to maximise "endowments" or modify the "entitlement set" that were typically considered to be morally just by the *poor themselves.* It is important to add, however, that Sen has come round to some of these criticisms. In his book *Hunger and Public Action* (with Jean Dreze) he discusses the routine violence deployed by dominant social groups to actively deny access to food (Drèze and Sen, *The Amartya Sen and Jean Drèze Omnibus*). These acknowledgements suggest that entitlements can be eroded or violated rather than merely "lacking" in the first place (Sen, *Poverty and Famines,* 49). The fact that some people are denied entitlement also leaves the ground open for an alternative concept of justice, including the recognition of a "right to food" (Sen, "The Right Not to Be Hungry").

205. When asked whether it was desirable to maintain a broad distinction between paupers and criminals, Edward Twisleton responded "I do not know that I would draw a very broad distinction: there should be some distinction, and I think there is a sufficient distinction in giving paupers the power to leave the workhouse whenever they please on giving three hours notice" (quoted in Scrope, *The Irish Poor Law,* 46). Likewise, George Cornewall Lewis regarded the duration and voluntary nature of confinement as the distinguishing factor between the workhouse and the prison: "There is . . . one great and essential difference between a prison and a workhouse, that a prison is a place where a man is confined till his sentence has expired; whereas a workhouse is a place where a man is only confined till he will undertake to maintain himself" ("Remarks on the Third Report of the Royal Commissioners on the Condition of the Poor in Ireland, by G. C. Lewis," 260).

206. The distinction between "disorderly" and "refractory" behaviour is spelled out in Rules 26 and 27 of "Sixth Annual Report of Commissioners of Inquiry into the Administration and Practical Operation of the Poor Laws";

"Orders of Poor Law Commissioners to Unions in Ireland," 610; Gerard O'Brien, "Workhouse Management," 127.

207. Article 43 of the Poor Law states that pregnant women were not to be punished by confinement or by alteration of diet. See also Article 44; "Orders of Poor Law Commissioners to Unions in Ireland," 610; Gerard O'Brien, "The Poor Law," 48.

208. McLoughlin, "Workhouses," 726.

209. Scrope, *Some Notes of a Tour,* 25.

210. Quoted in Scrope, *The Irish Poor Law,* 30.

211. S. G. Osborne, *Gleanings,* 7.

212. Ibid., 7, 10, 22, 40, 133, 169. Osborne continued: "A state of things which treats large bodies of women as mere animals, except in the matter of apparently caring less for their lives than most men do their dogs" (190).

213. Ibid., 126.

214. Scrope, *The Irish Poor Law,* 51, 46.

215. Agamben, *The Open,* 38. "In our culture," proclaims Agamben, "the decisive political conflict, which governs every other conflict, is that between the animality and the humanity of man" (80). I would certainly want to qualify this lofty claim, although it is primarily intended as a comment about the nature of racism and the power to construct what counts as human.

216. Trevelyan, *The Irish Crisis,* 158.

217. Trevelyan, *The Irish Crisis,* 185; see also Burn, "Free Trade in Land," 61–74.

218. S. G. Osborne, *Gleanings,* 120.

219. Hoppen, *Ireland since 1800,* 61; Crawford, "Food and Famine," 64. I discuss the common but misguided charge of anachronism in the introduction.

220. Žižek, "From Politics to Biopolitics," 509; see also P. Fitzpatrick, "Bare Sovereignty," 1–20.

221. Mbembe, "Necropolitics."

222. Bataille, *The Accursed Share,* 198.

223. S. G. Osborne, *Gleanings,* 30.

CHAPTER FIVE. THE "UNGOVERNED MILLIONS"

This chapter is a significantly revised and expanded version of Nally, "'Eternity's Commissioner,'" 313–35.

1. See R. F. Foster, "'We Are All Revisionists Now'"; Whelan, "The Revisionist Debate in Ireland."

2. Mbembe, "Necropolitics," 18.

3. Quoted in Kinealy, "'The Famine Killed Everything,'" 29.

4. Trevelyan, *The Irish Crisis,* 1.

5. Gregory, *The Colonial Present,* 256.

6. Nicholls, *A History of the Irish Poor Law,* 389, 404.

7. Surprisingly, Carlyle's memoirs of his travels, and his various political pamphlets on Ireland, have attracted little scholarly attention. The few scholars who have taken the time to study Carlyle's observations on Ireland are remarkably divergent in their summaries. Clayton Mackenzie highlights "the hyperbolic verbal texture of the argument" as well as Carlyle's "powerful and frightening views" ("Thomas Carlyle's 'the Negro Question,'" 221–22). In stark contrast, K. J. Fielding notes "Carlyle's active understanding and sympathy for Ireland" ("Ireland," 131). Malcolm Brown claims that Carlyle's thoughts on Ireland "intertwined platitude and hysteria," while Andrew Hadfield and John McVeagh note Carlyle's "bitter reaction to a bitter land," adding rather perfunctorily that the text "still retains its power to puzzle and antagonise the reader" (Brown, *The Politics of Irish Literature,* 118; Hadfield and McVeagh, *Strangers to That Land,* 23).

8. Elden, "The War of Race," 125–51.

9. Dugger, "Black Ireland's Race," 464; McLean, *The Event and Its Horrors,* 34–49.

10. Engels later recanted. See Martin, "Blood Transfusions," 83–102.

11. Here my reading owes a debt to Thomas C. Holt's discussion of race and the problem of regulating free labour in *The Problem of Freedom,* 21–41.

12. Morrow, "Thomas Carlyle," 654. Morrow notes that Carlyle advocated a "capitalized agrarian economy," but he then rather strangely suggests that Carlyle's views were *not* "refracted through the icy prism of political economy" (656).

13. Dugger, "Black Ireland's Race," 466.

14. Backus, *The Gothic Family Romance,* 33–34.

15. The Duke of Wellington, for example, viewed the Repeal Association as a revolutionary "war of extermination" against the Irish Protestants and British interest in Ireland in general. See Gray, "Wellington," 203–26.

16. Arendt, *The Origins of Totalitarianism,* 127 ff.

17. Vanden Bossche, *Carlyle,* vii–ix, 90–141. I am greatly indebted to this remarkable study.

18. Ibid., 117.

19. Ibid., 117–25; Seigel, "Carlyle and Peel"; N. Young, *Carlyle,* esp. chap. 17.

20. Vanden Bossche, *Carlyle,* 126.

21. Quoted in N. Young, *Carlyle,* 197–98. Note Carlyle only mentions the pernicious effect of Irish *men,* in marked contrast to the image of the deathly— and deadly—"Irish widow" of *Sartor.* Moreover, the gendered tropes of misrule and contagion were grounded in the very homes of the English elite in the figure of the Irish wet nurse. See Jones and Stallybrass, "Dismantling Irena."

22. Carlyle, *Occasional Discourse,* 9.

23. Mary Poovey has written with considerable insight on the conflation of the (emigrant) Irish body, the diseased body, and the burgeoning problem of inner-city degradation in industrialised Manchester (*Making a Social Body,* 55–72). See also Kearns and Laxton, "Ethnic Groups as Public Health Hazards"; T. Osborne, "Security and Vitality"; Morrow, "Thomas Carlyle," 647.

24. Quoted in Hollander, "Ford Madox Brown's Work," 115. See also Martin, "Blood Transfusions."

25. Carlyle, "Repeal of the Union," 275.

26. The other two guests were John Pigot (1822–71), who was the son of the Irish Chief Baron, wrote for the *Nation* under the pen name "Fermoy," and afterward became a successful advocate at the Indian Bar; and John O'Hagan (1822–90), who edited the pro-O'Connell newspaper, *Newry Examiner,* and later headed the Land Commission. C. G. Duffy, "Conversations and Correspondence," 120–23.

27. Quoted in Seigel, "Carlyle and Peel," 198.

28. C. G. Duffy, "Conversations and Correspondence," 130.

29. It is difficult to assess Carlyle's appeal for these two young men. Joel Hollander speculates that both Duffy and Mitchel perceived Carlyle to be "the voice of revolution" and therefore "minimized their political differences with the older man" ("Ford Madox Brown's Work," 112). Interestingly, Duffy later blamed Carlyle for having "taught Mitchel to oppose the liberation of the negroes and the emancipation of the Jews." Carlyle replied that Mitchel would be "found right in the end" (quoted in Park, "Thomas Carlyle and the Jews," 6). Brown agrees: "he [Mitchel] resembled Carlyle himself, whose downward path from *Chartism* to the *Latter Day Pamphlets* after the shocks of 1848 was an exact parallel to Mitchel's course from the *United Irishman* to the *Southern Citizen*" (*The Politics of Irish Literature,* 142–43). See also Fielding's relevant but misguided assessment of Carlyle and Mitchel's friendship in "Ireland." Jules Seigel offers a particularly useful discussion of the Young Irelanders and Carlyle in "Carlyle and Peel." See also J. Quinn, "John Mitchel."

30. Ryals and Fielding, *The Collected Letters,* 21:24 and 24:192.

31. Ibid., 21:25, 47. See also Morrow, "Thomas Carlyle," 650.

32. His brief visit prompted Carlyle's wife Jane to write, "Irland [*sic*] *Young* and *Old* is surely too large a thing to be *done* in a couple of days! I know you *beat the world* for the quantity of even *correct* impressions which you bring away . . . but the material and spiritual aspect of Irland should be looked at more leisurely even by *you*" (Ryals and Fielding, *The Collected Letters,* 21:44).

33. Ryals and Fielding, *The Collected Letters,* 21:112–13.

34. Carlyle's library in Chelsea included James Fraser's oft-cited *Hand Book for Travellers in Ireland* and a collection of tracts by Jasper W. Rogers. See Vanden Bossche, *Carlyle,* 199n51; Kaplan, *Thomas Carlyle.*

35. Quoted in C. G. Duffy, "Conversations and Correspondence," 131.

36. Vanden Bossche, *Carlyle,* 127–28. The Irish uprising of 1848 is detailed by Cecil Woodham-Smith in *The Great Hunger.* Its failure demonstrated the Young Irelanders' complete incomprehension of the extent of suffering in the Irish countryside.

37. These articles included "Repeal of the Union"; "Legislation for Ireland"; "Ireland and the British Chief Governor"; and "Irish Regiments." Also, sometime between 1846 and 1848 Carlyle composed "Rakes of Mallow," which satirised the Irish aristocracy. See Vanden Bossche, *Carlyle,* 199n49.

38. Quoted in Tarr, "Thomas Carlyle," 256.

39. C. G. Duffy, "Conversations and Correspondence," 455.

40. Spenser, *A View of the State of Ireland,* 12.

41. Quoted in Martin, "Blood Transfusions," 88.

42. Having "no resource in poor rates levied upon their own landlords," wrote the *Times* in 1828, "they [the Irish] take their ample vengeance on those in England and overspreading Great Britain like locusts, they drag down the British labourer, by an unnatural competition, to a level of wages and misery unknown to preceding generations of Englishmen" (Anon., "Untitled," *Times* [London], April 5, 1828).

43. Vanden Bossche, *Carlyle,* 128–29.

44. Quoted in C. G. Duffy, "Conversations and Correspondence," 135.

45. Carlyle, *Reminiscences,* v.

46. Quoted in C. G. Duffy, "Conversations and Correspondence," 135.

47. In a letter to Duffy dated May 29, 1849, Carlyle remarked that he has read Jocelyn's *St. Patrick,* St. Patrick's own *Confessio,* and the "dreary commentaries" of the Bollandists, a coterie of Jesuit scholars, in preparation for a future tour in Ireland. Ibid., 136.

48. Quoted in ibid., 136.

49. Quoted in ibid., 136–38.

50. Quoted in ibid., 139.

51. Duffy's relationship with Carlyle was at most times good-natured, although during his tour Carlyle did refer to him rather brusquely to his wife: "Indeed I rather think of parting with Duffy before long; who (in my sleepless state, he being a sleeper) does me almost as much ill as good.—He is beginning the *Nation* again [re-established in 1849]; is the idol, and sacred martyr of all the repeal population, which I think means all the mere-Irish population taken together,—something sadly *canaillish* in that kind of relation; but it shews me at present the *inside* of repeal, and has its worth for awhile." And again on July 21 he wrote: "I meant partly to have staid *over* Sunday, and bidden Duffy adieu *by writing.* By speech will do perhaps better; and that I rather think must soon do: his traitorhood [at this point Duffy had been charged with treason and imprisoned] is likely to be much in my way henceforth; nor is he otherwise worth much to me" (Ryals and Fielding, *The Collected Letters,* 24:109, 140).

52. Quoted in C. G. Duffy, "Conversations and Correspondence," 127.

53. Carlyle's illness was the subject of many letters; however, the physical and physiological strain became more marked in later life.

54. The full quotation reads as follows: "have forcibly recalled all my remembrances, and thrown them down on paper since my return. Ugly spectacle: sad health, sad humour; a thing unjoyful to look back upon. The whole country figures in my mind like a ragged coat; one huge beggar's gabardine, not patched or patchable any longer: far from a joyful or beautiful spectacle" (*Reminiscences*, vi).

55. Ryals and Fielding, *The Collected Letters*, 24:109.

56. Ibid., 119.

57. Ibid., 24:95; C. G. Duffy, "Conversations and Correspondence," 140. See also Froude's preface to Carlyle, *Reminiscences*, v–vii.

58. C. G. Duffy, "Conversations and Correspondence," 140–41.

59. Brown, *The Politics of Irish Literature*, 119.

60. Quoted in C. G. Duffy, "Conversations and Correspondence," 135.

61. Nicholls, *A History of the Irish Poor Law*, 404.

62. Gray, "Punch and the Great Famine." In 1849 Russell informed Lord Clarendon that "The great difficulty this year respecting Ireland is one which does not spring from Trevelyan or Charles Wood but lies deep in the breasts of the British people. It is this—we have granted, lent, subscribed, worked, visited, clothed the Irish; millions of pounds worth of money, years of debate etc.—the only return is calumny and rebellion—let us not grant, clothe etc. any more and see what they will do" (quoted in Kinealy, *The Great Irish Famine*, 88).

63. Naper, *An Appeal to Irishmen*, 25.

64. Quoted in G. Bernstein, "Liberals, the Irish Famine and the Role of the State," 518.

65. Quoted in Tarr, "Thomas Carlyle," 255. Elsewhere Carlyle declared that "there is decidedly no danger of our wanting food, if we do not want good sense and industry first" (*Indian Meal*, 561).

66. Boime, "Ford Madox Brown."

67. J. W. Foster, "Encountering Traditions," 27.

68. Carlyle, *Reminiscences*, 17.

69. It is noticeable that Carlyle switches to language far less flattering. In a characteristic outburst, the Irish politician Isaac Butt is described as a "terrible black burly son of earth: talent visible in him, but still more animalism; big bison-head, black, not *quite* unbrutal: glad when he went off." Elsewhere in *Reminiscences* the Irish are dismissed as "yellow-faced"; "clean-dirty face wrinkled into stereotype"; "second-class"; "vernacular aspect"; and "potato culture" (ibid., 2, 54, 59, 64, 72, 73).

70. At a late stage during his second tour (Sunday, July 29) Carlyle and Duffy were joined by William Edward Forster (1818–86). In September and October 1846 Forster toured the south and west of Ireland; and again in January

the following year Forster accompanied his father to Connemara as a distributor of the Society of Friends' relief fund for the famine. Forster later served as the Chief Secretary for Ireland (1880–81), where his repression of Parnell and the Land League earned him the nickname "Buckshot Forster." Forster described Carlyle as "the greatest modifying force of this century." Reid, *Life of the Right Honourable William Edward Forster,* 116–30.

71. Carlyle, *Reminiscences,* 204, 83–84.

72. Ibid., 201–2.

73. C. G. Duffy, "Conversations and Correspondence," 280.

74. Carlyle, *Reminiscences,* 145–46.

75. Ibid., 79–80.

76. Vanden Bossche, *Carlyle,* 134.

77. C. G. Duffy, "Conversations and Correspondence," 291–92.

78. Ibid., 280, 290–92.

79. This essay was a response to Duffy's own article in the *Nation* entitled "Wanted, a Few Workmen." Both are reprinted in ibid., 434–37, 439–40.

80. Quoted in ibid., 440.

81. Whelan, *The Tree of Liberty,* 57. As Whelan argues, the symbolism of the Tree of Liberty was easily grafted onto an existing "May bush" tradition, in which the colour green also had a powerful resonance. "In August 1795, soldiers had to be called out from Cork to Blarney 'to prevent the planting of a tree of liberty, adorned with ribbons and mounted with a red cap by Irish carmagnoles.' The tree was 'a finely grown birch tree, the most stately found in the wood,' and its planting was accompanied by 'the playing of the Marseillaise, Reveil le Peuple, Ça Ira etc' by a special requisitioned group of blind pipers" (85). See also J. W. Foster, "Nature and Nation."

82. Ryals and Fielding, *The Collected Letters,* 24:256.

83. Carlyle, *Reminiscences,* 242–43.

84. Carlyle, *Reminiscences,* 178–79. See also J. W. Foster, "Encountering Traditions," 28.

85. Quoted in C. G. Duffy, "Conversations and Correspondence," 439–40.

86. T. C. Foster, *Letters,* 49, 218.

87. Ibid., 296.

88. Quoted in C. G. Duffy, "Conversations and Correspondence," 452.

89. Quoted in Vanden Bossche, *Carlyle,* 129.

90. Ibid., 125–41.

91. By this stage Carlyle had already published his article "Repeal of the Union." Mill took exception to his former friend's opinions and published a rebuttal entitled "England and Ireland," 307–08. For discussion see Harnick, "Point and Counterpoint"; Steele, "J. S. Mill and the Irish Question"; C. Mackenzie, "Thomas Carlyle's 'The Negro Question.'"

92. Ryals and Fielding, *The Collected Letters,* 24:193.

93. Quoted in C. G. Duffy, "Conversations and Correspondence," 577; see also Carlyle, *Occasional Discourse,* 6, 10.

94. Quoted in C. G. Duffy, "Conversations and Correspondence," 577. Nassau Senior described Irish labourers in strikingly similar language. See Senior, *Journals, Conversations and Essays,* 1:44–45.

95. Carlyle, *Occasional Discourse,* 8, 12, 13, 43.

96. See Holt, *The Problem of Freedom*; Lloyd, *Irish Times,* 46.

97. Carlyle, *Occasional Discourse,* 9.

98. Carlyle, *Reminiscences,* 53.

99. Carlyle, "Repeal of the Union," 275; Carlyle, *Occasional Discourse,* 29.

100. In this context we might note Vanden Bossche's remark that Carlyle's anticipation that he would find little or no new knowledge in Ireland was not only fulfilled but desperately desired. See Vanden Bossche, *Carlyle,* 129.

101. Quoted in Martin, "Blood Transfusions," 88. At Westport Carlyle commented that "No rents; little or no *stock* left, little cultivation, docks, thistles; landlord sits in his mansion, for reasons, except on *Sunday*: we hear of them 'living on the rabbits of their own park.' Society is at an *end* here, with the land uncultivated, and every second soul a pauper.—'Society' *here* would have to eat itself, and end by cannibalism in a week, if it were not held up by the rest of our empire still standing afoot!" (Carlyle, *Reminiscences,* 206). The trope of cannibalism is very suggestive; after all, as Sharman Apt Russell reminds us, "hunger ends in a body forced to cannabilize itself" (Russell, *Hunger,* 11).

102. Agamben, *Homo Sacer,* 153.

103. See Lloyd, "The Political Economy of the Potato." For a Marxist reading of Foucault, see Harvey, "The Body as an Accumulation Strategy."

104. Fegan, *Literature and the Irish Famine,* 98.

105. Arendt, *On Violence,* 75.

106. Ibid., 75–76.

107. Quoted in Lloyd, *Irish Times,* 46. For similar reasons Carlyle has been called an intellectual ancestor of fascism. See Park, "Thomas Carlyle and the Jews."

108. D. Scott, "Colonial Governmentality."

109. Compare Olund, "From Savage Space to Governable Space."

110. F. Mackenzie, "Selective Silence," 101.

111. Ó Gráda, *Black '47 and Beyond,* 222.

112. While Carlyle was untypical in many respects, he was also highly respected and influential. As Peter Park explains, "Carlyle was no marginal figure, no obscure crackpot agitator, but a respected and influential Victorian British historian and social critic, admired as a prophet of moral earnestness and social concern even by contemporaries who disagreed with most of his specific philosophical and political views" (Park, "Thomas Carlyle and the Jews," 18).

113. T. C. Foster, *Letters,* 404. Foster also shared Carlyle's abhorrence of Irish "oratorical elegancies": "How many rigmarole speeches in Conciliation-hall will manufacture one bale of cloth?" (443).

CHAPTER SIX. THE ANGEL OF PROGRESS

1. Marx, *Capital,* 1:652.
2. Smyth, "Introduction," 8.
3. Miller, *Emigrants and Exiles,* 137; Kinealy, *A Death-Dealing Famine,* 151; Ó Gráda, *Black '47 and Beyond,* 227.
4. Miller, *Emigrants and Exiles,* 132.
5. Ibid., 128. "In short," Miller summarises, "as a result of death, emigration, eviction, and ruthless consolidation of smallholdings and cottiers' plots, Ireland's commercial farming sector had by the mid-1850s inherited much of the land formerly held by those who before the Famine had struggled tenaciously to retain it for subsistence" (290).
6. Lloyd, "After History," 56. See also P. Duffy, *To and From Ireland.*
7. Kinealy, *A Death-Dealing Famine,* 151.
8. Ó Gráda cites Garrett Fitzgerald's figure in *Black '47 and Beyond,* 216; Miller, *Emigrants and Exiles,* 89.
9. See related comments in Eagleton, *Heathcliff and the Great Hunger,* 12.
10. Whelan, "Pre- and Post-Famine Landscape Change," 31.
11. Miller, *Emigrants and Exiles,* 26, 79.
12. Kevin O'Rourke cites Solar's estimate that *net* potato yields per acre in the post-Famine period were 38 percent lower than before 1845 ("The Economic Impact of the Famine," 310–11).
13. Kennedy et al., *Mapping the Great Irish Famine,* 176–77; Kinealy, *A Death-Dealing Famine,* 153.
14. Miller, *Emigrants and Exiles,* 290. The diminution in pig rearing between 1847 and 1851 was more marked at 30 percent (Forbes, *Memorandums Made in Ireland,* 1:306). Forbes commented that "Since the failure of the potato crop, and consequent famine in 1847, when the whole race was devoured, the cottagers have not been able to buy or maintain pigs, there having been considerable destruction of the potato crops since" (38).
15. Kennedy et al., *Mapping the Great Irish Famine,* 193.
16. See chapter 4. The caveats I identified there must apply to the following figures as well.
17. Kennedy et al., *Mapping the Great Irish Famine*; Kinealy, *A Death-Dealing Famine,* 153; Marx, *Capital,* 1:652.
18. Senior, *Journals, Conversations and Essays,* 1:256–57.
19. Whelan, "Pre- and Post-Famine Landscape Change," 30.

20. Catherine Nash provides an illuminating discussion of how these "visionary geographies" were intensely debated in the post-Famine period. Nash cites William Bulfin's rejection of the "bullockdom, grazierdom, and grazierocracy" that he believed followed in the wake of conquest. Nash also shows how alternative visions animated the discourse of Irish nationhood and rural reform. See Nash, "Visionary Geographies," 56.

21. Marx, *Capital,* 1:665. Mitchel wrote, "The more sheep we have, the fewer human creatures are left to wear the wool or eat the flesh. Ajax was mad when he mistook a flock of sheep for his enemies; but we will never be sober until we have the same way of thinking" (*The Last Conquest of Ireland,* 665).

22. Kinealy, *The Great Irish Famine,* 213, 254n6.

23. Hill, *Facts from Gweedore,* xv.

24. Robert Smith, a Clerk of Peace in County Monaghan, gave the following account of rural violence in the wake of land clearances: "I was informed that upwards of twenty families were turned out, and in the other case more than thirty. The consequence was, that the persons so dispossessed did not submit quietly, and in revenge cut the tails off the cattle of the proprietor of the estates, and committed various outrages. In the other case, the people who were turned out mustered a strong armed force, and at night attacked the persons who had been put into possession, whereby some lives were lost. I should here observe, that previous to these occurrences, the country in which this has happened had been peaceable" ("Protection of Life [Ireland] Bill," *House of Commons Debate,* April 3, 1846, Col 85 cc492–569).

25. Scrope, *A Plea for the Rights of Industry in Ireland,* 46; Scrope, *Plan for a Poor Law for Ireland,* 38; Scrope, *The Rights of Industry,* 23. Recalling the words of Shakespeare ("he takes my life who takes the means whereby I live"), Scrope concluded, "The peasantry of Ireland view the matter in this light . . . they feel the continuance of the system of *clearing* estates now in progress, to be a question of life or death to them" (Scrope, *Plan for a Poor Law for Ireland,* 36). See also Lewis, *On Local Disturbances in Ireland.* For discussion see Clark and Donnelly, *Irish Peasants.*

26. Butt, *Land Tenure in Ireland,* 65. According to J. F. Lalor, the Irish people owed "no obedience to laws enacted by another nation without our assent; nor respect to assumed rights of property which are starving and exterminating our people" (*Collected Writings,* 85).

27. Hill, *Facts from Gweedore,* 9.

28. "Royal Commission of Inquiry into State of Law and Practice in Respect to Occupation of Land in Ireland, Digest of Evidence, Part I," 435; "Royal Commission of Inquiry into State of Law and Practice in Respect to Occupation of Land in Ireland," 1136.

29. Carlyle, *Reminiscences,* 247.

30. Senior suspected, however, that Irishmen could not be easily converted into Yorkshiremen because they lacked "the intellectual and moral

capital—the skill, and industry, and submission to law, both of farmers and of labourers—which produce the comfort of the unpauperised districts of England" (*Journals, Conversations and Essays,* 1:162).

31. The trope of "enterprising philanthropy" perfectly illustrates the conflation of humanitarian and market values. Forbes, *Memorandums Made in Ireland,* 1:260–61, 263.

32. Ibid., 1:296.

33. "Report of the Select Committee of the House of Lords on Colonization from Ireland; Together with the Minutes of Evidence," 15.

34. Trevelyan, *The Irish Crisis,* 1.

35. Trevelyan, "Distress in Ireland."

36. Anon., "Untitled," *Times* (London), July 5, 1849.

37. Johnson, *A Tour in Ireland,* 298; "First Report of the Royal Commission on Condition of Poorer Classes in Ireland," 9.

38. "First Report of the Royal Commission on Condition of Poorer Classes in Ireland," 13, 17.

39. Woodham-Smith, *The Great Hunger,* 26. In fact, as Charles Le Quesne pointed out, the Irish census of 1841 revealed that the proportion of people per square mile was less than that of England (*Ireland and the Channel Islands,* 89 ff).

40. "Royal Commission of Inquiry into State of Law and Practice in Respect to Occupation of Land in Ireland," 29.

41. "Royal Commission of Inquiry into State of Law and Practice in Respect of Occupation of Land in Ireland, Digest of Evidence, Part I," 411; Mitchel, *The Last Conquest of Ireland,* 72; Mitchel, *Jail Journal,* xxxviii.

42. Mitchel, *The Last Conquest of Ireland,* 72. The figure is increased to two million in his *Jail Journal.*

43. Quoted in Woodham-Smith, *The Great Hunger,* 373; see also Gallagher, *Paddy's Lament,* 84.

44. Senior, *Journals, Conversations and Essays,* 1:252–55; Thornton, *Over-Population and Its Remedy*; Gray, *Famine, Land and Politics,* 56.

45. Although Mill felt that the Irish "are confessedly among the most backward of the European populations in the Industrial virtues," unlike many of his contemporaries he believed that the introduction of a new class of peasant proprietors would be more effectual than "the transformation of the cottiers into hired labourers" (*Principles of Political Economy,* 1:406–8). That is, he favoured peasant proprietorship over forced proletarianisation. See also Bell, "John Stuart Mill on Colonies."

46. Caird, *The Plantation Scheme,* 170.

47. "Royal Commission of Inquiry into State of Law and Practice in Respect to Occupation of Land in Ireland," 16.

48. S. J. Connolly, *Divided Kingdom,* 360.

49. Marx and Engels, *Ireland,* 191.

50. Mitchel, *Jail Journal,* xxx, xxxiv.

51. Póirtéir, *Famine Echoes.* See also Whelan, "Pre- and Post-Famine Landscape Change," 32. The possibilities and difficulties of working with the folk archive are helpfully discussed in Ó Gráda, *Black '47 and Beyond,* 194 ff.

52. Dorian, *The Outer Edge of Ulster,* 230. Commenting on the Famine the Quaker Jonathan Pim described how "The bonds of natural affection were loosened. Parents neglected their children—children turned on their aged parents" (quoted in Crawford, "William Wilde's Table," 24).

53. Ó Gráda, *Black '47 and Beyond,* 211.

54. Póirtéir, *Famine Echoes,* 272 ff; E. M. Quinn, "Entextualising Famine."

55. Smyth, "Introduction," 8. Ó Gráda cites these words from an Irish ballad: "Ní Bhedh I Éirinn ach daoine aosta, i mbun staoic ag aoireacht cois fallaí i ndrúcht; Ní bheidh pósadh in aon bhall ná suim ina dhèanamh, Ach 'tabhair dom an sprè' agus 'raghad anonn'" [Ireland will be left with only the elderly, tending livestock by wall in the morning dew; there will be no marriages, nor interest in them, but "give me the dowry" and I'll head off]. Ó Gráda, *Black '47 and Beyond,* 226.

56. The song is called "Amhrain an Ghorta" [The Famine Song] and is discussed by Ó Gráda in *Black '47 and Beyond,* 221–22.

57. Kinealy, *A Death-Dealing Famine,* 153.

58. Bowen, *Souperism.* Johnson discusses efforts to proselytise on Edward Nagle's Achill Island colony (*A Tour in Ireland,* 242 ff). See also Branach, "Edward Nagle."

59. Hoppen, *Ireland since 1800,* 32.

60. As Hoppen helpfully observes, "For Lalor the 'people' were essentially the farmers; for Davis they were Celtic rustics rather than deracinated townsfolk; for O'Connell they were, above all else, Catholics" (*Ireland since 1800,* 35).

61. Daniel O'Connell died of ill health en route to Rome in 1847. He was seventy-two years old. John Mitchel, Thomas Francis Meagher, and William Smith O'Brien were tried for sedition and transported. John Blake Dillon fled to the United States. Between July 1848 and April 1849 Charles Gavan Duffy was arraigned five times but never convicted. Eventually, in April 1849 he was discharged. Believing that there was no hope left for the Irish cause, he departed for Australia with his family, where he began an illustrious political career. On religion and the Famine see Kerr, *The Catholic Church*; Kerr, *A Nation of Beggars?*

62. Kinealy, *The Great Irish Famine,* 216.

63. The conduct of the British government during the Famine became a recurring motif of the Irish Land League. At a meeting in Navan, County Meath, for example, Parnell reminded his audience that Disraeli had declared that "there were many things which had done less harm and more good than the

Irish Famine." And at Beaufort, County Kerry, he asked the meeting: "Can it be expected this time in the 19th century our people will allow themselves to be driven from their farms as in 1848?" (Irish Land League Carton 1, INL 1/213 and INL 1/174–196, National Archives of Ireland).

64. It is interesting in this context to note the comments of a prominent landlord who described how his tenants behaved very kindly toward him and that "this good feeling would have continued had they not been taught by Davitt to consider rent a robbery and to hate landlords and Protestants" (Ffolliott, "Reminiscences").

65. Marx, *Capital,* 1:666; Davitt, *The Fall of Feudalism,* 116–17.

66. S. J. Connolly, "The Great Famine and Irish Politics."

67. Lalor put this succinctly when he declared, "had the people of Ireland been the landlords of Ireland, not a single human creature would have died of hunger" (*Collected Writings,* 62).

68. Mitchel, *The Last Conquest of Ireland,* 218–19. Mitchel's estimate is close to Mokyr's upper-bound figure of almost 1.5 million deaths. In fairness, however, the census commissioners were not unaware that their estimate, "without making any allowance for a natural and ordinary increase of population, conveys but very inadequately the effect of the visitation of famine and pestilence" (quoted in Nicholls, *A History of the Irish Poor Law,* 387). Mitchel was clearly taking aim at a particular form of governmentality thoroughly on show in the commissioners' final remarks: "In conclusion, we feel it will be gratifying to your Excellency to find that although the population has been diminished in so remarkable a manner by famine, disease and emigration between 1841 and 1851, and has been since decreasing, the results of the Irish census of 1851 are, on the whole, satisfactory, demonstrating as they do the general advancement of the country" (quoted in Kinealy, *This Great Calamity,* 296).

69. Mokyr, *Why Ireland Starved,* 266. Mokyr's analysis is widely regarded as the best estimate to date. This does not mean that his figures are unproblematic. In fact, Mokyr registers a number of "ambiguities," some of which have been discussed by James Donnelly. Donnelly skips over one of Mokyr's most important qualifications, however: most computations of excess mortality—including Mitchel's estimate—assume that mortality and emigration were mutually exclusive (Donnelly, "Excess Mortality," 352, 356). In other words, excess mortality rates are usually calculated by subtracting the number of emigrants. As Mokyr recognises, "the procedure employed completely ignores all those who died at sea or shortly after arrival due to famine-related causes" (*Why Ireland Starved,* 271). Given the fact that emigrant mortality rates could be quite high (as high as 17 percent among emigrants to British North America in 1847, if we are to take the government's own estimates at face value), this lends a downward bias to Mokyr's estimates. See "First Report from the Select Committee

of the House of Lords, on Colonization from Ireland; Together with the Minutes of Evidence," 47.

70. The point about George Bentinck's criticisms of the government's performance draws on Kinealy, *The Great Irish Famine,* 49.

71. Ibid., 49.

72. Butt, *A Voice for Ireland,* 20.

73. This point has been made in other colonial contexts. See Gregory, *The Colonial Present.*

74. It is sometimes suggested that too many accounts of the Famine focus on Trevelyan's influence (for example, Bourke, *"The Visitation of God"*; Haines, *Charles Trevelyan*). There are, however, good reasons for this emphasis. Peter Gray's work shows that Trevelyan's brand of "evangelical providentialism" had a broad base in the more important government offices, while Woodham-Smith demonstrates how Trevelyan was able to marginalise dissent and consolidate treasury control. She also documents a revealing episode in which Trevelyan attempted to press-gang Alfred Power, the government's newly appointed Poor Law commissioner, into carrying out orders. In defence Power was compelled to seek legal advice on treasury authority. Gray, *Famine, Land and Politics,* 16 and passim; Woodham-Smith, *The Great Hunger,* 378.

75. Quoted in Woodham-Smith, *The Great Hunger,* 378; see also Donnelly, *The Great Irish Potato Famine,* 26.

76. Quoted in Kinealy, *A Death-Dealing Famine,* 145. George Nicholls later opposed the Rate-in-Aid Act and the deliberate effort "to make the property of Ireland answerable for the relief of Irish poverty." Although no champion of the Irish, Nicholls considered the Famine to be a "common cause," and his words echo Butt's criticisms regarding the convenient setting aside of the Act of Union in order to "compel" the Irish toward improvement. Nicholls, *A History of the Irish Poor Law,* 356–57. This episode is discussed more fully in chapter 4 of this volume.

77. Hall, *Life and Death in Ireland,* 72–73.

78. Ibid., 74.

79. Tuke, *A Visit to Connaught,* 29.

80. S. G. Osborne, *Gleanings,* 256–58; Hall, *Life and Death in Ireland,* 73.

81. Le Quesne, *Ireland and the Channel Islands,* 74. James Warren Doyle described political economists in withering terms: "They are men who calculate human labour, and human life, as they do bales of cotton and quarters of wheat; who look upon the labouring classes as articles of merchandize, or machines for creating wealth, and who would calculate on the extinction by hunger of a surplus population, as the house-wife calculates the lives of bees to be smothered for their honey" (Doyle, *A Letter to Thomas Spring Rice,* 56).

82. Le Quesne, *Ireland and the Channel Islands,* 116–17.

83. Ibid., 93.

84. See Blacker, *Prize Essay*, 31; Blacker, *An Essay on the Best Mode of Improving*, 5.

85. Blacker, *Prize Essay*, 14. Blacker believed that smallholdings held considerable advantages over larger farms: "The great value of this subdivision of land in Ireland, which produces a regular gradation from the very smallest to the very largest holdings, may be seen by the numerous instances which may be adduced of small cotters advancing themselves, by their industry and economy, from the possession of a mere hut and potato-garden to the operation of farms, more or less extensive. This arises from their being able to rise by easy stages . . . to rank and respectability. This advantage the English labourer rarely possesses, from the great size of the farms" (Blacker, *An Essay on the Best Mode of Improving*, 38).

86. Scrope, *How Is Ireland to Be Governed?* 27–28.

87. Senior, *Journals, Conversations and Essays*, 1:171, 174. In defence Scrope condemned the "illiberal" explanations of "shallow observers" who blamed Irish underdevelopment on the barbarous nature of the Irish. In his view Irish poverty was a consequence of the "most destructive and suicidal social arrangements." Scrope also vehemently condemned land clearances, describing the policy as an "overstraining of the rights of property which cannot be defended by the principle of justice" (Scrope, *The Rights of Industry*, 22). In a related article Scrope pointed out that legal checks on expropriation were an essential feature of English common law and should be extended to Ireland: "'De-population'— the pulling-down of houses and clearing of lands from the small occupying farmers, for the purpose of their consolidation—was by the common law of this country for several centuries considered an offence even amounting to an unclergyable felony—that many statutes were passed expressly to restrain the practice—that Sir Edward Coke names it as one of those 'offenses against the pubic weal which the king cannot pardon'—that the Judges on proceeding to their circuits were repeatedly enjoined to make enquiry into and punish such practices—and that in numerous instances the parties guilty of them, though the note and consideration, were punished by heavy fine and imprisonment, and required to build the houses they had pulled down, and restore the farms as they had been set with them" (Scrope, *A Plea for the Rights of Industry in Ireland*, 73–74).

88. Nash, "Cultural Geography," 221.

89. Loomba, *Colonialism/Postcolonialism*, 29.

90. The term "strategies of moral avoidance" is from Pogge, *World Poverty and Human Rights*, 6.

91. Somerville, *Letters from Ireland*, 14.

92. I am drawing inspiration from Lefebvre, *The Production of Space*; and T. Mitchell, *Rule of Experts*.

93. Arnold, *Famine*, 73.

94. Trevelyan, *The Irish Crisis,* 144–45.

95. Trevelyan supported such ventures, although he felt the policy ultimately failed. Significantly, assisted emigration had been tried as a famine relief strategy in 1822, when Ireland suffered a partial failure of the potato harvest. See Trevelyan, *The Irish Crisis,* 147; "Report of the Select Committee of the House of Lords on Colonization from Ireland; Together with the Minutes of Evidence," 6.

96. "First Report from the Select Committee of the House of Lords, on Colonization from Ireland; Together with the Minutes of Evidence," 49, 52.

97. On the Removal Laws see Kinealy, "Was Ireland a Colony?" 59.

98. "Report of the Select Committee of the House of Lords on Colonization from Ireland; Together with the Minutes of Evidence," 7. Robert Torrens echoed this claim: "If Irish wages are not raised to an equality with English wages, English wages must fall to an equality with Irish wages. But the consequences of such a fall in English wages we dare not even contemplate. The Celt must be raised to the Saxon, not the Saxon brought down to the Celt" (Torrens, *The Budget,* 114). For an exemplary discussion of assisted emigration and colonisation, see Brantlinger, *Rule of Darkness,* 109–34.

99. On the regulation of refugees, see Hyndman, *Managing Displacement.*

100. Nicholls, *A History of the Irish Poor Law,* 314.

101. Mitchel, *The Last Conquest of Ireland,* 108.

102. Haggard and Noland, *Famine in North Korea,* 44. In *The Origins of Totalitarianism,* Arendt brilliantly demonstrated the intellectual affinities between classical liberalism, colonialism, and totalitarianism. Aspects of Arendt's thesis have been provocatively extended by Traverso, *The Origins of Nazi Violence.* See also Žižek, *Violence.*

103. Hoppen, *Ireland since 1800,* 49.

104. Kinealy, *The Great Irish Famine,* 122. In fact, it was emergency legislation of this sort that toppled Tory power in 1846, thus paving the way for the Whigs. The role of emergency legislation deserves more space than I can afford here, and it is certainly the case that use of exceptional legislation has affinities in other colonial situations. See Hussain, *The Jurisprudence of Emergency;* and Townshend, "Martial Law."

105. Elden, "Plague, Panopticon, Police," 244.

106. Ohlmeyer, "A Laboratory for Empire?"

107. Davis, *Late Victorian Holocausts,* 11–15; Watts "Black Acts"; Watts, *Silent Violence.*

108. Davis, *Late Victorian Holocausts,* 31. Both Watts and Davis are working from a critical Marxist tradition that is unfortunately neglected in the more recent accounts of the Great Irish Famine. Reviewing the Famine period, the Irish socialist James Connolly warned, "No man who accepts capitalist society and the laws thereof can logically find fault with the statesmen of England for

their acts of that awful period . . . They acted consistently upon the lines of capitalist political economy. Within the limits of that social system and its theories their acts are unassailable and unimpeachable; it is only when we reject the system and the intellectual and social fetters it imposes that we really acquire the right to denounce the English administration of Ireland during the famine as a colossal crime against the human race. The non-socialist Irish man or woman who fumes against the administration is in the illogical position of denouncing an effect of whose cause he is a supporter. That cause was the system of capitalist property" (J. Connolly, *Labour in Ireland,* 162, 173). For a brilliant discussion of Connolly's thought, see Lloyd, *Irish Times,* 101–26.

109. Butt, *A Voice for Ireland,* 8, 10.

110. Ibid., 10. Modern historians usually follow variations of this argument, though not always. Reviewing Woodham-Smith's *The Great Hunger,* the English historian A. J. P. Taylor declared, "The English governing class ran true to form. They had killed two million people." The best estimates show that Taylor's figure of two million, even if averted births are included, is erroneous. Quoted in Donnelly, "The Administration of Relief, 1847–51," 330.

111. Gray, "Ideology and the Famine," 103.

112. Marcus, "Famine Crimes," 245. See also de Waal, *Famine Crimes*; Edkins, "Mass Starvations."

113. The debate on "human rights" is far from straight forward. For provocative assessments, see Orford, *Reading Humanitarian Intervention*; Rancière, "Who Is the Subject of the Rights of Man?"; Žižek, "Against Human Rights." With regard to famine, see Huish, "Human Security or Food Security"; Sen, "The Right Not to Be Hungry."

114. Marcus, "Famine Crimes," 247.

115. Ibid., 246.

116. Marcus stresses the role of government but neglects the parts played by private citizens, merchants, and semiofficial relief organisations. To be fair, Marcus is not unaware of these shortcomings, and he specifically defines what he means by the term "government official" (ibid., 247n19).

117. Agamben, *Means without Ends,* 124–25.

118. Agamben, *Homo Sacer,* 114. Agamben is drawing on Arendt's report on the banality of evil in *Eichmann in Jerusalem.* This account continues to generate great confusion and controversy even though Arendt's overarching message — that evil seldom arrives in the package one might expect — was a very simple one. For discussion see Herman, "The Banality of Evil."

119. The cited phrase is from Pogge, *World Poverty and Human Rights,* 59.

120. Quoted in Keen, *The Benefits of Famine,* 12.

121. Doyle, *A Letter to Thomas Spring Rice,* 75–76.

122. Ibid., 64. Doyle was clear in his convictions: "if the law which the lesser good of society, suppose *property,* could not be observed without the sac-

rifice of the greatest good, which is *life,* then the law of property should yield, and that which regards the preservation of life should be observed." Later in the same article he was even more explicit: "If, then, the right of every individual to preserve life, (a right which he never did or could abdicate,) be incontestable; if no man can deny this right, neither can any man deny that the governing power in a state is entitled and obliged to provide, in one shape or other, for the preservation of the lives of its subjects; whereas, if it neglect to do so, it must either punish, as crimes, what in reality are not offences against the laws of nature, or it must permit what are called theft, robbery, violence, and even bloodshed, when these happen to be committed by its subjects, driven to the committal of them by extreme want." As a Catholic bishop Doyle felt compelled to add: "All consideration of religion is excluded from the foregoing argument . . . What, therefore, we are bound in charity to perform, we are also generally obliged in justice to fulfil" (72, 74–76).

123. Pogge, *World Poverty and Human Rights,* 23, 15.

124. Wood, *Empire of Capital,* 78; see also Araghi, "The Great Global Enclosure."

125. Dean, "Powers of Life"; Mbembe, "Necropolitics"; Bauman, *Wasted Lives.*

126. Foucault, *The History of Sexuality,* 138; see also Dean, "Four Theses"; Santiago-Valles, "'Bloody Legislations,'" 36.

127. Giroux, *Stormy Weather,* 13; emphasis added.

128. As Chomsky reminds us, "There have been quite a few experiments in economic development in the modern era, and though it is doubtlessly wise to be wary of sweeping generalisations, still they do exhibit some regularities that are hard to ignore. One is that the designers seem to come out quite well, though the experimental subjects, who rarely sign consent forms, quite often take a beating" ("Free Trade and Free Markets," 357).

OFFICIAL PUBLICATIONS

[For British parliamentary reports, the title of the investigation is followed by the session date; bill or paper number in parentheses or command number in brackets; and the volume number of the bound set of Parliamentary Papers.*]*

"Census of Ireland 1851: Part VI, General Report." *British Parliamentary Papers* 1856 [2134] xxxi.

"Correspondence between Poor Law Commissioners of Ireland and Inspectors Relative to the Statements in Extract from Book, Entitled, *Gleanings in the West of Ireland.*" *British Parliamentary Papers* 1851 (218) xlix.

"Eighth Report from the Select Committee on Poor Laws (Ireland); Together with Minutes of Evidence." *British Parliamentary Papers* 1849 (259) xv.

"Fifth Report from the Select Committee on Poor Laws; Together with the Minutes of Evidence." *British Parliamentary Papers* 1849 (148) xv.

"First Annual Report of the Commissioner for Administering Laws for the Relief of Poor in Ireland." *British Parliamentary Papers* 1847–8 [963] xxxiii.

"First Report from the Select Committee of the House of Lords, on Colonization from Ireland; Together with the Minutes of Evidence." *British Parliamentary Papers* 1847–48 (415) xvii.

"First Report of the Royal Commission on Condition of Poorer Classes in Ireland." *British Parliamentary Papers* 1835 (369) xxxii.

"Letter from Nassau W. Senior to His Majesty's Principal Secretary of State for the Home Department on the Third Report from the Commissioners for the Inquiring into the Condition of the Poor Law in Ireland." *British Parliamentary Papers* 1837 [69] li.

"Orders of Poor Law Commissioners to Unions in Ireland." *British Parliamentary Papers* 1844 (577) xl.

"Remarks on the Third Report of the Royal Commissioners on the Condition of the Poor in Ireland, by G. C. Lewis." *British Parliamentary Papers* 1837 [91] li.

"Report of George Nicholls on Poor Laws, Ireland." *British Parliamentary Papers* 1837 [69] li.

"Report of the Select Committee of the House of Lords on Colonization from Ireland; Together with the Minutes of Evidence." *British Parliamentary Papers* 1847 (737) (737–II) vi.

"Royal Commission of Inquiry into State of Law and Practice in Respect to Occupation of Land in Ireland." *British Parliamentary Papers* 1845 [605], [606] xix.

"Royal Commission of Inquiry into State of Law and Practice in Respect to Occupation of Land in Ireland, Digest of Evidence, Part I." *British Parliamentary Papers* 1847 (002) xxxv.

"Second Annual Report of Commissioners of Inquiry into the Administration and Practical Operation of the Poor Laws." *British Parliamentary Papers* 1836 (595) xxix.

"Second Report of the Select Committee on State of Disease, and Condition of Labouring Poor in Ireland." *British Parliamentary Papers* 1819 (409) vii.

"Select Committee on Condition of Labouring Poor in Ireland and on Application of Funds for Their Employment." *British Parliamentary Papers* 1823 (561) vi.

"Select Committee on State of Poor in Ireland, and Means of Improving Their Condition." *British Parliamentary Papers* 1830 (667) vii.

"Sixth Annual Report of Commissioners of Inquiry into the Administration and Practical Operation of the Poor Laws." *British Parliamentary Papers* 1840 [245] xvii.

"A Statute of the Fortieth Year of King Edward III, Enacted in a Parliament Held in Kilkenny, A.D. 1367, before Lionel Duke of Clarence, Lord Lieutenant of Ireland." *CELT: Corpus of Electronic Texts,* University College Cork, Ireland. Text ID Number: T300001.001. Accessed April 22, 2010.

"Third Report of Evidence from the Select Committee on the State of the Poor in Ireland. Minutes of Evidence." *British Parliamentary Papers* 1830 (665) iv.

"Third Report of the Royal Commission on Condition of Poorer Classes in Ireland." *British Parliamentary Papers* 1836 [43] xxx.

PRINTED PRIMARY SOURCES

Acraeus. *God's Laws Versus Corn Laws: A Letter to His Grace the Archbishop of Canterbury from a Dignitary of the English Church.* London: Houlston and Stoneman, 1846.

Anonymous. "Famine in Ireland!" *Black Dwarf* 8, no. 19 (1822): 680–84.

Anonymous. "Famine in the South of Ireland." *Fraser's Magazine for Town and Country* 35, no. 208 (1847): 491–504.

Anonymous. *Ireland in 1804.* Edited by Seamus Grimes. Dublin: Four Courts Press, 1980.

Anonymous. *Ireland's Hour.* London: Thomas Hatchard, 1850.

Anonymous. *Strictures on the Proposed Poor Law for Ireland: As Recommended in the Report of George Nicholls, Esq.* London: J. Ridgway, 1837.

Anonymous. "Untitled." *Times* (London), April 5, 1828.

Anonymous. "Untitled." *Times* (London), February 6, 1844.

Anonymous. "Untitled." *Times* (London), July 5, 1849.

Anonymous. "The Working of the Irish Poor Law." *Times,* July 5, 1849.

Ashworth, John Hervey. *The Rambles of an Englishman in the West; or, the Saxon in Ireland.* Boston: Patrick Donahue, 1850.

Balch, W. M. S. *Ireland as I Saw It: The Character, Condition and Prospects.* London: Putnam, 1850.

Barrow, John. *A Tour Round Ireland, through the Sea-Coast Counties, in the Autumn of 1835.* London: J. Murray, 1836.

Beaumont, Gustave de. *Ireland: Social, Political, and Religious.* Edited by T. Garvin and A. Hess. Translated by W. C. Taylor. London: Belknap Press of Harvard University Press, 2006.

Bennett, Arthur. *John Bull and His Other Island.* 4 vols. London: Simpkin Marshall Hamilton Kent, 1890.

Bennett, William. *Narrative of a Recent Journey of Six Weeks in Ireland.* London: C. Gilpin, 1847.

Bentham, Jeremy. *A Fragment on Government.* Cambridge: Cambridge University Press, 2005.

Bicheno, J. E. *Ireland and Its Economy: Being the Result of Observations Made in a Tour through the Country in the Autumn of 1829.* London: J. Murray, 1830.

Bigelow, Andrew. *Leaves from a Journal; or, Sketches of Rambles in North Britain and Ireland.* Edinburgh: Oliver and Boyd and G. and W. B. Whittaker, 1824.

Blacker, William. *An Essay on the Best Mode of Improving the Condition of the Labouring Classes of Ireland.* London: R. Groombridge and Sons, 1846.

———. *Prize Essay, Addressed to the Agricultural Committee of the Royal Dublin Society, on the Management of Landed Property in Ireland, the Consolidation of Small Farms, Employment of the Poor, etc., etc.* Dublin: W. Curry and Jun, 1834.

Bowring, John, ed. *The Works of Jeremy Bentham Published Under the Superintendence of His Executor John Bowring.* 11 vols. Edinburgh: William Tait, 1843.

Butt, Isaac. *Land Tenure in Ireland: A Plea for the Celtic Race.* 3rd ed. Dublin: J. Falconer, 1866.

———. *"The Rate in Aid": A Letter to the Right Hon. the Earl of Roden, K.P.* Dublin: James McGlashan, 1849.

———. *A Voice for Ireland: The Famine in the Land, What Has Been Done and What Is to Be Done.* Dublin: James McGlashan, 1847.

Burke, Edmund. *Thoughts and Details on Scarcity. Originally Presented to the Right Hon. William Pitt, in the Month of November, 1795.* Montana: Reprinted by Kessinger Publishing, n.d.

Burritt, Elihu. *A Journal of a Visit of Three Days to Skibbereen, and Its Neighbourhood.* London: Charles Gilpin, 1847.

Caird, James. *The Plantation Scheme, or, the West of Ireland as a Field for Investment.* Edinburgh: London, 1850.

Campbell, Thomas. *A Philosophical Survey of the South of Ireland: In a Series of Letters to John Watkinson, M.D.* Dublin: Printed for W. Whitestone, W. Sleater, D. Chamberlaine, J. Potts, T. Wilkinson, [and 13 others], 1778.

Carlyle, Thomas. "Indian Meal." *Fraser's Magazine* 39, no. 233 (1849): 561–63.

———. "Ireland and the British Chief Governor." *Spectator,* May 13, 1848, 463–64.

———. "Ireland Not the Bravest." *Nation.* May 29, 1847, 537.

———. "Irish Regiments (of the New Aera)." *Spectator,* May 13, 1848, 464–65.

———. "Legislation for Ireland." *Examiner,* May 13, 1848, 308.

———. *Occasional Discourse on the Nigger Question.* 2nd ed. London: Thomas Bosworth, 1853.

———. *Reminiscences of My Irish Journey in 1849.* London: Sampson Low, 1882.

———. "Repeal of the Union." *Examiner,* April 29, 1848, 275–76.

Carter, Nathaniel Hazeltine. *Letters from Europe, Comprising the Journal of a Tour through Ireland, England, Scotland, France, Italy, and Switzerland, in the Years 1825, '26, and '27.* 2nd ed. New York: C. and H. Carvil, 1829.

Davitt, Michael. *The Fall of Feudalism in Ireland, or the Story of the Land League Revolution.* London: Harper and Brothers, 1904.

Dorian, Hugh. *The Outer Edge of Ulster: A Memoir of Social Life in Nineteenth-Century Ireland.* 1890. Edited by Breandán Mac Suibhne and David Dickson. Dublin: Lilliput Press, 2000.

Douglass, Frederick. "Thoughts and Recollections of a Tour in Ireland." *AME Church Review* 3 (1886): 136–45.

Doyle, James Warren. *A Letter to Thomas Spring Rice on the Establishment of a Legal Provision for the Irish Poor and on the Nature and Destination of Church Property.* London: J. Ridgeway, 1831.

Dufferin, Lord, and G. F. Boyle. *Narrative of a Journey from Oxford to Skibbereen During the Year of the Irish Famine.* Oxford: John Henry Parker, 1847.

Duffy, Charles Gavan. "Conversations and Correspondence with Thomas Carlyle." *Contemporary Review* 61 (1892): 120–52, 279–304, 430–56, 577–608.

———. "Ungrateful Ireland." *The Nineteenth Century* 82 (1883): 1003–29.

Ffolliott, John. "Reminiscences of Colonel John Ffolliott of Holybrook House, Co. Sligo [c. 1880–1890]." National Library of Ireland, MS 21,192.

Forbes, John. *Memorandums Made in Ireland in the Autumn of 1852.* 2 vols. London: Smith, Elder, and Company, 1853.

Foster, Thomas Campbell. *Letters on the Condition of the People of Ireland.* London: Chapman and Hall, 1847.

Glassford, James. *Notes on Three Tours in Ireland, in 1824 and 1826.* Bristol: W. Strong and J. Chilcott, 1832.

Gregory, William. *Sir William Gregory, K.C.M.G., Formerly Member of Parliament and Sometime Governor of Ceylon.* London: J. Murray, 1894.

Griscom, John. *A Year Comprising a Journal of Observations in England, Scotland, Ireland, France, Switzerland, the North of Italy, and Holland.* 2 vols. New York: Collins and Company, 1823.

Hall, Spencer T. *Life and Death in Ireland: As Witnessed in 1849.* Manchester England: J. T. Parkes, 1850.

Healy, T. M. *Why There Is an Irish Tenant Land Question and an Irish Land League.* Dublin: M. H. Gill and Son, 1881.

Hill, Lord George. *Facts from Gweedore.* 1887. Edited by E. Estyn Evans. 5th ed. Belfast: Institute of Irish Studies, 1971.

Hoare, Sir Richard Colt. *Journal of a Tour in Ireland, A.D. 1806.* London: W. Miller, 1807.

Hughes, John. *A Lecture on the Antecedent Causes of the Irish Famine in 1847: Delivered under the Auspices of the General Committee for the Relief of the Suffering Poor of Ireland, Delivered at the Broadway Tabernacle, March 20th, 1847.* New York: Edward Dunigan, 1847.

Inglis, Henry D. *Ireland in 1834: A Journey Throughout Ireland, during the Spring, Summer, and Autumn of 1834.* 2 vols. 3rd ed. London: Whittaker, 1835.

Johnson, James. *A Tour in Ireland with Meditations and Reflections.* London: S. Highley, 1844.

Knox, Robert. *The Races of Men: A Philosophical Enquiry into the Influence of Race over the Destinies of Nations.* London: Henry Renshaw, 1862.

Kohl, J. G. *Ireland, Scotland, and England.* London: Chapman and Hall, 1844.

Lalor, James Fintan. *Collected Writings, 1918.* Edited by L. Fogarty. Introduction by John Kelly. Preface by Arthur Griffith. Washington, DC: Woodstock Books, 1997.

Le Quesne, Charles. *Ireland and the Channel Islands; or, A Remedy for Ireland.* London: Longman, Brown, Green, and Longmans, 1848.

Lewis, George Cornewall. *On Local Disturbances in Ireland; and on the Irish Church Question.* London: B. Fellowes, 1836.

Lovett, Richard. *Irish Pictures Drawn with Pen and Pencil.* London: Religious Tract Society, 1888.

Mac Hale, John. *The Letters of the Most Reverend John Mac Hale, D.D. under Their Respective Signatures of Hierophilos; John, Bishop of Maronia; Bishop of Killala; and Archbishop of Tuam.* Dublin: James Duffy, 1847.

Maginn, Edward. *The Great Letter of the Right Rev. Dr. Maginn, on the Transporring* [sic] *Scheme.* Dublin: William J. Battersby, 1847.

Malthus, Thomas Robert. *An Essay on the Principle of Population; or, A View of Its Past and Present Effects on Human Happiness; With an Inquiry into Our Prospects Respecting the Future Removal or Mitigation of the Evils Which It Occasions.* 4 vols. 6th ed. London: John Murray, 1826.

Martineau, Harriet. *Illustrations of Political Economy, No. IX. Ireland: A Tale.* Boston: Leonard C. Bowles, 1833.

———. *Letters from Ireland.* London: J. Chapman, 1852.

Mathieson. G. F. G. *Journal of a Tour in Ireland, during the Months of October and November 1835.* London: Bentley, 1836.

McCulloch, J. R. *A Descriptive and Statistical Account of the British Empire: Exhibiting Its Extent, Physical Capacities, Population, Industry, and Civil and Religious Institutions.* 2 vols. 4th ed. London: Longman, Brown, Green and Longmans, 1854.

————. *The Principles of Political Economy with Some Inquiries Respecting Their Application.* 5th ed. Edinburgh: Adam and Charles Black, 1864.

Mill, John Stuart. "England and Ireland." *Examiner,* May 13, 1848.

————. *Principles of Political Economy with Some of Their Applications to Social Philosophy.* 2 vols. London: Longmans, Green, Reader, and Dyer. 1871.

Mitchel, John. *Jail Journal.* Dublin: M. H. Gill and Son, 1913.

————. *The Last Conquest of Ireland (Perhaps).* Glasgow: R. & T. Washbourne Ltd., n.d.

Naper, James Lenox William. *An Appeal to Irishmen to Unite in Supporting Measures Formed on Principles of Common Justice and Common Sense for the Social Regeneration of Ireland.* London: Ridgway, 1848.

Nicholls, George. *The Farmer's Guide: Compiled for the Use of the Small Farmers and Cotter Tenantry of Ireland.* Dublin: Alexander Thom, 1841.

————. *A History of the Irish Poor Law.* 1856. New York: Augustus M. Kelley, 1967.

————. *Poor Laws, Ireland. Three Reports by George Nicholls, Esq., to Her Majesty's Principal Secretary of State for the Home Department.* London: Printed by W. Clowes and Son for Her Majesty's Stationery Office, 1838.

Nicholson, Asenath. *The Bible in Ireland ("Ireland's Welcome to the Stranger or Excursions through Ireland in 1844 and 1845 for the Purpose of Personally Investigating the Condition of the Poor").* With an introduction by Alfred Tresidder Sheppard. New York: John Day Company, 1927.

O'Connell, Catherine M. *Excursions in Ireland during 1844 and 1850. With a Visit to the Late Daniel O'Connell, M.P.* London: R. Bentley, 1852.

O'Donoghue, D. J. *Sir Walter Scott's Tour in Ireland in 1825.* Glasgow: Gowans and Gray, 1905.

Osborne, Sidney Godolphin. *Gleanings in the West of Ireland.* London: Boone, 1850.

Parnell, Anna. *The Tale of the Land League: A Great Shame.* National Library of Ireland, MS 12,144.

Peel, Robert. *The Speeches of the Late Right Honourable Sir Robert Peel Delivered in the House of Commons, with an Explanatory Index, Volume IV, 1842–1850,* London: George Routledge and Co, 1853.

Plumptre, Anne. *Narrative of a Residence in Ireland during the Summer of 1814, and That of 1815.* London: Colburn, 1817.

Pückler-Muskau, Hermann Fürst Von. *Tour in England, Ireland, and France, in the Years 1828, and 1829. With Remarks on the Manners and Customs of the Inhabitants, and Anecdotes of Distinguished Public Characters. In a Series of Letters.* Philadelphia: Carey Lea and Blanchard, 1833.

Reid, T. W. *Life of the Right Honourable William Edward Forster, Vol I.* London: Chapman and Hall, 1888.

Ritchie, Leitch. *Ireland, Picturesque and Romantic.* London: Longman, Orme, Brown, Green and Longmans, 1838.

Rogers, Jasper W. *Facts for the Kind-Hearted of England! As to the Wretchedness of the Irish Peasantry, and the Means for Their Regeneration.* London: J. Ridgway, 1847.

————. *The Potato Truck System of Ireland: The Main Cause of Her Periodical Famines and of the Non-Payment of Her Rents.* London: J. Ridgway, 1847.

Rusk, Ralph L. *The Letters of Ralph Waldo Emerson, Volume 4.* New York: Columbia University Press, 1939.

Ryals, Clyde De L., and Kenneth J. Fielding. *The Collected Letters of Thomas and Jane Carlyle, Volumes 21 and 24.* Durham: Duke University Press, 1995.

Scrope, George Poulett. *How Is Ireland to Be Governed? A Question Addressed to the New Administration of Lord Melbourne in 1834 with a Postscript in Which the Same Question Is Addressed to the Administration of Sir Robert Peel in 1846.* London: James Ridgway, 1846.

————. *The Irish Poor Law: How Far Has It Failed? And Why?* London: James Ridgway, 1849.

————. *Plan for a Poor Law for Ireland with a Review of the Arguments For and Against.* London: James Ridgway and Sons, 1834.

————. *A Plea for the Rights of Industry in Ireland, Being the Substance of Letters Which Recently Appeared in the Morning Chronicle, with Additions.* London: James Ridgway, 1848.

————. *A Plea for the Rights of Industry Part III. On the Best Forms of Relief to the Able-Bodied Poor.* London: James Ridgway, 1848.

————. "Poor Laws for Ireland." *Quarterly Review* 44 (1831): 511–54.

————. *The Rights of Industry, or the Social Problem of the Day. As Exemplified in France, Ireland, and Britain.* London: James Ridgway, 1848.

————. *Some Notes of a Tour in England, Scotland, and Ireland: Made with a View to the Inquiry Whether Our Labouring Population Be Really Redundant? In Letters to the Editor of the "Morning Chronicle."* London: James Ridgway, 1849.

Senior, Nassau. *Journals, Conversations and Essays Relating to Ireland.* 2 vols. London: Longmans Green and Company, 1868.

Smith, Adam. *An Inquiry into the Nature and Causes of the Wealth of Nations.* 5th ed. Edited by Edwin Cannan. London: Methuen and Company, 1904.

Society of Friends. *Transactions of the Central Relief Committee of the Society of Friends during the Famine in Ireland in 1846 and 1847.* Dublin: Hodges and Smith, 1852.

Somerville, Alexander. *Letters from Ireland during the Famine of 1847.* Edited by K. D. M. Snell. Dublin: IAP, 1994.

Spenser, Edmund. *A View of the State of Ireland.* 1633. Edited by Andrew Hadfield and Willy Maley. London: Blackwell, 1997.

Stark, Archibald G. *The South of Ireland in 1850: Being the Journal of a Tour in Leinster and Munster.* Dublin: J. Duffy, 1850.

Stark, W., ed. *Jeremy Bentham's Economic Writings.* 3 vols. London: George Allen and Unwin, 1952.

Thackeray, William Makepeace. *The Irish Sketch Book of 1842.* London: John Murray Ballantyne Hanson, 1985.

Thomson, David, and Moyra McGusty, eds. *The Irish Journals of Elizabeth Smith, 1840–1850.* Oxford: Clarendon Press, 1980.

Thornton, William Thomas. *Over-Population and Its Remedy; or An Inquiry into the Extent and Causes of the Distress among the Labouring Classes of the British Islands and into the Means of Remedying It.* London: Longman, Brown, Green, and Longmans, 1846.

Tonna, Charlotte Elizabeth. *Letters from Ireland, MDCCCXXXVII (1848).* New York: Charles Scribner, 1856.

Torrens, Robert. *The Budget: A Series of Letters on Financial, Commercial, and Colonial Policy by a Member of the Political Economy Club.* London: Smith, Elder and Company, 1841.

———. *Colonization of South Australia.* London: Longman, Rees, Orme, Brown, Green, and Longman, 1835.

———. *Plan of an Association in Aid of the Irish Poor Law.* London: Longman, Orme, Brown, and Green, 1838.

Trench, William Steuart. *Realities of Irish Life.* 3rd ed. London: Longmans, Green, and Company, 1869.

Trevelyan, Charles E. "Distress in Ireland." *Times* (London), October 12, 1847.

———. "The Great Irish Famine." *Times* (London), June 29, 1880.

———. *The Irish Crisis.* London: Longman, Brown, Green, and Longmans, 1848.

———. "Threatened Famine in Bengal." *Times* (London), November 27, 1873.

Trollope, Anthony. *The Irish Famine: Six Letters to the Examiner, 1849/1850.* Edited by Lance O. Tingay. London: Silverbridge, 1987.

Tuke, James H. *A Visit to Connaught in the Autumn of 1847: A Letter Addressed to the Central Relief Committee of the Society of Friends.* London: Charles Gilpin, 1847.

Venedey, Jacob. *Ireland and the Irish during the Repeal Year, 1843.* Translated by William Bernard MacCabe. Dublin: James Duffy, 1844.

Wheatley, John. *An Essay on the Theory of Money and Principles of Commerce, Volume 2.* London: T. Cadell, 1822.

———. *A Letter to His Grace the Duke of Devonshire on the State of Ireland and the General Effects of Colonization.* Calcutta: Baptist Mission Press, 1824.

———. *A Letter to the Lord Grenville, on the Distress of the Country.* London: J. Ridgeway and Sons, 1816.

Wiggins, John. *The "Monster" Misery of Ireland: A Practical Treatise on the Relation of Landlord and Tenant, with Suggestions for Legislative Measures, and the Management of Landed Property, the Result of above Thirty Years' Experience and Study of the Subject.* London: Richard Bentle, 1844.

[Wilde, W. R.]. "The Food of the Irish." *Dublin University Magazine* 44, no. 253 (1854): 127–46.

Young, Arthur. *Arthur Young's Tour in Ireland (1776–1779).* 2 vols. Edited with introduction and notes by Arthur Wollaston Hutton, with a bibliography by John P. Anderson. London and New York: G. Bell and Sons, 1892.

SECONDARY SOURCES

Abraham, John. *Food and Development: The Political Economy of Hunger and the Modern Diet.* London: World Wide Fund for Nature, 1991.

Agamben, Giorgio. *Homo Sacer: Sovereign Power and Bare Life.* Translated by Daniel Heller-Roazen. Stanford: Stanford University Press, 1995.

———. *Means without Ends.* Translated by Vincent Binnetti and Cesare Casarino. Minneapolis: University of Minnesota Press, 2000.

———. *The Open: Man and Animal.* Stanford: Stanford University Press, 2004.

———. *Remnants of Auschwitz: The Witness and the Archive.* Translated by Daniel Heller-Roazen. New York: Zone Books, 2002.

———. *State of Exception.* Translated by Kevin Attell. Chicago: University of Chicago Press, 2005.

Ambirajan, S. *Classical Political Economy and British Policy in India.* Cambridge: Cambridge University Press, 2008.

———. "Malthusian Population Theory and Indian Famine Policy in the Nineteenth Century." *Population Studies* 30, no. 1 (1976): 5–14.

Anbinder, Tyler. "Lord Palmerston and the Irish Famine Emigration." *Historical Journal* 44, no. 2 (2001): 441–69.

Anderson, James. "Rundale, Rural Economy and Agrarian Revolution: Tirhugh, 1715–1855." In *Donegal: History and Society, Interdisciplinary Studies on the History of an Irish County,* edited by M. Dunlevy, W. Nolan, and L. Ronayne, 447–69. Dublin: Geography Publications, 1995.

Andrews, John H. *A Paper Landscape: The Ordnance Survey in Nineteenth-Century Ireland.* Oxford: Clarendon Press, 1975.

Araghi, Farshad. "The Great Global Enclosure of Our Times: Peasants and the Agrarian Question at the End of the Twentieth Century." In *Hungry for Profit: The Agribusiness Threat to Farmers, Food, and the Environment,* edited by F. Magdoff, J. B. Foster, and F. H. Buttel, 145–60. New York: Monthly Review Press, 2000.

Arendt, Hannah. *Eichmann in Jerusalem: A Report on the Banality of Evil.* New York: Viking Press, 1964.

———. *The Human Condition.* Chicago: University of Chicago Press, 1958.

———. *On Violence.* New York: Harcourt Brace and World, 1970.

————. *The Origins of Totalitarianism.* New York: Harcourt, 1976.

————. *Responsibility and Judgement.* Edited by Jerome Kohn. New York: Schocken Books, 2003.

Arnold, David. *Famine: Social Crisis and Historical Change.* Oxford: Basil Blackwell, 1988.

Backus, Margot Gayle. *The Gothic Family Romance: Heterosexuality, Child Sacrifice and the Anglo-Irish Colonial Order.* Durham: Duke University Press, 1999.

Barber, Sarah. "Settlement, Transplantation and Expulsion: A Comparative Study of the Placement of Peoples." In *British Interventions in Early Modern Ireland,* edited by C. Brady and J. Ohlmeyer, 280–98. Cambridge: Cambridge University Press, 2005.

Barnard, Toby. *Improving Ireland: Projectors, Prophets and Profiteers, 1641–1786.* Dublin: Four Courts, 2008.

————. *The Kingdom of Ireland, 1641–1760.* New York: Palgrave Macmillan, 2004.

Barnett, Clive. "'Sing Along with the Common People': Politics, Postcolonialism, and Other Figures." *Environment and Planning D: Society and Space* 15 (1997): 137–54.

Bataille, Georges. *The Accursed Share: An Essay on General Economy.* Vol. 2, *The History of Eroticism,* and vol. 3, *Sovereignty.* Translated by R. Hurley. New York: Zone Books, 1993.

Bauman, Zigmund. *Wasted Lives: Modernity and Its Outcasts.* Cambridge: Polity Press, 2006.

Beames, Michael. "Cottiers and Conacre in Pre-Famine Ireland." *Journal of Peasant Studies* 2, no. 3 (1975): 352–54.

Beaud, Michel. *A History of Capitalism, 1500–2000.* Delhi: Aakar Books, 2001.

Bell, Duncan. "John Stuart Mill on Colonies." *Political Theory* 38, no. 1 (2010): 34–64.

Bender, Jill. "The Imperial Politics of Famine: The 1873–74 Bengal Famine and Irish Parliamentary Nationalism." *Éire-Ireland* 42, no. 1/2 (2007): 132–56.

Benjamin, Walter. *Illuminations.* Edited and with an introduction by Hannah Arendt. Translated by Harry Zohn. New York: Schocken Books, 1989.

————. *Reflections: Essays, Aphorisms, Autographical Writings.* Edited and with an introduction by Peter Demetz. Translated by Edmund Jephcott. New York: Schocken Books, 1978.

Bernstein, George L. "Liberals, the Irish Famine and the Role of the State." *Irish Historical Studies* 24, no. 116 (1995): 513–36.

Bernstein, J. M. "Bare Life, Bearing Witness: Auschwitz and the Pornography of Horror." *Parallax* 10, no. 1 (2004): 2–16.

Bhabha, Homi. *The Location of Culture.* London: Routledge, 1994.

Bhatia, B. M. *Famines in India: A Study of Some Aspects of the Economic History of India with Special Reference to Food Problems, 1860–1990.* Delhi: Konark Publishers, 1991.

Black, R. D. Collison. *Economic Thought and the Irish Question, 1817–1870.* Cambridge: Cambridge University Press, 1960.

Boal, Iain, T. J. Clark, Joseph Matthews, and Michael Watts. "Afflicted Powers: The State, the Spectacle and September 11." *New Left Review* 27 (May/June 2004): 5–21.

Boime, Albert. "Ford Madox Brown, Thomas Carlyle, and Karl Marx: Meaning and Mystification of Work in the Nineteenth Century." *Arts Magazine* 56 (1981): 116–25.

Bourke, Austin. *"The Visitation of God"? The Potato and the Great Irish Famine.* Dublin: Lilliput Press, 1993.

Bowen, Desmond. *Souperism: Myth or Reality.* Cork: Mercier, 1970.

Boyce, D. G. *Nineteenth-Century Ireland: The Search for Stability.* Dublin: Gill and Macmillan, 1990.

Boylan, Ciara. "Victorian Ideologies of Improvement: Sir Charles Trevelyan in India and Ireland." In *Ireland and India: Colonies, Culture and Empire,* edited by Tadhg Foley and Maureen O'Connor, 167–78. Dublin: Irish Academic Press, 2007.

Boylan, Thomas A., and Timothy P. Foley. "A Nation Perishing of Political Economy?" In *"Fearful Realities": New Perspectives on the Famine,* edited by Chris Morash and Richard Hayes, 138–50. Dublin: Irish Academic Press, 1996.

———. *Political Economy and Colonial Ireland: The Propagation and Ideological Function of Economic Discourse in the Nineteenth Century.* London: Routledge, 1992.

Brady, Ciaran. *The Chief Governors: The Rise and Fall of Reform Government in Tudor Ireland, 1536–1588.* Cambridge: Cambridge University Press, 1994.

Branach, Niall R. "Edward Nagle and the Achill Island Mission." *History Ireland* 8, no. 3 (2000): 16–22.

Brantlinger, Patrick. *Rule of Darkness: British Literature and Imperialism, 1830–1914.* Ithaca, NY: Cornell University Press, 1988.

Brass, Paul R. "The Political Uses of Crisis: The Bihar Famine of 1966–1967." *Journal of Asian Studies* 45, no. 2 (1986): 245–67.

Brennan, Lance. "The Development of the Indian Famine Code." In *Famine as a Geographical Phenomenon,* edited by B. Currey and G. Hugo, 91–112. Dordrecht: D. Reidel, 1984.

Brown, Malcolm. *The Politics of Irish Literature: From Thomas Davis to W. B. Yeats.* Seattle: University of Washington Press, 1972.

Burke, Helen. *The People and the Poor Law in 19th Century Ireland.* Sussex: Women's Education Bureau, 1987.

Burn, W. L. "Free Trade in Land: An Aspect of the Irish Question." *Transactions of the Royal Historical Society* 31, no. 4 (1948): 61–74.

Bush, Ray. *Poverty and Neoliberalism: Persistence and Reproduction in the Global South.* London: Pluto Press, 2007.

Busteed, Mervyn. "Identity and Economy on an Anglo-Irish Estate: Castle Caldwell, Co. Fermanagh, c. 1750–1793." *Journal of Historical Geography* 26, no. 2 (2000): 174–202.

———. "The Practice of Improvement in the Irish Context: The Castle Caldwell Estate in County Fermanagh in the Second Half of the Eighteenth Century." *Irish Geography* 33, no. 1 (2000): 15–36.

Butler, David J. *South Tipperary, 1570–1841: Religion, Land and Rivalry.* Dublin: Four Courts Press, 2006.

Buzard, James. *The Beaten Track: European Tourism, Literature, and the Ways to Culture, 1800–1918.* Oxford: Clarendon Press, 1993.

Byrne, Joseph. *Byrne's Dictionary of Irish Local History from Earliest Times to c. 1900.* Cork: Mercier Press, 2004.

Canny, Nicholas. *The Elizabethan Conquest of Ireland: A Pattern Established.* Sussex: Harvester Press, 1976.

———. "The Permissive Frontier: The Problem of Social Control in English Settlements in Ireland and Virginia, 1550–1650." In *The Westward Enterprise: English Activities in Ireland, the Atlantic and America, 1480–1650,* edited by K. R. Andrews, N. P. Canny, and P. E. H. Hair, 17–44. Liverpool: Liverpool University Press, 1978.

Carroll, Clare. *Circe's Cup: Cultural Transformations in Early Modern Ireland.* Notre Dame, IN: University of Notre Dame Press, 2001.

Carroll, Clare, and Patricia King, eds. *Ireland and Postcolonial Theory.* Notre Dame, IN: University of Notre Dame Press, 2003.

Chomsky, Noam. "Free Trade and Free Markets: Pretense and Practice." In *The Cultures of Globalization,* edited by Frederic Jameson and Masao Miyoshi, 356–70. Durham, NC: Duke University Press, 1999.

Clark, Anna. "Wild Workhouse Girls and the Liberal Imperial State in Mid-Nineteenth Century Ireland." *Journal of Social History* 39, no. 2 (2005): 389–409.

Clark, Samuel, and James Donnelly Jr. *Irish Peasants and Political Unrest, 1780–1914.* Dublin: Gill and Macmillan, 1983.

Clarkson, L. A. Review of *A Death-Dealing Famine: The Great Hunger in Ireland. Reviews in History,* no. 43 (July 1997). http://www.history.ac.uk/reviews/review/43 (accessed September 26, 2010).

Connell, Kenneth H. *The Population of Ireland, 1750–1845.* Oxford: Clarendon Press, 1950.

Connolly, Claire. "Theorising Ireland." *Irish Studies Review* 9, no. 3 (2001): 301–15.

Connolly, James. *Labour in Ireland: Labour in Irish History; the Reconquest of Ireland.* Dublin: Irish Transport and General Workers Union, 1944.

Connolly, S. J. *Divided Kingdom: Ireland, 1630–1800.* Oxford: Oxford University Press. 2008.

————. "The Great Famine and Irish Politics." In *The Great Irish Famine,* edited by Cathal Póirtéir, 34–49. Dublin: Mercier Press, 1995.

Corish, Patrick J. *The Irish Catholic Experience: The Historical Survey.* Dublin: Gill and Macmillan, 1985.

Crampton, Jeremy, and Stuart Elden, eds. *Space, Knowledge and Power: Foucault and Geography.* Aldershot: Ashgate, 2007.

Crawford, E. Margaret. "Food and Famine." In *The Great Irish Famine,* edited by Cathal Póirtéir, 60–73. Dublin: Mercier Press, 1995.

————. "William Wilde's Table of Irish Famines." In *Famine: The Irish Experience, 900–1900, Subsistence Crises and Irish Famines,* edited by E. Margaret Crawford, 1–30. Edinburgh: John Donald, 1989.

Cronin, Michael. *Translating Ireland: Translation, Languages, Cultures.* Cork: Cork University Press, 1996.

Crossgrove, William, David Egilman, Peter Heywood, Jeanne Kasperson, Ellen Messer, and Albert Wessen. "Colonialism, International Trade, and the Nation-State." In *Hunger in History: Food Shortage, Poverty and Deprivation,* edited by L. Newman, 215–40. Oxford: Basil Blackwell, 1990.

Crossman, Virginia. *Politics, Law and Order in Nineteenth-Century Ireland.* Dublin: Gill and Macmillan, 1996.

Crotty, Raymond. *Ireland in Crisis: A Study in Capitalist Colonial Undevelopment.* Dingle: Brandon, 1987.

Cullen, L. M. *An Economic History of Ireland since 1660.* London: B. T. Batsford, 1981.

Currie, Katie. "British Colonial Policy and Famines: Some Effects and Implications of 'Free Trade' in the Bombay, Bengal and Madras Presidencies, 1860–1900." *South Asia* 14, no. 2 (1991): 23–56.

Curtis Jr., L. Perry. *Apes and Angels: The Irishman in Victorian Caricature.* 2nd ed. London: Smithsonian Institute Press, 1997.

Curtis, Mark. *Unpeople: Britain's Secret Human Rights Abuses.* London: Vintage, 2004.

Daly, Mary. *The Famine in Ireland.* Dundalk: Dundalgan Press, 1986.

————. "Farming and the Famine." In *Famine 150,* edited by Cormac Ó Gráda, 29–47. Dublin: Teagasc, 1997.

Darby, H. C. "The Age of the Improver: 1600–1800." In *A New Historical Geography of England,* edited by H. C. Darby, 302–88. Cambridge: Cambridge University Press, 1973.

Davis, Mike. *Late Victorian Holocausts: El Niño Famines and the Making of the Third World.* London: Verso, 2001.

————. "The Origins of the Third World: Markets, States and Climate." *Corner House Briefing Papers* 27 (2002): 1–36.

Davitt, Michael. *The Fall of Feudalism in Ireland, or the Story of the Land League Revolution.* London: Harper and Brothers, 1904.

Dean, Mitchell. *The Constitution of Poverty: Toward a Genealogy of Liberal Governance.* London: Routledge, 1991.

———. "Four Theses on the Powers of Life and Death." *Contretemps* 5 (2005): 16–29.

———. "Powers of Life and Death Beyond Governmentality." *Cultural Values* 6, no. 1/2 (2002): 119–38.

Deane, Seamus. "Civilians and Barbarians." In *Irish Field Day: Field Day Theatre Company,* edited by Seamus Deane, 33–42. London: Hutchinson, 1985.

Derrida, Jacques. "Force of Law: The 'Mystical Foundation of Authority.'" *Cardozo Law Review* 11, nos. 5–6 (1989–1990): 919–1045.

Devereux, Stephen. "The Malawi Famine of 2002." *IDS Bulletin* 33, no. 4 (2002): 70–78.

———. "Sen's Entitlement Approach: Critiques and Counter-Critiques." *Oxford Literary Review* 29, no. 3 (2001): 245–63.

———. *Theories of Famine.* London: Harvester Wheatsheaf, 1993.

Devereux, Stephen, Paul Howe, and Luka Biong Deng. "The 'New Famines.'" *IDS Bulletin* 33, no. 4 (2002): 1–11.

Devine, T. M. *The Great Highland Famine: Hunger, Emigration and the Scottish Highlands in the Nineteenth Century.* Edinburgh: John Donald, 2004.

de Waal, Alex. *Famine Crimes: Politics and the Disaster Relief Industry in Africa.* Oxford: African Rights and International African Institute in association with James Curry and Indiana University Press, 2002.

———. *Famine That Kills: Darfur, Sudan.* Oxford: Oxford University Press, 2005.

Dickson, David. *Arctic Ireland: The Extraordinary Story of the Great Frost and Forgotten Famine of 1740–41.* Belfast: White Row Press, 1998.

———. "The Other Great Irish Famine." In *The Great Irish Famine,* edited by Cathal Póirtéir, 50–59. Dublin: Mercier Press, 1995.

———. "The Potato and Diet before the Famine." In *Famine 150,* edited by Cormac Ó Gráda, 1–27. Dublin: Teagasc, 1997.

Donnelly, James S. "The Administration of Relief, 1846–7." In *A New History of Ireland.* Vol. 5, *Ireland under the Union, I: 1801–1870,* edited W. E. Vaughan, 294–306. Oxford: Clarendon Press, 1989.

———. "The Administration of Relief, 1847–51." In *A New History of Ireland.* Vol. 5, *Ireland under the Union, I: 1801–1870,* edited by W. E. Vaughan, 316–31. Oxford: Clarendon Press, 1989.

———. "Excess Mortality and Emigration." In *A New History of Ireland.* Vol. 5, *Ireland under the Union, I: 1801–1870,* edited by W. E. Vaughan, 350–56. Oxford: Clarendon Press, 1989.

———. "Famine and Government Response, 1845–6." In *A New History of Ireland.* Vol. 5, *Ireland under the Union, I: 1801–1870,* edited by W. E. Vaughan, 272–85. Oxford: Clarendon Press, 1989.

————. "A Famine in Irish Politics." In *A New History of Ireland*. Vol. 5, *Ireland Under the Union, I: 1801–1870,* edited by W. E. Vaughan, 357–71. Oxford: Clarendon Press, 1989.

————. *The Great Irish Potato Famine*. Stroud: Sutton, 2002.

————. "'Irish Property Must Pay for Irish Poverty': British Public Opinion and the Great Irish Famine." In *"Fearful Realities": New Perspectives on the Famine,* edited by Chris Morash and Richard Hayes, 60–76. Dublin: Irish Academic Press, 1996.

————. "The Journals of Sir John Benn-Walsh Relating to the Management of His Estates, 1823–64." *Journal of the Cork Historical and Archaeological Society* 79, no. 230 (1974): 86–123.

————. "Landlords and Tenants." In *A New History of Ireland*. Vol. 5, *Ireland under the Union, I: 1801–1870,* edited by W. E. Vaughan, 332–49. Oxford: Clarendon Press, 1989.

————. "Mass Eviction and the Great Famine: The Clearances Revisited." In *The Great Irish Famine,* edited by Cathal Póirtéir, 155–73. Dublin: Mercier Press, 1995.

————. "Production, Prices, and Exports, 1846–51." In *A New History of Ireland*. Vol. 5, *Ireland under the Union, I: 1801–1870,* edited by W. E. Vaughan, 286–93. Oxford: Clarendon Press, 1989.

————. "The Soup Kitchens." In *A New History of Ireland*. Vol. 5, *Ireland under the Union, I: 1801–1870,* edited by W. E. Vaughan, 307–15. Oxford: Clarendon Press, 1989.

Dowley, Leslie J. "The Potato and the Late Blight in Ireland." In *Famine 150,* edited by Cormac Ó Gráda, 49–65. Dublin: Teagasc, 1997.

Drèze, Jean, and Amartya Sen. *The Amartya Sen and Jean Drèze Omnibus: Poverty and Famines; Hunger and Public Action; India: Economic Development and Social Opportunity.* Oxford: Oxford University Press, 2008.

Driver, Felix. *Power and Pauperism: The Workhouse System, 1834–1884.* Cambridge: Cambridge University Press, 1993.

Duarte, André. "Hannah Arendt, Biopolitics, and the Problem of Violence: From Animal Laborans to Homo Sacer." In *Hannah Arendt and the Uses of History: Imperialism, Nation, Race and Genocide,* edited by R. H. King and D. Stone, 191–204. New York: Berghahn Books, 2007.

Duffield, Mark. "Governing the Borderlands: Decoding the Power of Aid." *Disasters* 25, no. 4 (2001): 308–20.

————. "Humanitarian Intervention: The New Aid Paradigm and the Separate Development." *New Political Economy* 2, no. 2 (1997): 336–41.

Duffy, Patrick J., ed. *To and From Ireland: Planned Migration Schemes, c. 1600–2000.* Dublin: Geography Publications, 2004.

Duffy, Seán. *The Concise History of Ireland*. Dublin: Gill and Macmillan, 2005.

Dugger, Julie M. "Black Ireland's Race: Thomas Carlyle and the Young Ireland Movement." *Victorian Studies* 48, no. 3 (2006): 461–85.

Duncan, James S. *In the Shadows of the Tropics: Climate, Race and Biopower in Nineteenth Century Ceylon*. Aldershot: Asgate, 2007.

Dunlop, Robert. "The Famine Crisis: Theological Interpretations and Implications." In *"Fearful Realities": New Perspectives on the Famine,* edited by Chris Morash and Richard Hayes, 164–74. Dublin: Irish Academic Press, 1996.

Eagleton, Terry. *After Theory*. London: Penguin Books, 2004.

———. "Afterword: Ireland and Colonialism." In *Was Ireland a Colony? Economics, Politics and Culture in Nineteenth-Century Ireland,* edited by Terrence McDonough, 326–33. Dublin: Irish Academic Press, 2005.

———. *Heathcliff and the Great Hunger: Studies in Irish Culture*. London: Verso, 1995.

———. *Literary Theory: An Introduction*. 2nd ed. Minneapolis: University of Minnesota Press, 1998.

Eagleton, Terry, Frederic Jameson, and Edward Said. *Nationalism, Colonialism, and Literature*. Minneapolis: University of Minnesota Press, 1990.

Edkins, Jenny. "Humanitarianism, Humanity, Human." *Journal of Human Rights* 2, no. 2 (2003): 253–58.

———. "Legality with a Vengeance: Famines and Humanitarian Relief in 'Complex Emergencies.'" *Millennium: Journal of International Studies* 25, no. 3 (1996): 547–75.

———. "Mass Starvations and the Limitations of Famine Theorising." *IDS Bulletin* 33, no. 4 (2002): 12–18.

———. *Whose Hunger? Concepts of Famine, Practices of Aid*. Minneapolis: University of Minnesota Press, 2000.

Edsall, Nicholas C. *The Anti-Poor Law Movement, 1834–44*. Manchester: Manchester University Press, 1971.

Edwards, Ruth Dudley, and Bridget Hourican. *An Atlas of Irish History*. 3rd ed. London: Routledge, 2005.

Eiriksson, Andres. "Food Supply and Food Riots." In *Famine 150,* edited by Cormac Ó Gráda, 67–93. Dublin: Teagasc, 1997.

Elden, Stuart. "The Constitution of the Normal: Monsters and Masturbation at Collège De France." *Boundary 2* 28, no. 1 (2001): 91–105.

———. "Plague, Panopticon, Police." *Surveillance and Society* 1, no. 3 (2003): 240–53.

———. "The War of Race and the Constitution of the State: Foucault's «*Il faut défendre la société*» and the Politics of Calculation." *Boundary 2* 29, no. 1 (2002): 125–51.

Escobar, Arturo. *Encountering Development: The Making of the Third World*. Princeton, NJ: Princeton University Press, 1995.

Fabian, Johannes. *Out of Our Minds: Reason and Madness in the Exploration of Africa*. Berkeley: University of California Press, 2000.

———. *Time and the Other: How Anthropology Makes Its Object*. New York: Columbia University Press, 1983.

Fanon, Frantz. *The Wretched of the Earth.* New York: Grove Press, 1963.

Farmer, Paul. "An Anthropology of Structural Violence." *Cultural Anthropology* 45, no. 3 (2001): 305–25.

Fegan, Melissa. *Literature and the Irish Famine, 1845–1919.* Oxford: Clarendon Press, 2002.

Ferreira, Patricia. "'All but 'A Black Skin and Wolly Hair': Frederick Douglass's Witness of the Irish Famine." *American Studies International* 37, no. 2 (1999): 69–83.

Fielding, K. J. "Ireland, John Mitchel and His 'Sarcastic Friend' Thomas Carlyle." In *Scottish Studies 14, Literatur in Kontext—Literature in Context: Fetschrift Für Horst W. Drescher,* edited by Joachem Schwend, Susanne Hageman, and Hermann Volkel, 131–43. Frankfurt: Peter Lang, 1992.

Fitzpatrick, David. "Famine, Entitlements and Seduction: Captain Edmond Wynne in Ireland, 1846–1851." *English Historical Review* 110, no. 437 (1995): 596–619.

———. "Ireland and the Empire." In *The Oxford History of the British Empire.* Vol. 3, *The Nineteenth Century,* edited by Andrew Porter, 495–521. Oxford: Oxford University Press, 1999.

Fitzpatrick, Peter. "Bare Sovereignty: Homo Sacer and the Insistence of Law." *Theory and Event* 5, no. 2 (2001): 1–20.

———. "'These Mad Abandon'd Times.'" *Economy and Society* 30, no. 2 (2001): 255–70.

Flood, Jeanne A. "The Forster Family and the Irish Famine." *Quaker History* 84, no. 2 (1995): 116–30.

Foster, John Wilson. "Encountering Traditions." In *Nature in Ireland: A Scientific and Cultural History,* edited by John Wilson Foster and Helena C. G. Chesney, 23–70. Dublin: Lilliput Press, 1997.

———. "Nature and Nation in Nineteenth Century Ireland." In *Nature in Ireland: A Scientific and Cultural History,* edited by John Wilson Foster and Helena C. G. Chesney, 409–39. Dublin: Lilliput Press, 1997.

Foster, R. F. *Modern Ireland, 1600–1972.* London: Allen Lane, 1988.

———. "'We Are All Revisionists Now.'" *Irish Review* 1 (1986): 1–5.

Foucault, Michel. *Abnormal: Lectures at the Collège De France, 1974–1975.* Edited by Arnold I. Davidson. Translated by Graham Burchell. New York: Picador, 2004.

———. *The Birth of the Clinic: An Archaeology of Medical Perception.* Translated by A. M. Sheridan Smith. New York: Vintage Books, 1975.

———. *Discipline and Punish: The Birth of the Prison.* Translated by Alan Sheridan. New York: Vintage, 1979.

———. "Governmentality." In *Essential Works of Foucault, 1954–1984.* Vol. 3, *Power,* translated Robert Hurley et al., edited by James D. Faubion, 201–22. New York: New Press, 1994.

———. *The History of Sexuality.* Vol. 1, *An Introduction.* translated by Robert Hurley. New York: Vintage Books, 1980.

———. "The Political Technology of Individuals." In *Essential Works of Michel Foucault, 1954–1984.* Vol. 3, *Power,* translated Robert Hurley et al., edited by James D. Faubion, 403–17. New York: New Press, 1994.

———. "Security, Territory, and Population." In *Essential Works of Foucault, 1954–1984.* Vol. 1, *Ethics, Subjectivity and Truth,* translated Robert Hurley et al., edited by Paul Rabinow, 67–71. New York: New Press, 1997.

———. *Security, Territory, Population: Lectures at the Collège de France, 1977–1978.* Edited by A. I. Davidson. Translated by G. Burchell. New York: Palgrave Macmillan, 2007.

———. *Society Must Be Defended: Lectures at the Collège De France, 1975–1976.* Edited by Arnold I. Davidson. Translated by David Macey. New York: Picador, 2003.

Frank, Andre Gunder. "The Development of Underdevelopment." *Monthly Review* 184 (1966): 17–31.

Frankel, Oz. "Blue Books and the Victorian Reader." *Victorian Studies* 46, no. 2 (2004): 309–18.

Freeman, T. W. "Land and People, c. 1841." In *A New History of Ireland.* Vol. 5, *Ireland under the Union, I: 1801–1870,* edited by W. E. Vaughan, 242–71. Oxford: Clarendon Press, 1989.

Friel, Brian. *Translations.* London: Faber and Faber, 1981.

Gallagher, Michael. *Paddy's Lament: Ireland, 1846–1847, Prelude to Hatred.* New York: Harcourt Brace Jovanovich, 1982.

George, Susan. *How the Other Half Dies: The Real Reasons for World Hunger.* New York: Penguin, 1980.

Gibbon, Peter. "Colonialism and the Great Starvation in Ireland 1845–9." *Race and Class* 17, no. 2 (1975): 131–39.

Gibbons, Luke. *Transformations in Irish Culture.* Notre Dame, IN: University of Notre Dame Press, 1996.

Gillingham, John. "Images of Ireland, 1170–1600: The Origins of English Imperialism." *History Today* 37, no. 2 (1987): 16–22.

Giroux, Henry A. *Stormy Weather: Katrina and the Politics of Disposability.* London: Paradigm, 2006.

Graham, B. J. "The High Middle Ages: c. 1100 to c. 1350." In *A Historical Geography of Ireland,* edited by B. J. Graham and L. J. Proudfoot, 58–98. London: Academic Press, 1993.

Gray, Peter. "Famine and Land in Ireland and India, 1845–1880: James Caird and the Political Economy of Hunger." *History Journal* 49, no. 1 (2006): 193–215.

———. *Famine, Land and Politics: British Government and Irish Society, 1843–1850.* Dublin: Irish Academic Press, 1999.

————. "Famine Relief Policy in Comparative Perspective: Ireland, Scotland and Northwestern Europe, 1845–1849. *Éire-Ireland* 32, no. 1 (1997): 86–108.

————. "Ideology and the Famine." In *The Great Irish Famine,* edited by Cathal Póirtéir, 86–103. Dublin: Mercier Press, 1995.

————. *The Making of the Irish Poor Law, 1815–43.* Manchester: Manchester University Press, 2009.

————. "'Potatoes and Providence': British Government Responses to the Great Famine." *Bullán: An Irish Studies Journal* 1, no. 1 (1994): 75–90.

————. "Punch and the Great Famine." *History Ireland* 1, no. 3 (1993): 26–33.

————. "'Shovelling Out Your Paupers': The British State and the Irish Famine Migration, 1846–50." *Patterns of Prejudice* 33, no. 4 (1999): 47–65.

————. "Wellington and the Government of Ireland, 1832–46." In *Wellington Studies III,* edited by C. M. Woolgar, 203–26. Southampton: Hartley Institute, 1996.

Green, David R. "Pauper Protests: Power and Resistance in Early Nineteenth-Century London Workhouses." *Social History* 31, no. 3 (2006): 137–59.

Greenblatt, Stephen. *Marvelous Possessions: The Wonder of the New World.* Chicago: University of Chicago Press, 1991.

Gregory, Derek. *The Colonial Present: Afghanistan, Palestine, Iraq.* Oxford: Blackwell, 2004.

————. "Cultures of Travel and Spatial Formations of Knowledge." *Erdkunde* 54 (2000): 297–319.

————. "Edward Said's Imaginative Geographies." In *Thinking Space,* edited by Nigel Thrift and Mike Crang, 302–48. London: Routledge, 2000.

————. "(Post)Colonialism and the Production of Nature." In *Social Nature,* edited by Bruce Braun and Noel Castree, 84–111. Oxford: Blackwell, 2001.

Griffin, Brian. "'Such Varmint': The Dublin Police and the Public, 1838–1913." *Irish Studies Review* 13 (1995/96): 21–25.

Habib, Irfan. "Capitalism in History." *Social Scientist* 23, nos. 7–9 (1995): 15–31.

Hacking, Ian. "Biopower and the Avalanche of Printed Numbers." *Humanities in Society* 5, nos. 3/4 (1982): 279–95.

————. "How Should We Do the History of Statistics?" In *The Foucault Effect: Studies in Governmentality with Two Lectures and an Interview with Michel Foucault,* edited by Graham Burchell, Colin Gordon, and Peter Miller, 181–96. London: Harvester Wheatsheaf, 1991.

————. "Making up People." In *Reconstructing Individualism: Autonomy, Individuality and the Self in Western Thought,* edited by Morton Sosna, Thomas C. Heller, and David E. Wellbery, 222–36. Stanford: Stanford University Press, 1986.

Hadfield, Andrew. "Rocking the Boat: A Response to Hiram Morgan." *Irish Review* 14 (1993): 15–19.

Hadfield, Andrew, and John McVeagh, eds. *Strangers to That Land: British Perceptions of Ireland from the Reformation to the Famine.* Gerrards Cross: Colin Smythe, 1994.

Haggard, Stephen, and Marcus Noland. *Famine in North Korea: Markets, Aid, and Reform.* New York: Columbia University Press, 2007.

Haines, Robin. *Charles Trevelyan and the Great Irish Famine.* Dublin: Four Courts Press, 2004.

Hall-Matthews, David. "Colonial Ideologies of the Market and Famine Policy in Ahmednagar District, Bombay Presidency, c. 1870–1884." *Indian Economic and Social History Review* 3 (1999): 303–33.

Harnick, Phyllis. "Point and Counterpoint: Carlyle and Mill on Ireland in 1848." *Carlyle Newsletter* 7 (1986): 26–33.

Harrington, John P., ed. *The English Traveller in Ireland: Accounts of Ireland and the Irish through Five Centuries.* Dublin: Wolfhound Press, 1991.

Harvey, David. "The Body as an Accumulation Strategy." *Environment and Planning D: Society and Space* 16, no. 4 (1998): 401–21.

———. *The Conditions of Postmodernity.* Oxford: Blackwell, 1989.

———. *The New Imperialism.* Oxford: Oxford University Press, 2003.

———. *Spaces of Hope.* Berkeley: University of California Press, 2000.

Herman, Edward S. "The Banality of Evil." In *Triumph of the Market: Essays on Economics, Politics and Media,* edited by Edward S. Herman, 97–101. Boston: South End Press, 1997.

Hill, Christopher V. "Philosophy and Reality in Riparian South Asia: British Famine Policy and Migration in Colonial North India." *Modern Asian Studies* 25, no. 2 (1991): 263–79.

Hilton, Boyd. *The Age of Atonement: The Influence of Evangelicalism on Social and Economic Thought, 1795–1865.* Oxford: Oxford University Press, 1988.

Himmelfarb, Gertrude. *The Idea of Poverty: England in the Early Industrial Age.* New York: Vintage Books, 1985.

Hobsbawm, Eric J. *Industry and Empire.* London: Penguin Books, 1979.

Hollander, Joel A. "Ford Madox Brown's Work (1865): The Irish Question, Carlyle, and the Great Famine." *New Hibernia Review—Irish Eureannach Nua* 1, no. 1 (1997): 100–119.

Holt, Thomas C. *The Problem of Freedom: Race, Labour, and Politics in Jamaica and Britain, 1832–1938.* Baltimore, MD: John Hopkins University Press, 1992.

Hooper, Glenn, ed. *The Tourist's Gaze: Travellers to Ireland, 1800–2000.* Cork: Cork University Press, 2001.

Hoppen, K. Theodore. *Ireland since 1800: Conflict and Conformity.* London: Longman, 1999.

Horden, Peregrine, and Richard Smith, eds. *The Locus of Care: Families, Communities, Institutions, and the Provision of Welfare since Antiquity.* London: Routledge, 1998.

Howe, Paul. "Reconsidering 'Famine.'" *IDS Bulletin* 33, no. 4 (2002): 19–27.

Howe, Stephen. *Ireland and Empire: Colonial Legacies in Irish History and Culture.* Oxford: Oxford University Press, 2000.

Howell, Philip. "Foucault, Sexuality, Geography." In *Space, Knowledge and Power: Foucault and Geography,* edited by J. W. Crampton and S. Elden, 291–316. Burlington, VT: Ashgate.

————. *Geographies of Regulation: Policing Prostitution in Nineteenth-Century Britain and the Empire.* Cambridge: Cambridge University Press, 2009.

Huish, Robert. "Human Security or Food Security in Geographical Study: Pragmatic Concepts or Elusive Theory." *Geography Compass* 2, no. 5 (2008): 1386–1403.

Hussain, Nasser. *The Jurisprudence of Emergency: Colonialism and the Rule of Law.* Ann Arbor: University of Michigan Press, 2004.

Hyndman, Jennifer. *Managing Displacement: Refugees and the Politics of Humanitarianism.* Minneapolis: University of Minnesota Press, 2000.

Jeffery, Keith, ed. *An Irish Empire: Aspects of Ireland and the British Empire.* Manchester: Manchester University Press, 1996.

Jones, Ann Rosalind, and Peter Stallybrass. "Dismantling Irena: The Sexualizing of Ireland in Early Modern England." In *Nationalisms and Sexualities,* edited by Andrew Parker, Mary Russo, Doris Sommer, and Patricia Yaeger, 157–71. New York: Routledge, 1992.

Joyce, James. *Ulysses.* London: Penguin Books, 1992.

Kalpagam, U. "Colonial Governmentality and the 'Economy.'" *Economy and Society* 29, no. 3 (2000): 418–38.

————. "Colonial Governmentality and the Public Sphere in India." *Journal of Historical Sociology* 15, no. 1 (2002): 35–58.

Kaplan, Fred. *Thomas Carlyle: A Biography.* Ithaca, NY: Cornell University Press, 1983.

Kearns, Gerry. "Bare Life, Political Violence, and the Territorial Structure of Britain and Ireland." In *Violent Geographies: Fear, Terror, and Political Violence,* edited by D. Gregory and A. Pred, 7–35. New York: Routledge, 2006.

————. "'Educate That Holy Hatred': Place, Trauma and Identity in the Irish Nationalism of John Mitchel." *Political Geography* 20 (2001): 885–911.

————. *Geopolitics and Empire: The Legacy of Halford Mackinder.* Oxford: Oxford University Press, 2009.

————. "Ireland after Theory." *Bullán: An Irish Studies Journal* 6 (2002): 107–14.

————. "Making Space for Marx." *Journal of Historical Geography* 10, no. 4 (1984): 411–17.

Kearns, Gerry, and Paul Laxton. "Ethnic Groups as Public Health Hazards: The Famine Irish in Liverpool and Lazaretto Politics." In *The Politics of the Healthy Life: An International Perspective,* edited by Esteban Rodríguez-Ocaña, 13–40. Sheffield: European Association for the History of Medicine and Health Publications, 2002.

Keating, John. *Irish Famine Facts.* Dublin: Teagasc, 1996.

Keen, David. *The Benefits of Famine: A Political Economy of Famine and Relief in South-western Sudan, 1983–1989.* Princeton, NJ: Princeton University Press, 1994.

Kelleher, Margaret. "The Female Gaze: Asenath Nicholson's Famine Narrative." In *"Fearful Realities": New Perspectives on the Famine,* edited by Chris Morash and Richard Hayes, 119–30. Dublin: Irish Academic Press, 1996.

————. *The Feminization of Famine: Expressions of the Inexpressible?* Cork: Cork University Press, 1997.

Kennedy, Liam. *Colonialism, Religion, and Nationalism in Ireland.* Belfast: Institute of Irish Studies, 1996.

Kennedy, Liam, Paul S. Ell, E. M. Crawford, and L. A. Clarkson, eds. *Mapping the Great Irish Famine: A Survey of the Famine Decades.* Dublin: Four Courts Press, 1999.

Kenny, Kevin. "Ireland and the British Empire: An Introduction." In *Ireland and the British Empire,* edited by Kevin Kenny, 1–25. Oxford: Oxford University Press, 2004.

Keogh, Dáire, and Kevin Whelan, eds. *Acts of Union: The Causes, Contexts and Consequences of the Act of Union.* Dublin: Four Courts Press, 2001.

Kerr, Donal A. *The Catholic Church and the Famine.* Dublin: Columbia Press, 1996.

————. *A Nation of Beggars? Priests, People, and Politics in Famine Ireland, 1846–1852.* Oxford: Oxford University Press, 1994.

Kiberd, Declan. *Inventing Ireland: The Literature of the Modern Nation.* London: Vintage, 1996.

Kincheloe, Pamela J. "Two Visions of Fairyland: Ireland and the Monumental Discourse of the Nineteenth-Century American Tourist." *Irish Studies Review* 7, no. 1 (1999): 41–51.

Kinealy, Christine. *A Death-Dealing Famine: The Great Hunger in Ireland.* London: Pluto Press, 1997.

————. "'The Famine Killed Everything': Living with the Memory of the Great Hunger." In *Ireland's Great Hunger: Silence, Memory, and Commemoration,* edited by David A. Valone and Christine Kinealy, 53–67. New York: University Press of America, 2002.

————. "Food Exports from Ireland, 1846–47." *History Ireland* 5, no. 1 (1997): 32–36.

————. *The Great Irish Famine: Impact, Ideology and Rebellion.* Palgrave: New York, 2002.

————. "'The Historian Is a Haunted Man': Cecil Woodham-Smith and the Great Hunger." *New Hibernia Review* 11, no. 4 (2007): 134–52.

————. "Peel, Rotten Potatoes and Providence: The Repeal of the Corn Laws and the Irish Famine." In *Free Trade and Its Reception,* edited by Andrew Marriso, 50–62. London: Routledge, 1998.

————. "The Poor Law during the Great Famine: An Administration in Crisis." In *Famine: The Irish Experience, 900–1900, Subsidence Crises and Irish*

Famines, edited by E. Margaret Crawford, 157–75. Edinburgh: John Donald, 1989.

———. "The Role of the Poor Law during the Famine." In *The Great Irish Famine,* edited by Cathal Póirtéir, 104–22. Dublin: Mercier Press, 1995.

———. *This Great Calamity: The Irish Famine, 1845–52.* Boulder, CO: Roberts Rinehart, 1995.

———. "Was Ireland a Colony? The Evidence of the Great Famine." In *Was Ireland a Colony? Economics, Politics and Culture in Nineteenth-Century Ireland,* edited by Terrence McDonough, 48–65. Dublin: Irish Academic Press, 2005.

Klein, Bernhard. *Maps and the Writing of Space in Early Modern England and Ireland.* New York: Palgrave, 2001.

Klein, Naomi. *The Shock Doctrine: The Rise of Disaster Capitalism.* London: Allen Lane, 2007.

Kleinman, Arthur, and Joan Kleinman. "The Appeal of Experience; the Dismay of Images: Cultural Appropriations of Suffering in Our Times." *Daedalus* 125, no. 1 (1996): 1–23.

Kurlansky, Mark. *Non-Violence: The History of a Dangerous Idea.* London: Jonathan Cape, 2006.

Lebow, Ned. "British Images of Poverty in Pre-Famine Ireland." In *Views of the Irish Peasantry,* edited by Robert E. Rhodes and Daniel J. Casey, 57–85. New Haven, CT: Archon Books, 1977.

———. *White Britain and Black Ireland: The Influence of Stereotypes on Colonial Policy.* Philadelphia: ISHI, 1976.

Lee, Joseph. "The Famine as History." In *Famine 150,* edited by Cormac Ó Gráda, 159–77. Dublin: Teagasc, 1997.

Leerssen, Joep. *Mere Irish, Fíor Gael: Studies in the Idea of Irish Nationality, Its Development and Literary Expression Prior to the Nineteenth Century.* Cork: Cork University Press, 1996.

———. *Remembrance and Imagination: Patterns in the Historical and Literary Representation of Ireland in the Nineteenth Century.* Cork: Cork University Press, 1996.

Lefebvre, Henri. *The Production of Space.* Translated by Donald Nicholson-Smith. Oxford: Blackwell, 2000.

Legg, Stephen. "Foucault's Population Geographies: Classifications, Biopolitics and Governmental Spaces." *Population, Space and Place* 11, no. 3 (2005): 137–56.

———. *Spaces of Colonialism: Delhi's Urban Governmentalities.* London: Blackwell, 2007.

Lemke, Thomas. "'The Birth of Bio-Politics': Michel Foucault's Lecture at the Collège De France on Neo-Liberal Governmentality." *Economy and Society* 30, no. 2 (2001): 190–207.

Lengel, Edward G. *Ireland through British Eyes: Perceptions of Ireland in the Famine Era.* Wesport, CT: Praeger, 2002.

Lennon, Joseph. "Irish Orientalism: An Overview." In *Ireland and Postcolonial Theory,* edited by Clare Caroll and Patricia King, 129–57. Notre Dame, IN: University of Notre Dame Press, 2003.

Li, Tania Murray. *The Will to Improve: Governmentality, Development, and the Practice of Politics.* Durham, NC: Duke University Press, 2007.

Lloyd, David. "After History: Historicism and Irish Postcolonial Studies." In *Ireland and Postcolonial Theory,* edited by Clare Carroll and Patricia King, 46–62. Notre Dame, IN: University of Notre Dame Press, 2003.

———. "Colonial Trauma/Postcolonial Recovery." *Postcolonial Studies* 2, no. 2 (2000): 212–28.

———. "Cultural Theory and Ireland." *Bullán: An Irish Studies Journal* 3, no. 1 (1997): 87–92.

———. *Irish Times: Temporalities of Modernity.* Dublin: Field Day, 2008.

———. "The Political Economy of the Potato." *Nineteenth-Century Contexts* 29, nos. 2–3 (2007): 311–35.

Loomba, Ania. *Colonialism/Postcolonialism.* New York: Routledge, 1998.

Lowe, W. J. "Policing Famine Ireland." *Eire-Ireland* 24, no. 4 (1994): 47–67.

Luxemburg, Rosa. *The Accumulation of Capital.* Translated by Agnes Schwarzschild, with an introduction by Joan Robinson. London: Routledge, 1951.

MacCarthy, B. G. "Thackeray in Ireland." *Studies: An Irish Quarterly Journal* 40 (1991): 55–68.

MacCarthy-Morrogh, Michael. "The English Presence in Early Seventeenth Century Munster." In *Natives and Newcomers: The Making of Irish Colonial Society, 1534–1641,* edited by Ciaran Brady and Raymond Gillespie, 171–90. Dublin: Irish Academic Press, 1986.

MacDonagh, Oliver. *Early Victorian Government, 1830–1870.* New York: Holmes and Meier, 1977.

———. *Ireland: The Union and Its Aftermath.* Dublin: University College Dublin Press, 2003.

Mackenzie, Clayton. "Thomas Carlyle's 'The Negro Question': Black Ireland and the Rhetoric of Famine." *Neohelicon* 24 (1997): 219–36.

Mackenzie, Fiona. "Selective Silence: A Feminist with Environmental Discourse in Colonial Africa." In *The Power of Development,* edited by Jonathan Crush, 100–114. London: Routledge, 1995.

Mamdani, Mahmood. "Karamoja: Colonial Roots of Famine in North-East Uganda." *Review of African Political Economy* 9, no. 25 (1982): 27–33.

Marcus, David. "Famine Crimes in International Law." *American Journal of International Law* 97, no. 2 (2003): 245–81.

Margaroni, Maria. "Care and Abandonment: A Response to Mika Ojakangas' 'Impossible Dialogue on Biopower: Agamben and Foucault.'" *Foucault Studies* 2 (2005): 29–36.

Martin, Amy E. "'Becoming a Race Apart': Representing Irish Racial Difference and the British Working Class in Victorian Critiques of Capitalism."

In *Was Ireland a Colony? Economics, Politics and Culture in Nineteenth-Century Ireland,* edited by Terrence McDonough, 186–211. Dublin: Irish Academic Press, 2005.

———. "Blood Transfusions: Constructions of Irish Racial Difference, the English Working Class, and Revolutionary Possibility in the Work of Carlyle and Engels." *Victorian Literature and Culture* 32, no. 1 (2004): 83–102.

Marx, Karl. *Capital.* 3 vols. London: Lawrence and Wishart, 1954.

Marx, Karl, and Friedrich Engels. *The Communist Manifesto.* New York: Bantam Classic, 2004.

———. *Ireland and the Irish Question.* Edited by C. Desmond Greaves. London: Lawrence and Wishart, 1971.

Mbembe, Achille. "Necropolitics." *Public Culture* 15, no. 1 (2003): 11–40.

McCarthy, Pete. *McCarthy's Bar.* London: Hodder and Staughton, 2000.

McClintock, Anne. *Imperial Leather: Race, Gender and Sexuality in the Colonial Context.* London: Routledge, 1995.

McDonough, Terrence, ed. *Was Ireland a Colony? Economics, Politics and Culture in Nineteenth-Century Ireland.* Dublin: Irish Academic Press, 2005.

McDonough, Terrence, and Eamonn Slater. "Colonialism, Feudalism and the Mode of Production in Nineteenth-Century Ireland." In *Was Ireland a Colony? Economics, Politics and Culture in Nineteenth-Century Ireland,* edited by Terrence McDonough, 27–47. Dublin: Irish Academic Press, 2005.

McDowell, R. B. "Ireland on the Eve of the Famine." In *The Great Famine: Studies in Irish History, 1845–52,* edited by R. Dudley Edwards and T. Desmond Williams, 10–19. 1956. Reprint, Dublin: Lilliput Press, 1994.

———. *The Irish Administration, 1801–1914.* London: Routledge and Kegan, 1964.

McLean, Stuart. *The Event and Its Horrors: Ireland, Famine, Modernity.* Stanford: Stanford University Press, 2004.

McLoughlin, Dymphna. "Women and Sexuality in Nineteenth Century Ireland." *Irish Journal of Psychology* 15, nos. 2–3 (1994): 266–75.

———. "Workhouses." In *The Field Day Anthology of Irish Writing.* Vol. 5, *Irish Women's Writing and Traditions,* edited by A. Burke, S. Kilfeather, M. Luddy, M. Mac Curtain, G. Meaney, M. Ní Dhonnchadha, M. O'Dowd, and C. Willis, 722–40. New York: New York University Press, 2002.

———. "Workhouses and the Irish Female Paupers." In *Women Surviving: Studies in Irish Women's History in the 19th and 20th Centuries,* edited by Maria Luddy and Cliona Murphy, 117–47. Dublin: Poolbeg, 1990.

McLoughlin, Thomas. *Contesting Ireland: Irish Voices against England in the Eighteenth Century.* Dublin: Four Courts Press, 2004.

McVeagh, John. *Irish Travel Writing: A Bibliography.* Dublin: Wolfhound Press, 1996.

Mehta, Uday Singh. *Liberalism and Empire: A Study in Nineteenth-Century British Liberal Thought.* Chicago: University of Chicago Press, 1999.

Meillassoux, Claude. "Development or Exploitation: Is the Sahel Famine Good Business?" *Review of African Political Economy* 1, no. 1 (1974): 27–33.

Mignola, Walter. *The Darker Side of the Renaissance: Literary, Territoriality and Colonization.* Ann Arbor: University of Michigan Press, 1995.

Miller, Kerby A. *Emigrants and Exiles: Ireland and the Irish Exodus to North America.* Oxford: Oxford University Press, 1985.

Millman, Sara, Stanley M. Aronson, Lina M. Fruzzetti, Marida Hollos, Rose Okello, and Van Whiting Jr. "Organization, Information, and Entitlement in the Emerging Global Food System." In *Hunger in History: Food Shortage, Poverty and Deprivation,* edited by Lucile F. Newman, 307–30. Oxford: Basil Blackwell, 1990.

Mintz, Sidney W. *Sweetness and Power: The Place of Sugar in Modern History.* New York: Penguin, 1986.

Misra, Kavita. "Productivity of Crises: Disease, Scientific Knowledge and State in India." *Economic and Political Weekly* 35, nos. 43–44 (2000): 3885–97.

Mitchell, Don. "Dead Labor and Political Economy of Landscape — California Living, California Dying." In *Handbook of Cultural Geography,* edited by Kay Anderson, Mona Domosh, Steve Pile, and Nigel Thrift, 233–48. London: Sage, 2003.

Mitchell, Timothy. *Colonising Egypt.* Berkeley: University of California Press, 1991.

———. *Rule of Experts: Egypt, Techno-Politics, Modernity.* Berkeley: University of California Press, 2002.

Mokyr, Joel. *Why Ireland Starved: A Quantitative and Analytical History of the Irish Economy, 1800–1850.* London: George Allen and Unwin, 1983.

Morash, Chris. "Mitchel's Hunger." In *Theorising Ireland,* edited by Claire Connolly, 114–24. London: Macmillan, 2003.

Morash, Chris, and Richard Hayes, eds. *"Fearful Realities": New Perspectives on the Famine.* Dublin: Irish Academic Press, 1996.

Morgan, Hiram. "Mid-Atlantic Blues." *Irish Review* 11 (1991): 50–55.

Morrissey, John. "Contours of Colonialism: Gaelic Ireland and the Early Colonial Subject." *Irish Geography* 37, no. 1 (2004): 88–102.

———. "Cultural Geographies of the Contact Zone: Gales, Galls and the Overlapping Territories in Late Medieval Ireland." *Social and Cultural Geography* 6, no. 4 (2005): 551–66.

———. "Geography Militant: Resistance and the Essentialisation of Identity in Ireland." *Irish Geography* 37, no. 2 (2004): 166–76.

Morrow, John. "Thomas Carlyle, 'Young Ireland' and the 'Condition of Ireland Question.'" *Historical Journal* 51, no. 3 (2008): 643–67.

Murphy, Ignatius. *Before the Famine Struck: Life in West Clare, 1834–1845.* Dublin: Irish Academic Press, 1996.

Nally, David. "The Biopolitics of Food Provisioning." *Transactions of the Institute of British Geographers* 36, no. 1 (2010):37–53.

————. "'Eternity's Commissioner': Thomas Carlyle, the Great Irish Famine and the Geopolitics of Travel." *Journal of Historical Geography* 32, no. 2 (2006): 313–35.

————. "Maintaining the Marches: Seigneur, Sept and Settlement in Anglo-Norman Thomand." In *Clare: History and Society,* edited by P. Nugent and M. Lynch, 27–60. Dublin: Geography Publications, 2008.

————. "'That Coming Storm': The Irish Poor Law, Colonial Biopolitics, and the Great Famine." *Annals of the Association of American Geographers* 98, no. 3 (2008): 714–41.

————, ed. "Considering the Political Utility of Disasters." *Geographical Journal* 174, no. 3 (2008): 284–87.

Nash, Catherine. "Cultural Geography: Postcolonial Geographies." *Progress in Human Geography* 26, no. 2 (2002): 219–30.

————. "'Embodying the Nation'—The West of Ireland Landscape and Irish Identity." In *Tourism in Ireland: A Critical Analysis,* edited by Barbara O'Connor and Michael Cronin, 86–112. Cork: Cork University Press, 1993.

————. "Visionary Geographies: Designs for Developing Ireland." *History Workshop Journal* 45 (1998): 49–78.

Neilson, Brett. "Potenza Nuda? Sovereignty, Biopolitics, Capitalism." *Contretemps* 5 (2005): 63–78.

Newsinger, John. "The Great Irish Famine: A Crime of Free Market Economics." *Monthly Review: An Independent Socialist Magazine* 47, no. 11 (1996): 11–20.

Nichols, Kenneth W. *Gaelic and Gaelicised Ireland in the Middle Ages.* Dublin: Gill and MacMillan, 1972.

Norton, Desmond. "On Lord Palmerston and the Irish Famine Emigration." Centre for Economic Research Working Paper Series (WP01/19). Department of Economics, University College Dublin, 2001.

O'Brien, George. *The Economic History of Ireland in the Eighteenth Century.* London: Maunsel and Company, 1918.

————. *The Economic History of Ireland from the Union to the Famine.* London: Longmans, Green, 1921.

O'Brien, Gerard. "The Poor Law in Pre-Famine Ireland: A Case History." *Irish Economic and Social History* 12 (1985): 33–49.

————. "A Question of Attitude: Responses to the New Poor Law in Ireland and Scotland." In *Economy and Society in Scotland and Ireland, 1500–1939,* edited by Rosalind Mitchison and Peter Roebuck, 160–70. Edinburgh: John Donald, 1988.

————. "Workhouse Management in Pre-Famine Ireland." *Proceedings of the Royal Irish Academy C* 86, no. 3 (1986): 113–34.

O'Connor, John. *The Workhouses of Ireland: The Fate of Ireland's Poor.* Dublin: Anvil Books, 1995.

Ó Criomhthain, Tomás. *The Islandman.* Translated by Robin Flower. London: Oxford University Press, 1951.

O'Faoláin, Sean. *The Irish.* London: Penguin, 1980.

O'Farrell, Patrick. *England and Ireland since 1800.* Oxford: Oxford University Press, 1975.

Ogborn, Miles. *Global Lives: Britain and the World, 1550–1800.* Cambridge: Cambridge University Press, 2008.

————. "Writing Travels: Power, Knowledge and Ritual on the English East India Company's Early Voyages." *Transactions of the Institute of British Geographers* 27 (2002): 155–71.

Ó Gráda, Cormac. *Black '47 and Beyond: The Great Irish Famine in History, Economy, and Memory.* Princeton, NJ: Princeton University Press, 1999.

————. *Famine: A Short History.* Princeton, NJ: Princeton University Press, 2009.

————. *The Great Irish Famine.* London: Macmillan, 1989.

————. *Ireland Before and After the Famine: Explorations in Economic History, 1800–1925.* 2nd ed. Manchester: Manchester University Press, 1993.

Ó Gráda, Cormac, and Jean-Michel Chevet. "Famine and Markets in *Ancien Régime* France." *Journal of Economic History* 62, no. 3 (2002): 706–33.

O'Hearn, Denis. "Ireland in the Atlantic Economy." In *Was Ireland a Colony? Economics, Politics and Culture in Nineteenth-Century Ireland,* edited by Terrence McDonough, 3–26. Dublin: Irish Academic Press, 2005.

Ohlmeyer, Jane. "'Civilizinge of Those Rude Parts': Colonization within Britain and Ireland, 1580s-1640s." In *The Oxford History of the British Empire.* Vol. 1, *The Origins of Empire: British Overseas Enterprise to the Close of the Seventeenth Century,* edited by Nicholas Canny, 124–47. Oxford: Oxford University Press, 1998.

————. "A Laboratory for Empire? Early Modern Ireland." *Ireland and the British Empire,* edited by Kevin Kenny, 26–60. Oxford: Oxford University Press, 2003.

Ojakangas, Mika. "Impossible Dialogue: Agamben and Foucault." *Foucault Studies* 2 (2005): 5–28.

Olund, Eric. "From Savage Space to Governable Space: The Extension of the United States Judicial Sovereignty over Indian Country in the Nineteenth Century." *Cultural Geographies* 9 (2002): 129–57.

O'Muirithe, Diarmuid. *A Seat Behind the Coachman: Travellers in Ireland, 1800–1900.* Dublin: Gill Macmillan, 1972.

O'Neill, Tim P. "Famine Evictions." In *Famine, Land, and Culture in Ireland,* edited by Carla King, 29–70. Dublin: University College Dublin Press, 2000.

Orford, Anne. *Reading Humanitarian Intervention: Human Rights and the Use of Force in International Law.* Cambridge: Cambridge University Press, 2003.

O'Rourke, John. *The History of the Great Irish Famine of 1847, With Notices of Earlier Irish Famines* Dublin: Bibliobazaar, 2007. 3rd ed. published in 1902.

O'Rourke, Kevin. "The Economic Impact of the Famine in the Short and Long Run." *American Economic Review* 84, no. 2 (1994): 309–13.

Osborne, Thomas. "Security and Vitality: Drains, Liberalism and Power in the Nineteenth Century." In *Foucault and Political Reason: Liberalism, Neo-Liberalism and Rationalities of Government,* edited by Andrew Barry, Thomas Osborne, and Nikolas Rose, 99–121. London: University College London Press, 1996.

O'Sullivan, Patrick, and Richard Lucking "The Famine World Wide: The Irish Famine and the Development of Famine Policy and Famine Theory." In *The Irish World Wide: History, Heritage, Identity.* Vol. 6, *The Meaning of Famine,* edited by P. O'Sullivan, 195–232. London: Leicester University Press, 2000.

Ó Tuathaigh, Gearóid. *Ireland before the Famine, 1798–1848.* 2nd ed. Dublin: Gill and Macmillan, 2007.

Oxford Dictionary of National Biography. Oxford: Oxford University Press, 2004.

Park, T. Peter. "Thomas Carlyle and the Jews." *Journal of European Studies* 20 (1990): 1–21.

Patel, Raj. *Stuffed and Starved: From Farm to Fork, the Hidden Battle for the World Food System.* London: Portobello Books, 2007.

Pitts, Jennifer. *A Turn to Empire: The Rise of Imperial Liberalism in Britain and France.* Princeton, NJ: Princeton University Press, 2005.

Pogge, Thomas. *World Poverty and Human Rights: Cosmopolitan Responsibilities and Reforms.* Cambridge: Polity, 2002.

Póirtéir, Cathal. *Famine Echoes.* Dublin: Gill and Macmillan, 1995.

———. Introduction to *The Great Irish Famine,* edited by Cathal Póirtéir, 9–17. Dublin: Irish Academic Press, 1995.

Polanyi, Karl. *The Great Transformation: The Political and Economic Origins of Our Times.* Boston: Beacon Press, 2001.

Poovey, Mary. *Making a Social Body: British Cultural Formation, 1830–1864.* Chicago: University of Chicago Press, 1995.

Post, John D. *The Last Great Subsistence Crisis of the Western World.* London: John Hopkins University Press, 1977.

———. "Nutritional Status and Mortality in Eighteenth-Century Europe." In *Hunger in History: Food Shortage, Poverty, Deprivation,* edited by Lucile F. Newman. Oxford: Basil Blackwell, 1990.

Prakash, Gyan. *Another Reason: Science and the Imagination of Modern India.* Princeton, NJ: Princeton University Press, 1999.

Pratt, Mary Louise. *Imperial Eyes: Travel Writing and Transculturation.* London: Routledge, 1992.

Proudfoot, L. J. "Landownership and Improvement, c. 1700 to 1845." In *Down: History and Society, Interdisciplinary Essays on the History of an Irish County,* edited by L. J. Proudfoot, 203–37. Dublin: Geography Publications, 1997.

———. "Spatial Transformation and Social Agency: Property, Society and Improvement, c. 1700 to 1900." In *An Historical Geography of Ireland,* edited by B. J. Graham and L. J. Proudfoot, 219–57. London: Academic Press, 1993.

Quinn, David Beers. *The Elizabethans and the Irish*. Ithaca, NY: Cornell University Press, 1966.

———. "Sir Thomas Smith (1513–77) and the Beginnings of English Colonial Theory." *Proceedings of the American Philosophical Society* 89, no. 4 (1945): 543–60.

Quinn, Eileen Moore. "Entextualising Famine, Reconstititing Self: Testimonial Narratives from Ireland." *Anthropological Quarterly* 74, no. 2 (2001): 72–88.

Quinn, James. "John Mitchel and the Rejection of the Nineteenth Century." *Eire-Ireland* 38 (2003): 90–108.

Rancière, Jacques. "Who Is the Subject of the Rights of Man?" *South Atlantic Quarterly* 103, no. 2/3 (2004): 297–310.

Rangasami, Amrita. "'Failure of Exchange Entitlements' Theory of Famine: A Response." *Economic and Political Weekly* 20, no. 41 (1985): 1747–52, 1797–801.

Rashid, Salim. "The Policy of Laissez-Faire during Scarcities." *Economic Journal* 90, no. 359 (1980): 493–503.

Raulff, Ulrich. "An Interview with Giorgio Agamben." *German Law Journal* 5, no. 5 (2004): 609–14.

Redford, Bruce. *Venice and the Grand Tour*. New Haven, CT: Yale University Press, 1996.

Richards, Evelleen. "The 'Moral Anatomy' of Robert Knox: The Interplay between Biological and Social Thought in Victorian Scientific Thought." *Journal of the History of Biology* 22 (1989): 373–436.

Roberts, Paul. *The End of Food: The Coming Crisis in the World Food Industry*. London: Bloomsbury, 2008.

Roberts, Wade. "Sovereignty, Biopower and the State of Exception: Agamben, Butler and Indefinite Detention." *Journal for the Arts, Sciences, and Technology* 3, no. 1 (2005): 33–40.

Rodden, John. "'The Lever Must Be Applied in Ireland': Marx, Engels, and the Irish Question." *Review of Politics* 70 (2008): 609–40.

Roncaglia, Alessandro. *The Wealth of Ideas: A History of Economic Thought*. Cambridge: Cambridge University Press, 2005.

Rone, J. S. C. "Thackeray and Ireland." *Irish Book Lover* 3 (1912): 3–4.

Rose, Nikolas. *Powers of Freedom: Reframing Political Thought*. Cambridge: Cambridge University Press, 1999.

Russell, Sharman Apt. *Hunger: An Unnatural History*. New York: Basic Books, 2005.

Ryan, W. P. *The Irish Labour Movement: From the 'Twenties to Our Day*. Dublin: Talbot Press, n.d.

Ryle, Martin. *Journeys in Ireland: Literary Travellers, Rural Landscapes, Cultural Relations*. Aldershot: Ashgate, 1999.

Said, Edward. *Culture and Imperialism*. New York: Vintage Books, 1993.

————. *Orientalism.* New York: Vintage Books, 1979.

————. "Representing the Colonized: Anthropology's Interlocutors." *Critical Inquiry* 15 (1989): 205–25.

Santiago-Valles, Kelvin. "'Bloody Legislations,' 'Entombment,' and Race Making in the Spanish Atlantic: Differentiated Spaces of General(ized) Confinement in Spain and Puerto Rico, 1750–1840." *Radical History Review* 96 (2006): 33–57.

Scott, David. "Colonial Governmentality." *Social Text* 43 (1995): 191–220.

Scott, James C. *The Moral Economy of the Peasant: Rebellion and Subsistence in Southeast Asia.* New Haven, CT: Yale University Press, 1976.

————. *Seeing Like a State: How Certain Schemes to Improve the Human Condition Have Failed.* New Haven, CT: Yale University Press, 1998.

Seigel, Jules. "Carlyle and Peel: The Prophet's Search for a Heroic Politician and an Unpublished Fragment." *Victorian Studies* 26, no. 2 (1983): 181–95.

Sen, Amartya. *Development as Freedom.* New York: Anchor Books, 2000.

————. *Identity and Violence: The Illusion of Destiny.* New York: W. W. Norton, 2006.

————. *Poverty and Famines: An Essay on Entitlements and Deprivation.* Oxford: Clarendon Press, 1981.

————. "The Right Not to Be Hungry." In *The Right to Food,* edited by K. Tomaševski and P. Alston Dordrecht, 69–81. The Hague: Martinus Nijoff, 1984.

————. "Starvation and Exchange Entitlements: A General Approach and Its Application to the Great Bengal Famine." *Cambridge Journal of Economics* 1, no. 1 (1977): 33–59.

Sharma, Sanjay. *Famine, Philanthropy and the Colonial State: North India in the Early Nineteenth Century.* Oxford: Oxford University Press, 2001.

Shenton, Robert, and Michael Watts. "Capitalism and Hunger in Northern Nigeria." *Review of African Political Economy* 6, no. 15 (1979): 53–62.

Smith, Sidonie. *Moving Lives: Twentieth Century Women's Travel Writing.* Minneapolis: University of Minnesota Press, 2001.

Smyth, William J. "Introduction: Remembering the Great Irish Famine, 1845–1851." *Journal of Economic Studies* 24, no. 1/2 (1997): 4–9.

————. *Map-Making, Landscapes and Memory: A Geography of Colonial and Early Modern Ireland, c. 1530–1750.* Cork: Cork University Press, 2006.

————. "Semi-Colonial Ireland." In *Home and Colonial: Essays on Landscape, Ireland, Environment and Empire in Celebration of Robin Butlin's Contribution to Historical Geography,* edited by Alan Baker, 53–65. Historical Geography Research Series, no. 39. London: HGRG, 2004.

Solar, Peter. "The Great Famine Was No Ordinary Subsistence Crisis." In *Famine: The Irish Experience, 900–1900, Subsidence Crises and Irish Famines,* edited by E. Margaret Crawford, 112–33. Edinburgh: John Donald, 1989.

————. "The Potato Famine in Europe." In *Famine 150,* edited by Cormac Ó Gráda, 112–27. Dublin: Teagasc, 1997.

Spitz, Pierre. "Livelihood and the Food Squeeze." *Ceres: FAO Review on Agriculture and Development* 81 (May/June 1981): 27–30.

———. "The Public Granary." *Ceres: FAO Review on Agriculture and Development* 72 (November/December 1979): 16–19.

———. "The Right to Food in Historical Perspective." *Food Policy* 10, no. 4 (1985): 306–16.

———. "Right to Food for Peoples and for the People: A Historical Perspective." In *The Right to Food,* edited by P. Alston and K. Tomaševski, 169–86. The Hague: Martinus Nijoff, 1984.

Steele, E. D. "J. S. Mill and the Irish Question: The Principles of Political Economy, 1848–1865." *Historical Journal* 13, no. 2 (1970): 216–36.

Stokes, Eric. *The English Utilitarians and India.* Oxford: Clarendon Press, 1959.

Stoler, Ann Laura. *Race and the Education of Desire: Foucault's History of Sexuality and the Colonial Order of Things.* London: Duke University Press, 1995.

Tarlow, Sarah. *The Archaeology of Improvement in Britain, 1750–1850.* Cambridge: Cambridge University Press, 2007.

Tarr, Rodger L. "Thomas Carlyle and Henry M'Cormac." *Studies in Scottish Literature* 5, no. 4 (1968): 253–56.

Thomas, Nicholas. *Colonialism's Culture: Anthropology, Travel and Government.* Princeton, NJ: Princeton University Press, 1994.

Thompson, E. P. *The Making of the English Working Class.* London: Penguin, 1991.

———. "The Moral Economy of the English Crowd in the Eighteenth Century." *Past and Present* 50, no. 1 (1971): 76–136.

———. "Time, Work-Discipline, and Industrial Capitalism." *Past and Present* 38, no. 1 (1967): 56–97.

Tilly, Louise A. "Food Entitlement, Famine and Conflict." *Journal of Interdisciplinary History* 14, no. 2 (1983): 333–49.

Tóibín, Colm, and Diarmuid Ferriter. *The Irish Famine: A Documentary.* London: Profile Books, 2002.

Townshend, Charles. "Martial Law: Legal and Administrative Problems of Civil Emergency in Britain and the Empire, 1800–1940." *Historical Journal* 25, no. 1 (1982): 167–95.

———. *Political Violence in Ireland: Government and Resistance since 1848.* Oxford: Clarendon Press, 1983.

Traverso, Enzo. *The Origins of Nazi Violence.* London: New Press, 2003.

Tribe, Keith. *Genealogies of Capitalism.* New Jersey: Humanities Press, 1981.

Vanden Bossche, Chris R. *Carlyle and the Search for Authority.* Columbus: Ohio State University Press, 1991.

Vaux, Tony. *The Selfish Altruist: Relief Work in Famine and War.* London: Earthscan, 2001.

Vernon, James. *Hunger: A Modern History.* Cambridge, MA: Belknap Press of Harvard University Press, 2007.

Vincent, Joan. "A Political Orchestration of the Irish Famine: County Fermanagh, May 1847." In *Approaching the Irish Past: Historical Anthropology through Irish Case Studies,* edited by M. Silverman and P. H. Gulliver, 75–98. New York: Columbia University Press, 1992.

Waters, Hazel. "The Great Irish Famine and the Rise of Anti-Irish Racism." *Race and Class* 37, no. 1 (1995): 95–108.

Watts, Michael. "Black Acts." *New Left Review* 9 (May/June 2001): 125–39.

———. "The Demise of the Moral Economy: Food and Famine in the Sudo-Sahelian Region in Historical Perspective." In *Life before Drought,* edited by E. Scott, 124–48. Boston: Allen and Unwin, 1984.

———. "Entitlements or Empowerment? Famine and Starvation in Africa." *Review of African Political Economy* 18, no. 51 (1991): 9–26.

———. *Silent Violence: Food, Famine, and Peasantry in Northern Nigeria.* Berkeley: University of California Press, 1983.

Whelan, Kevin. "'Come All You Staunch Revisionists': Towards a Post-Revisionist Agenda for Irish History." *Irish Reporter* 2 (1991): 23–26.

———. "The Memories of 'The Dead.'" *Yale Journal of Criticism* 15, no. 1 (2002): 59–97.

———. "The Modern Landscape: From Plantation to the Present." In *Atlas of the Irish Rural Landscape,* edited by F. H. A. Aalen, K. Whelan, and M. Stout, 67–103. Cork: University College Cork Press, 1997.

———. "The Other Within: Ireland, Britain and the Act of Union." In *Acts of Union: The Causes, Contexts and Consequences of the Act of Union,* edited by Dáire Keogh and Kevin Whelan, 13–33. Dublin: Four Courts Press, 2001.

———. "Pre- and Post-Famine Landscape Change." In *The Great Irish Famine,* edited by Cathal Póirtéir, 19–33. Dublin: Mercier Press, 1995.

———. "The Revisionist Debate in Ireland." *Boundary 2* 31, no. 1 (2004): 179–205.

———. *The Tree of Liberty: Radicalism, Catholicism and the Construction of Irish Identity, 1760–1830.* Cork: Cork University Press, 1996.

———. "Writing Ireland: Reading England." In *Ireland in the Nineteenth Century: Regional Identity,* edited by Leon Litvack and Glenn Hooper, 185–98. Dublin: Four Courts Press, 2000.

Wilmot, Sarah. *"The Business of Improvement": Agriculture and Scientific Culture in Britain, c. 1700–1870.* Historical Geography Research Series, no. 24. London: HGRG, 1990.

Wood, Ellen Meiksins. "The Agrarian Origins of Capitalism." In *Hungry for Profit: The Agribusiness Threat to Farmers, Food, and the Environment,* edited by F. Magdoff, J. B. Foster, and F. H. Buttel, 23–42. New York: Monthly Review Press, 2000.

———. *Empire of Capital.* London: Verso, 2003.

Woodham-Smith, Cecil. *The Great Hunger.* London: Hamish Hamilton, 1962.

Woods, Christopher. "American Travellers in Ireland before and during the Great Famine: A Case Study of Culture-Shock." In *Literary Interrelations, Ireland, England, and the World: National Images and Stereotypes,* edited by Heinz Kosok and Wolfgang Zazh, 77–84. Tubingen: Gunter Nam Verlag, 1987.

Woods, C. J. "Review Article: Irish Travel Writings as Source Material." *Irish Historical Studies* 28, no. 110 (1992): 171–83.

Young, Liz. "Spaces of Famine: A Comparative Geographical Analysis of Famine in Ireland and the Highlands in the 1840s." *Transactions of the Institute of British Geographers* 21 (1996): 666–80.

Young, Norwood. *Carlyle: His Rise and Fall.* London: Duckworth, 1927.

Young, Robert. *Postcolonialism: An Historical Introduction.* Oxford: Blackwell, 2001.

Žižek, Slavoj. "Against Human Rights." *New Left Review* 34 (July/August 2005): 115–31.

———. "From Politics to Biopolitics . . . and Back." *South Atlantic Quarterly* 103, no. 2/3 (2004): 501–21.

———. *Violence: Six Sideways Reflections.* London: Profile, 2009.

DAVID P. NALLY

is a University Lecturer and Fellow of Fitzwilliam College
at the University of Cambridge, England.